METHUEN'S MANUALS OF MODERN PSYCHOLOGY

EDITED BY H. J. BUTCHER

Personality Assessment: a Critical Survey

Personality Assessment
A Critical Survey

BY

PHILIP E. VERNON

Professor of Educational Psychology,
University of Calgary

METHUEN & CO LTD

11 New Fetter Lane EC4

First published in 1964
Second impression 1965
Third impression 1966
Fourth impression 1969
Fifth impression 1972
SBN 416 27020 4

First published as a Social Science Paperback in 1969
Second and third impressions 1972
Fourth impression 1973
SBN 422 72560 9

© *1963 by Philip E. Vernon*
Printed in Great Britain by
Butler & Tanner Ltd, Frome and London

Distributed in the USA by
HARPER & ROW PUBLISHERS, INC.
BARNES & NOBLE IMPORT DIVISION

CONTENTS

Part III. Objective Approaches to Personality

Part IV. Practicable Methods of Assessment

FOREWORD

This book is neither a psychological theory of personality, nor an account of personality tests. Many other authors have discussed these topics and, in the case of testing, I myself published a survey ten years ago, entitled *Personality Tests and Assessments*. There is very little overlapping between that book and this. My chief aim here is to reach a balanced viewpoint, in the light of research evidence, regarding the best approach to diagnosing and assessing people's personalities for such practical purposes as counselling, guidance and selection. This will, I hope, provide a useful background, or a philosophy (in the loose sense of the word), for vocational, educational and clinical psychologists, or others concerned with selecting or advising people.

For over 30 years I have been perturbed by the conflicting claims of clinically oriented psychologists on the one hand and psychometrically oriented psychologists on the other hand, and their criticisms of each other. Neither side, it would seem, has succeeded in providing acceptable and practicable methods of diagnosis which are consistently more accurate than the unsophisticated methods that we ordinarily use in understanding people in daily life. A year's Fellowship at the Center for Advanced Study in the Behavioral Sciences, at Stanford, California, in 1961–2, gave me the opportunity to study the whole matter afresh, and to try to get down to basic difficulties.

In Part I, then, I consider the remarkable facility we have for judging people's motives and traits in everyday social intercourse or in interviews. Research is summarized on the many biases and inaccuracies that occur in such judgments, on the nature of so-called social perception and insight, and on the characteristics of 'good judges' of personality. Whether our interpretations of people are explicable in terms of learned associations and inference, or whether we possess a special capacity for 'intuition', is a controversial problem; but I argue that the processes involved are essentially the same as those involved in perception of the physical world.

The clinical psychologist or psychiatrist, with his more sophisticated knowledge of human motives derived from Freudian or depth psychology, should be capable of more accurate diagnoses of, and predictions about, people; but this is not borne out by the experimental evidence. In an attempt to find out why, I show that there is considerable support from experimental studies for many of the concepts of depth psychology. In contrast, theories about the long-term effects of upbringing in infancy on the adolescent or adult personality have received little confirmation. Nor can it be claimed that the depth-psychological approach is substantiated by its success in treating neurotic patients or maladjusted children. An alternative framework for understanding people in terms of their Self-concepts and attitudes is outlined, and this appears to yield more fruitful therapeutic results, as in Rogers's non-directive type of therapy. Likewise vocational counselling, which makes little reference to unconscious mechanisms, is demonstrably successful. Other chapters in this Part II deal with the nature of clinical exploration, with the scientific status of depth psychology, and with the aims and methods of projective tests. The weight of evidence shows that these latter should not be used for practical assessment purposes, though they can be of value in clinical exploration and in experimental research.

In Part III, I take up the psychometric approach, with particular reference to the work of Eysenck and Cattell, and their claim that personality should be viewed as a number of objectively measurable traits or factors. The main weakness in this approach is that people's responses to objective tests and personality questionnaires are so dependent on their attitudes to the testing situation and on various 'response sets', that the results are highly unstable. The statistical or actuarial method of making predictions about people has a very limited application, hence we are forced back on to more subjective assessments. However, it is possible to measure some relatively stable behaviour patterns, attitudes, interests and self-concepts; and the diagnostician or assessor should use these as far as possible, rather than trying to penetrate to deeper, unconscious, motivations. This Part includes, also, a discussion of the nature of 'validity', and a general theory of the relation between internal dispositions in the personality, outer behaviour, and the conceptual structures of the person himself and of those who are trying to assess him.

The final Part describes those tests, or other techniques, of assessing a person's major trends which appear most promising in the light of the previous discussion. These include the constitutional or body type, certain perceptual or cognitive tests, time-sampling and other records of behaviour, 'situational' tests; questionnaire tests for a number of self-concepts, interests and attitudes; also the Q-sort, semantic differential, Rep test, and related techniques. I have not, however, attempted to specify how the diagnostic interview should be conducted, nor how the data from such tests or interviewing should be combined in reaching decisions about the person; in other words, this is not a 'how to do it' manual.

I am fully aware that the book raises more controversial problems than it solves, and that it contains innumerable loose ends. No one person could possibly hope to digest and summarize all the relevant evidence; and I have inevitably laid myself open to the charge of selecting the evidence that suits me, and neglecting (or displaying my ignorance of) conflicting theories and findings. I can only answer that I have tried to examine current approaches to personality assessment as impartially as possible, to achieve a balanced synthesis, and to suggest possible lines of advance.

While the book is addressed primarily to psychology students, most of it should be intelligible to others who are concerned with assessment of their fellow-men – doctors, teachers, ministers, social workers, personnel officers, etc. Chapters 4, 10 and 13 are definitely more technical than the rest, and the non-psychologist might be advised to read only the summaries of these. All the chapters are fully summarized in the Introduction, in order to help the reader pick and choose. In each chapter, also, the more technical accounts of experimental investigations are printed in smaller type, so that the 'skimmer' can omit them.

I cannot adequately express my gratitude to the Center for Advanced Study, to Ralph Tyler and his staff, for making the book possible. Equally, I should thank the Institute of Education, University of London, for allowing me this year's study leave. I am particularly grateful, also, to Gordon Allport, my sister Magdalen D. Vernon, and my colleagues Doris M. Lee and Robert Andry, for reading and criticizing several chapters. My wife gave invaluable help in typing the first draft and in preparing the index; and Miss D. Brothers was mainly responsible for typing the revised manuscript. Acknowledgment is due to Dr F. Heider for permission to copy the Figure on p. 27.

P. E. V.

December 1962

Chapter 1

INTRODUCTION
AND GENERAL SUMMARY

Our daily lives are largely made up of contacts with other people, during which we are constantly making judgments of their personalities and accommodating our behaviour to them in accordance with these judgments. A casual meeting of neighbours on the street, an employer giving instructions to an employee, a mother telling her children how to behave, a journey in a train where strangers eye one another without exchanging a word – all these involve mutual interpretations of personal qualities.

Success in many vocations largely depends on skill in sizing up people. It is important not only to such professionals as the clinical psychologist, the psychiatrist or the social worker, but also to the doctor or lawyer in dealing with their clients, the business man trying to outwit his rivals, the salesman with potential customers, the teacher with his pupils, not to speak of the pupils judging their teacher. Social life, indeed, would be impossible if we did not, to some extent, understand, and react to, the motives and qualities of those we meet; and clearly we are sufficiently accurate for most practical purposes, although we also recognize that misinterpretations easily arise – particularly on the part of others who judge us!

Errors can often be corrected as we go along. But whenever we are pinned down to a definite decision about a person, which cannot easily be revised through this 'feed-back', the inadequacies of our judgments become apparent. The hostess who wrongly thinks that the Smiths and the Joneses will get on well together can do little to retrieve the success of her party. A school or a business may be saddled for years with an undesirable member of staff, because the selection committee which interviewed him for a quarter of an hour misjudged his personality; and most marriages which break down do so because the partners wrongly believed that they understood and liked each other's personality.

1

Just because the process is so familiar and taken for granted, it has aroused little scientific curiosity until recently. Dramatists, writers and artists throughout the centuries have excelled in the portrayal of character, but have seldom stopped to ask how they, or we, get to know people, or how accurate is our knowledge. However, the popularity of such unscientific systems as Lavater's physiognomy in the eighteenth century, Gall's phrenology in the nineteenth, and of handwriting interpretations by graphologists, or palm-readings by gipsies, show that people are aware of weaknesses in their judgments and desirous of better methods of diagnosis. It is natural that, in the present century, they should turn to psychology for help, in the belief that psychologists are specialists in 'human nature'.

This belief is hardly justified: for the primary aim of psychology has been to establish the general laws or principles underlying behaviour and thinking, rather than to apply these to concrete problems of the individual person. A great many professional psychologists still regard it as their main function to study the nature of learning, perception and motivation in the abstracted or average human being, or in lower organisms, and consider it premature to try to put so young a science to practical uses. They would disclaim the possession of any superior skill in judging their fellow-men. Indeed, being more aware of the difficulties than is the non-psychologist, they may be more reluctant to commit themselves to definite predictions or decisions about other people. Nevertheless, to an increasing extent psychologists are moving into educational, occupational, clinical and other applied fields, where they are called upon to use their expertise for such purposes as fitting the education or job to the child or adult, and the person to the job. Thus a considerable proportion of their activities consists of personality assessment, and the main object of this book is to evaluate the methods available to them. It will be appropriate, then, to begin by listing the kinds of situations in which they make decisions about people. These situations can be broadly categorized under three headings: Selection, Counselling or Guidance, and Research.

Selection. 1. Choosing, or promoting a man for a particular job: e.g. managing director, headmaster. Technical qualifications may be important, but these can be fairly adequately assessed from the candidates' records, and the more crucial issue is which candidate possesses the most suitable combination of personality qualities.

2. Admission of men and women for training as officers in the

Services, as doctors, nurses, lawyers, school-teachers, salesmen, etc., where again the 'wrong kind' of personality may prove disastrous.

3. Admission to advanced schooling or university education, where the supply of places is limited and it is necessary to select those with sufficient perseverance, personal stability, and interest – in addition to sufficient ability – to profit.

4. In the field of psychopathology: identifying those patients whose personality disturbance justifies some rather drastic and irreversible treatment such as electroconvulsive therapy or leucotomy.

5. Transfer of mentally retarded or maladjusted children to some special form of schooling, or residential care, where again provision is limited, and where the proposed treatment carries serious implications for the child and his family.

6. Allocation of criminals and delinquents to special types of detention, probation or release on parole, where a wrong assessment may likewise have serious social consequences.

7. Screening of recruits by a short test or preliminary interview with a view to referring possible cases of mental disorder or maladjustment for more detailed study, e.g. by psychiatrists. It would be wasteful and impractical to submit all recruits, over 90% of whom may be reasonably normal, to skilled psychiatric examination.

Counselling. 8. Providing a person with normative information on his interests, attitudes, and other qualities (i.e. showing him how he compares with people of similar age, sex, etc.) in order to help him to make wise educational or vocational decisions.

9. Counselling or psychotherapy of maladjusted persons based more on clinical interview methods than on testing, with the aim of promoting self-understanding and resolution of personality conflicts.

10. A counsellor or clinical psychologist collects similar material but uses it to make up his own mind as to what kind of treatment will best suit an educationally retarded, maladjusted or delinquent child or adult patient. This is similar to Nos. 4, 5 or 6, but is more exploratory, less drastic or irreversible. Alternatively, he may pass on his findings regarding the personality to the child's parents or teachers, or to a court of law, or to a hospital psychiatrist, leaving it to them to decide the appropriate treatment.

Research. 11. Surveying the effects of some form of treatment or instruction, generally with a view to making practical recommendations. For example, evaluating the effects on pupils' personalities and attitudes of different kinds of schooling, of violent TV programmes, or of different techniques of child upbringing; assessing the changes brought about by various psychotherapies.

12. Miscellaneous issues of public concern where practical decisions have to be taken, and where a knowledge of personality differences would be useful. Thus it may be asked whether certain personality types are more liable than others to ethnic, fascist or communist prejudice, more susceptible to special kinds of advertising and propaganda, weaker in industrial or military morale, more liable to accidents, etc.

The role of contemporary psychology in personality decisions. To all of these and other situations in daily life, psychologists have made some contributions, but their success is so limited, in comparison with what they have achieved in the fields of abilities and training, that most people continue to rely mainly on unscientific methods of assessment. The past third of a century has seen a tremendous amount of work on personality tests, and on carefully controlled experimental studies of personality. Investigations of personality by Freudian and other 'depth' psychologists and psychiatrists have an even longer history. And yet psychology seems to be no nearer to providing society with practicable techniques which are sufficiently reliable and accurate to win general acceptance. It is true that counsellors are working full-time in most American schools and colleges, and that child guidance and vocational guidance are developing so rapidly in Europe that it is difficult to meet the demand for trained personnel. But the soundness of their methods and the value of their work are under constant fire from other psychologists, and we shall see below that it is far from easy to prove their worth.

The growth of psychology in the present century has probably helped responsible members of society to become more aware of the difficulties of assessment. But it is not much use telling employers, the Services, educationists and judges how inaccurately they diagnose the personalities with which they have to deal unless psychologists are sure that they can provide something better. Even when university psychologists themselves appoint a new member of staff, they almost always resort to the traditional techniques of assessing the candidates through interviews, past records, and testimonials, and probably make at least as many bad appointments as other employers do. However, a large amount of experimental development of better methods has been carried out since 1940 by groups of psychologists in the Armed Services and in the Civil Service, and by such organizations as the (British) National Institute of Industrial Psychology and the American Institute of Research. It is hoped in this book to show which of their techniques are most promising and worth more extensive application.

In some ways, popular interest in psychology, and its potential applications to practical decisions, has been embarrassing and even harmful. The personnel manager and the teacher, possessing very little psychological training (and even some industrial and educational psychologists who ought to know better), are tempted to procure tests which claim to measure good adjustment or other traits or interests, and to give them to employees and school pupils, without realizing the precautions that are necessary if they are to have any reliability. W. H. Whyte, in *The Organization Man*, has trenchantly criticized this all-too-common misapplication of testing. Many of the discoveries of depth psychology are equally open to abuse, for example in the handling of maladjusted children at school, or in so-called motivation research on consumer preferences.

Ethical considerations. One of man's strongest motives is the maintenance and enhancement of his Ego. Hence any attempt by psychologists and others to study his personality more closely with a view to controlling his freedom of action is likely to be resented. Many serious thinkers, therefore, are shocked by the invasions of privacy which are implied by the kind of situations we have listed above, and are inclined to regard any scientific investigation of the person as unethical, particularly if done without his consent, or, in the case of children, without the consent of their parents.

One can sympathize with this point of view, and with the underlying fear that unscrupulous politicians or employers might use the results of scientific research on personality to manipulate man against his will. But surely the answer is that the good of civilized society already demands some control over the freedom of its members. Thus, we think it right to refuse to employ persons with unsuitable qualities in important posts, and to care for the deviant (criminal or psychopathological cases) in prisons and hospitals. Again, teachers, ministers and the law are already interfering with the parents' rights to bring up their children as they wish. If these things are being done ineffectively it seems obscurantist to object to the psychologist's attempt to improve our methods.

Secondly, psychologists have generally shown themselves more aware of the need to serve the individual's best interests than have other 'manipulators' or decision-makers. They have an ethical code similar to that of the doctor,* which emphasizes this responsibility, though admittedly there are many doubtful cases. For example, a lecturer in psychology wishes to demonstrate to his students, or to carry out research on, personality inventories. How far is he justified in invading their privacy by applying these highly personal question-naires, perhaps making them aware of abnormal tendencies which had not previously occurred to them; and may not his own reactions to some students be biased by his knowledge of their responses to tests of very dubious validity? Many other problems arise in con-nection with the communication of the results of personality studies to employers and teachers. But there is good reason to think that, as the science of personality assessment becomes more advanced, the practitioners will formulate even more adequate principles and safeguards.

The nature of personality. This book does not attempt to offer a novel psychological theory of personality. It draws on the contributions of those who have studied personality from many different theoretical viewpoints, and tries to reconcile the frequently conflicting evidence. In the course of these discussions, a tentative eclectic picture will emerge which, it is hoped, will be acceptable to occupational and educational psychologists and to counsellors generally (cf. especially Chapter 14). But for the moment we will make do with Harsh and Schrickel's phrase (1950): personality is 'that which characterizes an individual and determines his unique adaptation to the environ-ment'. More colloquially, personality means – what sort of a person is so-and-so, what is he like? At the same time we usually restrict the term to the relatively permanent emotional qualities underlying the person's behaviour, his drives and needs, attitudes and interests, and distinguish it from his intellectual and bodily skills and cognitive characteristics.

---

* Cf. American Psychological Association. *Standards of Ethical Behavior for Psychologists* (1958). In the *Handbook of Research Methods in Child Development* (ed. P. H. Mussen 1960), the ethical considerations involved in studying the per-sonalities of young children are frequently stressed. In Britain, the British Psycho-logical Society keeps a constant check on undesirable practices through its Com-mittee on Professional Conduct; and its Committee on Test Standards is con-cerned with the proper application, and the sale to qualified persons only, of personality and other psychological tests.

SUMMARY OF LATER CHAPTERS

Parts I, II and III of this book deal respectively with the approaches to personality of the lay or psychologically unsophisticated individual (naïve interpretation), of the clinical psychologist or psychiatrist who is influenced by Freudian or depth psychological theories of human nature, and of the psychological tester or psychometrist who aims to measure people's traits or other personality characteristics scientifically. The fourth Part describes some methods of studying people which appear most promising for the practical purposes outlined above, in the light of the weaknesses of both clinical and psychometric techniques brought out in Parts II and III.

PART I. *Naïve interpretations of personality*

Chapter 2. **Perceptions and misperceptions of people.** In daily life, and in such situations as the selection interview, we judge people by observing their outer appearance and expressions, how they behave in various contexts, and what they or others tell us about them. However, we do not so much observe or perceive particular cues as such, but immediately interpret these as expressing underlying intentions and dispositions. Much as the ordinary processes of perception serve to sort out our complex physical environment into a lot of stable objects, so we see people as motivated beings, like ourselves, each possessing a stable and organized structure of traits, interests and abilities, which constitute his personality. A reciprocal interaction occurs between any two persons: each realizes that he is being observed and evaluated by the other, and tries to behave in such a way as to create a favourable impression of his personality; at the same time he tries to penetrate the disguises or façades that the other is displaying.

There are many reasons why one's judgments of people's personalities (or of one's own) disagree with those of others, or measure up badly to external criteria: for example the tendency to over-generalize from insufficient observation and to oversimplify; also inflexibility in accepting fresh evidence and undue egocentricity or self-reference. Different observers differ characteristically in their modes of perception, and there is evidence that perception may be distorted by the perceiver's motivation and attitudes. In particular, each of us builds up theories or stereotypes of human nature, in terms of which we sort people and make predictions about them. Despite the crudity of these theories they serve many useful purposes in everyday social contacts.

B

Chapter 3. **Theoretical considerations.** Two main types of explanation of our perception and interpretation of the emotions and dispositions of others are distinguished: *inference* theories, based on association and the processes of social learning and reinforcement; and *intuition* theories (including instinctive reactions, empathy, physiognomic perception and *Verstehen*) which invoke an unlearned capacity for understanding others. The former is generally favoured by those who study personality *nomothetically*, i.e. as an object possessing universal properties which can be measured scientifically; the latter by those who approach it *idiographically*, i.e. as an unique individual structure. These approaches are characteristic, respectively, of the experimental psychologist or psychometrist, and of the clinical psychologist. They are considered in detail in Parts III and II below.

Here it is argued that the contradiction between inference and intuition theories is unnecessary; for even in the perception of objects psychologists no longer draw a hard-and-fast line between the reception of sense data and inferences regarding the sources of the data. Thus the perception of people does not differ essentially from perception in general. It appears to be intuitive because it generally depends to a greater extent on affective reactions and on less explicit or rational processes of sorting the incoming cues and inferring from them. A brief account is included of its development in lower animals and young children.

Chapter 4. **Experimental investigations of personality judgments.** This chapter sketches the current state of research on judgments of personality by acquaintances, interviewers or other non-expert observers. Although no particular physical feature is a valid indicator of any personality trait or ability, judgments based on the pattern of the features and on expressive movements (including vocal characteristics, handwriting, etc.) have been shown to have appreciable validity, for example by the matching method. These expressive cues, however, derive from many sources and levels of the personality, and therefore provide no sure guide to inner personality dispositions.

Ratings or assessments based on extended acquaintanceship and collected under controlled conditions can be useful for research purposes; but judgments provided by a variety of untrained acquaintances are of very little practical value to the selector or counsellor.

The ability to judge emotional expressions, individual personality, or group characteristics, has been intensively investigated, and some indications of the characteristics of the 'good judge' of people have been obtained. However, accuracy depends greatly on the type of judgment, and most studies have shown serious methodological weaknesses. Much depends on the generally favourable or unfavourable standards that the judge adopts, the extent to which he spreads out or differentiates among individuals, on his tendency to judge others as like himself, on the accuracy of his stereotypes about people in general as well as on his perception of deviations from these stereotypes.

The poor reliability and validity of judgments based on interviews are well known, though they can be reduced, and useful results obtained, under controlled conditions. Moreover the interview is likely to remain the chief tool for assessing people in a majority of selection and counselling situations because of its flexibility and acceptability.

PART II. *The clinical psychologist's understanding of personality*

Chapter 5. **Reliability and validity of depth psychological interpretations.** Clinical psychologists and psychiatrists use much the same processes as the lay or naïve judge in interpreting personality, but employ far more sophisticated theories or constructs of the nature of human motivation, based on Freudian or other schools of depth psychology. How far it is necessary and useful to postulate unconscious or repressed motives and defence mechanisms in order to understand and influence people is the main issue of this Part.

A good deal of inconsistency occurs in psychiatric diagnoses of mental patients; but more serious evidence of the unreliability of clinical judgment is obtained when clinicians attempt to predict such practical outcomes as vocational suitability, prognoses of mental illness or recidivism among delinquents and criminals. Inaccuracies in such judgments have been demonstrated by investigations in the armed forces, in the selection of psychiatrists and clinical psychologists for training, and in various researches summarized by P. E. Meehl. These latter studies indicate that the clinical type of prediction is weak because the clinician does not know the precise significance of the various cues on which he bases his judgment, and because he combines or weights them inefficiently.

Hence statistical or actuarial prediction based on a few objectively measurable cues is more accurate in those situations where it can be applied than the far more detailed and intensive, but subjective, assessments by the clinician.

Chapter 6. Fundamental concepts of depth psychology. Depth psychology should be valued more for the fruitfulness of its hypotheses and for its use in therapeutic treatment than for its contribution to practical assessment. To an increasing extent experimental psychologists are drawing on depth constructs of motivation in their theories of learning and development, and providing scientific support for the explanatory value of, e.g., unconscious affective and cognitive processes, regression, repression and other defence mechanisms. Indeed it is possible to view neurosis as the conditioning of maladjustive habits, and psychotherapy as a process of relearning which might become more effective if experimentally established principles of learning were more explicitly recognized and applied. Though the clinical or depth psychologist and the contemporary behaviour theorist differ in many respects, they both stress the importance of primary and acquired drives, and the shaping of behaviour patterns by factors in early upbringing.

Depth psychology further includes a variety of theories or developmental propositions regarding the effects of child-rearing practices and parental attitudes. However, these have seldom been formulated sufficiently precisely to be confirmed by scientific investigations. The effects of early weaning, strict toilet training, mother-child separation, disciplining, etc. on *current* behaviour patterns can be observed, but most of the findings concerning *later* personality characteristics are negative. Although research is beginning to unravel some of the complex influences of upbringing on aggressive and moral behaviour and attitudes, these results are largely explicable in terms of learning throughout childhood, with less emphasis on the biological drives and the fantasies and conflicts of infancy that are postulated by more extreme psychoanalytic doctrine. It is not necessary to assume that the experiences and adjustments of early childhood persist as such in the Unconscious and underly all later motivations, nor that present behaviour (whether neurotic symptoms or conscious strivings) is always an expression of deeper dispositions which must be brought into the open if personality is to be understood. More stress is now being laid on cultural forces in development, and on later acquired or autonomous motives. However, both depth psychology and learning theory still consider a man's personality as a product of his past, and do not sufficiently recognize the positive forces towards self-actualization and the importance of forward-looking goals.

Chapter 7. **Self-theories as an alternative approach to explaining personal behaviour.** The Neo-Freudians such as Adler, Horney, From and Sullivan represent intermediate viewpoints between depth and Self-theories. C. R. Rogers, in his 'client-centred' therapy, opposes the customary diagnosis of a patient and the explanation of his condition in terms of any system of constructs, Freudian or otherwise. In the permissive atmosphere of non-directive counselling, the client or patient brings up his own problems, is helped to clarify his feelings, and effects his own reintegration of his conflicting perceptions and goals. Several other writers have conceived personality in terms of the ways the person perceives himself, other people and his environment, and their views are outlined, including Snygg and Combs' phenomenology, G. Kelly's psychology of personal constructs (and its extension by Harvey, Hunt and Schroder), and Leary's interpersonal diagnosis.

Several different aspects or meanings of the 'Self' are distinguished. A person's Self-concepts and Super-ego are built up gradually during childhood and adolescence through the influence of linguistic and social training, through identifications with parents and peer groups, and the acquisition of social roles. A model or scheme of the personal conceptual system is proposed, which includes these several aspects, together with concepts of, and attitudes towards, other people and environment. A person's constructs or theories about his Self and environment are classified under four main levels:

1. Social selves and impersonations+ public attitudes.
2. The conscious Self + private attitudes.
3. The 'insightful' Self, e.g. as realized through non-directive analysis.
4. The depth Self as formulated in terms of Freudian or other unconscious mechanisms.

The 'effective Self' or phenomenal field which really determines the person's perceptions and behaviour, and which might be inferred by an unbiased and omniscient observer, includes all of these. It should, however, be distinguished from the personality.

Chapter 8. **The effectiveness of psychotherapy and counselling.** It has been surprisingly difficult to prove satisfactorily that treatment of neurotic or psychotic patients, or of disturbed and delinquent children, by professional experts on a basis of depth theories or other psychological systems, are more effective than the naïve methods of everyday life. There is very little proof also that any particular method of treatment is superior to others. Comparisons by Eysenck and Levitt of the later outcome among maladjusted adults and children respectively indicate just about the same 'recovery' or 'improvement' rate of around two-thirds both among treated and untreated cases. Studies of personality counselling of adolescents, and of remedial work with school children, have likewise yielded essentially negative results. But it is seldom possible to secure really comparable control groups, and there are many technical snags, for example in defining and measuring 'improvement'. 'Adjustment' is an evaluative rather than a scientific conception, and more promising evidence is obtained by studying the changes in people's Self-concepts. (However, it has been objected that such changes represent mere 'verbal conditioning'.) Rogers and his followers have carried out studies of the therapeutic process by recording and analysing therapeutic interviews (e.g. classifying linguistic features or the content of patients' utterances), and in particular have explored the technique of the Q-sort for demonstrating improved self-acceptance and self-insight. Probably other systems of therapy bring about similar changes, since the crucial factor appears to be the kind of interpersonal relationship established between client and therapist, rather than the latter's psychological theories or techniques.

More definite proof is available of the value of guidance or counselling in producing better vocational adjustment among young adults; and this holds good not only for counselling in America, which favours non-directive techniques, but also for the more directive type of advice given by British vocational psychologists. It is noteworthy that these counsellors seldom make much use of depth theories in studying their clients' personalities.

Chapter 9. **The scientific status of clinical methods and depth psychology.** Depth or other psychological theories should not be regarded as 'true' or 'false', or as capable of being proved or disproved by verbal arguments. It is possible and useful to have several alternative theories, provided they introduce order into some part of the phenomena that have been observed and stimulate further research and suggest further relationships that can be investigated. A serious weakness in some of the constructs and generalizations of depth psychology is that they are too imprecise to lead to specific expectations which can be tested out or falsified. It is incorrect to regard clinical psychology as unscientific because it does not conform to the more rigid hypothetico-deductive model of some of the older sciences. To a considerable extent the clinician does follow the paradigm of observing, classifying and generalizing, proposing hypotheses regarding his patient, and testing them out. But in so far as he is interpreting the individual case, the processes involved are less explicit, more idiographic, than the rational and replicable inferences of the scientist. Such data also provide a somewhat insecure basis for scientific generalizations, partly because of the nature of the clinical relationship and the therapeutic session, but partly because of resistances among many clinicians to, or a lack of understanding of, the nature of scientific evidence and experimental controls.

The bearings of this discussion and of the preceding four chapters on the value of the clinical approach to personality assessment are finally discussed. The clinical approach is essentially exploratory, flexible, adapted to investigating and helping to modify the motivations and conceptual structure of the person. But this does not mean that it has any advantage in predicting definite outcomes such as vocational suitability, or in making non-exploratory, irreversible decisions. For such purposes, an approach based on more direct predictions from observed behaviour and conscious attitudes and goals is likely to be superior, since it avoids complex interpretations involving theories regarding the deeper layers of personality.

Chapter 10. **Projective techniques.** Projective techniques are favoured by clinical psychologists as revealing covert dynamic forces in the personality through their expression in fantasy, creative activity, play, or free associations to verbal or inkblot stimuli. However, the processes involved in the production of responses might be accounted for in terms of other theories besides the psychoanalytic, for example learning theory or perceptual theories. Thus there are variations between testers, not only in methods of administration of such widely used tests as Rorschach Inkblots, Thematic Apperception and Sentence Completion, and in scoring or categorizing the responses, but also particularly in the interpretation of the scores and of the overall pattern. Recent work has shown that the techniques are unreliable also because responses are much affected by situational factors such as the Subject's moods, his conception of the object of the test, and his reaction to the personality of the tester. Though not normally fakable nor liable to ordinary 'social desirability' effects, they certainly reflect the current situation as well as more enduring personality trends.

They can legitimately be employed as exploratory instruments in therapy, alternatively to verbal techniques. But the congruence of the cues they yield with the clinical picture does not provide acceptable evidence of their validity for diagnostic assessments. Correlations between scores (particularly the formal Rorschach scores) and other tests or estimates of traits, motives, abilities, etc., or with criteria of vocational suitability, are generally poor; and there is little improvement when the tester attempts to estimate these variables from the overall pattern. Even with clinical criteria (e.g. using Q-sorts) validity coefficients tend to average around 0·2, and vary considerably from one tester-interpreter to another. Global matching of projective test interpretations with clinical diagnoses or personality sketches gives strongly positive results, but this seems to be due to the projective test revealing a few correct details about one Subject, other details about another. Also there is little consistency from one interpreter to another, and even less between testers employing different techniques. Some, though not all, of this evidence can be discounted since the techniques are intended to touch off covert trends, i.e. deeper motives and mechanisms rather than overt behaviour. The 'construct validity' approach, which attempts to test out deductions from the hypotheses on which the techniques are based, gives a good deal of positive support, particularly when the instrument (e.g. TAT pictures, Story Completions, or play situations) are specifically designed to elicit some particular motive or attitude. Thus these latter instruments have considerable value in experimental and developmental studies of motivation. But responses to the present general tests derive from so many sources, situational, peripheral and central, and there is so large a subjective element in interpreting them, that one is forced to conclude that they should not be used for diagnosing the 'total personality'.

PART III. *Objective approaches to personality*

Chapter 11. **Measurements of traits and factors.** A considerable diversity of viewpoints on personality may be found among those who approach it nomothetically; and the various techniques of studying it have grown up rather haphazardly. However, there would be general agreement in regarding man as an object of scientific study, whose attributes – habits, behaviour tendencies, etc. – can be classified under broader headings or traits, which can be sampled and measured by suitable tests. An early study by the present writer appeared to show that it was possible to reach a rather complete objective survey of personality by sorting the results of a large battery of tests and ratings into clusters or 'trait-composites'. But a major problem in this area is one of taxonomy: that is, determining the main dimensions of human personality differences, and at the same time discarding heterogeneous traits that do not represent consistent behaviour tendencies. This is a problem which would appear to be soluble by multiple factor analysis, though in fact different factorists have arrived at very different conclusions. This chapter concentrates chiefly on the contributions of Guilford, Eysenck and Cattell.

The work of H. J. Eysenck. Eysenck favours a hierarchical picture of personality organization, specific habits being grouped under traits, traits under a few major 'types'. His choice of types or main dimensions is guided by widely recognized group differences (e.g. between neurotics, psychotics and normals) or by psychological theory (e.g. Hullian learning theory of drive and excitation-inhibition). His three type-factors of neuroticism-stability, introversion-extraversion and psychoticism-normality are claimed to synthesize the results of other factorial investigations, and also to make possible the reduction of qualitative psychiatric descriptions to an objective, quantitative, system. Likewise in the area of social attitudes, the manifold results of previous investigations are reduced by him to two factors: radicalism-conservatism and toughness vs. tender-mindedness. His work is strongly antithetical to that of clinical psychologists, and some of his findings have been criticized by other psychometric and experimental psychologists. But the main weakness would appear to be the instability of his and others' test results, which implies that personality factors cannot be measured in the same consistent fashion as ability factors.

The work of R. B. Cattell. Cattell's investigations cover a far wider range of factors, which he considers as fundamental or 'source' traits within the individual, provided they are repeatedly established by a variety of measuring techniques and isolated by oblique rotation to 'Simple Structure'. His main list of factors is derived from 'Life Record' or 'L' data, i.e. ratings of sets of traits chosen to cover the whole personality domain; and he has been less successful in duplicating these with factorizations of 'Q' (questionnaire) or 'T' (objective performance test) data. Second-order analysis of these factors yields a grouping which corresponds closely with Eysenck's introversion-extraversion and neuroticism-stability. Cattell has further analysed the domain of motives, attitudes and interests (ergs and sentiments), preferring objective tests at various levels – overt and covert – to questionnaires and inventories. And he has developed far-reaching techniques for factorizing the personality structure within the individual, for studying group or situational differences, etc. Here too the results appear too unstable to provide a practicable and adequately valid system for assessment purposes.

Chapter 12. **Test-taking attitudes and spurious factors.** The greatest amount of work in the personality field has been done with questionnaires, inventories, social attitude scales, etc., which show useful validity for many purposes, but whose liability to distortions by the Subjects have long been recognized. These distortions are most marked when there are incentives to create a favourable impression (e.g. selection situations), though they are present too in counselling or survey situations where the Subject is guided more by his self-concepts of his traits or attitudes than by the content of the questions as such. As a result, reliabilities are generally quite high, but inter-correlations between tests or attitudes aimed at different variables are affected. Attempts to correct for faking by Lie scales, or forced-choice devices, are only partially successful.

This tendency to give socially desirable responses is but one of a variety of test-taking attitudes. Responses to projective and objective tests are likewise affected by the Subject's conception of the test and its object, his desire to display a personality suitable to the occasion or to his own self-picture, and by so-called response sets. The latter are 'stylistic consistencies', the most noticeable being the tendency of some persons to accept many more statements as applying to themselves than others do (acquiescence), or to choose more extreme responses than others, regardless of the content of the statements. Acquiescence and extremeness particularly affect the F-scale for measuring fascist or authoritarian attitudes, and other scales where all the items are couched in the same direction; and acquiescence plays a considerable part in the Minnesota Multiphasic Personality Inventory (MMPI), where a high 'Yes'-rate produces a high score on scales connected with psychotic abnormality, and a high 'No-rate' a low score on scales connected with neurotic symptoms. However, response sets cannot be distinguished sharply from significant personality traits. Acquiescence is linked with lack of inhibition, with superficial, uneducated, and to some extent with psychotic and extraverted, trends; while social desirability is linked with non-neuroticism. There is no satisfactory way of separating the sets from personality components. Hence the major factors postulated by Eysenck, Cattell and others represent trivial stylistic consistencies to an unknown degree. Similarly any personality factor derived from questionnaire or objective test scores is liable to reflect the method of testing and the Subject's habits of response to this method as much as they do inner personality dispositions.

Chapter 13. **The concept of validity, and other technical considerations.** What a test measures can seldom be determined from its content or logical make-up; we too often over-generalize from the name given to it. Hence external validity is normally demanded in the form of correlations with objectively specifiable outcomes, or with other evidence of the trait, etc., which the test claims to measure. The latter type of validation is never satisfactory, since the criterion is 'notional'. Factorial validation too is unacceptable, since significant factors can be distinguished from 'method' factors only on a basis of content or notional validity. The construct-validation approach is valuable in the personality area; but theory is too apt to outrun fact. Thus this approach has to revert eventually to meaningful relations with external criteria. It is argued that a test should be thought of as measuring only itself, and that its validity resides in the inferences that can be made from it which have been experimentally substantiated. In addition to the richness of its correlates with behaviour, the stability or repeatability of these associations with minor variations in experimental conditions is of crucial importance.

Actuarial or empirical validation. Many psychometrists believe that all assessment problems can be handled on the actuarial model, i.e. by finding an optimally weighted battery of tests or signs for measuring any specified outcome; likewise that valid tests are best constructed by selecting items which correlate optimally with a criterion (or differentiate between two or more criteria). The forced-choice device for reducing halo or social-desirability effects, and other empirically developed correction scores, imply this same belief. While this approach works under certain limited circumstances – namely recurrent situations where a constant outcome is to be predicted for very large numbers of persons – it normally breaks down because of the instability of test-criterion or item-criterion correlations. Regression weights or difference scores inevitably possess low reliability; hence actuarial batteries, or empirically constructed tests, seldom retain useful validity. A few exceptions occur, e.g. the Strong Vocational Interest Blank (VIB), where large numbers of items are related to stable Self-concepts.

Other problems of validation. The 'pay-off' or value of a test depends not only on its correlation with a criterion, but upon the circumstances in which it is applied, for example the Selection Ratio (in educational or vocational selection) or the Base Rate (in clinical diagnosis); upon whether the interests of the Subject or of the selectors are the primary concern; and upon whether it is more obnoxious to select the wrong individuals, or to reject the wrong ones. Again incremental validity (adding useful information to already available techniques) or differential validity (differentiating between two or more outcomes) are very different from raw validity. Irreversible final decisions or the straight prediction of outcomes are generally less effective than exploratory methods, or 'adaptive' treatments. Thus while the actuarial model is the most efficient for such decisions, it does not apply to a majority of personality assessment situations. We are forced back on more clinical or subjective syntheses of test data, though these should be guided as far as possible by actuarial considerations, i.e. by tests with known correlates.

Chapter 14. **The personality system.** This chapter aims not so much to provide a theory or even a definition of personality as to delimit the data with which the personality assessor must concern himself, and to discuss the units or categories in terms of which he can describe it. The conception of traits (or of depth-psychological mechanisms) – i.e. of Inner Dispositions – will continue to be useful, especially in describing abilities, interests and attitudes, and biogenic or physiological factors, all of which can be fairly well defined operationally. But it is unsatisfactory for general personality description: (a) because it involves non-operational theoretical constructs which are anybody's choice: (b) because behaviour varies too widely in different situations to be covered adequately by a limited number of traits, etc., although certainly showing some stability and consistency: (c) because it has not worked; it has failed to yield any satisfactory system of assessment.

In the writer's view it is preferable to think of personality as a kind of chain or system of interactions. Inner Dispositions, including the Self-sentiment and Super-ego, constitute one hypothetical portion. This together with External Stimulation (the objective situation which is interpreted by the Outer-directed Construct system) interact with the Personal Conceptual system to produce Behaviour and Utterances (which are objective). Behaviour and Utterances in turn are interpreted by the Construct systems of other observers, or of the Self, as emanating from Inner Dispositions. This system can and should be studied by the assessor at many points; it is insufficient to investigate: External Stimulation → Objective Behaviour and Utterances (the actuarial or Behaviourist approach), or the Self-system alone.

Statistical factors do not provide adequate units and certainly do not directly represent Inner Dispositions. A possible categorization might be in terms of Murray's needs (Inner Dispositions), alpha press (External Stimulation) and beta press (Outer-directed Constructs). However, preference is given to F. Allport's theory of 'teleonomic trends', i.e. to the categorization of the person in terms of what he is trying to do. This reduces theorizing regarding Inner Dispositions and allows for situational variations. But at present it lacks an adequate taxomony and gives little clear guidance as to how a person's main trends are to be diagnosed.

PART IV. *Practicable methods of assessment*

Chapter 15. **Tests and observations of behaviour.** No attempt is made to give an exhaustive survey of assessment techniques; nor is any radically fresh approach suggested as capable of overcoming the difficulties of assessment. But post-war research has greatly advanced our knowledge both of personality organization and of the uses and limitations of different methods. Hence it is worth describing some of the more promising and practicable methods of arriving at measures with rich and stable correlates which can be of use to the assessor, and which may help to reduce his reliance on more subjective interview judgments.

Though physical and sensory factors may be psychologically significant in the individual case, almost the only physical measure likely to be of value as an indicator of potential personality trends is the somatotype (the initial claims for this must be considerably scaled down). The relations of ability factors, e.g. Thurstone's or

Guilford's, or of measures of maturity, complexity and organization of thought, to personality are still obscure.

Techniques of observing and codifying behaviour which are more direct than the ordinary personality rating, and less dependent on the trait-concept, include time-sampling (especially with young children), and Stott's 'Social Adjustment Guides'. Measures based on qualitative aspects of behaviour in performance tests (such as the Porteus Maze Q-score) are worth further development. Situational tests, e.g. the Leaderless Group Discussion technique, are being widely used in selection for high-grade appointments, and seem capable of making a distinct contribution, though there are numerous difficulties such as fakability, expense, and dependence on relevant job experience. Their superficiality is a positive advantage, and they have shown useful validity in eliciting stable trends, either in social behaviour or in individual methods of coping with jobs. Nevertheless they could benefit from better focusing on particular job requirements and better standardized techniques of scoring.

Chapter 16. Self-report tests. These tests can provide convenient measures of certain aspects of the Concept system, which possess very real advantages of norming and statistical reliability. Some of the merits and demerits of the MMPI and other commonly employed multiple personality inventories are pointed out. Specifications are suggested for an improved test. It should include items to yield control measures of acquiescence and the social-desirability tendency. Items should be chosen to cover a variety of clinically useful variables, and based on reactions to a wide range of everyday life situations. Instead of empirically derived scoring keys, the items should be cluster-analysed in several population samples, to yield some half-dozen scores representing stable Self-concepts; and the external correlates of these should be determined by comparisons with numerous objective criteria.

There is a still stronger case for attitude and interest tests, although they require supplementation by interview or other qualitative techniques. The main difficulty is to choose the most basic or useful list – whether to separate vocational from avocational interests, or interests from attitudes and values (since all of these overlap with one another and with personality measures), or to separate environment-type from need-type (outer- from inner-defined) variables. For example, the question of the relative usefulness of Eysenck's two attitude dimensions, of the construct of authoritarianism, or of

Rokeach's dogmatism vs. open-mindedness, is far from settled. Though no single solution may be satisfactory, it is suggested that a group test should cover some dozen major interests and attitudes, leaving detailed exploration for individual techniques. A wide range of item-types should be included and, once again, stable scales – rather than the items – would be correlated with external criteria. Combinations of such scales might be expected to duplicate many of the variables covered by current tests of interests, attitudes and values.

Chapter 17. **The study of personal concepts.** This chapter is concerned with several methods of studying a person's attitudes and concepts in terms of his own categories rather than of categories imposed by the psychologist's theories – methods which are also, for the most part, more direct and more verbal than the typical projective device. A number of suggestions are made for applying Q-sort technique in ordinary vocational and personality counselling, though little information is available regarding the psychological significance of the various Discrepance scores that might be calculated, factorized, etc.

Similarly, the vocational and clinical uses of Osgood's Semantic Differential for mapping a person's concepts have as yet been little explored. This promises to cover a wider range of attitudes than the Q-sort, but is more troublesome to apply. G. Kelly's Rep test permits of the greatest degree of flexibility for the Subject to define his own conceptual dimensions. But there seems to be no way of using its findings other than idiographically; also it deals only with constructs about people, not about jobs, goals, etc.

Autobiographical materials are valuable to the counsellor, though probably too heterogeneous for systematic content analyses to be profitable. A compromise proposed by the writer is to ask counsellees to write briefly on their likes and dislikes regarding the world in which they live and about themselves. These could be content-analysed, scored and normed, and their construct validity investigated, while yet providing rich clinical material. Despite the objections to projective devices, both picture description and drawings might usefully elicit somewhat less censored attitudes than the above techniques.

Part I

Naïve Interpretations of Personality

Chapter 2

PERCEPTIONS AND
MISPERCEPTIONS OF PEOPLE

Our first task will be to study the processes whereby the ordinary man judges the personalities of those he meets. What theories of personality does he assume, and how can we account for his successes and his failures? This topic received comparatively little attention until the post-war years. In the 1920's and 30's psychologists were more concerned with the reliability and accuracy of the interview, of ratings or of judgments of expressions. And they demonstrated repeatedly the fallibility and bias of our judgments of ourselves and others. Much ingenuity, also, went into investigations of the characteristics of the 'good' or 'poor' judge of personality (cf. Chap. 4). However, in the 1950's there began a spate of publications on *how* we judge, under the headings 'person perception' or 'social perception'. The suitability of these terms might be queried in so far as we interpret, judge, analyse and evaluate, over and above seeing or perceiving people's characteristics. It is not only in Britain that the problem was neglected until fairly recently.* Its popularization in America was due largely to immigrants from Europe, including Heider and Ichheiser, W. Wolff and Arnheim, and the leading Gestalt psychologists.

Our ignorance of how we interpret. The ordinary adult or child cannot formulate explicitly how he interprets, any more than he can explain how he walks or reads; though if pressed he could mention some of the signs or *cues* he uses: that when people blush they are embarrassed, if they yawn they are tired or bored, and so on. And he can often produce saws or generalizations which, he believes at least, guide his understanding: 'children should be seen but not heard', 'you can't teach an old dog new tricks', 'most actors and actresses are

* A notable exception was Oldfield's (1941) brief but important book on interviewing which included a careful analysis of the psychological processes involved, in addition to suggestions on how an employment interview should be conducted.

unstable', 'Jews are clever but unreliable', and so forth. Much as a child learns and applies grammatical rules without having been taught grammar, when he says: 'I eated my dinner', so we shall find that A judges B, and B judges A, according to quite systematic though implicit (i.e. largely unconscious) principles. At the same time, much of what we have to say in this chapter must seem platitudinous if it is to describe correctly something we are doing all the time.

Our unsophisticated Mr or Mrs A does not think of interpretation as a problem. He or she *sees* B as 'irritated', 'looking for something', 'domineering', just as he or she sees them 'walk', or hears them 'shout', and sees a chair as solid and brown and 3 feet tall. True, B is more variable, complicated and unpredictable than things are, but that is because B is regarded as a person with thoughts and feelings like A's. He is a self-activating being, and he is not entirely unpredictable if A understands him aright. A thinks of himself as consistent and logical, and expects B to be the same. Note that 'being a person' is a matter of degree rather than of kind, depending on the extent to which people affect us personally. The teeming millions of China, India and Africa tend to seem more 'object-like', less human than dwellers in our own slums, than even our pet dog. And slum-dwellers, or strangers seen in a bus, have less person-quality than our acquaintances.

Now a moment's thought will show that B's 'domineeringness' or his subjective states cannot be physical stimuli which are directly seen, that they are somehow inferred from B's behaviour. But thinking a stage further, we realize that perhaps this is not so different from the perception of physical objects. The 'solidity' of the chair is not given either; it is an inference from A's past experience of touching and handling chairs. In both instances A assigns 'dispositional qualities' to the percept (Heider, 1958). The chair looks comfortable – it possesses the quality or trait of comfortableness; B looks amiable – he has a disposition or trait of amiability. And just as A's judgment of the chair is usually borne out when he subsequently sits in it, so his readings of B's dispositions, thoughts and feelings normally seem to be confirmed. At the same time, these qualities are definitely referred to the object or person. If A is pricked, the sensation of pain is subjective – it happens to him; but he regards the sharpness of the pin as objective. So too is B's amiability.

Behaviour is 'explained' by references to intentions. Dispositions and traits, intentions, motives and attitudes, interests and abilities play a crucial part in our interpretations of people, since it is these that give consistency and stability to what might otherwise be a chaotic series of actions. If an observer from another planet saw B preparing a meal or arguing with his teenage son, the successive bits of behaviour might seem fragmentary, arbitrary and inexplicable; but to A, who realizes the underlying intention, they fall into line. A similar observation was made by Hebb (1946) when studying chimpanzees, namely that records of their specific actions were meaningless, but they became intelligible when grouped into general categories and related to preceding actions. It was impossible to give a complete description without resorting to anthropomorphic interpretations of the animals' wants and feelings. Others have shown that certain sequences of physical stimuli readily evoke animistic impressions of causation and motivation.

In a long series of experiments on the perception of moving squares, Michotte (1946) found that one square was seen as 'launching' or 'pushing' or 'carrying along' a second one, and concluded that we have an innate disposition to perceive mechanical causality directly. In other situations, purpose or 'intentionality' might be inferred. Similarly,

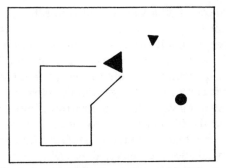

Fig. 1. Apparent behaviour of geometrical figures.
(From Heider and Simmel, 1944.)

Heider and Simmel (1944) presented a short film in which two triangles and a circle moved in or out of a rectangle with a door in it. Almost all his observers described one triangle as 'chasing' or 'hitting' the other, the circle as 'hiding to escape'. The large triangle was 'aggressive', the smaller 'heroic', the circle 'timid and feminine'.

F. From (1960) goes so far as to claim that it is impossible for us to perceive behaviour as such; what we think we see always depends on the intention that we ascribe to the person. And if he should act in some unexpected fashion, we say that he has made a mistake or changed his mind, not that we were wrong in our interpretation.

Invariance of dispositional qualities. Behaviour is variable also in the sense that many different actions seem to stem from the same disposition. B's amiability may be shown at one time by his facial expression or tone of voice, at other times by the opinions he states in a discussion, or by various kindly acts that he performs towards C or D. The same end may be achieved by diverse means. Likewise there is no one definable pattern of behaviour which is always recognized as a cue for amiability, or other such traits, but rather a kind of theme with variations. Indeed the significance of any one cue depends a good deal on the circumstances. An action which is kind to C, who is a weak and undeserving person, might be taken to imply currying favour if performed for D, who is a popular and powerful person. Note, moreover, that dispositional qualities – traits, abilities, interests and the like – are assumed to persist in the individual whether or not he is displaying them at the moment. We recognize that, under conditions of stress, he may behave out of accord with these qualities.

This invariance or stability in the trait or intention, despite variable appearances and temporary lapses, is particularly striking in the interpretation of people; but it occurs also in our identification of objects, for example in so-called phenomenal regression and the 'constancy phenomenon'. A circular white dinner-plate, a foot across, is seen as such whether it constitutes a large stimulus close to the eyes, or a tiny stimulus 30 feet away, when it is a narrow ellipse seen on its side, and even when the illumination is so dim that it reflects no more light into the eye than a dull grey surface. Similarly a person's physical characteristics are perceived as highly constant. When he walks from a spot 10 feet away to another 20 feet away, he certainly does not appear to halve his size. However, constancy is limited; for if we see people from the top of a tall building, they tend to lose this human or person quality, and look like ridiculous ants. Again, while constancy of colour can be demonstrated, and is certainly a dispositional quality of the object, yet a blue dress will become greenish in yellow illumination, and a human face looks ghostly in the light of mercury vapour lamps.

Ittelson and Slack (1958) and Cantril (1957) report experiments in which perceptual distortions were induced by wearing aniseikonic lenses, or by viewing people in an Ames distorted room. They claim to have found greater stability or freedom from distortion in perceiving familiar people than strange people, and greater for persons in authority than for less important people, though the differences were fairly small.

A number of other parallels between Gestalt characteristics in visual perception and characteristics of person perception have been pointed out, e.g. by Heider (1958) and McLeod (1960). True, considerable caution is needed before assuming that the perception of personal qualities is essentially identical with the perception of meaningless shapes. Yet equally it might be questioned whether perceptual phenomena observed under controlled laboratory conditions fully cover the normal perception of objects and occurrences in our everyday environment.

Cues and their interpretation. What are the cues or stimuli on which our judgments of people are based? The following list is modified from Ichheiser (1949):

1. *Static or physical factors:* facial appearance, physique, also such modes of expression as clothes, personal adornment, furnishings of home, etc. Although, as we shall see, these are quite inaccurate a-indicators of enduring personality traits, they do enable A to classify B's social *roles*. By identifying his sex, age, often his nationality and social class, or his job, he can anticipate the patterns of behaviour and attitudes associated with these categories, and adapt his own behaviour accordingly.

2. *Dynamic or expressive factors:* movements of the features and limbs, vocal and speech qualities. These allow A to judge temporary moods with some facility, but he is also likely to extrapolate and interpret such enduring dispositional qualities as energy, vivacity, caution, seriousness, insincerity, etc.

3. *Content factors: What* he does rather than how he does it. In this and the preceding category, it may be impossible to specify just what cues are operating. They may influence A subconsciously, or produce an affective rather than a cognitive response. Rommetveit (1960) provided an experimental demonstration of this process of 'discrimination without awareness'. But this feature too is not peculiar to the interpretation of persons. We are seldom aware of the bases of our judgments of spatial characteristics such as distance and solidity. The tennis player would find it hard to specify how he tells what kind of shot his opponent is playing; still less could he analyse all the components that make up his responses, i.e. his own strokes.

4. *Situational factors:* the context in which the behaviour occurs, whether realized or not.

5. *Communications from other people:* what A has previously heard about B.

6. *Communications from the person himself.* This category is usually regarded as the least trustworthy, not to be taken at its face value, unless it is backed up by previous knowledge of B's sincerity, by evidence of behaviour (No. 3) and judgments of expression (No. 2), for example, the definiteness and clarity of his speech and its relevance, the keenness and interest he displays. Indeed, in contacts between persons other than close friends and relatives, the participants normally take it for granted that each is 'playing a part', that the visible expressions, actions and speech are chosen to create a favourable impression and to ward off, as far as possible, any revelation of the 'real' self or Ego.

Much as perception of the world around us is inextricably entangled with inferences based on past experience, so too, even in quite casual social contacts, we carry out elaborate analyses of, and inferences from, the cues that others present. Heider (1958) provides a detailed description of the components which seem to enter into these judgments.*

As an example, let us suppose that A is visiting B's home and observes him adjusting the television set for a ballet programme. He weighs up *situational factors* that help or hinder (age of set, positioning, etc.) and may ascribe B's success or failure in part to *luck* (e.g. interference conditions). He also tends to differentiate between 'can', 'tries', 'wants', and 'why'. Failure may be due to lack of skill – he *cannot*; or to lack of persistence and keenness – he does not *try* and this is because he does not *want* it sufficiently. But in addition 'want' is complex. The reason 'why' or the goal may be:

i) B's own wish, or interest in ballet. This may be subdivided into intrinsic attractiveness – the ballet is 'good' in the same way as sugar is sweet; and idiosyncratic attraction – B's particular taste.

ii) Some temporary feeling rather than an enduring disposition, e.g. he is tired, or upset by some extraneous circumstance.

iii) Some secondary motive – e.g. to appear cultured, although he will be bored.

iv) He is asked to by the other guests or knows they would

---

* Both Heider's account, and our own brief summary, consist too largely of 'armchair' speculation, and more empirical data on the kinds of analyses that different judges carry out are badly needed.

appreciate it, i.e. the degree of provocation as distinct from personal responsibility. If, in A's estimation, B would not find the action *personally satisfying*, then he is absolved, and this forms one of the most crucial elements in any judgment. Thus, if A had said that he would prefer to watch a political broadcast, he would be angered by B's action, unless he believed that B was not *at fault*, or realized that he had *tried*, but *could not* through lack of skill or situational handicaps.

A similar analysis might be made of the interviewer's interpretation of a candidate's motivations in an employment interview. Indeed, the good interviewer will try to establish much more explicitly the parts played by luck, opportunity, ability, superficial and deeper motives, in exploring the candidate's previous successes or failures.

Types of social interactions. However, the components that A looks for, and his interpretations, may vary considerably with the type of social interaction between A and B, i.e. with the situation or context (cf. Sarbin, Taft and Bailey, 1960; Jones and Thibaut, 1958). We may distinguish the following:

1. Giving and receiving information, e.g. a social survey interview, a purchase in a shop, etc. Here, A is particularly on the lookout for B's reliability, candour, his objectivity, prejudice, his relevant knowledge and experience. In the survey situation, B is suspicious of any threat to his values, intrusions on his personal affairs, and thereıore attempts to assess A's role and his motive for making the inquiry.

2. Social rituals, e.g. meeting people at a cocktail party. These might well be compared to dogs sniffing each other's tails, the object being simply to assess status or dominance and role. A looks for cues which will tell him who B is, in order to behave appropriately, while also striving to maintain his own position in the social hierarchy. Each also avoids expressing any attitudes strongly, being reluctant to give away cues to his own personality until he knows that the other will not disapprove.

3. Obtaining support for one's attitudes and values. A wishes to know if B thinks as he does; if not, he will tend to devaluate B as a person. Is he compatible as a friend or work-mate; does he flatter A's self-esteem and help or hinder his needs? In most ordinary social intercourse between acquaintances the approach is strongly normative; each is assessing the other in terms of good or bad.

4. Persuading people to do a job, buy something, etc. Here A looks for evidence of B's competence and dependability, his persuasibility

and willingness, and his interest in his (A's) goals. Conversely, B is concerned with A's reliability in describing the proposition and his personal disinterestedness.

5. Directing people and being directed, e.g. the employer-employee, parent-child, or other such situations. A is primarily concerned with B's responsibility and his values or standards which he wishes to modify. But he usually takes careful account also of abilities and personal dispositions so as to avoid antagonizing B against the values he wants to communicate. Likewise, B assesses which approach to A will placate him and minimize the extent of the blow to his self-esteem.

6. Purposive analysis, as by a doctor, psychologist, social worker, counsellor, teacher, lawyer, novelist. This is a more logical and deliberate, if less evaluative, study of B's motives. Here, even more than in No. 1, B is on the alert to reveal only those cues which he is willing that A should know, and is concerned about A's trustworthiness and approval of him.

Note that in all these contacts there is an interplay; they are not just a matter of B providing stimuli for A. By addressing or answering someone, and letting him see us perform any action, we are revealing ourselves to his evaluation and, in a way, laying ourselves open to potential attack. Thus, we seldom look directly at another, or like to be looked at, for long, and are apt to become paralysed with stage-fright if, at a public function, large numbers of people are able to attack us with their eyes.

Many social situations, of course, contain two or more of these types. Thus the selection interview falls primarily under No. 6, but would include much of Nos. 2, 3 and 4. As Oldfield (1941) points out, the interviewer's main object should be to stimulate the candidate to display his 'attitudes'*, through first establishing good rapport, then introducing a series of topics on which he will talk spontaneously, sometimes by arguing or stating his own attitudes, or by a variety of other tactics.

The synthesis of impressions. So far we have been concerned with the analytic aspects of interpreting people. But it should be stressed that the observer always tends to see the subject as a unitary whole, how-

---

* It is not entirely clear what Oldfield means by attitudes; they are not just sentiments, beliefs and values (as in common American usage), but appear to include more general personal dispositions such as cautiousness, domineeringness, introversion, etc. They are both states of mind in the candidate and qualities of his behaviour.

ever fragmentary the cues. He is not a sum of his physical, dynamic and other qualities any more than a chair is perceived as an addition of certain dimensions and colours. At first sight (or on first hearing about him from others) he is an individual, and the information about more detailed qualities which is obtained from subsequent cues is integrated into this whole. Inconsistencies, variability or unintegratedness may indeed be perceived, but these tend to make us search for deeper motives or traits which reconcile them. As Bartlett (1932) described in his work on perception of, and memory for, complex drawings and stories, there is an 'effort after meaning', a striving towards an integrated structure or good Gestalt. Links are more readily established because any one cue often carries multiple meanings and implications. Thus, if A sees that B is a cripple or a negro, or is told that B is a professor, he at once expects a whole series of qualities which he associates with these roles.

This is illustrated by an experiment in which Haire and Grunes (1950) presented the following list of items to a group of college students, and asked them to describe what sort of person this man was:
'Works in a factory, reads a newspaper, goes to movies, average height, cracks jokes, strong and active.'
To a second similar group the same list was presented, but with the insertion of an additional word: 'intelligent'.
The first group had little difficulty in picturing the man, usually in rather patronizing tones, but the second group found it much harder to integrate the qualities. Some subjects denied the intrusive item, e.g. 'He is intelligent, but not too much so, since he works in a factory'; others promoted him to foreman, i.e. denying that he was a worker; and others qualified it so as to render it harmless, e.g. 'He is intelligent but doesn't possess the initiative to rise above his group.'

Asch (1946) showed that the significance of any one trait is affected by others with which it is associated. As in visual or auditory perception the whole is more than the sum of its parts. For example, to two groups he presented lists of traits differing in one item:

intelligent, skilful, industrious, warm, determined, practical, cautious.
intelligent, skilful, industrious, cold, determined, practical, cautious.

asking them to write 'a characterization' of the person. He found that this alteration of one term produced a basic change in the subjects' impressions, and went on to show by similar experiments that some traits are more influential or central, while others are more peripheral and easily altered.

Asch's work has been justly criticized by Luchins (1948) on the grounds of the artificiality of experimental technique and poor control of conditions. Luchins points out that we do not normally perceive discrete qualities in people and then integrate them, nor even necessarily make use of the notion of traits at all in arriving at our impressions (unless told to by an investigator). However he does not deny the tendency to organize our impressions, though the structure may be looser and more inconsistent as between different judges than Asch and others have claimed.

In another study with adjectives, similar to Asch's, Wishner (1960) pointed out that those traits are most affected which correlate most highly with the altered item. In other words, this type of experiment does not necessarily support the view that A's synthesis of B's characteristics constitutes an unique Gestalt (cf. also Bruner et al., 1958).

An experiment by H. H. Kelley (1950) seems to bear a closer resemblance to real-life situations. A new instructor was introduced to a group of students by means of a brief sketch which included the words, either 'a warm person' or 'a cold person'. After a class discussion period with him they rated him on a series of traits, and those whose preliminary cue was 'warm' assessed him as more considerate, informal, social, popular, and humorous than those whose cue was 'cold'. Moreover, 56% of the former judges actually participated in the discussion as against 32% of the latter. However, ratings on intelligence, generosity, dominance, and getting ahead, were little affected by this cue. It did not merely raise or lower the judges' all-round halo, but mainly influenced their perception of a cluster of related personality traits.

What we seem to arrive at is a mental image or model of the person, or as Oldfield calls it, a *homunculus*, which guide our reactions to him in any future situation.* Thus, if A's first impression of B includes the idea of 'pushingness', he will behave differently to him throughout that meeting, or at subsequent meetings. And though he will modify, clarify and expand his image as further cues are received, the initial judgment often remains dominant. The homunculus may or may not incorporate verbalized labels or names of traits, attitudes, etc., or visual images. Indeed it is as much an affective concept or senti-ment towards the person (in McDougall's sense – a crystallization of feelings) as a cognitive picture. If A is asked for an opinion of B, he refers to it in formulating his answer, and if A is a job interviewer, he will try to match this 'working model' (cf. Wilson, 1945) against what he considers to be the job requirements. We should note, too, that the homunculus is not usually constructed by conscious de-liberation – it forms itself; and just because it is a synthesis, it would

* Cf. also H. S. Sullivan's (1933) concept of a 'personification'.

be very difficult for A to state on just what cues any particular feature is based. However, the scientifically minded vocational or clinical interviewer will often do his best to 'validate' or test out his analysis of B's motivations by seeking additional evidence. For example, he will suspend judgment on B's 'pushingness' until he has probed further into his past career and present relations with people.

Personality displays. Complementary to the process of interpretation is the process whereby each participant attempts to influence the other's judgment by displaying an acceptable and impressive personality (cf. Goffman, 1956). Not only in important situations like the selection interview, but in trivial social contacts, B impersonates, or puts on what he considers an appropriate front or façade for A. Indeed it might be said that we change our personalities to suit the occasion as women change their clothes, but much more rapidly and with less conscious deliberation. To some extent B may calculate or plan to create a particular effect on A, but it is largely an automatic adjustment to the particular social situation and to B's assessment of A's expectations. Note also that we have taboos against discussing this; it would be as impolite to admit that we are not behaving 'naturally' as it would be to talk about our private sexual or excretory functions. Moreover, the barriers against all these topics tend to be raised or lowered simultaneously; we behave more naturally and are more willing to discuss both impersonations and sex with our wives or with a psychotherapist than with a stranger. (A particularly interesting social phenomenon, analysed in great detail by Goffman, is the assumption of mutual 'fronts' by two or more people, as when husband and wife back one another up at a party, or the sales staff in a shop combine to impress the customer.) Yet at the same time the participants are generally aware of what is going on, and do their best to penetrate the other's disguise.

Young children, of course, are not conversant with these rituals, and have to be kept out of adult functions because they are apt to give away information about their parents' private behaviour. However, they become indoctrinated remarkably early. Even at 3 years they are being taught to behave more circumspectly when visitors arrive. By 7 years they are displaying different personalities when the teacher is present or absent, and soon they are putting on 'fronts' to other children appropriate to their own age. For example, they despise certain games or toys as babyish in front of their peers, though liking to play with them privately.

Two important points must be held over for later discussion. First: is there a real, natural or undisguised personality? Even when B is performing before a completely trusted friend or psychotherapist, or before no one at all, is he not his own audience, putting on behaviour which approximates to his internal standards and values, in just the same way as he adapts to others' expectations? And secondly, despite the variations with different audiences, is there not a fair degree of consistency – a personal style which he cannot readily disguise? Clearly, some traits, e.g. abilities and interests, are less modifiable than others. Some people, also, are less willing to modify and more rebellious against putting on conventional displays than others are.

MISINTERPRETATIONS OF PERSONALITY

Oversimplification. Let us consider now the main sources of errors and biases that are only too apt to arise in so complex a process as the interpretation of personality. A useful account is given by Ichheiser (1949), and at the head of his list is the tendency to oversimplify people, to exaggerate their consistency or invariance.

In our perception of the physical world, we usually assume that the mind's eye, as it were, somehow mirrors or photographs external reality directly. But it would be more correct to say that we merely use the incoming stimuli to construct a picture or model of the world which best serves our practical needs. M. D. Vernon (1952) points out that the essential function of perceiving is to maximize its stability and consistency, to see (and hear or feel) it as a world of familiar and enduring objects, while also developing sufficient sensitivity to be able to respond to any unfamiliarities or changes that might be potentially harmful or significant to us. Similarly, it is of the utmost importance to us personally, and to the stability of society, that people should be consistent and simple beings, who stay the same in different surroundings or at different times. Both in object perception and personality interpretation we do not like ambiguity, complexity or unusualness, and therefore simplify down to what is essential from our standpoint. Hence the well-known tendency to see people in blacks *or* whites, as goodies or baddies, to overestimate their unity and to ignore their subtler variations. Normally A meets B only in a limited context, and extrapolates, assuming that B will be the same in other circumstances. The teacher sees a boy as badly behaved in school, and imputes his mother's favourable opinion of him at home to prejudice; and the mother reciprocates. Even the novelist or bio-

grapher, who appeals to us through his sensitivity to motives, is apt
to simplify his characters down to a single theme (for example,
Dickens and Emil Ludwig). The writer such as Boswell, who gives
us the rich unintegratedness of a personality, is the exception (cf.
Allport, 1961a). Most of us simply cannot hold the innumerable cues
that a person provides in mind, and therefore have to select and
over-generalize.

In so far as we ignore situational variations, we tend to overweight
'personal responsibility' (cf. p. 31) in analysing the sources of
people's actions. Oversimplification is often associated with the kind
of animism which Piaget has described in children's thinking – the
tendency to attribute natural occurrences to human agencies rather
than to physical factors. In children, this probably arises because
their basic experiences of movement occur when *they* push or pull
things. To quote an example from Watts (1944): if a young child is
asked – 'The clock stopped because . . . ?', he is likely to give such
answers as, 'Because father dropped it.' Not until 7 or 8 years or later
will impersonal, mechanical causes be invoked. As adults we are less
anthropomorphic about physical events, but we are still apt to attribute complex social and economic occurrences to the personalities
of certain individuals: for example the rise of fascism and all that it
entails to the personal qualities of Mussolini and Hitler, or the
difficulties of a commercial firm to the inefficiency of the manager,
and so on. Similarly in everyday affairs, we are usually satisfied with
imputing the behaviour of those we meet to a few stock motives or
dispositions.

Rigidity. The exaggeration of personal consistency implies, too, that
we are remarkably impermeable to contradictory evidence. Often we
simply do not see behaviour, or hear speech, which does not fit in
with our conception of a person, much as we don't see an object
placed in an unusual context in the game of Hunt-the-Thimble.
When tape recordings are made of vocational or social-survey interviews, it is often found that the interviewer, A, so largely anticipates
what he is expecting B to say that he either does not allow him to
complete, or even ignores, his answers (Kahn and Cannell, 1957).
And if B gives qualified, uncertain or reluctant answers, A tends to
sharpen or improve them in his recollection. Obviously this is a
serious difficulty in inquiries into people's opinions on political,
social and moral issues, since more often than not their attitudes *are*
confused, ambiguous and inconsistent.

In an experiment by Stanton and Baker (1942), five experienced interviewers were told to find out from a group of students which of a series of geometrical designs they had been shown previously. The interviewers were working from keys which supposedly gave the 'correct' responses for each student. But even when the keys were false, they still tended to obtain positive results; i.e. they unwittingly recorded the students as recognizing the designs which they, the interviewers, believed to be correct.

Often, again, we resist admitting changes in the personalities of our acquaintances, as when our children grow up, or a friend alters markedly through going to university, getting married, or moving to a new job. We are not, of course, entirely impervious to contradictory evidence; indeed, with children, we expect them to change to some extent with growth. However, Ichheiser points out that what we perceive 'in principle' may differ from what we interpet 'in fact'. A may acknowledge *theoretically* that B differs from what he thought, and yet *effectively* behave towards him as before. Often, indeed, we are genuinely unaware of our effective attitudes and would indignantly disclaim our snobbishness or our prejudice against negroes. This distinction may be related to that drawn earlier between the affective and the more cognitive, verbalizable aspects of the homunculus.

To a large extent people back us up in our interpretations, since they show us these aspects of their personalities of which they think we will approve. A does not realize that he himself is an important element in the situation to which B is reacting. This happens in the selection interview, where the candidate is extremely sensitive to what he thinks the interviewer wants, and chooses his answers in the light of any hints he can get from the interviewer's questions, tone of voice, manner, even pauses (the 'frigid silence'), and other expressions of which the interviewer may be quite unaware. But the same is true of everyday social intercourse and of long-term contacts. The boy who is regarded as a delinquent at school tends to live up to his reputation. The unemployed man realizes that many think of him as unemployable (they attribute his position to his 'own fault' rather than to situational factors), and this lowers his security and self-esteem until he accepts their judgment and actually becomes more and more unemployable.

Egocentricity and projection. Experimental studies of personality ratings show that a major component in our judgments of almost any trait is the 'halo' – a general good or bad impression (cf. p. 59). In part this derives from oversimplification, or failure to recognize that people can be high in some desirable traits, low in others. But in addition there is a strong tendency to evaluate people along the single dimension of how they affect us, and to assume egocentrically that most of their actions are directed towards helping or harming us. We dislike ambiguity also, and are apt to polarize people; they must be for us or against us, not qualified in their approval. If one is harmed by a person one doesn't know or whom one dislikes, e.g. if he steps on one's toe on a bus, it is a sign of his malignancy (personal responsibility), whereas if a friend does the same action, it is excused and attributed to situational factors or luck.

Again, we expect people's attitudes, beliefs and habits to be similar to our own; and if this is falsified we regain our peace of mind by concluding that there is something wrong with them – they are queer, outsiders, etc. This assumption that all right-minded people think as we do has been called 'projection'. However, as Cattell (1951) and Murstein and Pryor (1959) point out, the term projection has been variously interpreted. The present phenomenon should be distinguished both from Freudian projection – the attribution to others of our repressed impulses, and from the influence of personal factors on the perception of ambiguous stimuli, which occurs in projection tests (Chap. 10). Note that our values are another example of constancies or absolutes, which we regard as independent of people's wishes. Meat *must* be eaten with cutlery, boys *should* fight for dominance and girls *shouldn't*, royalty *is* to be respected, just as grass *is* green, and a plate seen sideways on *is* circular.

This egocentricity in interpreting others is more marked among young children, as Piaget has shown, and among less educated people. The more sophisticated and insightful, possibly because they themselves have richer personalities, are better able to differentiate their evaluations from mere personal compatibility. For example they are more tolerant of foreigners, less apt to devaluate introverts if they themselves are extraverted, or conservatives if they are radicals, and vice versa.

Howard and Berkowitz (1958) set up an experimental situation in which college students heard a number of evaluations of their performance at a complex task, and assessed these for accuracy. It was found that they regarded both over- and under-evaluations as inaccurate; i.e. they did not accept praise which exceeded their own levels of aspiration.

This experiment suggests that Heider and Ichheiser (whom we have largely followed in analysing personality interpretation) tend to exaggerate our egocentricity. However, the conditions of the experiment were rather different from those of everyday social interactions. The students were well educated and it was not their values which were being approved or disapproved. Thus it is hardly surprising that they put more trust in their own internal standards of performance than in the evaluations by onlookers.

Frameworks of interpretation. A number of lines of evidence indicate that it would be a mistake to reduce our guiding principle of judgment to a single dimension of congeniality-uncongeniality, or goodness-badness. Osgood's work (1957) on the 'semantic differential', and George Kelly's (1955) studies of personal constructs show that different people have varied 'frames of reference', or attitude systems.

Osgood took a series of concepts: 'My father, Confusion, Lady, Sickness, Hatred, etc.', and had them rated by groups of subjects on a number of adjectival scales such as rough vs. smooth, thick vs. thin, large vs. small, etc. The subjects did not find this unduly difficult and gave fairly consistent judgments.

When correlations were calculated between the adjectival scales, there was considerable overlapping; and by factor analysis it was shown that they could be reduced to three main dimensions:

I. Evaluative: good-bad, beautiful-ugly, clean-dirty, fair-unfair, etc. In numerous investigations this has always proved to be the most outstanding factor.

II. Potency: large-small, strong-weak, heavy-light, etc.

III. Activity: fast-slow, active-passive, excited-calm, etc.

In other words, our classificatory system, either for people's traits or for other abstract concepts, though largely evaluative, does recognize other aspects and dimensions.

A later analysis by Osgood (1962) of a more heterogeneous set of 40 epithets, applied to 40 concepts about people, yielded a larger number of significant factors, at least six of which could be identified as follows: 1. Moral evaluation; 2. Rationality; 3. Uniqueness or Unusualness; 4. Excitable-calm; 5. Sociable-introverted; 6. Tough-sensitive.

These dimensions still represent the average attitudes of many judges, and one may doubt the adequacy of Osgood's technique for revealing the richness of individual frameworks, despite his demonstration of a high degree of consistency, even among judges of different ethnic backgrounds. A combination of his approach with that of Kelly, where each individual chooses his own effective dimensions (cf. p. 284) might be more fruitful. One might expect different individuals to have widely varying conceptions of 'good'. For example, the rebellious intellectual looks for unconventionality rather than conformity, and the schoolboy who is unconcerned about his mother's dimension of social respectability instead refers the actions and speech of other boys to his own value of 'good at football, rags the teacher, vs. bookworm'. Again people who are strong in Spranger's aesthetic, theoretical or religious, values will judge others according to different criteria.

The 'new look' in perception. Recent years have seen a spate of work on affective or motivational factors influencing our perception of objects, pictures, words etc. (cf. Blake and Ramsey, 1951; Jenkin, 1957). People tend to recognize more readily words that refer to their values than those that don't, and to set up defences against stimuli that arouse unpleasant associations. If hungry, they are more apt to see images of food in weakly structured perceptual situations. These phenomena are more complex than was originally assumed, and their explanation more controversial (cf. W. P. Brown, 1961). Other writers, including M. D. Vernon (1955) and Gibson (1951), point out how small and inconsistent are the effects in contrast to the effects of perceptual constancy, or of variations in the experimental instructions. They can generally be demonstrated only in situations where it is difficult to perceive realistically. But for this very reason we might expect them to assume importance in interpreting people. If Mr A has had a tiring and frustrating day at work and has to entertain Mr and Mrs B as guests in the evening, he is likely to regard them with a more jaundiced eye. Perhaps it would be difficult to prove here that A really perceives the B's differently – that he is not merely feeling and reacting differently. However, it has been shown, for example, that people prejudiced against negroes actually misperceive pictures or incidents involving whites and negroes (Allport & Postman, 1947). Similarly Murray (1933) found that children who had just experienced a frightening situation – a game of 'Murder' – tended to interpret pictures of people as being more malicious than normally. It is probable, then, that our attitudes and values arouse expectations and sensitize us to certain cues from people, or make us repress other cues.

Naïve personality theories and stereotypes. More generally, each of us, in the course of his lifetime, seems to build up a rough-and-ready set of theories or schemata of human nature, of how and why various kinds of people react to various situations. We possess a considerable repertoire of concepts about motivation and personality, although much of it is but weakly formulated or verbalizable. Probably our schemata are based largely on analysing ourselves and observing others, but also on discussions about people and on what we were taught in childhood, at school and elsewhere, on novels, stories and newspapers, cinema films, plays, and television. All these help to develop categories for interpreting others which will, of course, differ from one judge to another despite a fair amount of consensus attributable to common cultural values and mutual discussions. Among other things our theories tell us that certain traits go with others – that a well-educated person is likely to be more intelligent, reliable, perhaps more interested in books and less in sports, than an ill-educated, and so on. These theories guide our understanding of people's intentions and enable us to anticipate their behaviour – so much so that when people from foreign countries or from a different social class do not fulfil our expectations we are apt to think them peculiar, aimless, or even immoral.

Another prominent feature of our theories is what social psychologists call 'stereotyping' – that is we see a person as a specimen of a certain group and attribute to him all the characteristics that we associate with that group. If A has heard that B is a Jew, or rightly or wrongly identifies him as Jewish, he tends to expect various traits and attitudes and consequently usually finds evidence of these. We have stereotypes or expected roles for people of different ages, for the two sexes, for many occupational groups – doctors, ministers, teachers, army officers, etc., for interest groups – athletes, aesthetes, socialists, and for various personality types – the hen-pecked husband, the shy intellectual, the efficient organizer, etc.

Normally, on first meeting, as pointed out above, we try to fit a person into one or more of our pigeon-holes or stock personalities, on the basis of physical cues or previous communications, and these do indeed allow us to go quite a long way in adjusting our behaviour to suit them and in making predictions about them. Social psychologists have too often given the impression that stereotypes are fictitious and biased. But while it is true that they are always over-simplified, often irrational or based on hearsay or other unreliable fragments of evidence, and thus lead us, for example, to misinterpret foreigners, negroes, and other 'out-groups', yet at least as often they help us to get to know people more quickly, and promote common reactions among members of the in-group who share the same stereotypes. For example, social intercourse would become chaotic if we did not straight away react differently to a 60-year-old and a 6-year-old, to a society hostess and a prostitute. Moreover stereotypes are misnamed in that we habitually use them as starting points, when we have nothing else to go on, and are often willing to modify them – to recognize that B differs from 'the typical' Jew, etc.

Nevertheless, they do often act as barriers to understanding, particularly because the process of stereotyping is reciprocal. Not only may the secondary school teacher oversimplify and misinterpret a pupil through thinking of him as 'a teen-ager', but the pupil likewise pigeon-holes the teacher, and each tends to react in accordance with the other's expectations until some measure of trust and recognition of individuality is built up between them. One of the reasons for the unsatisfactoriness of the short selection interview is that it is seldom able to progress much beyond this exchange of stereotypes, particularly since the role of employer (or personnel officer) and candidate are strongly demarcated. Wide differences in social class, age, interests, speech patterns and so forth obviously make for difficulty in the interpretation of cues. For example, the style of haircut is interpreted very differently by the teen-ager and the teacher.

Perceptual styles. A factor neglected so far is differences in 'perceptual styles'. Several references have been made to intolerance of ambiguity. Frenkel-Brunswik (1949) claims that this is a perceptual and personality variable; that people who show rigidity and insistence on definite categories in their perceptions and thinking also tend to show authoritarian prejudice and ethnic intolerance, usually due to insecurity in their own personality make-up. The work of Klein (1951) has suggested a distinction between sharpeners and levellers – those who tend to accentuate unusual features, say in perceiving a diagram, and those who level down such features so as to make the perception more conventional and acceptable. It may be that sharpeners are more aware of inconsistencies in others' personalities and more interested in probing their sources. However, this is purely hypothetical: there is as yet little convincing evidence that the way we see and interpret people is linked with the way we see objects.* Indeed it is by no means certain that these styles are consistent or general over a wide range of visual phenomena.

Nevertheless we do find individual differences in methods of viewing personalities. Some appear to be satisfied with describing people in terms of relatively superficial traits and interests: others look for

* Harvey *et al.* (1961) claim that persons whose conceptual structure falls at different developmental levels from the concrete to the abstract show characteristic differences in interpreting others (cf. p. 113, also Chap. 15).

deeper motivations, perhaps because they have a strong, neurotically based, need to analyse people (cf. Taft, 1960). There are variations also in the treatment of cues, some obtaining a more synthetic or global impression, others inferring particular traits from particular impressions or behaviour. And Oldfield (1941) points out that interviewers vary widely in the use they make of different kinds of evidence. Rosenzweig's (1945) classification of reactions to frustration may also be relevant, though again we know of no direct evidence. He suggests that, in a frustrating situation, some people tend to blame others or the environment (extrapunitive); some find fault with themselves (intropunitive); while some tend to evade or minimize the frustration (impunitive). These might conceivably be connected with the tendency, noted above, to underestimate situational factors in favour of personal responsibility, also the attribution of malignancy to those who step on our toes, literally or metaphorically.

Finally, we should not forget Jung's four types of mental function – thinking, feeling, sensation and intuition; though there is little experimental proof that these operate as consistent 'styles'. The thinker would try to understand people logically, the sensation type would perceive literally in terms of concrete actions; the feeling type values others with reference to effects on himself, and the intuitive person tries to perceive their essential nature through non-analytic processes. Jung believes that when one type of function is strongly developed in an individual, another would be repressed. Thus one might expect considerable discrepancies in the way different individuals perceive a mutual acquaintance, as also between psychologists who interpret personality from different theoretical standpoints, such as the empirical-psychometric, and the subjective-clinical.

Interpretations of self. It would be premature at this stage to discuss fully our self-concepts or analyses of our own motives. But it should be pointed out how largely self-perception follows the same lines as interpetations of others. One's homunculus is, of course, much more vivid and of more consuming concern than anyone else's, and it is based on direct awareness of one's feelings rather than on the physical and expressive cues listed above (p. 29, Nos. 1 and 2).* However, a person certainly weighs the significance of his own actions, the situational factors and others' opinions (Nos. 3, 4 and

* The work of Wolff (1943) and Huntley (1940) shows that we are often not consciously aware of our own expressive cues, e.g. we do not recognize our own voices, while also evincing strong affective attitudes towards them.

5) in judging himself. We overestimate the constancy of our own personalities more than that of others, but allow for greater temporary variations with mood, fatigue, etc; and rather than over-simplify, we seem to over-elaborate our motives. We give far more credit to situational factors in adverse situations, instead of blaming 'can', 'tries', or personal responsibility, and correspondingly more credit to the latter, less to the environment, when things go well.

Belief in the correctness of our interpretations. Finally, in this chapter, it should be asked why we remain generally satisfied with our interpretations of people we meet, despite all the variations and possibilities of error, and despite our realization that people are playing a part and are trying to impress or deceive us, as we do to them. The fact is that to a large extent it works; in so many instances it is confirmed by later evidence. We can tell when our child is hurt, a shop salesman is helpful, a neighbour lowbrow and so forth. Normally there is a lot of feed-back; B indicates to A by his subsequent behaviour that A has read him aright, or if not A is quickly able to correct or cover up minor misjudgments. Not only our experience shows us that we are often justified, but also there is 'consensual validation' – that is, others arrive at the same judgments. A group of cronies quickly agree that the new family across the street is snobbish. The group forgets, however, that their own attitudes are likely to be fairly similar, otherwise they would not be friendly, and that, therefore, they may all have made the same misinterpretation. Again, we have seen that personality interpretation is closely bound up with our self-esteem. We cannot afford to be wrong since this would mean that we do not know who is for us, who against us. Thus we are likely to rationalize or repress any evidence that we have misjudged another person. If A_1 and A_2 disagree about B, each tends to ascribe it to the other's bias or ignorance.

Chapter 3

THEORETICAL CONSIDERATIONS

Certain contemporary writers such as McLeod (1960) maintain that we perceive people's inner states – their intentions, feelings, motives and dispositions or personal qualities – in the same way as we perceive the physical world. To others this would seem to be a misuse of the word perception, since clearly an elaborate process of analysis, inference and evaluation is involved in the former, over and above the reception of cues from the people we observe. Unlike the visual perception of objects, there appears to be little direct connection between the shape or form of the cues and the observer's awareness; or, as Ichheiser puts it, there is a lack of 'natural harmony' between the person's expressions and the interpreter's impressions. Indeed as often as not the expressions are a mask for very different feelings, as when we thank someone for an unwanted birthday gift, or are being interviewed for a job. Yet, to some extent at least, the observer can penetrate through this mask.

We have pointed out, however, that object perception is not just a kind of reflection or picturing in the observer's mind of physical stimuli from the environment. It is a constructive mental activity whereby the observer processes, codes and transforms his sensations in such a way as to resolve the world into intelligible and stable entities. McLeod describes it as the process whereby objects and events, including their qualities and meanings, dispositions and relations, become present, here and now, to the observer. Such a description would seem to apply quite aptly also to the perception of personal qualities. Moreover the 'coding' stage in object perception normally leads over without a break into further analyses and inferences much as it does in person perception. For example I do not merely perceive that it is raining, but instantly realize that this will affect my plans for today, much as A instantly modifies his behaviour to B when he perceives him as being in a bad temper. At the same time it was noted, in Chapter 2, that person perception manifests much of the immediacy, and the resolution of variable cues into underlying constancies, that characterize object perception.

46

Many of our difficulties in accounting for both phenomena seem to arise largely from the persistence of the associationist tradition in general perceptual theory, according to which the reaction of the senses to physical stimuli is primary, and any awareness of meanings and relations is based on secondary, inferential processes. But if we agree with the Gestalt psychologists in rejecting this view, it becomes more reasonable to group the perception of the physical world, and the perception of emotions, intentions and traits under the same theoretical model. However we should also admit that a great deal more empirical evidence is needed regarding their precise resemblances and differences.

Inference theories. Allport (1961a) has closely examined the controversies over the nature of our perception of personal qualities and points out that most explanations either stress inference and learning, or else minimize these in favour of some kind of immediate awareness or intuition. This dichotomy is largely, though not necessarily, linked with preference for the nomothetic vs. idiographic, or psychometric vs. clinical approach to personality, which we have already outlined. Inference theory may take the following forms:

1. B looks annoyed to me because, from childhood up, unpleasant consequences have often followed when adults frowned, shouted or acted in this manner. (This would be ordinary learning through reinforcement.) If he frequently behaves in this way, I infer that he is irritable in personality.

2. B looks angry because, when I have felt angry myself, I have acted in the same way as he is doing. I have been taught labels for my own feelings as well as hearing them applied to the cues presented by others.

3. B is probably angry because he is reacting to a situation which has frustrated me, I infer that his feelings will be similar. (Inference by analogy.)

4. B makes me feel small and insignificant, therefore he is a domineering or tactless person.

5. These and similar judgments have been reinforced when correct since they have helped me to adjust to the current social situation, to get on with people. If incorrect, they have led to various unpleasant consequences, hence I have abandoned them.

In other words, as a result of experience, we have learned to associate certain visual and vocal cues with our own and others' responses to emotion-provoking situations. But while learning is certainly important, none of these views – singly or in combination – appears adequate, since we do not normally find ourselves inferring in this way. That is, we do not first perceive the cue, then deduce from it, except perhaps in situations where the cues are complex and contradictory and we are forced to puzzle out B's feeling or intention. Equally, of course, in object perception, we do not perceive the cues to depth or solidity and infer from these, except under unusual circumstances. Another argument is that young children who have acquired little experience appear to be able to react immediately, for example, to 'sense' that father is in a bad temper and refrain from bothering him. And it is claimed by Estes (1938) and Allport that judges who do adopt an analytic, reflective kind of observation of people are often less accurate in assessing them than those who react by more global, intuitive processes.

Non-inferential theories. Some of the contrasting explanations are as follows:

6. It was suggested by Charles Darwin that our major emotional expressions are vestiges of instinctive biological reactions. Thus the dog bares its teeth when about to attack; we tend to make similar muscular contractions when angry, and it may be that our recognition of these cues is equally instinctive. This theory is generally rejected, not merely because it could apply only to a few of the more primitive emotions, but because there is much evidence of variations in the conventional expressions of emotions in different cultures, suggesting again that these are learned. However, the objection may be overdone. Children do show pain or sorrow by crying, pleasure by smiling, and the well-defined startle reflex, all the world over. Moreover it has been found that blind children exhibit many of the same expressions, which they could not possibly have learned by visual association, though less uniformly than sighted children (Thompson, 1941).

7. We often empathize or mimic the movements of people engaged in some activity, for example, straining upwards when watching a high-jumper make a tremendous effort to clear the bar, and these movements may evoke in us the same feelings. Thus, we may see a person as 'relaxed' because we are unconsciously imitating his posture. Lipps, who originated this theory, used it to explain our attribution of emotional qualities to works of art – soaring spires, sprightly melodies, etc. Similarly, it would seem that we project the

feelings on the person rather than feeling our own kinaesthetic sensations and inferring that the person is similar.

8. Both Werner (1948) and the Gestalt psychologists consider that 'physiognomic' perception – i.e. the seeing of emotional qualities in people's expressions, works of art or physical objects – is a direct and primitive process, not based on empathy or on learned associations. We see a stormy landscape as threatening with the same immediacy as an infant perceives a parent as angry. However, the evidence for the primitive nature of this type of perception is far from satisfactory, and Honkavaara's (1961) investigations suggest that, on the contrary, it may be a rather sophisticated perceptual response.

A favourite instance among Gestalt psychologists is that people find little difficulty in deciding which of the following figures is called 'takete' and which one 'maluma':

Fig. 2. Maluma   Takete

and that some 90% or more agree. But Honkavaara found that only 9% of 5- to 6-year-old children answered 'correctly', and over half answered: 'Don't know'. Even from about 9 to 14 years, only one-half to two-thirds were correct, though very few 'didn't know'.

Honkavaara obtained many affective, as well as literal, responses among young children to pictures of faces and other expressive cues, but not physiognomic ones. This may link up with Bullough's (1908) claim that the 'characterizing' type of appreciation of works of art is the most aesthetically developed, and quite distinct from the subjective appreciation of the feelings aroused, or objective appreciation of the work's technical features.

9. Many German writers such as Spranger (1928) postulate a special faculty of insight or *Verstehen*, whereby we comprehend the person as an integrated whole; this they differentiate sharply from scientific or analytic understanding. The Gestalt psychologists – Köhler, Koffka, Arnheim – likewise emphasize the immediate perception of structures, but regard the process as in no way different from our ordinary perception of visual or other Gestalts. The term

'intuition' is unpopular among American and British psychologists because it seems to imply some mysterious and inexplicable capacity, independent of past experience; it is not open to introspection and cannot be substantiated by any rational argument, but rather bases its claims on the strong conviction that the intuitive person feels in the rightness of his judgments.

Allport himself takes up a middle position, admitting that we make a great deal of use of learned experience and inference and yet pointing out that these cannot account for the way in which we perceive a person and his intentions as a unique and organized system, a self-activating structure independent of our own feelings and associations; nor for the direct and immediate character of these judgments. Sarbin, Taft and Bailey (1960) are strongly critical of Allport's views, believing that all the phenomena cited under the heading of intuition can be reduced to the same kind of inferential processes that occur in everyday perception. Their theory is too elaborate to give here in detail, but, shorn as far as possible of its technical terminology, they would claim that in interpreting people we 'process' incoming stimuli, sorting and classifying them just as we do in perceiving objects. In the course of our lives we build up a network of concepts or postulates about the physical world or about human nature, both from cultural influences and from personal experience – e.g. 'chocolates are good to eat', 'frowning faces are associated with anger', or such stereotypes as 'athletes are unintelligent'.

These guide our interpretation or attribution of meaning to the incoming stimuli or cues. The fundamental units in this operation are what Bartlett and Piaget have called *schemata* – Sarbin *et al.* prefer 'modules'; others refer to 'constancies', 'expectancies', 'coding systems'. As pointed out in Chapter 2, the visual sensations of any object or event are so varied that we must suppose that the growing infant constructs a sort of model or schema of the 'real object', probably largely on the basis of motor explorations (which yield more constant impressions) and sometimes through learning the label or name for the object. Such a schema produces an expectation of 'what to look for' in the flood of incoming stimuli, and embodies all his past experience of its various appearances. Eventually, then, any fresh appearance of it is – to use Sarbin's term – *instantiated*, that is, immediately subsumed under, or identified, by means of the schema, and thereby assigned the characteristics of the class to which it belongs. Though the process occurs at a pre-conscious level it follows quite logical principles, e.g.: 'All chocolates are good to eat.

This object is instantiated as a chocolate. Therefore it is good to eat';
'This man is an athlete and therefore unintelligent'.

Obviously in most perceptions and interpretations, multiple inferences or long chains of deduction may be involved. The mind
seems to work, in many ways, like a computing machine; concepts
and postulates are like the instructions fed into the machine, and
when a problem is given to it, in the form of perceptual cues, it comes
out with the answer that best fits the instructions, or possesses the
greatest probability under the circumstances. Those judgments of
people that we call intuitive are essentially the same as any others,
but they depend on less fully instantiated, i.e. unconscious, cues, and
are processed by less explicit concepts and principles. As Taft states
elsewhere (1960), we use ourselves as a frame of reference to a much
greater extent than in object perception. Probably these judgments
carry their sense of immediacy and conviction because of empathic
components, i.e. kinaesthetic and affective responses in the judge.
But Sarbin and his colleagues maintain that they are no more 'creative'
or 'unique' than any other perceptions. They are equally dependent
upon sorting the individual according to his resemblance to previously observed classes of individuals, and thus inferring his
structure of personal dispositions.

Possibly this theory sounds far too mechanical, too simplified, to
be adequate, though this is partly because our exposition is over-
simplified. It is, of course, regarded as inadequate by Allport and
others who are sympathetic to idiographic views. And yet, to the
present writer, it seems to go a long way towards reconciling the
divergences between the more extreme inferential and intuitional
theories. It has the great merit of accepting perception as a molar process whereby we see structured wholes, not elementary sensations,
and thereby makes it possible to consider interpretations of people as
following the same principles as any other kind of perception (as we
have attempted to do throughout these chapters). The writer would
agree with Meehl (1961) that it is most seriously at fault in imposing
a particular logical model on the mind's sorting mechanisms; it con-
fuses psychological with logical processes. Meehl shows that even
professional logicians are far from agreed that this model of thinking
is the only way of arriving at conclusions. The theory might seem
inadequate also in explaining the creativeness and uniqueness of
personality interpretations. But to the present writer these features
too are characteristic of object perception – they are aspects of the
mind's everyday computing capacities. Suppose one sees for the first

time a house in an unfamiliar architectural design; the eyes scan it, taking in and sorting (instantiating) various cues, but one quickly arrives at an overall impression or 'understanding' of an organized structure – a new and creative experience. Indeed we possess a variety of processing skills, which are like our motor skills, e.g. fast bowling, in that we cannot pick out the component elements and that, the better developed they are, the less conscious we are of them. But this does not mean that they are mysterious or different in kind from more mundane perceptual or motor capacities which can more easily be understood in terms of a mechanical model like a computer.

The genesis of person interpretation. Hebb and Thompson (1954) describe how the higher mammals and birds, at least, respond to various emotional expressions in their own species, young birds to their parent's warning cry, dogs to threatening growls, etc. Disinterested concern for the distress of other members can be observed with porpoises as well as chimpanzees. Köhler and Yerkes give instances of empathy or spontaneous imitation among apes and of their reactions to human emotional expressions, and Hebb recorded many teasing or deceitful actions to a man behaving timidly, more nervous ones when the man was displaying boldness. Chimpanzees even have the capacity to act in one way towards a human while intending to treat him differently, for example, hiding a mug of water as a visitor approaches and then drenching him. Both they and dogs obviously learn to respond differently to different human personalities; and R. E. Miller et al. (1959) showed that rhesus monkeys can learn to discriminate colour slides of emotional expressions in their own species.

It seems probable then that human interpretative abilities are attributable partly to the maturation of innate tendencies, partly to such non-symbolic forms of learning as lower animals are capable of. The fact that these abilities are not present at birth, and develop slowly, does not mean that they depend wholly upon the kinds of learning suggested by inference theories.

Actually there is a serious dearth of reliable information regarding interpretations among young children. By about 2 months, babies are beginning to show an interest in people by smiling when they approach, and by 4 months to take special pleasure in the mother. It is well attested also that they react to differences in adult handling, behaving differently to a confident from an awkward person, to a warm and loving from a coldly efficient or unloving person. It is often said that they can discriminate a kind facial expression or tone of voice from a frowning face or angry tone; but it seems more likely that they are merely responding positively to any familiar human-like stimulus (cf. Spitz, 1945), negatively to a strange or startling one. Individual people are certainly beginning to be discriminated by about 9 months.

However, we must recognize that the infant has no perceptual awareness like our own; he does not differentiate 'things out there' from internal impressions or feelings. Rather there seems to be a vague, global consciousness of comfort or discomfort, which gradually differentiates into feelings accompanying feeding, wetness, Mother, handling and other stimuli. In other words: 'Meanings always precede objects in perception' (Stone and Church, 1957). Specific reflex responses are made to particular stimuli, and as his brain matures he shows increasing interest in observing, exploring and experimenting with a wider range of stimuli. But as external stimulation is continuously changing (both the environment itself and his own head and body movements), he seeks constancies – his mother's voice, his rattle which he can see, hear and manipulate, cause to approach and recede, disappear and reappear. Thus he gradually detaches recognizable parts of the environment by making selective responses to them, building up schemata, and – with the advent of language – labelling them. Perhaps this process of sorting out and objectifying a world of things is not so different from what adults do when coping with complex, unfamiliar situations, e.g. learning to look for geological specimens, or to operate some machine. Accompanying this analysis are the synthetic processes of associating and grasping relations between parts, that is the development of higher-order concepts and meanings.

During the second year, there is rapid growth in distinguishing people and their actions, though more in terms of affective impressions and sentiments than as physical objects – whether they gratify or frustrate his needs. Hand in hand with this, as we shall see later, is the acquisition of a conception of his own self as a person separated from objects and persons outside him. Among other young children he spends a great deal of time observing them, or he plays parallel to them, but only begins to make tentative interchanges. Emotional contagion can be observed – a direct response of distress or excitement when *they* are distressed or excited. But it is not usually till 3–4 years that he shows sympathetic or leadership behaviour which imply sensitiveness to another's emotions as different from his own.

From then on, also, we observe a series of identifications, through which he acquires sex and other roles that largely underly his social skills. However, Piaget's investigations show that the realization of a variety of viewpoints – that others do not perceive as he does – is a particularly difficult acquisition. The egocentricity that Piaget describes in children clearly enters into many of the misinterpretations that we have noted among adults. We attain objectivity in our perception of things because we are forced to by the physical pressures of the external world; thus the baby is 'punished' by the consequences if he treats his rattle as something eatable. In the social sphere, learning is much more difficult since the pressures are more complex and indirect. A child's correct interpretation of his parents' or peers' moods and intentions are indeed 'rewarded', while incorrect ones lead to trouble; but usually the connection between the error and its social consequences is a subtle one, and long-term rather than immediate (cf. Rommetweit, 1960). Sometimes the 'punishment' consists in the person finding that he is out of step, that others are interpreting certain cues differently from him. But we have also seen that he is likely to have resistances against admitting misjudgments.

Such experimental investigations in this area as have been carried out with children have tended to show that their judgments of emotional expressions from photographs are much less accurate than those of adults, and that there is an improvement with age which parallels, and is fairly closely correlated with, general intellectual development (Gates, 1923; Honkavaara, 1961). Similarly their sociometric judgments of peers, or their ratings, tend to show greater unreliability and stronger halo effects (Watts, 1941). But much of this is surely attributable to the artificial and abstract nature of the task, to having to verbalize names for expressions and personality traits. General observation would suggest that children of, say, 4–8 years can distinguish the moods and intentions of adults and peers with remarkable success (though also often erroneously) and react appropriately to different personalities. But much more investigation of the processes involved in these natural interpretative situations is needed.

Chapter 4

EXPERIMENTAL INVESTIGATIONS OF PERSONALITY JUDGMENTS

So far we have made occasional references only to the enormous wealth of experimental literature bearing on judgments of emotions, motivation and personality qualities by naïve observers – i.e. by psychologically untrained persons such as most employment interviewers, teachers, fellow-students, etc. Useful accounts of personality ratings and other methods of assessment can be found in many books, e.g. those by Cronbach (1960), Anastasi (1961), Freeman (1955), Allen (1958), Guilford (1959) and Vernon (1953). Our aim here is to summarize the present position, and to draw attention to a few trends of importance in current research.

Static features and personality. It should hardly be necessary to point out that no specific physical feature, such as size of forehead or jaw, or the colour of hair or eyes, has any uniform significance as an indication of personality; yet many people still believe in these external physiognomic signs. One exception, to be discussed later (p. 253), is the somatotype or type of body physique, which is probably linked with the endocrine balance and may, therefore, give some indication of basic temperamental tendencies. At the same time, age, sex, bodily health and grooming largely determine our stereotypes and judgments of status, in terms of which we initially classify people. Further, it often happens that particular physical features may be of great concern to the person himself (e.g. good looks, excessive shortness, obesity, or a deformity), and thus be significant in the individual personality.

Normally we seem to depend more on the pattern or overall expression of the features and bodily appearance than on specific signs. Early experiments, in which judgments of photographs were compared with test scores (e.g. for intelligence) or with ratings by close acquaintances, showed such judgments to possess virtually no validity. There is a fair amount of agreement between different judges – that is, they have a common stereotype as to what the intelligent or unintelligent individual looks like, though it happens to be unjustified.

Secord *et al.* (1954) obtained ratings of photographs by groups of 16–20 students on (*a*) a series of physical characteristics, such as curvature of the mouth, age, etc., and (*b*) on 35 personality traits. The authors claim considerable agreement in both types of judgment, though the average intercorrelation between any pair of judges is likely to be only about 0·38. A number of significant correlations between the physical and personality attributes were noted, e.g. mouth curvature with 'easygoing': +0·70. But the main finding was that both sets of attributes could be grouped into clusters, which yielded more consistent and meaningful physical and psychological relationships. Some half-dozen types of expression were thus isolated:

Warm, likeable, cheerful
Conscientious, intelligent, studious
Arrogant, conceited, sly
Alert, self-confident, energetic
Proud, reserved
Meek vs. aggressive, determined

Note that these are the main personality expressions that judges tend to distinguish; but they too represent stereotypes – there was no independent evidence that the individuals who were photographed possessed these traits. Another interesting finding was that the judges gave their personality assessments about twice as quickly as the physical ones. This bears out the claim that we sort or code the cues into impressions of personality qualities directly, rather than inferring from physical signs.

The matching method and its alternatives. In so far as we see a person's expression and his personality structure as wholes or Gestalten, the method of correlating physical signs with separate traits (even when combining them into clusters or factors) may not be the most appropriate. The matching method was advocated as an alternative by this writer in 1936. Here the judge is presented with a small group of, say, half a dozen photographs, and character sketches of each person, though in a different order, and tries to identify or match one set with the other. If several judges match several such sets, the percentage by which their correct judgments exceed chance (in this case, one sixth), can be expressed as a coefficient comparable to a correlation. Numerous investigations have shown that photographs and other modes of expression (voices, handwriting, literary style, drawings and projective material such as Rorschach protocols) can be matched with personality descriptions decidedly better than would appear likely from correlational studies of isolated personality attributes (cf. Allport and Cantril, 1934; Vernon, 1935).

Though the method has had quite wide application, it is not without its difficulties. It depends not only on the perceptive ability of the particular judges but, to a large extent, on the heterogeneity of the persons being judged. Sometimes it is deceptive in that successful matching may be based, not on comparing the expression with the personality as a whole, but on some trivial detail, e.g. a reference to age, health, neatness. As Cronbach (1948) points out, its strength is also its weakness; because the judgment is global, it gives no information on what aspects of personality or expression were taken into consideration.

Cronbach therefore advocates a modified technique* whereby the personality descriptions of each set of three persons are split into their component statements, and each statement is ticked by several judges as fitting, doubtful or not fitting each of the three photographs (or other expressive material). The statistical significance of the number of correct choices is given by chi-squared, and this can be converted to a phi-coefficient; moreover the results can be calculated separately for different kinds of personality qualities. Cronbach applied the technique to the Rorschach protocols of nine persons and found a preponderance of correct choices of statements in eight cases. But judgments from the Rorschach of traits such as originality were more often valid than those concerned with accuracy, social relations or drive; and judgments about persistence and emotional control actually showed negative validity (a preponderance of misidentifications).

This is fairly similar to the method used in many studies of social insight (cf. below), namely predicting a person's responses to a number of items in a personality or attitude questionnaire. An alternative approach would be that of the 'Q-sort' (Stephenson, 1953), where the judge sorts a series of statements into piles varying from those most applicable, to those least applicable, to a given person. This too allows for patterning or structure within the individual personality and avoids the artificiality of having to compare a lot of people on one abstracted trait at a time.

Expressive movements. In judging people we normally rely more on the dynamic or expressive, than on static, features – facial movements, gestures, postures, vocal qualities and style of speech. As far back as 1933 Allport and Vernon showed that there is considerable

* For further development of the method, cf. Henry and Farley (1959).

reliability and generality or clustering in such movements; individuals tend to be consistently expansive or forceful or rapid in a variety of actions carried out by varied muscle groups. This was confirmed by Eisenberg (1937), who also found that individuals selected by a personality inventory as strongly dominant or retiring showed certain differences in movement patterns. Matching experiments have frequently yielded positive results, though the coefficients tend to be low to moderate. Despite many attempts to validate graphological analyses by such methods (thus avoiding the fallacy of correlating specific graphic signs with particular traits), there is still no convincing evidence that handwriting provides a particularly fruitful approach to personality diagnosis.

While there can be no doubt of the existence of styles or patterns of expressive movement, characteristic of the individual person, such movements are influenced by many other factors – cultural or occupational conventions, age, sex, health, physical and muscular build, and temporary moods and intentions. It would appear also that the same personality trend, e.g. shyness or inferiority, may express itself in different ways in different persons, or in the same person at different times; and that expression may be rather direct in some persons, more compensatory in others. The fact is that there has been so little scientific investigation of the nature of the connections betweer. expressive styles and personality dispositions, that it is hardly surprising that their interpretation is chancy – valuable in some cases, deceptive in others.

> An illustration of the complexity of relationships is given by a study of doodling by Wallach and Gahm (1960). Seventy-six students were encouraged to doodle while listening to music, as 'a test of creative imagination', and the area of their productions was measured. This area gave a low positive correlation of 0·36 with Eysenck's MPI measure of extraversion; but the mean score was high only for non-neurotic or low-anxious extraverts, not for anxious ones; and it was high also among anxious introverts, for whom doodling presumably represented a compensation for inhibited overt expression.

Ratings of personality. The general principles of obtaining reliable ratings of people's traits are well established, and there has been little fresh development since World War II. They are particularly convenient for research purposes, e.g. where some criterion is needed against which to validate tests, or where the effects of some kind of treatment on personality development are to be surveyed. For it is then usually possible to get two or more judges to assess all subjects (or comparable judges to assess sub-groups), and to arrange for them to observe systematically rather than relying on impressionistic recollections. The judges can be made aware of the difficulties, and instructed in interpreting the traits uniformly, and their variations of standards controlled.

Even with these precautions and with carefully prepared graphic or other scales, it is clear – from the moderate correlations usually obtained between independent raters, and from the excessive over-lapping of ratings on different traits known as halo effect – that there is a large subjective component in the results. Bayroff *et al.* (1954) conclude, as the result of a large-scale trial in the American army, that the variance attributable to the rater is much greater than that attributable to the method of rating – graphic scale, forced choice, etc. It seems best to regard ratings, not so much as summaries of objectively observed behaviour, as rationalizations abstracted from the rater's overall picture (his homunculus) of the subject. Cattell (1957) dissents from the view that ratings consist largely of halo, since he finds it possible by factor analysis to extract from them a dozen or so different personality factors (cf. Chap. 11). Other investigators, however, seldom duplicate more than a few of his factors, and in many studies (where admittedly, conditions were less carefully controlled than in Cattell's work) only two or three significant factors emerged. These tend to correspond quite closely to Osgood's three semantic factors (cf. p. 40). Thus there is usually a prominent good vs. bad factor including such traits as emotional stability and reliability, and an extravert-introvert dichotomy, or some variant of active-potent vs. passive-weak.

There is no way of eliminating generalized bias or halo, despite ingenious attempts by Chi (1937) and Johnson and Vidulich (1956), since every correlation between traits represents a mixture of:

(i) genuine overlapping between the types of behaviour in the subjects, (ii) common evaluative attitudes of the raters and common cultural theories regarding the inter-relations of traits, and (iii) idiosyncratic attitudes and theories in particular raters.

The present writer's inclination is to include in any list of traits to be rated several which will chiefly measure liking-disliking, and to hold this constant by partial correlation or factor analysis before interpreting other factors that may be present.

Practical applications of ratings. The value of reports in the form of ratings on persons requiring selection or counselling is much more dubious, since these normally have to be provided by miscellaneous raters over whom the psychologist has very little control. Both their standards and their interpretations of trait-names vary widely.

A. Walker (1955) analysed a series of ratings and other entries on the Cumulative Record cards of 10–11-year children, given by a number of different teachers, and found that they amounted to little more than general impressions of scholastic success. The first factor obtained loadings of 0·79 to 0·92 on IQ, English achievement, perseverance and self-confidence ratings, etc., and its variance was 8 times as large as that of all other factors combined. Walker concluded that the separate personality assessments, when assigned by miscellaneous judges, are not capable of giving any consistent information on any additional personality factor.

Some improvement is possible with better designed rating scales which break down general trait-names into half a dozen or so more specific and concrete descriptions of behaviour. These can be ticked for presence or absence, or coarsely graded, so as to reduce variability in the interpretation of finer steps. Sometimes, also, it is possible to 'key' these by validating them against an external criterion – as in the Haggerty–Olson–Wickman (1930) Behavior Rating Schedules, and Stott's (1958) Bristol Social Adjustment Guides (cf. p. 259). A particular item then contributes to a score for, say, maladjustment, not because the rater thinks it implies maladjustment, but because a preponderance of maladjusted children are known to be credited with that item by typical raters. (But cf. the discussion of empirical keying in Chapter 13.)

The best form of report to employers, selectors or psychological counsellors (e.g. by a school, or by testimonial writers) is likely to be a fairly brief third-person questionnaire covering well-defined behaviours, to which the writer is invited to append a free personality sketch, commenting on and supplementing his ratings. The testimonial has a particularly bad reputation among psychologists. Yet, when written confidentially, and when the points it is supposed to cover are clearly specified, it surely provides more guidance to the selectors and more hints worth following-up in interview, than does any set of scores on a rating scale.

Ability to judge. Large individual differences are always observed in success at any task involving judgments of people, and these have been subjected to a great deal of experimental investigation. It was hoped not only to specify the characteristics of the good or poor judge of personality, but also to throw light on the nature of social sensitivity or empathy, self-insight, projection, identification, and other interpersonal processes. In fact, the results have been highly contradictory and inconclusive, and have contributed very little to our knowledge of how to judge people better. The earlier work is well summarized by Notcutt and Silva (1951), Bruner and Tagiuri (1954), and Taft (1955), who attribute the variability in findings partly to the variations in techniques and in the kinds of qualities judged. These include:

1. Identifying emotions displayed in photographs; the criterion may be the label given by the person portrayed, or the experimenter's own specification, or a description of the situation to which the person is responding.
2. Matching photographs, handwritings, voices, etc. to occupations, brief or full character sketches or previous knowledge of the persons.
3. Ratings or rankings of acquaintances, compared with group judgments or with test scores. Self-ratings are often similarly evaluated.
4. Predicting responses of persons to personality or attitude tests from observation of filmed interviews or other performances, case studies, handwritings, etc.
5. Predictions of group responses, e.g. proportions of peers or of people in general who accept certain attitude statements.
6. Subjective assessment by clinicians of self- or social-insight shown in autobiographic, TAT or clinical protocols, or in role-playing.

The correlations between different measures, though usually positive, are often low – which implies that there may be no such thing as good judgment or social insight in general. However, this arises partly because most of the separate measures are weak in consistency and stability; and this is to be expected in so far as all measures of accuracy, are, in effect, difference scores – the difference between the judges' interpretations of a person and some criterion – and difference scores always have low reliability (cf. p. 224).

Crow and Hammond (1957) presented films of 10 patients being interviewed by doctors to students who judged their responses to the Strong Interest Blank and MMPI, and self-ratings. Few of the intercorrelations of the 15 possible measures of social perception were significant, and there was little agreement with the scores obtained on repeating the judgments after six months, except in the case of so-called stereotype scores – that is, the accuracy in predicting the typical response of the averaged patient.

On the other hand Cline (1955), and Cline and Richards (1960), using similar material from rather heterogeneous interviewees, have built up a series of tests with acceptable reliability, including a multiple-choice test of 'post-diction' of behaviour; that is, items were constructed separately for each interviewee describing his known behaviour in specific situations. Good correlations were obtained also between the accuracy scores of the same judges interpreting different individuals.

Different types of judgment. In 1955, Cronbach subjected the concepts involved in this type of research and the methods adopted to an extremely penetrating and critical analysis, which throws considerable doubt on the validity of all the claims that have been made (cf. also Gage and Cronbach, 1955; Bronfenbrenner et al. 1958). He insists that, just because a test *looks* as though it involves something in the nature of insight, etc., this does not justify inferring that the findings apply to other kinds of judgment obtained under different conditions. Not only are there variations in the 'input' – the material presented to the judges, and the 'out-take' – the interpretations they are required to make, but also in the kind of person or persons judged, e.g. strangers or close acquaintances. The judge may attempt to estimate the typical behaviour or feelings of people in general, of a particular category (e.g. other college students), of individual members of this category, or to estimate variations from such normal behaviour either within a category or an individual. Each of these skills may be socially useful, but there is no reason to assume that one implies the others, i.e. that they are closely correlated. Bronfenbrenner adds that A's sensitivity to B's feelings about A or about himself, other people and things may all differ; and that understanding of B's feelings may not be the same as predicting about him or responding appropriately to him.

Taft suggests that judgments may be global or empathic in some situations, analytic and inductive in others, and that these might be expected to yield relatively independent scores. However, he admits to finding little supporting evidence in the literature, and it may be that some judges are more inclined one way or the other, whatever the task. Vernon (1933a) thought that different skills would be involved in judging (a) friends, (b) strangers, (c) self; but though his investigation showed differences in personality patterns among the most successful on these different kinds of tasks, there was no clear statistical clustering of the separate kinds of judgment.

Statistical artifacts and response sets. Cronbach pointed out that many experiments have yielded fallacious results because judges differ in the way they apply a rating scale – i.e. in the mean and variance of their judgments. Such idiosyncrasies or response sets (cf. p. 206) may markedly affect their accuracy scores. Suppose, for example, they are estimating answers to a personality questionnaire for emotional stability: some will tend to impute strongly unstable answers to all persons, others to impute more stable answers. Some, again, will spread out the scores of those they are judging more widely than others. Even if they should rank the persons correctly in *order* of instability, their deviations in what Cronbach calls Elevation and Differential Elevation would lower their accuracy scores. Again, if they are required to judge several traits or items in one or more persons, some judges will give more uniform judgments of all the traits in any one person (i.e. strong halo effect), whereas others will differentiate and see the persons as more complex. Those who over-differentiate, either between persons or traits, generally tend to get lower accuracy scores.

> In a further experiment with medical students, Crow (1957) compared a group who had received special clinical instruction in doctor-patient relations with a control group, and found that the former actually showed less improvement than the latter on his test of judging patient responses to questionnaires. The reason for this was that their training had made them more responsive to individual differences, hence the variance of their judgments increased to a dangerous extent. Arnhoff (1954) similarly reports that trained psychiatrists and clinical psychologists show wider variance in judging whether the vocabulary responses of mental patients manifest disordered thinking, and thus score no higher in this test of clinical insight than unsophisticated students.

'Projection' phenomena. Several early studies indicated some relation between possession of a trait and ability to judge it in others, and Sears (1936) claimed to have demonstrated a tendency for projection of undesirable traits. Thus students who were rated high on such traits as bashfulness and stinginess, and who were also low in insight, were more apt to attribute these traits to others. Whether we tend to see people in terms of our own dominant characteristics, or project on to others those motives which are repressed in ourselves, was undecided. Weingarten (1949) denied the operation of a compensatory mechanism, but found that judges whose autobiographies showed insecurity and lack of insight were more likely to discover problems and tensions in judging motivational problems of others.

Hastorf and Bender (1952, 1953, 1955) reported several studies of judgments by students of their associates' responses to attitude and personality items. They noted a tendency for A's judgment of B and C to correlate more closely with one another, *and* with A's actual responses, than with B's or C's actual responses. This they attributed to self-projection, and they attempted to hold it constant in order to obtain a purer measure of empathy or social sensitivity. However, there was very poor consistency in the judgment scores, apart from that for projection.

Scodel and Mussen (1953) picked out pairs of authoritarian and non-authoritarian students on the basis of the Californian F-test, and instructed them to get acquainted by discussing, for example, Television, for 20 minutes. Each then assessed the other's responses to the F-test and to the MMPI. The authoritarians were found to be far more liable to misperceive their new acquaintances, by imputing attitudes to them similar to their own. There was little difference, however, between the groups in prediction of MMPI results. Similarly, Vroom (1959) found that supervisors predicted the responses to attitude items of workers whom they liked as being much more similar to their own, than in the case of workers whom they disliked. This tendency was most marked for items that dealt with 'central', as contrasted with 'peripheral' dispositions.

However, Gage and Cronbach now point out that most of these findings are, if not spurious, very difficult to interpret. They all involve (*a*) the judges' own responses or self-ratings, (*b*) the actual responses of other persons, (*c*) the judges' estimate of (*b*). The resemblance of (*b*) to (*c*) is taken to show accuracy, and (*a*) to (*c*) to show projection. But there will normally be a considerable resemblance of (*a*) to (*b*), since most people – particularly those congenial to one another, tend to answer questionnaires, or to assess the desirability or undesirability of personality traits, fairly similarly. This (*a*)(*b*) correlation, therefore, must affect the others; actual similarity, projection and accuracy are not independent variables. And the person who is most like others in his responses will naturally appear to judge them best.

Similar artifacts are likely to have been involved (i) in Adams' (1927) investigation (backed up by Vernon, 1933a) claiming that good judges of self tend to be extraverted and socially minded, whereas good raters of others are more detached; (ii) in investigations which appear to show that leaders or those who win sociometric acceptance are good at judging the sociometric choices or opinions of their peers; (iii) in studies which attempt to measure identification by comparing the self-descriptions of sons with their descriptions of their fathers (cf. Bronfenbrenner, 1958), and many others.

Stereotype vs. differential accuracy. Gage (1952) seems to have been the first to realize that, in judging individuals, we may rely largely on a stereotype of what such individuals in general are like.

In his experiments, students were asked to fill out part of the Kuder Interests test for unknown students whom they observed carrying out various prearranged activities; they also estimated the responses of a typical male, or female, student. It was found that the stereotype predictions correlated more highly than did the individual predictions with the unknown persons' actual responses.

An alternative method of arriving at a stereotype is to take the judge's modal or pooled prediction regarding a number of persons, differential accuracy then being measured by the correctness of the deviations predicted for each individual from this mode (cf. Gage and Cronbach's discussion). Bronfenbrenner (1958), Cline and Richards (1960, 1961) and others have confirmed that sensitivity to the 'generalized other' is distinct from differential or interpersonal sensitivity, though both are valuable skills in judging people in everyday life. Cline and Richards further suggest that when psychiatrists and psychologists are found to give no better, or even poorer, judgments than laymen, it is because they fail to make sufficient use of the stereotype. The trained judge may be superior in interpersonal accuracy and (as already pointed out) he is more adventurous in his diagnoses, seeing people as more complex and differentiated; but he would do better if he realized that all members of a certain type or category of persons tend to behave very much alike.

Similarly, Hathaway (1956) suggests that judgments may be based on:

1. specific inferences from one piece of behaviour to another;
2. general classifications, behaviours characteristic of sex, age, occupation, or other groups;
3. projective processes – the judge sees the person as like or unlike himself;
4. 'intuition', where the source of the judgment cannot be specified.

In a test similar to those used in studies of paranormal cognition, he found that judges were able to guess the Subjects' choices slightly better than chance by knowing his or her sex, but did not improve on this score through seeing the Subject make the choice. Such a test is, of course, hardly parallel to a personality judging situation; but Hathaway stresses the value of his (*b*) category in clinical diagnosis also.

'Built-in' personality theories. Any judgment of a person on two or more traits or items implies a set of correlations in the judge's mind between these traits. For example, the classical research by Wickman (1928) showed that teachers tend to associate 'maladjustment' with 'disorderliness', whereas psychiatrists associate 'maladjustment' with 'withdrawingness'. Thus the judgments they make of children would be bound to differ and, according to the nature of the criterion, the teachers' or the psychiatrists' accuracy scores would suffer. Such theories are responsible also for the halo phenomenon, and, as pointed out in Chapter 2, they underly our stereotypes and classificatory categories.

Discussion. The general conclusion that Cronbach draws from this analysis is that most personality judgments depend far more on the perceiver than on the person perceived. And this obviously has important implications for studies involving ratings, for selection interviews or counselling, and indeed for personality theory generally. Cronbach (1955, 1958) urges that experimenters should give up studying the imprecise concept of judging ability or social perception in general, and analyse it into the various components he has listed. He provides techniques whereby the D^2 statistic – the generalized distance between predicted scores or responses and the criteria – can be broken down into Elevation and Differentiation measures and correlation terms representing Stereotype and Differential Accuracies. In this way he hopes to quantify the individual judge's perceptual map of people. With minor modifications these techniques have been successfully applied in a series of studies by Cline and Richards (1960, 1961).

Are we to conclude that the technical hurdles which blocked progress in the study of social perception have now been cleared away, and that rapid advances are to be expected? Or, on the other hand, might we not question whether the whole area has not been shown to be so complicated that it is hardly possible to interpret the true psychological significance of any experimental findings? Murstein and Pryer (1959) comment on the growing aridity of research on social perception and projection.

An important point to remember is that Cronbach's and Bronfenbrenner's analyses are *a posteriori*. They show that personality judgments in controlled experimental situations can be effectively resolved into such-and-such variables; but they do not tell us much about how judges normally carry out their task. Obviously judges do not usually distinguish consciously between stereotype and individual predictions, between variances and assumed correlations – any more than the person carrying out an ability test is conscious of applying so much Verbal, Reasoning, Spatial or other ability factors. There is a certain danger, then, in reifying the components, just as there is in the mental testing field. The psychologist sometimes forgets, also, that placing people on numerical scales, or answering questionnaires on their behalf, are rather artificial activities, which differ a good deal from the sort of judgments we commonly make in daily life or which the clinician makes in counselling. Thus it may be that halo, projective tendencies and response sets such as over- or under-differentiation appear to play so prominent a part largely because the exigencies of the experiments force the subjects to verbalize and quantify subtle feelings and subconscious inferences (as Rommetweit suggests, 1960).

Hastorf, Richardson and Dornbusch (1958) agree that the experimenter's variables may often seem irrelevant to the judges; the latter might prefer to answer some of the questions about some of the persons, others about other persons. In an early study of personality ratings of young children, Conrad (1932) asked his raters to star any trait which seemed to them to be of 'central or dominating importance' in a particular child. The inter-rater agreement on these starred traits was much higher than on the less outstanding traits. Against this, there have been several studies (e.g. Holtzman and Sells, 1954) in which the judges were invited to distinguish the judgments in which they felt confidence from those of which they were less certain; but it was seldom found that the former were any more accurate than the latter. Nevertheless there is much to be said for trying to secure more spontaneous data, and Richardson and Hastorf (1961) have shown that good use can be made of reports given by judges in their own words, which are subsequently coded and analysed by the experimenter.

They have applied this technique extensively to 10–11-year children, simply asking each to: 'Tell me about –' a child he knows well; 'Tell me more' – etc. Each child describes himself and three others. A series of classificatory categories, in terms of which children make their discriminations, has been developed, and interesting differences are emerging between the sexes, between physically handicapped and normals, and between children of different socio-economic and sociometric status. Moreover the material allows some analysis of stereotype and projective components. For example, there is more overlapping of categories when A describes B_1 and B_2 than when A_1 and A_2 independently describe B; and the large element of overlapping when A_1 describes B_2 and A_2 describes B_1 presumably represents the common cultural baseline in terms of which all A's perceive the behaviour of all B's.

It should not be impossible to make a similar attack on social interactions involving mutual judgments in everyday situations (e.g. interviewing). Possibly Bales's (1950) categories for analysing verbal communications would be a useful starting point, though one would hope that non-verbal as well as verbal processes could be systematically observed.

The good judge of personality. Bruner and Taguiri (1954), Taft (1955, 1956, 1960) and Allport (1961a) agree fairly closely on a number of qualities which have been shown experimentally to correlate with judging ability. It is true that the various investigations have used extremely multifarious criteria and techniques, and that almost all of them are open to the weaknesses that Cronbach has pointed out. Indeed Cronbach goes so far as to doubt whether there is any consistent ability apart from response sets and similar artifacts. Nevertheless Taft is justified in arguing that there is a good deal of concordance in the findings, and that, despite the importance of situational and specific factors in different kinds of judgments, there is some generality.

We know that judging ability tends to increase with age among children, and that it usually correlates slightly with intelligence (except where the judges are rather homogeneous intellectually). Most studies have indicated little sex difference, and in those where women have done better, the difference has been small. Bronfenbrenner *et al.* (1958), however, claim marked differences in personality between men who are good at judging other men, or women, and women judging other women, or men. Similarity of the judge to the persons judged is clearly important, if only because they are likely to share common stereotypes. Hence judgments of members of unfamiliar cultural groups are likely to be seriously at fault, and older adults of high socio-economic status are unlikely to be the best interviewers for appointing young candidates of varied background to a job.

A significant number of studies has indicated a link with artistic and literary interests, though we do not know whether, as might be expected, they are more related to Differential than to Stereotype accuracy. The disturbing effects of dogmatic, authoritarian attitudes are confirmed by Cline (1955), who obtained a correlation of −0·46 between the F-scale and his scores based on predicting the test responses of persons filmed in interviews. Estes (1938), Luft (1950), Taft and others had found psychiatrists and clinical psychologists inferior to artists and laymen and even to physicists and experimental psychologists, but Cline did obtain somewhat better results from clinically experienced judges. Probably a good deal depends on the nature of the task and, as we have seen, the type of score adopted. Bieri and Blacker (1955, 1956) present some interesting evidence that the complexity or richness of the judges' concepts about people, as measured by Kelly's 'Rep' Test or by Rorschach, produce better judgments.

Taft's and others' experiments contradict the notion that the more neurotic or maladjusted are more sensitive to others, and Cline found that his better student judges tend to be sympathetic and affectionate, his poorer ones more dissatisfied, irritable and awkward. Similarly, Chance and Meaders (1960) found that students who could predict the responses of others on the Edwards Personal Preference Schedule were more warm and outgoing on the same test (though the spurious projection to which Cronbach draws attention was not controlled).

Diagnostic interviewing. There is little fresh evidence on the reliability and validity of the selection or counselling interview. Maccoby and Maccoby (1954) survey the many uses of interviewing and both they and Kahn and Cannell (1957) provide valuable advice on getting good rapport, on formulating questions, etc., particularly for research purposes; and draw attention to the defences and distortions that invariably arise from the status differences between interviewer and interviewee. Anstey and Mercer (1956) point out the extent to which important vocational decisions are taken by amateur, or occasional, interviewers, who have few qualms regarding their lack of skill or training. Their books gives detailed advice on tactics.

While we must agree that the interview is a time-consuming and expensive technique, that far too often it puts the interviewee in an unnatural situation where he is unlikely to display his normal dispositions, and that its results are untrustworthy, these defects have to be weighed against its versatility and universal acceptability.

Subsequent chapters will show that it is only in rare situations that a more efficient technique can be substituted. Evidence for the lack of agreement between independent interviewers or Boards, and for its weak predictive value, is well known (cf. Wagner, 1949; Vernon and Parry, 1949; Vernon, 1953), though this is sometimes exaggerated because the influences of selectivity or homogeneity in the experimental population are not allowed for. Critics tend to refer, also, to one or two investigations such as Kelly and Fiske's (described below, p. 84), which have not been replicated, and to ignore the consistently positive findings of, for example, British Civil Service selection and the National Institute of Industrial Psychology's vocational guidance interviews (cf. p. 135). Wagner (1949) and Yonge (1956) point out that the worst results tend to be obtained when miscellaneous interviewers, e.g. personnel managers, conduct interviews each in his own way, without any clear conception of what they are looking for. Again, the criteria for evaluating interview judgments are often inadequate. There are many instances in the literature of quite good validity. Thus, Yonge interviewed 47 employees without knowing their work records, and filled in a standard schedule for rating relevant attitudes. The scores on this schedule gave correlations averaging around 0·70 with supervisors' reports in several small sub-groups.

That a very common form of selection interview, namely the admission of students to teacher training, may be better than is often supposed, is brought out by Burroughs (1958). Several members of the staff of an Education Department were involved, and each rated the applicants whom he interviewed on a list of 15 qualities. When factorized, these qualities tended to cluster in groups: (1) Manner and voice; (2) Intellect, ability, maturity; (3) Enthusiasm, sincerity, suitability with children. Correlations with practical teaching success a year later, in three follow-up groups, ranged from 0·48 to 0·57, but these were based almost wholly on the first two clusters. The more personal qualities, though doubtless of greater importance, could not be adequately judged in the brief interview situation. Though these coefficients are by no means high, they are better than any that are consistently found for more objective personality or ability tests.

While there is much else to be said later, particularly about clinical and counselling interviews, it may be stated here that the selection interview is at its best when it is used: (a) for expanding, checking and probing the information previously provided by paper qualifications and biographical data; (b) for assessing particular qualities, mainly physical, social and intellectual, that have a good chance of expression during the interview situation. It is at its worst when it is conceived as a means for the interviewer: (*a*) to intuit or infer fundamental qualities of personality and character; (*b*) to weigh up and synthesize the evidence from diverse sources and reach a decision in the light of his 'experience' and judgment of job requirements.

Finally, we know that there are large variations in skill between different interviewers. Some hints for selection of good ones have emerged in previous sections of this chapter. So far there is no direct evidence that tests of judging ability, of intelligence, artistic interests, non-authoritarianism, out-goingness and similarity of background to the candidates, would actually work well. But it would be worth-while finding out.

Part II

*The Clinical Psychologist's Understanding
of Personality*

Chapter 5

RELIABILITY AND VALIDITY OF DEPTH-PSYCHOLOGICAL INTERPRETATIONS

Most people, at least among the better educated, are aware that they often fail to understand personality adequately, and tend to think that there are deeper motives which could be fathomed if they had greater insight. The parents of a problem child tell their doctor or the probation officer that they have tried every method of controlling Johnny and failed; and nowadays there is a growing willingness to consult the professionally trained psychiatrist or the psychologist at the Child Guidance Clinic. It seems fairly obvious to us, again, that the obsessional hand-washer or pyromaniac, or the soldier who develops a paralysis following the stress of battle without having received any physical injury, are suffering from deep-down mental difficulties.

In less extreme cases we often recognize that people are motivated by needs of which they are not fully aware; for example, that a 3-year-old may regress to babyish behaviour because he is jealous of the attention lavished on the younger brother or sister; that limelight behaviour may develop at school as a compensation for lack of progress in academic subjects, and so on. And we realize that traditional methods of control – rational argument, sympathy and reassurance, or punishment, do not always work. Then, too, we not only accept the pictures of tortuous motives portrayed by Shakespeare in Hamlet, Othello and other characters, by Dostoievski and more modern authors, but feel uplifted by their insights into human nature.

Much as we dislike to admit that our judgments of ourselves or others are at fault, we often do seek advice from people whom we think of as having valuable experience and insight – the doctor, lawyer, teacher, welfare-worker, and our older relatives. Indeed, such people were giving help, and were aware of some of the irrationalities of human motivation, at a time when professional psychologists confined their interests almost entirely to studying the simpler mental functions in the laboratory. So often, however, our advisers have a very limited acquaintance with human nature. They mix chiefly with others of the same social class, age and values. Thus there is reason to expect that the psychiatrist and psychologist will not only know a wider range of personality phenomena, but will have studied them more impartially and systematically.

At the same time there are many who reject this point of view, and not merely the ill-educated parent whose sole idea of controlling children is brute force. There are the authoritarian army officer, teacher, magistrate, etc., usually of the older generation, who inveigh against any 'softness' as encouraging malingering and delinquency. And we shall see that by no means all psychologists accept the validity of what has been called 'depth psychology' – the explanation of human behaviour in terms of unconscious instinctive urges and neurotic mechanisms or complexes.

> An alternative description is *dynamic psychology* or *psychodynamics*; but we shall avoid this term since it has been used so widely to apply to almost any branch of psychology concerned with drives and motives, or with frustrations and conflicts. Indeed, it has come to mean little more than 'up-to-date' or 'good'. *Clinical* psychology is a more acceptable alternative, though this may or may not stress the 'depth' dimension. *Psychoanalysis* is the original and basic brand of depth or clinical psychology, as put forward by Freud and his followers.

Depth psychology. We will not attempt any detailed outline of the theories of human nature developed by the psychoanalysts or other depth psychologists.* But perhaps we can characterize some of the main features in which they appear to go beyond our more naïve understanding, as follows:

1. Man, like other animals, is energized by a number of powerful biological drives or instincts, mainly of a sexual and aggressive nature, which demand gratification or reduction of tension. The term sex, however, includes many complex forms of drive, for example, the infant's sensuous pleasure in stimulation of 'erogenous' zones of the body; and in the course of development the instinct passes through a number of phases during which important character traits are laid down. Thus the kind of gratification and frustration at the

---

* Convenient secondary sources are C. S. Hall (1954), Hall and Lindzey (1957), J. A. C. Brown (1961) and T. M. French (1944).

oral stage is connected with talkativeness, optimism, and their opposites, at the anal stage with stubbornness, obsessional tidiness and concern over money. Such instinctual forces constitute, as it were, the universal and impersonal basis of human nature referred to as the *Id*.

2. These forces are held in check, not so much by cultural taboos and parental restrictions as by various defence mechanisms that the individual himself builds up in attempting to adjust to social pressures and frustrations, and to assuage the anxiety and guilt associated with instinctual gratification. The *Ego* is that part of the personality that copes with the real world, but in addition the child absorbs or *introjects* moral values or controls, to form the *Super-ego*. The Super-ego includes what we would naïvely call the 'conscience', but tends to be far stricter, more irrational and guilt-provoking than we realize. Some of the modes of adjustment adopted by the Ego in reconciling these pressures, and defending itself, include: *displacement* on to some substitute goal; *sublimation* or conversion into more constructive channels; *identification* with a parent or other persons, by imitating those features that may help towards his goals; *projection* of repressed impulses on to others, and *reaction-formation* or reversal, for example, denial of hostility by exaggerated affection; *fixation* or arrest at an early stage of development or *regression* to a more primitive stage; and the more familiar processes of *rationalization* and *compensation*. Of particular importance in the development of attitudes to the parents and to authority generally are the *Oedipus Complex* and complexes centred around fear of castration in boys and penis envy in girls.

3. We are not aware of these depths to our nature since we tend to repress our conflicts and anxieties into the unconscious sectors of the mind, and hence find it difficult to recall any memories much further back than five years. This explains too the opposition with which Freud's views were at first greeted. Yet the forces of the Id and Super-ego, and the adjustments that have been built up in the first few years of life, continue to exert a basic underlying influence on those secondary motives of which we are consciously aware.

4. Freud was the first psychologist to carry the principle of 'psychic determinism' to its logical conclusion, by insisting that nothing comes into the mind, or no action occurs, without a cause. Thus he found that not only dreams express a latent content of repressed wishes, usually in disguised or symbolic form, but also slips of the tongue or even apparent coincidences such as a series of

accidents. Hysterical and psychosomatic symptoms and the irrational compulsions and anxieties of the neurotic likewise represent the best adjustment he has been able to work out. Phenomena like these have, as it were, got past the repressing barriers and, therefore, with the aid of free association, provide the psychoanalyst with techniques for exploring the content of the unconscious mind.

Diversity of views. Freud's own views changed considerably through the years, and a number of variations exist among his followers, not to speak of the major dissensions with Jung and Adler. For example, there is less emphasis now on revealing the unconscious origins of symptoms as a means of bringing about a better integration of the personality, and more analysis of the patient's *present* values and feelings and his transference to the analyst. However, the more conservative 'wing', led for many years by Melanie Klein, still attaches primary importance to the aggressive fantasies and anxieties of the first year or two of life; whereas Anna Freud has been more concerned with studying the Ego's defences, i.e. the later transformations of the instincts. Others such as Suttie have disagreed with the Freudian derivation of altruistic tendencies and of the constructive features of human civilization from sexual repression, and have added more positive needs for love and activity.

An extremely wide range of views exists among contemporary clinical psychologists and psychiatrists – i.e. those persons who are most directly involved in the diagnosis and assessment of personality and with treating the emotionally disturbed in clinics and mental hospitals. On the whole it would be true to say that they pay more attention to the conflicts of the recollect-able period of childhood (say 3–11 years) and adolescence than to the infant stages, and look for causal factors chiefly in the family situation – in the irrational attitudes of the individual to his parents and siblings and of them to him – or outside the home. However, they would often admit that this is because they lack the training, and seldom have the time, to penetrate to deeper levels; that basically their conceptions of personality derive from the principles we have outlined above (albeit in grossly oversimplified form).

To a remarkable extent also, these conceptions have percolated into common usage and have influenced public attitudes to child-upbringing and delinquency. They are implicit in many books on educational psychology or on the development of the normal child (though criticized by others, e.g. Valentine, 1956). They are exemplified in countless novels, plays and movie-films, and are even employed by many advertisers in devising effective appeals to the public to buy their wares, under the name: motivational research.

Criticisms on naïve grounds. There is no point, then, in criticizing depth psychology theories on such grounds as their failure to accord with 'commonsense' knowledge of human nature, their over-emphasis on sex, on 'not frustrating the child' or 'getting rid of repressions'. On the one hand, 'commonsense' is no criterion; it does not reveal to us the physicist's conceptions of matter as consisting of electrons and protons, and there is no more reason why our naïve perceptions and working theories of personality should accord with those of the specialist. On the other hand, the violent opposition which characterized Freud's early work has largely disappeared; much of it is already acceptable, and much too is confirmed by unbiased observation of young children, for example, their unbridled sensuousness and aggression. (Even more direct illustrations of what personality is like 'with the lid off' are often provided by psychotic patients.)

A more plausible objection is that Freud exaggerates; he underestimates the resilience and easy adjustment of the normal child and adult, while providing valuable insight into the maladjustments of a relatively small proportion of neurotics. Indeed, his theories were based on analysing a limited number of middle-class Viennese patients and he has extended what he found to the whole human race. As Eysenck (1953) points out, the sexual attitudes and activities of the different social classes vary extremely widely; thus the psychiatrist and psychologist, who tend to come from a homogeneous class background, are liable to serious bias in applying these concepts to people from other cultures and classes.

It is indeed true that many children grow up to be reasonably adjusted citizens, although their parents and teachers know nothing of Freud and handle them by traditional methods; also that minor maladjustments are either outgrown, or corrected by 'talking-out', reassurance, and everyday rewards and punishments. But the depth psychologist could reasonably answer that we all do have neurotic trends in varying degrees, and that the apparent exceptions are individuals who were probably basically stable in innate temperament, and who were brought up in a secure atmosphere, so that they can cope readily with their anxieties and frustrations. He would add that 'surface' methods such as reasoning with, or spanking, the naughty child often fail to work, or may produce some apparent improvement while leaving the deeper conflicts unsolved. As for the efficacy of 'talking-out', it is characteristic of the neurotic to spend most of his life talking about his worries, since this excuses him from facing up to his real problems (cf. Leeper and Madison, 1959).

However, we will come back to a more thorough critical assessment of depth psychology when we have surveyed some of the evidence. Our prior consideration must be, not theoretical arguments, but: does it work? Does the adoption of these conceptions enable the clinical psychologist to make more accurate predictions about people, or to influence them more effectively? We shall first ask how consistent or reliable they are among themselves in the diagnosis either of abnormal or normal individuals.

Reliability of diagnosis. It is widely believed that the proportions of patients in mental hospitals diagnosed under the various nosological groups vary markedly with the psychiatrist who makes the diagnosis (cf. Ash, 1949; Mehlman, 1952). However, Schmidt and Fonda (1956) analysed the agreement between diagnoses of 426 typical patients made by 8 moderately experienced psychiatrists and the later (independent) official hospital diagnosis, and found agreement in 84% of cases on the major category; psychotic, organic or character disorders. On the 11 minor categories recommended by the American Psychiatric Association's Manual there was somewhat poorer agreement, 55%, particularly in classifying the characterological-neurological groups. However, such findings may be due less to the subjectivity of psychiatric judgment than to the imprecision of such categories as schizophrenia, hysteria, psychopathy, etc. As Szasz (1957) points out, they derive partly from pathological, partly from administrative and legal, partly from depth-psychological considerations. One cannot really say that schizophrenia 'exists', since to call a man a schizophrenic does not always imply that he possesses any definite attributes characteristic of a group of patients.

> Doering and Raymond (1934) noted as much variation when a single psychiatrist reclassified a number of symptoms from case histories as when this psychiatrist's judgments were compared with those of two colleagues, suggesting again that differences in viewpoint may be less serious than general looseness and uncertainty of terminology.

One might hope that a more objective and logical taxonomy of mental pathology might be reached through factor analysis. Somewhat discrepant schemes have been put forward by different factorists, but Wittenborn and Holzberg (1951a) and Lorr *et al.* (1957) agree fairly closely on the most suitable dimensions under which commonly recorded symptoms may be classified. Wittenborn's psychiatric rating scales (1955) are based on these, and offer promise of a much improved system of describing patients.

Whether clinical psychologists, with their more thorough training in academic psychology, and their access to objective test data, are any more reliable in their diagnoses, is not known. Naturally a psychologist's report on a patient is a complex and lengthy document, not just a nosological labelling, so that it would be difficult to prove how far other psychologists, seeing the same patient independently, would arrive at the same conclusions. Nevertheless this should be tackled by the techniques suggested earlier (pp. 56–7).

Studies of reliability in the Armed Forces. It becomes possible to evaluate agreement more precisely when the psychiatrist or psychologist, on the basis of his overall study of a group of individuals, commits himself to rating them on certain traits, on their suitability for employment, their psychiatric prognosis or some other outcome. Here the published figures are generally similar to those recorded for lay interviewers. Thus, N. Bartlett (1950) reports a correlation of only 0·39 between short psychiatric interviews of candidates for submarine training.

Hill and Williams (1947) compared the assessments of 541 RAF personnel who were seen by more than one of 37 psychiatrists. Classifications of the main 'reaction-types' – anxiety, depression, hysteria and others – were in agreement in 68½% of cases. This corresponds to a matching correlation coefficient of 0·76. However, judgments of 'neurotic predisposition' were more subjective, nearly half the men assessed as 'severe' by one psychiatrist being called 'mild' or 'nil' by another – corresponding to a tetrachoric correlation of 0·58.

The best recorded reliability is that obtained by Newman, Bobbitt and Cameron (1946) in the US Coast Guard, when two psychologists and a psychiatrist independently assessed the suitability of officer candidates and the correlations of the psychologists' judgments with the psychiatrist's were 0·81 and 0·86. Almost certainly these figures can be attributed to the careful definition beforehand, by the team, of just what qualities they were looking for.

Psychiatrists played an important part also in the War Office Selection Board procedures of the British Army from 1941 onwards (cf. Vernon and Parry, 1949). Officer candidates attended a typical

Board for three days in groups of 8 to 10, and during that time were given certain intelligence and personality tests and questionnaires, and put through a series of practical situational exercises by a (non-psychologist) Military Testing Officer, who observed their social and leadership reactions. They were also interviewed individually by the President of the Board (a senior Army officer) and by a psychiatrist, the latter's main function being to diagnose deeper motivations which might affect the candidate's social relations with other officers and the men under his command, and his reactions to the stresses of combat and Army life. Finally a conference was held among the members of the Board and an agreed recommendation made.

It was soon observed that the pass-rates for different Boards assessing similar candidates varied considerably, and in one experimental study with 116 candidates who were seen by a second Board two weeks after the first, $21\frac{1}{2}\%$ of those passed by one Board were rejected or deferred by the second; this represented a tetrachoric correlation of 0·67. In a more thorough investigation, using highly experienced staff, 125 candidates were assessed by two teams, and the overall agreement was quite high: a correlation of 0·80. The pairs of Military Testing Officers and psychologists reached a similar or even higher figure; but the correlation between the two psychiatrists was 0·65, the same as for the two Presidents. Admittedly this low reliability was obtained with only one pair, but it can be presumed that they were looking for much the same qualities in potential officers.

Validity studies. The problems of finding suitable criteria against which to validate the accuracy of clinical predictions are obviously manifold. Nevertheless a considerable amount of relevant evidence is available, some of it fairly favourable, a good deal of it not. In one study at an RAF station, 200 airmen were interviewed by a psychiatrist, who assessed their 'neurotic disposition'; they were then followed up through a tour of operations. Two or more neurotic symptoms had been noted among 69% of those who developed psychiatric breakdown, and among 20·4% of those who became casualties or had accidents, but among only 5·4% of those who successfully completed their tour. This corresponds to a tetrachoric correlation of 0·55 (cf. Hill and Williams, 1947).

In the Army a short psychiatric procedure was applied to 1,492 men selected for parachute training, and the psychiatrists themselves underwent the training in order to acquaint themselves with the job requirements. They graded the men on a 1 to 5 scale for suitability, and it was found that 3%, 7%, 10%, 23% and 46% of those classified in the five grades failed the training, corresponding to a validity coefficient of 0·58. However, this success may have arisen, in part, from taking account of the recruits' scores on tests of intelligence, mechanical and educational abilities. Further follow-up, a year later, showed a much lower association between the gradings and promotion on the one hand, or failure due to disciplinary, medical or training wastage on the other.

In the US Navy, Wittson and Hunt (1946, 1955) similarly demonstrated greater breakdown and disciplinary trouble rates among recruits recorded as showing neurotic symptoms during a brief psychiatric interview on entry.

In the War Office Selection Board follow-up studies it was not possible to separate off the contributions of the psychiatrist from those of the other members. Clearly the procedure as a whole succeeded in picking considerably larger numbers of officers who passed their training courses than did the traditional procedure of selection through interview by a senior Army officer alone, or by a Board of military interviewers; and small but fairly consistent correlations were obtained later between WOSB gradings and Training Unit results. Satisfactory ratings of efficiency at the job were much more difficult to obtain, and the finding that Commanding Officers were generally pleased with the material sent them by the WOSBs and Training Units cannot be accepted as evidence, in the absence of reports on a control group who had not been so selected. However, one study carried out on 500 officers just before the crossing of the Rhine did show some predictive value for the WOSB ratings, particularly among the younger men (cf. Vernon and Parry, 1949). Considering the imperfect reliability of the ratings, and the doubtless even greater subjectivity of the criteria, this result is fairly reassuring.

Another small-scale study, of 89 officers who underwent psychiatric breakdown within a year of passing their Board, showed that the psychiatrists and psychologists had given somewhat adverse reports in many instances – more than they had to normal acceptances; whereas the lay members of the Boards had not observed suspicious signs. (The psychologists had studied projection test material as well as aptitude scores, but had not seen the candidates.) However, the data is too meagre for any precise conclusions.

A more elaborate and more depth-oriented procedure was introduced by Murray and his colleagues for selecting men for special assignments (e.g. underground work in enemy territory; OSS

Assessment Staff, 1948). Naturally it was particularly difficult to obtain estimates of success at the job, though some positive evidence of validity was collected. More striking was one study which indicated that candidates selected by an abbreviated one-day procedure were, on the whole, better than those assessed on the intensive three-day procedure.

The selection of clinicians. A series of researches into the selection of doctors for psychiatric training was carried out at the Menninger Clinic under Holt and Luborsky (1958; cf. also Holt, 1958).

> Initially, the candidates were interviewed by psychiatrists and reported on by a clinical psychologist, each using his own favourite techniques, a final recommendation being reached by an Administrative Committee. It was found that 71% of those accepted as against 36% of those not recommended successfully qualified as psychiatrists; but the correlations with training performance for individual interviewers were very low, averaging from 0·24 to 0·27, with a range from zero to 0·52. Actually a single intelligence test, the Wechsler, gave as good a prediction of 0·27, even in this high-grade group. Next, a careful job-analysis was made of the qualities required for psychiatric work and training, for example by applying projection and other tests to known good and bad trainees; and a manual was written drawing attention to the more significant indicators in each test. Two psychologist judges who applied this information to predictions about another 64 trainees achieved correlations of 0·48 and 0·57, though the figures varied with different criteria, and for one psychologist they were as low as 0·22 with staff ratings. No objective test gave correlations higher than 0·20. However, we should note that the apparent superiority of the revised method may have been due not to any improvements in clinical interviewing but to basing the evaluation of the candidates to a greater extent on objectively validated test procedures.

The most frequently quoted research in this area is that reported by Kelly and Fiske (1951) into the selection of candidates for training as clinical psychologists. Information was collected on 76 to 93 candidates by means of standard ability and personality tests, projection techniques, situational tests and lengthy interviews. Assessments of proficiency were obtained after two and four years; but, as the accepted candidates were trained at several different institutions, the reliability of these criteria cannot have been high. The correlations between different predictors and the criteria were small, also, since they could be calculated only within this rather homogeneous, already selected, group, and they varied considerably for different criteria. Some of the pooled figures appear in Table I.

TABLE 1

AVERAGE VALIDITY COEFFICIENTS OF PROCEDURES USED IN
SELECTING CLINICAL PSYCHOLOGISTS

	Correlations 2 yr.	Correlations 4 yr.
Paper qualifications only judged by 2 psychologists	0·17	0·22
Paper qualifications and 1 hour's interview	0·15	0·25
Judgments based on paper qualifications + a number of objective tests only	0·27	0·29
Separate objective tests only: Miller analogies	0·17	0·30
Certain scores on Guilford–Martin Personality Inventory	0·22	0·16
Strong Interest Blank, scored for psychologists	0·25	0·20
Strong Interest Blank, scored for clinical psychologists	0·32	0·18
Judgments based on above data + a series of projection tests	0·29	0·26
Separate projection tests, each given by an independent tester		
Rorschach Inkblots	0·12	0·05
Thematic Apperception	0·11	0·12
Sentence Completion (group test)	0·19	0·21
Ditto + a further intensive interview	0·27	0·26
Judgments of a team based on all the above	0·24	0·30
Ditto after observing 'situations' test (final prediction)	0·20	0·33
Situations alone judged by 3 independent observers	0·27	0·22

These appear to indicate that the correlations for Paper Qualifications and for certain standard group tests are as high or higher than those for any of the more clinical procedures. The addition of the first or second interview does not add to, and even detracts from, the validity of prediction. The well-known projective techniques are particularly weak, and the simplest of them – Sentence Completion – seems better than the more complex. The Situations Test rating, based on observation of behaviour in standard social and clinical situations, is also quite promising. (cf. p. 261). Kelly and Fiske conclude that the more intensive techniques, in which the judges felt greatest confidence, work less well than the more superficial techniques; and this conclusion has been seized upon by critics as a complete disproof of the diagnostic value of the clinical approach. (cf. Eysenck, 1953; Sarbin *et al.*, 1960).

The writer is less convinced by this evidence, since the differences between the various coefficients are mostly too small to be statistically significant; only those differences exceeding 0·20, say, can be given much credence. Moreover, very different results were obtained from the application of some of the procedures to a similar sized group in the following year. Few of these results are published, but the coefficients seem to have been lower and more irregular; and they did not confirm the view that the more a clinician finds out about his candidate, the worse his judgments are.

In a further follow-up 5–6 years later (Kelly and Goldberg, 1959) some of the intelligence, interests and personality tests still gave significant correlations of 0·2 to 0·33 with various, not very satisfactory, criteria of professional competence. But not a single measure was consistently predictive for both groups of psychologists.

At the same time there is considerable plausibility in Kelly and Fiske's, and in Sarbin's, argument that the clinician collects such complex evidence that his weighing or synthesis of it is liable to go awry. Having little information on just which predictors are most significant he may put more trust in the poorer than in the better ones. Essentially he is trying to do the same job as a computing machine, that is to combine a variety of cues; only the machine is inevitably more efficient, given the same information, since it can take account of the validity of each cue and weight them in such a way as to yield the best possible prediction. Though the human brain can often surpass the machine in perceiving complex patterns, we know that it is less efficient in retaining and recalling information accurately and combining it.

The work of P. E. Meehl. Meehl has made a most important contribution to this topic with his book: *Clinical versus Statistical Prediction* (1954). By statistical or actuarial prediction he means that certain objectively ascertainable cues (whether test scores or facts from case histories, etc.) are recorded for a number of subjects, and their correlations with the criterion – the outcome to be predicted – are calculated. Knowing also the intercorrelations of these cues, a multiple correlation can be obtained which weights the several cues optimally. He has surveyed twenty researches in which this actuarial approach could be compared with a clinical approach, i.e. where a psychologist or other judge studied the same cues – usually with additional data – and attempted to reach an overall synthetic prediction of the same outcome. Actually the full multiple-correlation (or discriminant function) technique has seldom been applied in such comparisons. The weighting has been a theoretical or arbitrary one, which probably approximates closely to the optimal, but puts the actuarial appraisal at a slight disadvantage.* The important point is,

* It should be noted, on the other hand, that optimal weighting always exaggerates the multiple-correlation coefficient unless it is cross-validated or at least corrected for 'shrinkage'; i.e. the weights worked out from one group of subjects

however, that a uniform set of weights was applied to all subjects, whereas the clinician would be inclined to attach greater significance to some cues with one subject, other cues with another.

For example, Wittman (1941) investigated predictions of the likelihood of schizophrenic patients benefiting from shock treatment. The actuarial predictions were based on adding together items from a check list, while the clinical judgments were made by psychiatrists. Of the former predictions 81% turned out to be correct, of the latter 44%; and in a further similar study the figures were 68% and 41%. Again, Sarbin (1943) found that statistical predictions of students' college grades, on a basis of high school ranks and objective test scores, correlated 0·45 for men and 0·70 for women with the criterion. When counsellors likewise made predictions on the basis of the same information plus the scores on personality and interest tests and an interview, the corresponding coefficients were 0·35 and 0·69, that is, lower though not significantly so. Other investigations cited by Meehl were concerned with predicting vocational suitability, parole violations or adjustment of delinquents – i.e. a wide range of outcomes; and in the majority of these the clinical predictions were poorer than the actuarial.

A subsequent research by Wirt (1956) points in the same direction. Eight clinicians, who were expert in interpreting MMPI results, attempted to classify 38 neurotic patients, half of whom had benefited from psychotherapy, half were unimproved. On the average, they were successful with 20½ cases, when 19 would be expected by chance. The same patients had taken Barron's Ego-strength scale (made up of validated items from MMPI), and by dividing them at an appropriate cutting score, 30 of the 38 were correctly classified.

The most advanced applications of actuarial prediction are to be found in the field of delinquency.* Mannheim and Wilkins (1955) picked seven items which could be objectively assessed from the records of youths in English Borstals, and showed that, when properly weighted, they gave a correlation of 0·46 with later recidivism. Moreover, on applying this regression equation to a fresh group, the correlation remained at 0·48, and the failure rates for those with various actuarial scores, i.e. the proportions later reconvicted, were much the same. No systematic clinical evaluation was followed up, but predictions by the Governors and housemasters (who had access to all the same evidence)

---

should be applied to a second group. In so far as this precaution was not taken in all the studies, the actuarial success was unduly boosted; for the clinicians *were* employing previously determined, even if subjective, weights.

* The classical work of the Gluecks on prediction is not mentioned here, since they did not actually carry out a full regression analysis of objectively determined items. Their research published in 1950 reports the extent of differentiation between delinquents and non-delinquents by social background, family and educational data, and by psychiatric and other assessments. But no useful comparisons can be made since the psychiatrist presumably knew, or could easily guess, which boys were delinquent. The results with the Rorschach and somatotype are commented on in later chapters.

achieved validity coefficients of only 0·18 to 0·15. At the same time the authors were able to show that, within the 'border-line' group, for whom predictions based on previous record were most uncertain, items based on personality characteristics could usefully be taken into consideration.

Discussion of Meehl's findings. As with the Kelly and Fiske study, critical writers tend to exaggerate Meehl's conclusions by saying that all his comparisons showed the actuarial predictions to be equal or superior to the clinical. It would be more correct to state that half the comparisons definitely favoured the actuarial; in most of the remainder the clinical approach was insignificantly inferior or superior, or no conclusion was justified; in only one study – the prediction of the performance of nursing trainees from MMPI protocols – were the clinicians more successful. However, there was no clear tendency for any particular type of clinical prediction to be better than another, nor for psychiatrists, psychologists, counsellors or psychologically untrained persons such as doctors to be inferior or superior (if anything, psychiatrists do worst, psychologists relatively best).

Meehl himself in no way disputes the conclusion that the actuarial approach, when applicable, can do a better job. Rather, as an experienced psychotherapist, he is concerned to argue that the clinician does other jobs which could not be duplicated by a computer, nor put into the actuarial framework. At the moment clinicians are spending an enormous amount of time giving tests, trying to weigh up their results – individually or in case conference – where better predictions could be made by what Meehl (1956) calls 'cook-book' methods, i.e. by actuarial tables which summarize the established correlations between symptoms or scores and outcomes. They should be devoting themselves to therapy or research rather than to diagnosis or prognosis. Nor does he accept the depth psychologist's objection that human behaviour is not determined by the simple addition of particular traits and abilities; it is possible both to score configurationally, i.e. to feed certain patterns of scores or items into a computer, and to employ more complex statistical treatments, taking account of interactions, than the simple additive model of the regression equation or of factor analysis. (cf. also Hoffman, 1960). And it is still true that the additive treatment generally works.

To Sarbin, Taft and Bailey (1960) the results cited by Meehl confirm their view that all judgments of personality are essentially inferential, that indeed clinical inference is merely a form of actuarial. It tends to be less accurate because the clinician does not know the exact validities of his postulates – he has only a rough impression, a personal hunch, or an accepted dogma, that certain symptoms go with certain outcomes; and he over-generalizes, assuming that all persons possessing some attribute (e.g. a broken home) will do so-and-so, rather than thinking probabilistically. He then weights his data arbitrarily instead of inductively, the result being that the more data he has, the worse his prediction is. At the same time he obtains strong convictions of his capacity to understand and make predictions about people because his inferential processes are often incompletely formulated, subjective, and affective in nature.

We will attempt later to answer these arguments and to show more clearly what is the nature of the clinical approach. To summarize the position reached so far: there seems to be little proof that, by adopting depth conceptions of personality, it becomes possible to improve greatly on our naïve method of making predictions about people. Nor can the clinical psychologist do better in this respect than the statistical or experimental psychologist who consider man more as a scientific object, a kind of mechanism, than as a motivated being who needs to be understood. Indeed, clinical diagnosis seems to be most effective when the clinician's methods approach more closely to those of the statistically trained psychologist as in Newman, Bobbitt and Cameron's, and Holt's, researches.

Chapter 6

FUNDAMENTAL CONCEPTS OF
DEPTH PSYCHOLOGY

Although depth psychology appears to be of little help in improving our diagnoses of personality, this does not mean that it may not have other valuable practical applications. After all, the kinds of predictions discussed in the preceding chapter are somewhat narrow, artificial ones which the clinician might do better to avoid. His function is therapy, rather than forecasting vocational or other achievements. Thus we shall examine (in Chapter 8) the evidence bearing on the success of clinical methods in the treatment of emotionally disturbed children and neurotic adults, and on the value of different kinds of counselling. It will be shown that the effects of such treatment are rather different from what is commonly supposed, and that they do not necessarily 'cure' or 'improve' people any better than do the psychologically naïve methods which society conventionally employs.

We should, however, distinguish the applied or technological aspects of depth psychology such as clinical diagnosis and therapy, from the scientific aspects – that is the general propositions put forward by Freud and other leading writers. The success of clinical methods in understanding and helping people does not necessarily rest upon the soundness of these particular theories; nor, conversely, are the theories necessarily disproved if their technological applications fail to work out. Nevertheless they are obviously interlinked, and it would be as well to examine some of the concepts listed earlier (pp. 76–78), in the light of available observational and experimental evidence, before trying to make up our minds about the practical implications of depth psychology. For example, do such propositions as unconscious mental processes, repression, regression and character types rest purely on clinical generalizations or on Freud's fiat, or can we cite independent confirmation? For reasons of space, however, it will not be possible to do more than sketch some of the lines of investigation that seem most relevant, and (in Chapter 7) some of the alternative theoretical formulations proposed by 'non-depth' psychologists.

Unconscious mental processes. There is ample proof from hypnotic phenomena, that ideas or 'complexes' can influence our behaviour without our being consciously aware of their existence. For example, post-hypnotic suggestions can be implanted which are carried out by the subject who does not realize their origins, and Luria's (1932) experiments neatly illustrate the effects of unconscious, unadmitted guilt and anxiety. Thus we may reasonably accept the inference from observations of neurotics and normals that they are often motivated by unacknowledged dispositions, though it is more difficult to prove that psychologists can correctly diagnose these dispositions or bring them to the level of conscious awareness whether by free association, projective or other techniques. For example, it may be true that advertisers can sell more cars, cosmetics and foods by studying consumers' subconscious motives, but there is a conspicuous lack of published evidence comparing the effectiveness of such advertisements with that of more 'naïve' appeals to conscious needs.

It is likewise a commonplace of experimental psychology that many of the processes involved in perception, recall and thinking operate at preconscious levels – that we are largely unaware of the cues, the effects of previous experience, and the 'sets', which enter into our impressions and judgments. However, as Erickson (1958) shows in his discussion of the discrimination of sub-threshold stimuli, this does not imply the existence of an Unconscious as a kind of omniscient super-mind, lying behind and even plotting against the conscious mind. For example, there is very little experimental support for the notion of subliminal advertising – that people can be influenced through the reading by their unconscious minds of advertisements which are flashed upon a cinema or TV screen too rapidly for conscious perception (cf. McConnell *et al.*, 1958).

There is a third sense in which the concept of unconscious processes must be viewed with considerable caution – namely, the persistence of emotional traumata or other early experiences in virtually unaltered form in the unconscious regions of the mind, whence they can be resuscitated by appropriate techniques. Bartlett's (1932) investigations of remembering have demonstrated that it is exceptional for images to be recalled unchanged, that our memories normally fuse and become distorted so that what we recollect is a reconstruction fashioned out of a whole mass of past experiences and dispositions. They may bear very little resemblance to the original material, except under the rather unnatural circumstances in which rote memorization is conducted in schools or in psychological laboratories. Thus when a patient, as a result of psychotherapy, seems to bring up repressed material, it is not so much because his Unconscious is a repository for this material as that he is analysing and verbalizing a previously undifferentiated mass of affectively toned impressions. In very much the same way our motor habits and perceptual schemata are syntheses of experiences going right back to infancy, which could not possibly be analysed in accurate detail. Thus any effects of, say, maternal rejection in the first few years of life should be thought of as persisting in the Unconscious in much the same sense as the effects of learning tennis with a badly strung racket persist in an adult's tennis playing, or the effects of living in the tropics as an infant persist in the person's later health and physique. Though this does not, of course, explain why some images persist much more clearly than others, consciously or unconsciously, it has an obvious bearing on the apparent inability of depth psychologists to predict future behaviour or adjustment any better than, or as well as, the interpreter who concentrates more on present feelings and concepts.

Experimental studies of psychoanalytic concepts. When Sears reviewed these studies in 1944 he was forced to conclude that the experimentalist's techniques were too clumsy to cover the kind of thing the psychoanalyst was talking about. It was hardly to be expected that such highly charged emotional processes could be brought into the laboratory and studied under controlled conditions. True, strong motivations could be investigated with animals such as rats, but the depth psychologist would very pardonably doubt the relevance of findings based on lower animals to complex human processes. Nevertheless Sears was able to adduce a surprising amount of evidence from animal and human investigations which appeared to illustrate such mechanisms as repression, regression, fixation and projection, even if in emasculated form. Only in the case of sublimation did the evidence appear to be contrary: a direct inquiry from young unmarried males who were prominent in cultural activities indicated that they had in no way suppressed sexual needs, but gratified them through a number of channels.

Since that date there have been considerable advances, and it might be claimed that depth-psychological concepts are not merely acting as stimuli to research, but are being clarified and extended through direct research. The production of 'experimental neuroses' in animals through demanding unduly fine discriminations, or setting strong needs into conflict, may tell us little about humans; yet the conditions under which animals develop rituals, tics, or 'superstitions' are certainly of interest. Skinner's discovery of the greater stability (resistance to extinction) of habits such as bar-pressing in rats, through applying intermittent schedules of reinforcement, can be regarded as a major contribution to human dynamics. For example, it helps to explain why the spoiled or over-protected child who is too frequently reinforced shows less tolerance of frustration than the occasionally rewarded.

Repression and regression. Early studies of repression which attempted to show that pleasant memories were more readily recalled than unpleasant were highly unconvincing, if only because Freud's claims referred to repression of experiences that conflict with other dominant personality traits rather than merely to their unpleasantness. Somewhat more realistic were investigations such as those of Rosenzweig (1943), showing that ego-threatening experiences are apt to be forgotten; and there has been much study of the conditions under which the perception of anxiety-provoking verbal or other stimuli is inhibited. For examples of regressive phenomena we still have to turn mainly to experiments showing that rats revert to earlier habits when current ones are blocked, or to the classical study by Barker, Dembo and Lewin of the deterioration in organized, constructive behaviour among young children under frustration. But investigations of the arousal of aggression have gone far beyond the Lewin, Lippett and White observations of autocratically run and *laissez-faire* groups. There is much greater sophistication in the design of experiments, control of situational conditions and in the combined use of observational, projective, interview and other techniques (cf. Mussen, 1960). For example, Sears (1951) has shown that there is little overall association between observed aggressive behaviour among pre-school children and their production of aggressive fantasies in doll-play; but that a strong positive relation appears among children whose mothers punish them little or moderately for aggression, and a negative relation among children whose mothers punish them severely, i.e. when repression is likely to be operating (cf. also Lesser, 1957).

Behavioristic learning theory. Even more far-reaching are the attempts of such writers as Dollard and Miller (1950), Mowrer (1953), Shoben (1949, 1953) and Eysenck (1960a) to translate depth-psychological concepts into terms of modern learning theory. That is – neurosis is regarded essentially as acquired maladaptive responses and therapy as a process of reconditioning. Shoben, for example, describes the neurotic as one who has learned 'uncomfortable' social or interpersonal responses, including non-verbalized anxieties. In the permissive atmosphere of psychotherapy, less anxiety-laden and more rational responses are reinforced, and his 'comfortable' attitudes to the therapist are gradually generalized or transferred to other people. As Bandura (1961) points out, this approach suggests that psychotherapy works, not because the patient is gaining insight into his unconscious defences, but because the ordinary principles of learning are being applied, albeit rather inefficiently, and that success would be greater if the principles were acknowledged and used more systematically. Naturally the depth psychologist is inclined to be suspicious of this conception of treatment, in so far as it implies that the patient is a mechanical system, like a rat in a maze, which he, the psychologist, is trying to manipulate. He is apt to regard himself rather as a catalyst. Hence his actual behaviour during therapy is only vaguely defined and varies with his training and personal inclinations.

A number of different types of learning may be operating, or could be made to operate, including the straightforward processes of reward and punishment. However much the therapist tries to control expressions of approval and disapproval of the patient's attitudes and concepts, he can hardly help but show them by various subtle verbal or non-verbal cues. The patient is likely to absorb the therapist's theories and values not so much from what he says as from how he says it. Psychoanalysts reject the accusation that they employ suggestion, pointing out that the analysis of transference relationships is calculated to break down suggestive influences. Nevertheless suggestion is intentionally employed by other psychotherapists for certain types of patients, and may well enter unintentionally at other times.

Types of conditioning. 'Extinction conditioning' may also play a part. It is illustrated by the curing of motor habits such as typewriting errors, or tics, through practising them. If a patient is allowed to 'practise' his guilts or anxieties by bringing them up freely in therapy, reactive inhibition is likely to be built up against them. The same device appears to be operating in schools for maladjusted children, where they are freely permitted to act out their hostile or other fantasies. That counter-conditioning is often effective has been demonstrated in the treatment of enuresis, fetishes, alcoholism and phobias (cf. Wolpe, 1958; Eysenck, 1960a). For example, an alcoholic is given repeated drinks, accompanied by a drug which induces unpleasant vomiting, and this soon builds up a distaste for alcohol which is reported as being highly permanent. The enuretic sleeps with an absorbent pad which sets off an alarm bell and wakes him as soon as it is wetted by urine. Stone and Church (1957) criticize this technique on the grounds that learning to wake when wet is not the same as sleeping dry, and that the latter can be accomplished only if the child achieves the necessary feelings of security. Clinical psychologists would also urge that dealing with one symptom of an underlying neurotic condition, without getting to the root of the condition, would merely lead to the appearance of some new symptom which served the same unconscious motive. Certainly this is a strongly held dogma of depth psychology, and illustrative cases of symptom-substitution have often been described. But as Yates (1958) points out, it is not confirmed by follow-up evidence; some 70-80% of enuretics are permanently cured by conditioning, and there is no proof that clinical treatment is superior to, or even as effective as, this. True, such techniques are not always so effective, but it naturally takes time to investigate the appropriate reinforcement schedules and other conditions of successful learning.

Another point brought out by experimental studies of learning is that some people learn better by one technique, others by another. The clinician is apt to assume, perhaps unwittingly, that all cases of maladjustment are fundamentally similar and thus to favour one method of approach. Hence he tends to be much more successful with some types of patients than with others. Eysenck suggests a distinction between those who are already over-conditioned and those who are under-conditioned. The more introverted individual conditions easily and thus develops an over-strong Super-ego, manifested in anxiety or obsessional symptoms. Whereas the more extraverted person tends rather to behaviour disorders because his Id is not sufficiently socialized. Thus delinquency may arise more often from weak anticipations of punishment than from repressed aggression and insecurity (cf. Harsh and Schrickel, 1950). While no doubt this is an over-simplification, it does suggest a fruitful interaction of depth-psychological and learning theory hypotheses.

Behaviour theory and depth psychology. More generally it might be asked whether this view of therapy is not an attack on depth theories rather than a source of support? Thus when Eysenck and Yates reject the likelihood of alternative symptoms arising from unresolved conflicts, they state that neurosis *is* a learned pattern of maladjusted behaviour; in other words, it is nothing but symptoms. True the overt symptoms, e.g. enuresis, may be associated with learned anxieties, but the treatment of the one helps to reduce the other. It does not, as it were, leave them smouldering in the Unconscious, to flare up in another place. Lundin (1961) attempts to provide a completely behaviouristic account of personality, based largely on Skinner's work, in which he dispenses with all such conceptions of internal variable as motives, mechanisms, traits, etc. This is an extreme example of what Allport (1961a) refers to as the 'empty organism' view of personality. Yet in many respects such a theory is consonant with depth psychology; both are mechanistic in stressing the determination of behaviour by previous experience, and the shaping of the person by the way he is brought up. Lundin brings out the remarkable extent to which psychoanalytic conceptions of conflict, anxiety, displacement, etc. are illustrated in experiments on learning with rats and humans. Similarly, Hullian theory emphasizes the acquisition of social drives, which operate in much the same way as the depth psychologist's Super-ego and defence mechanisms; and it holds that learning occurs only through the reduction of tensions in these, or in the primary, biological drives. Moreover, although the therapist's concept of insight finds no place in S-R psychology, it obviously fits in with the field theorist's or Gestalt view of learning, as will appear in our next Chapter. Thus the earlier opposition between the experimental and the depth psychologist is breaking down, and there are few of the latter's dynamic concepts which do not link up with the former's interests.

Unfortunately, of course, the results of a controlled experiment seldom provide much guidance in making predictions about the individual case in an everyday life situation. It may be reasonable to hope that, in course of time, a combination of depth psychology with scientific experimentation will provide a sound basis for making correct decisions. But their application at the present time seems to be largely guesswork or unverified extrapolation. Let us turn then to another type of psychoanalytic proposition which Hartman and Kris denote as 'genetic'. The present writer prefers the term 'developmental' since, in some fields of psychology, genetic implies maturational, or inherited, as contrasted with environmental.

Developmental propositions. While many of the earlier Freudian statements on child development, derived from analyses of adults, tend to be confirmed by observations of children's behaviour, others, such as preference for the opposite-sex parent, the prevalence of castration anxieties, and the lack of sexual interests during the latency-period are not (cf. Farrell, 1951). The trouble is, however, to specify precise expectations when behaviour and feelings are so complex. Thus, observations such as Valentine's (1956) which appear to negate the Oedipus complex are hardly relevant if this complex is intended to refer to repressed attitudes rather than to conscious preferences. This difficulty continuously recurs. It is only too easy for the critic to pick out straw men and demolish them, i.e. to oversimplify some developmental proposition, and disprove it by inappropriate observations. At the same time, the critic is justified in asserting that the theory is insufficiently precise if it is so readily misinterpreted.

Child-rearing practices. The effects of various child-rearing practices are a case in point. Many doctors or infant welfare workers, not to speak of mothers, have taken Freud to mean that children who are breast-fed, fed on demand, weaned and toilet-trained gradually, and who receive much mothering, will grow up more secure and better adjusted than less indulged children. However, Orlansky (1949) shows how weak is the supporting evidence, and Sewell (1952) was unable to find anything more than chance relationships between such practices and personality characteristics. He interviewed the mothers of 162 American children aged 5-6, regarding upbringing, and assessed the children's personalities from tests, teachers' ratings and mothers' reports. Similarly, Peterson and Spano (1941) compared ratings of the behaviour of nursery-school children with records of the actual duration of breast-feeding which had been kept during infancy. Many of the correlations were in the reverse direction from that predicted by psychoanalytic theory; and overall there was no significant agreement. However, these results do not necessarily falsify Freudian theory, for, as Sewell points out, the practices as such may be less important than the emotional situation in which they operate, and the mothers' attitudes. If so, the theory has not been properly formulated. Alternatively, the methods of investigation may have been deficient. In Sewell's study, the mothers' recollections of rearing practices were probably far from reliable, and it is even possible that those who reported greater severity were merely being more frank about it.

Other studies of early weaning have indicated fairly definite effects on short-term oral behaviour, e.g. thumb-sucking, though not on long-term personality characteristics. One often-quoted research by Goldman-Eisler (1950) did indeed show a correlation in the expected direction with adult traits of optimism-pessimism (as measured by a self-rating inventory). But Eysenck (1952b) points out that other explanations might account for this; thus, more introverted mothers might have children similar to themselves, and also be more likely to wean them early.

Probably the most extensive investigation of child-rearing practices and attitudes is that of Sears, Maccoby and Lewin (1957), although, as this was based on interviews with 379 mothers of 5-year-old children, there was no independent evidence of the children's behaviour, nor later follow-up. The authors report no consistent effects of bottle- as against breast-feeding, and somewhat greater emotional upsets at the time of weaning when this takes place between 5 and 8 months than when it occurs either earlier or later. But they insist that relationships are seldom straight-forward; the effects of a given practice often vary with other conditions or with the type of child. For example, severe toilet-training goes with: quick cessation of bed-wetting if the mother shows considerable sex-anxiety but also warmth to the child; and very slow cessation of bed-wetting if the mother shows considerable sex-anxiety but also coldness to the child. Obviously the establishment of complex causal relations such as this will require lengthy research with very large numbers.

Mother-child separation. The work of Spitz, Goldfarb and Bowlby has suggested another rather concrete developmental theory: that separation from the mother (or a mother-figure) in the early years, and especially in the early months, of life leads to a lack of security which inhibits the development of sentiments of affection for others and causes retardation of intellectual growth. In a review of the literature Yarrow (1961) concludes that the case is proven, but fails to note that in very few of the published studies was there any control group. Thus it is quite possible that the intellectual deficiencies of the separated children might be attributable to genetic differences rather than to the deprivation as such. Yarrow does point out that the effects are very variable for different children, that they almost certainly depend on the age at separation, frequency or duration, and that there are various different kinds of separation, including: (a) institutionalization, e.g. of orphans; (b) temporary separation due to hospitalization of child or mother; (c) transfer of some or most maternal functions to other adults; (d) deprivation through rejection or other abnormal mother-child relationships. It is probable that (c) has little effect. Thus in the Israeli kibbutzim, the children are reared in small groups by a professional worker, but continue to have some leisure-time contacts with their mothers. Reports suggest that there may be some excess of psychological disturbances in childhood, but that they grow into mentally and physically healthy adults (cf. Caplan, 1954).

The intellectual and linguistic retardation of (a) institutionalized children appears to vary directly with the amount of reduction in normal perceptual and linguistic stimulation, hence it is possible that the lack of social and affectional stimulation likewise reduces social responsiveness or, according to some reports, increases 'affect hunger' and demands for attention. It is noteworthy that in a group of children studied by Anna Freud, who grew up under extreme deprivational conditions in war-time Europe, reasonable adult adjustment was achieved (cf. Stevenson, 1957). Hospitalization without the provision of an adequate mother-substitute seems apt to lead to a characteristic emotional trauma with subsequent rejection of the mother and difficulties of readjustment. But Bowlby (1956) himself has carried out a careful follow-up of such children 5–10 years later and found very little evidence of permanent intellectual, emotional or social impairment. He therefore advocates considerable caution in predicting ill-effects from the mere physical occurrence of mild amounts of deprivation.*

Various other examples could be quoted where psychiatrists have observed certain characteristics in the life-histories of neurotic children or adults and have attributed causal significance to these characteristics, when a fairly straightforward research with a control group would have shown them to occur just about as frequently in non-neurotics. One of the better attested findings is that mothers of

* For an up-to-date statement of Bowlby's claims, with supporting evidence, and with critical discussions by several authors, cf. Ainsworth, Andry et al. (1962).

male schizophrenics tend to be much more interfering, lacking in understanding, keeping them away from sex or independence, fearing sex themselves and despising their husbands, than mothers of normal or neurotic patients (Mark, 1953; McGhie, 1961). However, the pattern seems to differ in different social classes (Myers and Roberts, 1959).

Aggression, delinquency, prejudice. Some of the more satisfactory work has been done in the area of aggressive behaviour, as mentioned above, and there is considerable support for a connection between repressive parental attitudes in the home and concurrent behaviour at school (cf. Baldwin et al., 1945; Radke, 1946; Wittenborn et al., 1956).

Sears, Maccoby and Lewin (1957) again point out the complexity of relationships. Thus, they found that aggressiveness towards the parents was not increased by parental punitiveness unless the parents were also permissive about it; and it was lowest when the parents not only did not punish but did stop it (i.e. non-permissive). Further, the causal factors appeared to differ in respect of aggression to siblings, or to other children. A strong development of conscience by the age of 5 was associated with maternal warmth and negatively with rejection, but also showed interesting associations with type of control. High use of praise, reasoning with the child, or isolation as a form of punishment, all occurred more frequently among children 'with a conscience'; use of tangible rewards, deprivation of privileges, and especially physical punishment, were more likely to inhibit its development.

Attempts to trace back aggressive qualities in adolescents or adults, or high vocational achievement, to the type of home upbringing generally yield inconsistent results. In a rather thorough study of aggressively antisocial delinquents, Bandura and Walters (1959) interviewed 26 such boys, 26 controls and both parents of each. Many of the associations between home-rearing practices or parental attitudes and personality, hypothesized on the basis of depth and learning theories, were not confirmed. However, there was support for the view that delinquency arises from 'disruption of dependency relationships to the parents'. That is, the parents of delinquents had shown, and still did show, less warmth. In particular, the father was unsympathetic and the son did not identify with him. There was a greater tendency to use physical punishment and deprivation of privileges when the boys were young, and less reliance on reasoning, which may account for the boys' lack of internal standards of acceptable behaviour. However, parental control tended to be too inconsistent rather than too lax or too severe. Most noticeable, perhaps, was the consistent resistance of the boys to any form of socialization from very early years.

In a similar control-group study in England, Andry (1960) found that the adolescent's conscious attitudes to, and recollections of, his father are much more closely connected with juvenile delinquency than are maternal deprivation or rejection. Kohlberg (1963) brings out the highly contradictory results of numerous researches into the relation of moral attitudes and behaviour to variables in upbringing, but points out that psychoanalytic theory does stress the predominant importance of the father in the development of the conscience.

The factor of social class differences in child rearing, and its effects on method of resolving conflicts, was highlighted by Miller and Swanson (1960; also Swanson, 1961).

The mothers of about one hundred boys, around 13–15 years, were interviewed for their recollections on weaning, toilet-training and disciplining, and the boys were given a series of Story Completion projective tests, designed to bring out their responses to guilt- or anger-provoking situations. In some instances, situations were devised to arouse real feelings of guilt, anger or failure, and the *change* in type of response to the Story tests was analysed. Disciplinary methods (e.g. corporal, mixed or psychological) were clearly associated with social class, and a number of rather small associations were found which confirmed hypotheses based on psychoanalytic propositions. For example, 76% of middle-class as against 54% of working-class boys relied on inner standards when making moral judgments. Generally the middle-class boys tend to resort to displacement, repression or rejection in conflict situations, and to handle them conceptually, whereas the working-class boys are more apt to deny or evade the conflict, to turn aggression outwards rather than against the self, and to express it overtly. Similar effects were noted for disciplining by psychological as against physical methods.

The obvious weakness in this study is how far one can infer from projective responses to natural behaviour. However, in one instance it was shown that working-class background and corporal disciplining were associated with overt resentment of criticisms by school-teachers, as assessed by peer ratings.

A very different approach was employed by Hewitt and Jenkins (1946) in a study of child guidance cases in Chicago. By a modification of factor analysis, associations were found between types or clusters of home background items, and types of maladjustment. For example:

Unsocialized aggressive behaviour: (fighting, defiance, cruelty, etc.)	correlated with	Parental rejection: (illegitimacy, separation from both parents, mother hostile, etc.)

Socialized delinquency:
(truancy, stealing,) correlated
(bad companions, etc.) with

Parental negligence:
(unkempt home,)
(irregular routines,)
(bad area, etc.)

Over-inhibited:
(seclusiveness, worry-) correlated
(ing, sensitiveness) with

Family repression:
(mother dominating,)
(father inconsistent,)
(sibling rivalry, etc.)

and with

Physical deficiency:
(abnormal growth, tonsils)
(and adenoids, auditory)
(or speech defects, etc.)

The mean correlation between these maladjustment and environmental patterns was 0·52, whereas the cross-correlations (Unsocialized Aggression with Parental Negligence, etc.) averaged only ±0·18. As Eysenck (1960b) points out, the results prove nothing about the *causes* of maladjustment. The neglected children may have been more delinquent because of genetic differences, or the fact that they were delinquent may have increased parental neglect.

However, Wittenborn *et al.* (1956) succeeded in controlling the hereditary factor fairly effectively by comparing the personality characteristics of 5-6-year and 8-9-year adopted children with the attitudes and practices of their foster parents. Care was taken also to avoid 'contamination' of the data; i.e. the children's and the home characteristics were not both elicited from the mothers' reports. In the younger group, assessments of Child Rejection, Severe Toilet-training and Unsympathetic attitudes gave correlations around 0·3 to 0·4 with Aggressive and Compulsive Traits and Phobias in the children; in the older group the same parental attitudes correlated with Aggressive and Anxious characteristics. While the correlations are not high, they are of the same order as the correlations between socioeconomic + cultural level of a foster home and child I.Q.

One of the clearest associations claimed by Adorno *et al.* (1950), and confirmed by other investigators such as Allport and Kramer (1946), is that between authoritarianism or racial prejudice in adults and factors in upbringing. The authoritarian's home background is described as one where the family was autocratically organized, discipline was rigid, affection was conditional on approved behaviour.

and the child seemed to have reacted by a submissiveness which concealed strong hostility that was apt to be displaced on to non-parent figures. Now the weakness in this proposition is that the evidence about home upbringing was collected from the prejudiced subjects themselves (and the control group of 'democratic' adults), and it is only too probable that persons who possess a certain pattern of neurotic attitudes should conceive of their upbringing as distorted, whereas well-adjusted individuals should have happier views of their childhood and their parents. A further comment is suggested by studies of prejudice. By using quite simple attitude scales or opinion surveys, a vast amount of useful information has been collected on the distribution and the correlates of prejudice; whereas it is difficult to think of any scientific demonstration that the incidence of prejudice can be reduced, or better prediction or control achieved, through direct studies of the insecurities of children or the authoritarianism of parents.

Conclusion. Another approach is the comparative study of different cultures which favour different methods of child-rearing. Here too there have been incautious theories of child-restriction, weaning and other practices as 'producing' characteristic adult personality patterns, or determining the 'ethos' of the culture, which are readily confuted by pointing to other cultures that show the same practices but different personalities (cf. Orlansky, 1949; Inkeles and Levinson, 1954). Even if definite associations were proven, we would be faced with the problem of the hen and the egg. Does the culture produce the method of child-rearing or vice versa? There can be no doubt of the stimulating influence of psychoanalytic ideas on anthropological and sociological theory and research; though at the same time we find an undue readiness to assume that what are essentially group phenomena (e.g. cultural ethos, the development of civilized institutions, the causes of war, delinquency and prejudice) can be settled by intensive psychodynamic studies of individuals.

In concluding this section it would seem that depth-psychological constructs and propositions, despite their exploratory value, are mostly too vaguely formulated to allow concrete deductions regarding individuals or groups. We have indeed cited a number of positive results as fairly well established, but most of these appear to show the effects on later personality of parental attitudes and practices operating throughout childhood rather than in infancy. They are

H

more readily explicable in terms of ordinary learning theory than by unconscious mechanisms. Szasz (1957) argues that it is not possible to apply insights from psychoanalysis directly to problems of child-rearing or the disposition of criminals. Although we may justifiably hope that the interaction of these constructs with developmental and experimental studies will eventually provide the key to fuller understanding and control of human beings, there is little justification for thinking that we can already improve our predictions and decisions about people through studying their repressed motivations. Indeed it is questionable whether instinctive drives and defence mechanisms built up in early childhood should be regarded as more important determiners of the social behaviour, at least of relatively normal individuals, than later-developed motives. This point requires further discussion.

The importance of deeper dispositions. Two general assumptions are implicit both in the developmental propositions and in the diagnostic applications of depth psychology – assumptions which seem to be at variance with many of the facts. These are, first, the notion that personality is virtually determined by what happens to the instinctive urges in the first few years of life; and secondly, that the deeper dispositions or attitudes, deriving from this period, are more stable than those which are readily elicited; that indeed it is necessary to diagnose these in order to account for the inconsistencies and irrationalities in our conscious attitudes (cf. Rosenzweig and Kogan, 1949; Leeper and Madison, 1959). Bound up with the same dogma is the view, which we have already queried, that neurotic symptoms or 'strategies' are always expressions of deeper conflicts, and that the latter must be brought into the open for effective improvement in the former. Though these assumptions are highly plausible, they clearly require some qualifications. So far as stability goes, it is the abilities, interests, conscious goals, attitudes, prejudices and values, and aspects of the self-concept such as inferiority feelings, which show the greatest statistical reliability, and which correlate most consistently with normative, real-life criteria – not the constructs which the clinical psychologist diagnoses by interviews and projective techniques. Even the neuroses of adults or maladjustments of children are characterized by considerable changeability and a high spontaneous 'remission rate', as shown in Chapter 8 (cf. also Eysenck, 1960d). True, there are lifelong criminals, a few of whom seem to show deep-seated psychopathic or compulsive personalities; but many more are those whose criminality is continually reinforced by their social environment.

Determination by early experience. It is not entirely clear how far Freud implied that personality structure is fixed in the pre-school years. Thus, when common observation suggests that personality alters greatly with varied circumstances in later childhood, adolescence and adulthood, the depth psychologist can argue that he does not regard behaviour patterns as being fixed in childhood and recurring thereafter; rather the child acquires basic attitudes, e.g. towards authority, which transfer to, and influence, his reactions to later situations. According to Allport (1961a) and Harsh and Schrickel (1950), observation of infants during the first year or so of life, and our knowledge of their brain development, suggest that their existence is so largely vegetative that they would hardly be capable of the elaborate emotions and fantasies with which Melanie Klein and some other analysts credit them. However, the basic structures of cognition are laid down during that period (cf. the work of Hebb and Piaget); thus there is little reason to doubt that some organization of emotional attitudes occurs likewise, depending greatly on the affectional bonds with the adults. But it seems much more probable that fantasies regarding early child-parent relations are later fabrications and projections of present defence mechanisms. Indeed, a likely reason for the emphasis on early experience in depth-psychological theories is that patients like to talk about such experiences as a defence against facing their current difficulties (much as a mother ascribes her son's backwardness in school to his falling on his head when he was a baby.)

Importance of later motives. Allport has argued over many years that acquired motives may become self-supporting or 'functionally autonomous', and that personality is constructive, forward-looking, self-determining – not merely a resultant of the past. A boy may have decided originally to become, say a doctor, through identification with his father, but this develops and becomes a goal in its own right, which organizes all his activities for many years and itself controls other deeply rooted impulses. Such behaviour, Allport suggests, is flexible and creative, whereas behaviour that is primarily determined by neurotic fixations is compulsive and rigid, since it is merely repeating its origins. Both depth psychology and modern learning theories imply that secondary needs require periodic reinforcement or tension-reduction of the primary needs from which they derive. This may apply to laboratory-trained animals, but does not seem to be characteristic of human ideals and achievements; far from seeking reduction of tensions, people continually build up their own. However, no one has devised the crucial experiment to decide between these alternative views of motivation, which suggests (as shown in Chapter 9) that the arguments are more verbal than factual. Again it is only too easy for the depth psychologist to counter-attack by claiming that his opponent's preference for explanations in terms of conscious motives, or for the type of counselling which is carried out at relatively surface levels, are rationalizations that enable him to avoid anxieties regarding his own unconscious mechanisms.

However, it is clear that among the ranks of clinical psychologists themselves there is an increasing acknowledgement that Freud and Klein relied too heavily on biological determining factors and the influences of infantile adjustments, to the neglect both of the cultural forces in personality development and of the individual's own resources for positive growth. In other words, depth psychology has progressively moved closer to Allport's position, though there are still the traditionalists such as Glover (1961) who do not admit that the so-called Neo-Freudians are Freudians at all, and dubs them as sociologists.

Before proceeding to examine the effectiveness of clinical psychology in understanding and influencing people, we will outline some of the alternative psychological theories to which many psychologists, who are dissatisfied with classical depth theory, subscribe.

Chapter 7

SELF-THEORIES AS AN ALTERNATIVE APPROACH TO EXPLAINING PERSONAL BEHAVIOUR

The Neo-Freudians represent the transition from depth to self-psychology. Credit is generally given to Alfred Adler as the first revolutionary to realize that man is as much a product of his culture as of his psychological drives, and to urge that man self-consciously plans his own life. Adler's term: Individual Psychology, is significant, and his teachings have had a considerable influence upon many workers in child guidance (cf. Ansbacher, 1956). Even for Adler, however, the child is innately inferior and conscious of his own weakness; hence he develops a drive for coping with life -- a 'life-style' that persists in all his later adjustments. Karen Horney accepted the deterministic Freudian view that adult conflicts and neuroses arise from the totality of childhood experience, but urged that the inconsistent demands of Western culture are at least as influential as the sex instinct. For example, society's stress on Christian altruistic virtues *and* on the achievement of success through individual assertiveness create frustrations and anxieties which are solved by neurotic strategies. In Fromm's and in Sullivan's writings there is even more stress on sociological factors and on the building up by the neurotic of distorted patterns of relationships with people and conceptions of the Self. Each of these writers, of course, differed in important respects from the others (cf. Hall and Lindzey, 1957), but they all emphasized, in contradistinction both to Freudian and to modern learning theories, the view that the individual strives to actualize and to maintain the integrity of his personality.

The work of Carl Rogers. It is in Rogers' (1951) 'non-directive' approach to therapy that we find least concern about unconscious

107

motivations from the past, most interest in the client's conceptions of himself and the strongest belief in the self-realizing potentiality of a personality. Rogers by no means rejects Freudian explanations, but insists that the patient or client should find out his own explanation, instead of seeking it in the therapist's theories. The client must be understood in terms of his own frame of reference, not an outwardly imposed one, whether Freudian or otherwise. If he can learn to accept himself, which he will do in a completely permissive atmosphere, the natural progressive forces in personality will bring about greater harmony between his conflicting impulses; his own need for adjustment will be released, and he will grow to greater emotional maturity. Not only the neurotic, but also any normal individual who seeks for advice or counselling, realizes that there is disharmony between his perception of his own behaviour and his values or goals. The neurotic builds up defences and rationalizations as a way around his problems; he becomes rigid, unable to acknowledge his true feelings, and he resists any kind of attack on these subterfuges. With non-directive therapy, however, he comes to see that he has no need of rationalizations. He revises his concepts of himself and of others; for example, he realizes that the world is not threatening him, or that it does not owe him a living; that all men are not stern fathers, and so on. Simultaneously he comes to like and to accept himself. Incidentally, it is claimed, this produces more tolerance of, and better social relations with, others. The crucial factor in the neurotic, therefore, is his lack of understanding of the true nature of his problem. A very common case is the person who seeks vocational advice, expecting that the counsellor will provide a ready-made solution. But when helped to examine his own nature, he realizes the underlying conflicts and thus becomes capable of making his own decisions.

Rogers, Kell and McNeil (1948) attempted to assess the presence or absence of eight 'component factors', i.e. favourable or unfavourable sets of circumstances among two groups of 75 and 76 delinquents (aged 14 and 15 years), and correlated these with good or poor outcome 2 to 3 years later. During this interval the boys had mostly been on probation, in foster homes or institutions, i.e. they had not received any skilled therapy. Rogers expected such factors as Heredity, Family Circumstances and Economic-Cultural level to be most predictive. They did indeed give positive correlations of around 0·30 in one group, and 0·17 in the other. But much higher figures were obtained for Self-Insight (frank self-appraisal of own problems: r's of 0·84 and 0·41), and Social Adequacy (participation in group activities, etc.: r's of 0·55 and 0·36). These results led him to lay less stress on modifying the environment, more on changing the maladjusted individual's social adjustment and insight.

The nature of client-centred therapy. The client-centred therapist's role is that of a sympathetic and interested listener, who passes no value judgments, but shows that he respects whatever the client likes to bring up. The more the client gets to trust him, the more he will bring up real problems. Usually, after each statement, the therapist 'reflects back', that is, he restates in his own words what the client appears to be trying to say, with a view to clarifying his concepts, but not approving or disapproving them. The client, of course, continually tries to test him out, to elicit support or shock, but is continually forced back on his own resources. Rogers makes little use of free association and other Freudian techniques, since he regards these as invasions of the client's confidences before he is ready to volunteer them. Nor does he start off by making a detailed case history or reconstruction of the past; for the client is apt to think that this will provide the answer without further work on his part. Still less, of course, does the therapist put forward a diagnosis or specification of the problem. Tests are avoided in the early stages, though often applied later to give further information which may help the client in making rational decisions. The psychologist who thinks of vocational counselling in terms of measured abilities and traits is, in Rogers' view, prejudging the issue and imposing an arbitrary solution on the client. The therapist is neither a doctor who sets out to cure a patient, nor a scientist who is studying a human guinea-pig.

This does not mean that the therapist is passive any more than in other types of therapy. He needs at least as much perceptiveness as does the depth-oriented clinician, not only of the client's conscious attitudes, but of underlying motivations, of transference phenomena, etc. In his recent writings, Rogers (1960) has urged (with supporting experimental evidence) that effective treatment depends on the therapist's empathic understanding of the client, on his positive affective attitudes towards him, and on his own sincerity and congruence between his words and feelings. Although never offering advice, he is always willing to give information and, at suitable moments, to suggest courses of action between which the client must decide.

Rogers' approach is sometimes criticized as being too naïve, and as taking the client's statements too much at their face value. But in fact it differs markedly from the naïve approach of the lay counsellor

– the friend of the family, the doctor, or minister. Their methods are far from being non-directive, and consist largely in giving advice. A more valid criticism is that client-centred therapy involves a good deal more intervention than it alleges; reformulating or reflecting back invariably means selecting from, and interpreting, the client's utterances. However, many clinical psychologists and psycho-therapists (cf. Brammer and Shostrom, 1960) regard it as the most valuable approach for certain types of client and prefer other, more depth-oriented, approaches for other types. It is particularly suitable for educational and vocational purposes, where counselling can be conceived largely as a matter of rational problem-solving, and it seems to work best with clients of at least average intelligence and good verbal ability. Nevertheless, it can certainly be useful with the neurotic and the delinquent, and Rogers claims successful applications even with alcoholics and schizophrenics, while admitting that it may not be suitable for all kinds of personality disorders.

From our point of view this approach is especially important because, as shown in the next Chapter, there is more convincing experimental evidence for its effectiveness in bringing about personality changes than there is for other types of therapy. This does not necessarily mean that it is better than other types, but it does show that effective therapy does not necessarily depend on acceptance of any particular theory of unconscious personality dispositions.

Phenomenology. We shall deal more briefly with other formulations of Self-Theory, since their practical applicability seems more limited. Snygg and Combs (1949) provide a particularly clear statement of the phenomenological approach which conceives of personality wholly in terms of the individual's personal conception of the current situation – his phenomenal field. Their ideas derive partly from Rogers, partly from Lewin's topology and largely from P. Lecky's *Self-Consistency: A Theory of Personality* (1945). The individual's field consists of the Not-Self or Environment and the Phenomenal Self, as he sees them. When any stress or incongruity arises in the field, his need to maintain his own organization leads him to act in such a way as to regain consistency. From his point of view he is always consistent; he acts in such a way as the situation, in his view, demands. It is only because we judge him from outside without knowing all the components or 'differentiations' of his field that he appears inconsistent. True, he may admit that he acted in error; but then his field has now changed – the action was appropriate to his perception at the moment. Experimental psychologists and mental testers who study the individual externally cannot predict how he will react in any current situation; but the clever observer who correctly infers the nature of his field can do so. Snygg and Combs believe that this approach solves the problems of motivation and learning. There is only one motive, the need for personal adequacy and consistency. However, as the individual develops he makes more and more differentiations within his field, corresponding to percepts, habits, dispositions; and therefore tensions are apt to arise when his differentiations are inadequate for meeting threats to the Self, and there is conflict between his self-concepts and his perceptions of external reality. The value of therapy such as that of Rogers is that it provides a facilitating situation for the individual's drive to self-consistency, and so enables him to make better differentiations of himself and his perceived environment. It is not a matter of un-covering his various motivations and changing them, but of enabling him to recognize his true Self.

Criticisms. Phenomenology provides many new insights into problems with which classical psychology, with its abstractions such as cognition, motivation and learning, seems unable to cope. It is help-ful, also, to realize how often human misunderstandings arise because we do not want to admit the validity of other people's fields (e.g. teachers have little idea of what their instruction really means to children). But we would query whether it offers any advantages in studying personality. If a person's behaviour is determined wholly by his phenomenal field, this notion of 'field' lacks any explanatory value; it just *is* his total psychological processes. We cannot identify it simply with his conscious awareness. For though it is useful – even essential – to know what the person is thinking and feeling, when trying to explain his behaviour, his introspective report certainly does not give us a complete explanation. If Snygg and Combs had suc-ceeded in specifying all the components or differentiated parts of the phenomenal self, it seems unlikely that they could have avoided re-introducing the multiple motives, drives, attitudes, unconscious mechanisms and other intervening variables that they have tried to banish. Lewin's topological description of behaviour was similar. It helped to provide an illuminating picture of the vectors, barriers, etc., that influence the individual's reaction at the moment, but con-tributed little to our understanding of the more enduring components

of personality. In contrast, Festinger (1957) demonstrates the usefulness of the notion of 'cognitive dissonance', i.e. phenomenal incongruity, in a variety of socio-psychological areas, but considers the
need to reduce dissonance as only one among the major human
motives.

Snygg and Combs also provide no help towards more scientific
diagnosis. They admit that the person is not fully aware of his own
field. Thus the psychological diagnostician, who is trying to discover this person's characteristic differentiations, must infer them
indirectly and idiographically. He can use such techniques as
observation, interview, autobiography and impressions of others.
Standardized tests tend to fragment or break up the person's natural
organization, and they are often invalidated because they threaten
his self-concept; however, the meanings that various test stimuli have
for him, particularly projective ones, are said to be enlightening.

Kelly's psychology of personal construct. G. Kelly's (1955) system is
similar in many respects, though he shifts the locus of explanation
from perception to conception. The whole of the individual's psychological processes are thought of as arising directly from his constructs – the ways in which he interprets experiences and anticipates
events. As with the previous theory, the need for consistency among
the constructs, and their validity in enabling the person to predict or
control his environment, is thought to explain all phenomena of
motivation and learning. (When a man's anticipations are incorrect,
he tries to reconstrue – i.e. to learn fresh constructs.) The aim of the
clinician must be to see the patient in terms of the patient's constructs,
rather than imposing his own frame of reference. He can help the
patient formulate his poorly verbalized constructs more adequately
and encourage him to revise unduly rigid or conflicting ones. But
Kelly disagrees with Rogers' view that insight and the natural forces
of growth will be effective by themselves, The person is what he does;
he must test out his constructs. Hence Kelly advocates a more active
type of therapy, including experimentation with a variety of roles in
his daily life activities.

Kelly works out in detail a system of psychotherapy which avoids
assuming any universal causal agencies (such as the Super-ego,
Oedipus Complex, needs or traits), and instead classifies and plots the
dimensions of the person's own constructs. There seems to be no
evidence as to whether this is more, or less, effective than any other
system. But his major contribution probably lies in his method of

diagnosis, known as the Role Construct Repertory Test (or Rep Test), which we shall discuss later.

Harvey, Hunt and Schroder (1961). These authors have extended Kelly's ideas by classifying personal concepts or constructs under four main types which represent, in their view, stages of development from the concrete or simple to the abstract and complex.* Concepts are defined as the links between the situational and the personal or dispositional determinants of behaviour; they are the organized effects of past experience which determine how the person perceives and reacts. Regardless of the particular context, they show various formal or structural characteristics; for example, they vary in centrality vs. peripherality, in openness to modification vs. closedness, in compartmentalization, or integration, in directness or indirectness of expression. But, most important, are the main stages which characterize any kind of psychological development: the growth of a child's thinking and socialization, the formation of a new concept, progress in psychotherapy, or the formation of social groups. Depending, however, on the type of training, the development either of the person as a whole or of some of his concepts may be arrested at any of the lower stages, or at transitional levels between the stages. People tend to be consistent or general in their stage, though their concepts in different areas can vary or coexist at different stages.

The Table overleaf lists some of the characteristics of these stages in very abbreviated form, since it is impossible to do justice to the scheme in a restricted space.

This system allows the authors to integrate a tremendous range of evidence from developmental psychology (e.g. Piaget's stages, effects of home atmospheres, educational policies), social psychology (group influences, attitudes), psychopathology and psychotherapy, and personality testing. The authors suggest that our failure to find general answers to such problems as the effects of therapy, of home influences and training methods, etc., arises from neglecting to coordinate the kind of stimulation with the conceptual level of the particular persons, or with the degree of openness or closedness at this level.

It may be that the authors are over-ambitious and tend to over-

---

* A similar, though independent, formulation is put forward by Rokeach (1960), who classifies people's 'belief-disbelief systems', i.e. concepts and expectancies in terms of openness vs. closedness or dogmatism (cf. p. 275).

TABLE 2

OUTLINE OF HARVEY, HUNT AND SCHRODER'S DEVELOPMENTAL STAGES

Stages	Social-emotional characteristics	Characteristic thinking	Contributory type of upbringing	Psycho-pathological extremes	Neuroses characteristic of transitional levels
I	Authoritarian; identification with power	Stimulus-bound, rigid, absolutist; intolerance of ambiguity	Rejective, severe, restrictive	Schizo-phrenia	
					Obsessional, Compulsive
II	Rejecting dependence, people as threatening, extrapunitive	Negativistic, field-independent*	Unreliable, neglectful	Psychopathy, delinquency	
					Hysteria, Over asser-tiveness
III	Dependent, fear of rejection, self-blaming	Uncertainty, field dependent*	Permissive, over protective	Depression	
					Anxiety states
IV	Autonomy, self-reliant, secure, balance of impulses	Creative, flexible, based on abstract and informational standards	Warm, democratic	Integrated, non-psychotic	

*Cf. Witkin *et al.* (1954), also p. 255 below.

generalize: that people seldom think or adjust consistently in accordance with any one of these categories (or of the intermediate, and sub-categories that we have omitted for simplicity's sake). But they certainly present ideas which are stimulating to the educationist or the clinician, and demonstrate that one can fruitfully think of personality in terms of 'the stable conceptual systems emerging from interaction effects of training conditions and stages of development'.

Leary's interpersonal diagnosis. Yet another approach to diagnosis and therapy is that of T. Leary (1957), who follows Sullivan in conceiving maladjustment primarily as distorted relationships with others. He contrasts this with the traditional Freudian and psychiatric study of motives and mechanisms within the individual. Unlike the other writers we have mentioned, he considers it necessary to study interpersonal behaviour and attitudes at five different levels:

1. Public communications, including the person's overt behaviour and his impact on others.
2. Conscious descriptions – his self-report.

3. Private symbolizations – fantasies, projections, dreams.
4. Unexpressed unconscious – trends or theories which he avoids or distorts.
5. Values – the Super-ego, ideals (this might be considered the uppermost rather than the most repressed level).

Leary believes that at each level it is possible to classify or grade the person under eight variables (or sixteen, since every variable has a normal and an abnormal aspect); for example, Aggressive-Sadistic, Managerial-Autocratic, Co-operative-Overconventional, etc. These variables are intended to comprehend the whole range of inter-personal traits. We need not discuss the theoretical value, or possible therapeutic applications, of Leary's work; but we will return later (p. 279) to the methods whereby he grades or codes an individual patient in respect of these variables and levels.

The Self. Our survey of a number of theories suggests that a useful approach to personality may be based on a study of conscious atti-tudes and concepts rather than of deeper motivations. However, the notion of the Self has been approached from many different angles, and there is no comprehensive theory to link these together. Allport (1961a) and Lowe (1961) list the various meanings that can be attached to the term, including:

1. The Self as perceiver of the outer world and of internal thoughts and feelings. For Gestalt psychologists it is a segregated portion of the total phenomenal field; and F. C. Bartlett (1932) suggests that at some stage in evolution the organism becomes capable of 'turning around on itself' and of observing its own schemata.

2. A feeling of 'me' – a body sense, which is variously located, but often thought of as in the head.

3. The Self as an object or image which is perceived – an enduring object to which things are happening at the moment, and which embodies past experiences and future goals that set 'me' off from other people. Hilgard (1949) warns us that introspective speculation alone cannot yield a clear definition of Self. But he agrees that there is a unity which is bound together by continuity of memories, habits and motivational patterns.

4. The attitude or sentiment of self-esteem, which can feel threat-ened or humiliated, and which one strives to exalt. This capacity for self-evaluation is another aspect recognized by Hilgard. He points out that the Freudian mechanisms are comprehensible only if we

allow of a Self which is capable of guilt feelings, and which denies, or in various ways disguises, unwanted impulses in order to boost its self-esteem.

5. The Self as executive, or motivator, which wills *my* actions and fights for my ends. The layman is very apt to exaggerate this conception of the Self as agent, failing to recognize the extent to which his actions arise from all sorts of past experiences or dispositions and present stimuli, rather than from *his* decisions. Just as he perceives others as unitary individuals with personal responsibility for their actions (cf. Chap. 2), so he sees his Self as a kind of manikin who runs him. Psychologists generally shrink from this notion, which smacks of free-will as against determinism, and conceive of the Self rather as a group of inter-linked cognitive and affective processes. Allport, however, shows that some processes are more 'propriate' or central, others more peripheral, and that the former – including personal memories and aspirations, conscience and values, self-image and self-esteem – do, in combination, play the most important part in steering behaviour. When the individual is Ego-involved, it makes a crucial difference to his learning and perception, and generally increases the effectiveness of his thinking and acting. In Freud's writings too, the Ego was merely a reconciler between the Id, Super-ego and external pressures, which had no energy of its own. But his later followers accord it much greater potency, though without erecting it into an arbitrary, non-deterministic, agent.

Here we are more concerned with the self-image and attitude, (3) and (4), than with the problems of the Self's knowing and executive functions. How is this Self built up, and what is its relation to personality?

The formation of the Self. We have good grounds for believing that the Self does not exist in the infant, but is acquired gradually, largely as a result of social and linguistic training during the second and third years of life. In the pre-school child it is still a fluctuating quantity, as illustrated by the ease with which he takes on different roles in different games, and even in the adult it appears to recede in states of drowsiness. A combination of influences may be observed: the child hears adults refer to him as 'you' or 'John', and for a time often refers to himself as 'John' rather than 'I'. Once he becomes mobile he realizes more and more that he can control his movements and exert himself against external forces. (Gesell and Ilg, 1945, suggest too that this notion of power is stimulated by learning bowel control.) Further, he spends a great deal of time observing adults and other children, and their exertions of power, thus coming to think of them and himself as independent individuals. Bound up with the growing notions of Self are not only his limbs and body that feel and perform skilled actions, but also his possessions. At school, his clothes and home and relatives are different from others'; and later, his skills, ideas and attitudes likewise become incorporated as personal belongings that must be defended. Before the end of the second year of life he is evaluating his achievements, his conquests and defeats, and listening to others' evaluations, thus building up the notion of himself as worthy or unworthy, good or bad, clever or dull. Later, the class teacher's and other children's, evaluations become part of his self-sentiment. The process of identification, or imitating an admired person, also enters. A boy identifies with his father, and seems to do this unconsciously even if consciously he dislikes and rejects his characteristics. From 5 or 6 years on he predominantly identifies with the leaders of his peer-group, and thus acquires his sense of masculinity and most of his social and moral values.

Many sociologists and social psychologists tend to consider the Self simply as a product of the images other people have of him, and of his identifications and the roles that he acquires. But crucial as these are, we can hardly ignore the inner energizing forces – the drive to self-maintenance which is characteristic of all biological organisms and which, at the human level, seems to express itself as a striving for self-assertion and actualization. The person actively seeks out and selects or rejects cultural influences. Particularly during adolescence he questions such influences in his search for identity and self-determination, though admittedly his revolt often achieves little success. The issue of functional autonomy comes up again. At any age, the Ego that has been reached is not just a summation of its origins, but a self-sustaining set of dispositions which affects, as well as being affected by, its cultural environment.

Levels of the Self. Though we have so far talked of the Self as unitary, writers from William James on have pointed out that we have many different 'social selves', which we adopt when enacting our various social roles and interacting with different people. These, as we have seen, are only semi-calculated or consciously fabricated; they are largely habitual. And each of us feels that he has a 'real' core or central Self, distinct from such outer displays. Yet the central Self too is complex, with many parts that are often in conflict, but which are unified by a sense of identity or Self-hood. It contains impulses that sometimes seem to operate outside one's control, together with ideals, aspirations and standards (the Super-ego) that are set apart from the rest; and it varies to some extent with one's mood.

It may be useful to think of the Self as constituted in a series of conceptual levels. These should not, however, be confused with stages of development; they are more closely akin to Leary's levels than to Harvey's stages. These are summarized in Fig. 3, where it is shown that they apply also to the person's concepts of, and attitudes to, other people and his environment.

The Self-concept (including impulses and ideals)
1. Social Selves and impersonations
2. Conscious, private Self
3. Insightful Self
4. Repressed or depth Self

Concepts of, and attitudes to, other people and the environment
1. Public
2. Private
3. Insightful
4. Depth

Hilgard's 'inferred' or the 'effective' Self

The personal conceptual system (or Phenomenal Field)

Fig. 3. The personal construct system

The topmost level consists of a number of social or public selves and attitudes which we display to acquaintances and strangers, also to selection interviewers or to psychological testers who demand answers to personality inventories and attitude scales.

Next there is the major private Self, as one normally perceives and verbalizes or feels it. This is revealed, to a greater or lesser extent, to close friends.

Thirdly there is the Self that we realize when pressed to analyse more thoroughly, as when a friend points out inconsistencies, or when counselled by a follower of Rogers. Through considering our behaviour and fantasies as objectively as possible, we may achieve greater insight, and realize that we possess dispositions which are difficult to verbalize, or which we have previously rationalized and concealed from our own second level. This too is the level of attitudes to other people which Ichheiser refers to as 'in fact' (cf. p. 38), in contrast to the second level which we hold 'in principle'.

Fourthly, there is the picture of one's personality which is normally completely repressed, but which one reaches as a result of depth therapy, whether Freudian or other. Many clinical psychologists would hold that this level represents the greatest degree of 'self-insight', i.e. that it is in some sense more true than the other levels.

We would prefer to say that there are many possible conceptualizations. Each of the three 'upper' levels embodies a theory of how and why we behave and want to behave, and the same applies to the fourth – it represents the kind of theory advocated by Freud or Jung or Klein, etc. Maybe the uppermost layers contain the largest proportions of demonstrably false rationalizations, but our search, in these chapters, for demonstrable evidence of truth in the bottom level has not been very successful.

It is relevant here to refer to a research by Fisher (1956), in which a series of interpretative statements about a fictitious patient were assessed for 'depth' by experienced psychiatrists and by psychologists with a little therapeutic experience. They were also assessed for 'plausibility to the patient' by other psychologists and by students. There was good consistency within all the groups – a mean inter-rater correlation of 0·70. But the combined ratings for depth correlated 0·86 to 0·87 with combined ratings for implausibility, i.e. not much lower than the coefficient of 0·96 between the two sets of depth, or the two sets of plausibility ratings. We would not deduce that 'depth' is 'untrue'; but clearly it comes to much the same thing as implausibility or unacceptability to the conscious Self.

It is likely that people differ considerably in the level at which they habitually conceive themselves and others. Some are largely dependent on the current social context and sincerely believe in the top level Self and the public attitudes that they happen to have adopted as appropriate for the moment. Others are much more aware of the private Self as distinct from the outer displays, or have better insight into deeper impulses and defence mechanisms. Perhaps this corresponds rather closely with the conventional extravert-introvert dichotomy. The neurotic would be one whose conceptual levels (both self-concepts and outer-directed attitudes) are unusually disintegrated or compartmentalized, as Kelly, and Harvey et al., have described.

How are these Selves related to other writers' theories? Hilgard talks of the 'inferred Self' as providing the unifying concept in motivation – that is the effective Self as diagnosed by an informed and unbiased observer. This must surely include all levels; since dispositions from any level may affect our behaviour. If we add the outer-directed concepts to the inner-directed or Self-concepts, we obtain the overall conceptual structure which corresponds to Kelly's system of constructs, Rokeach's belief-disbelief system, or Snygg and Combs' phenomenal field. This conceptual structure should, however, not be confused with the personality, though it is an essential part of personality (cf. Chap. 14), and must indeed be taken into account in personality diagnosis. Our scheme further provides a useful approach to psychotherapy, reminding us that the picture which the client gives of his motivations, or which the therapist obtains, are largely subjective, or dependent on the conceptual structure of the observer; and that many other pictures, at different levels, are possible. Progress in therapy is obtained when the second-level, conscious, Self not only gets down to a third or deeper level of insight, but also achieves a closer approximation to the 'inferred' or 'effective' Self.

Chapter 8

THE EFFECTIVENESS
OF PSYCHOTHERAPY AND
COUNSELLING

Our main criterion for deciding how far depth psychology can help in understanding people must clearly be its effectiveness in improving their adjustment. The same is true of self-psychologies such as those of Rogers and Kelly. Indeed there are thousands of reports in the literature, either describing particular cases where better adjusted behaviour or increased insight are claimed as a result of clinical treatment, or giving statistics on improvement rates for groups of mental patients, delinquents, etc. Unfortunately, though, there is a conspicuous lack of comparative, well-controlled studies to show that one kind of treatment (e.g. depth-oriented) is more effective than another. True, it is extremely difficult to define 'improvement' in any precise manner, let alone measure it, and difficult to secure really comparable control groups. Hence a considerable number of investigations, some of which we will summarize first, have yielded almost wholly negative results; i.e. they have failed surprisingly to substantiate the value of psychological treatment. However, we shall see later that, with a more careful analysis of the nature of the problem and its methodology, considerable progress is being made. Particularly with the influx, in the post-war period, of well-trained psychologists into the clinical field, more and more well-planned studies are being published which do show what kind of changes are induced by therapy and counselling.

Eysenck's survey. In 1952, Eysenck administered a considerable shock to those who took for granted the effectiveness of psychotherapy. He claimed that the overall 'success rate' for patients given treatment privately, or in mental hospitals, is no higher than that for similar patients who were either treated by their own doctors without any depth-psychology training, or who received no treatment at all other than custodial care in hospital. In all cases the average proportions reported as recovered or improved were close to two-thirds. The doctor-treated group consisted of severe psychoneurotics who were receiving disability payments from an insurance company. After 2 years, 72% were back at work, and after 6 years, 90%. The figures for patients treated by psychotherapy were based on some 24 investigations, covering 8,000 cases. In most of these the treatment is described as 'eclectic', but five studies reported on improvement following full psychoanalysis, and here the success rate appeared to be lowest. However, this may have arisen merely because many of the patients cut short their analysis for financial or other reasons and had to be included among the failures.

Eysenck admits that there are many snags in comparing these groups, and he is careful to state that the findings do not *disprove* the value of psychotherapy, only that they fail to prove it and also fail to show any definite superiority of more over less intensive forms of treatment (cf. also Eysenck, 1953, 1955). Naturally his conclusions have been disputed, and Rosenzweig (1954) in particular believes that diagnoses of types of mental illness and their severity, and assessments of recovery, are so variable that the statistics are valueless. Indeed, they might be taken to show that the more intensive the type of therapy, the more rigorous are the standards of recovery that the therapist demands. To the present writer, however, the crucial point is that so little attempt had been made by the psychotherapists who initiated their various kinds of treatment to prove their worth. Experimentally trained psychologists do not advocate new devices in teaching, such as educational films, synthetic trainers and teaching machines, without taking some steps to validate their effectiveness; and doctors hesitate to recommend drugs which have not received experimental trials.

Levitt's investigations of child guidance. In 1957, Levitt published similar data for children given psychodynamic child-guidance treatment, comparing them with other similar cases who were accepted for treatment but never actually received any. Some 67% of the former were found to be much, or partially, improved shortly afterwards, and 78% several years later. But $72\frac{1}{2}$% of the untreated also 'recovered', and more did so in the longer time interval. A possible rejoinder here is that many of those who failed to take up treatment were less severe cases, who perhaps were already beginning to improve without it; but there is no evidence to back up such an assertion.

A more thorough follow-up by Levitt et al. (1959) traced 237 treated cases and 93 defaulters some 5½ years later. The treated had received at least 5 hours of therapy, and neither group had subsequently attended any clinic. Here it was shown that the control group matched the treated very closely on all available diagnostic and background data: i.e. they were certainly not less maladjusted initially. Some 26 indices of final adjustment were studied, including clinicians' judgments, reports by parents and by the children, scores on tests such as MMPI, and objective facts such as marriage or institutionalization. Overall, no more than chance differences were found between the treated and the untreated, and some of the small differences that did occur favoured the latter rather than the former.

Studies of adolescent counselling. Even more striking, perhaps, in that 'guided' and 'control' groups were entirely comparable, was the Cambridge-Somerville study of delinquency (Powers and Witmer, 1951).

Some 300 boys, many of whom seemed likely to become delinquent, were chosen (mostly at the ages of 7 to 10+), and given several years – up to 8 years in some cases – of guidance by counsellors. Their eventual delinquency rate, and assessments of social adjustment, were no better than those of the matched, unguided group. (It is claimed that the treated group, though committing numerous adolescent delinquencies, less often became hardened criminals, but the evidence presented is far from conclusive.) In both groups, two-thirds of those expected to become delinquent did not do so 'in any serious sense' (note the coincidence of this figure with that for treated and untreated child guidance cases and neurotics). Obviously it would be unfair to regard such case-work as 'therapy', though most of the counsellors were professionally trained. Also the control group members often had help from ordinary social agencies like youth clubs, or from friends and relations.

The most interesting conclusion, quoted by Allport (1960) – though not made in the original report, was that those counsellors who were trained professional social workers, strongly theoretically oriented, were on the whole less successful with their boys than the more informal and friendly ones who developed warm personal relationships.

A similar, though smaller-scale, investigation is reported by Rothney and Roens (1950).

They followed up 129 pairs of eighth-grade pupils, matched for age, sex and socioeconomic status. The groups were originally put forward by teachers as problems or retarded, or else as pupils of outstanding ability, who needed help; but only one member of each pair was given counselling on educational, personality, and vocational problems. Actually it was found that the counselled group produced slightly *more* course failures and drop-outs from school, at least in the first year or so. There was some evidence that the guided group achieved better academic adjustment later (e.g. more went on to college), though this is difficult to evaluate since some of the least adjusted were lost sight of. After about 5 years the survivors reported on their college or vocational plans, and the guided group showed greater purposiveness and realism in their plans, were more settled and stable. While this proves that they had discussed their plans with their counsellors and could formulate them more clearly, and perhaps had followed advice on rational choice of courses, the research does not seem to have yielded any convincing evidence of better personality adjustment in the guided than in the control group.

Other work on child guidance. In his early book, *The Clinical Treatment of the Problem Child* (1939), C. R. Rogers showed serious concern regarding the effectiveness of different types of treatment: institutional, foster-home, camps, changing the family situation, and therapy with the child. He points out the complete ineffectiveness of the traditional corrective institutions for delinquents, and the improved – though still high – recidivism rates with more enlightened methods of disposal and treatment. But obviously it is difficult to know, in such comparisons, whether it was not the less severe and hardened groups of boys who were assigned to the method of treatment that appeared to yield better results.

> Two small control-group studies are quoted. In one of these, recommendations for disposal of 107 delinquents were carefully planned before they appeared in court. Among 88 cases where the court followed the recommendation only 1 boy failed to adjust satisfactorily, whereas, in the 19 cases where the clinic's recommendation was disregarded, 12 or 63% were gross failures. In another study by Martens and Russ, 68 problem children were treated by a clinic for over two years, and showed considerable average improvement in scores on an adjustment rating scale, whereas with 50 other non-treated cases, claimed to be parallel, scarcely any improvement occurred. Though insufficient details are quoted to set this off against Levitt's results (*supra*), it at least showed that objective evidence of the value of treatment could be collected.

Now that psychological services are available to most English schools a large amount of data is being published on the successful treatment of educationally retarded children. True, the origin of much of this retardation is irregular schooling or inappropriate teaching, and the criterion of improvement is usually a gain in reading and arithmetic ages; but it is also true that most retardation is associated with emotional disturbance, and the more fully staffed clinics aim to readjust and not merely to coach backward children, indeed claiming that educational improvement will not occur without emotional treatment. Here too there are difficulties in assessing improvement, for example in distinguishing it from mere practice effect on the tests used or statistical regression effects (cf. Curr and Gourlay, 1953), but the weight of the evidence is that treatment helps. However, good results are obtained also by carefully selected teachers who give individual or small-group tuition in schools, but who have varying amounts of psychological training and who sometimes rely mainly on their own naïve psychological insights. There is no proof that fully trained psychologists, who combine remedial work with play therapy, or otherwise use depth-psychological concepts, are any more effective. Here also, however, problems of comparability of the treated children arise.

Phillips (1960) advocates 'a simple, matter-of-fact approach' to child guidance, as much on the grounds that it is more economical and reduces the drop-out rate, which is a prominent feature of full-scale depth-oriented guidance, as because of its efficiency. In his scheme of short-term therapy, treatment is started when parent and child first apply to the clinic – there is no lengthy period of diagnosis and case conferences. Appointments are given at about two-weekly intervals. Parents are provided with 'commonsense' explanations of the meaning of the child's disturbed behaviour; specific aims are set and regular routines are established (e.g. for home chores, homework, etc.); contact is made with the school, so as to arrange suitable treatment there.

In one follow-up of 30 cases who received an average of 17·5 depth-treatment interviews and of 27 others who, at the same clinic, received an average of 7·0 simplified therapy interviews, parents answered questions on present adjustment and the latter group clearly gave more satisfactory answers. Presumably the groups were comparable in initial severity, though the author does not demonstrate this. Critics might claim too that the criterion is inadequate, and that more careful study of the 'simplified' cases might have revealed unresolved maladjustments; but surely it is up to them to demonstrate the superiority, if any, of more intensive methods.

In another small-scale study by Seeman and Edwards (1954), poorly adjusted and retarded children received a daily session, over about 4 months, with a psychologist which was spent on reading, play and art activities. Compared with a matched control group there was a significant improvement in reading but an actual decline in adjustment as measured by the Rogers Personality Test – perhaps not a very satisfactory criterion.

Comment on psychiatric treatment. There is a very large literature on the treatment of psychotic and neurotic patients in mental hospitals, by psychiatric care, occupational, somato- and other therapies, some of it summarized by Zubin (1953), Hastings (1958), Fulkerson and Barry (1961). The findings are so inconsistent that Hastings is driven to admit that we still do not know for certain if any treatment for psychiatric illness is superior to the spontaneous remission rate. An area in which one might expect to find more convincing evidence of the value of depth-oriented therapies is that of psychosomatic illnesses. Few would deny that psychological factors play a tremendous part in many digestive disturbances, asthma, hypertension, enuresis, and that the causes are often unrealized or repressed by the sufferer. However, it is hardly possible to establish a one-to-one relation between any particular emotional condition or disturbance, or type of temperament, and a specific bodily expression (cf. L. J. Saul, 1944). Even more widely recognized is the skill of the good doctor in curing people's complaints less by physical treatment than by his psychological insight into their underlying anxieties and needs, i.e. by what is really psychotherapy. Yet here also there is a conspicuous lack of definite evidence as to how effectively, or why, it works.

Difficulties in evaluating therapeutic outcomes. In fact, the problem is much more complicated than would appear at first sight (cf. Zubin, 1953; Zax and Klein, 1960). Difficulties arise in:

a) obtaining large enough groups of sufficiently homogeneous types of patient. Not only the kind of illness, but its duration and severity of onset, the age and social background, etc. of the patient, markedly affect the results;

b) controlling the type of treatment. Obviously this varies with the psychiatrist or therapist as well as with the techniques he claims to use; and many other influences are operating in addition to the treatment that is being investigated;

c) obtaining properly matched control groups and denying them the proposed treatment, while yet keeping other influences comparable. Eysenck (1960d) points out that it is preferable to assign cases randomly to treated and control groups, rather than attempting to match discrete groups. And he advocates having more than one control group (much as in experiments on transfer of training), so as to isolate the effects of, e.g., hospitalization in addition to those of treatment. But while it may be possible to regiment human beings in accordance with the principles of experimental design in the psychological laboratory, or even in short-term experiments on drugs, it is not so easy with people who are desirous of protracted psychological help;

d) defining and measuring improvement.

Criteria of adjustment. Probably the chief inadequacy of most work in this field lies in the specification of improvement, cure, adjustment or change. It is only too likely that negative results have often been obtained through studying inappropriate outcomes. An enormous variety of criteria have been employed, and there is no reason to suppose that all of them will be uniformly affected by a particular treatment. What little evidence we have suggests some, but far from complete, overlapping among them. They include:

1. Psychiatric assessments of improvement. Obviously there is no way of controlling variations in standards. More accurate specifications of the person's mental condition may be made by check lists or rating scales (e.g. Wittenborn's, 1955), but these by no means eliminate the subjective element, particularly when the rater has a 'vested interest' in the outcome.

2. Removal of objectively observable symptoms. These are unlikely to be representative of the overall effects of treatment, and as Malan (1959) insists, they may disappear without affecting the patient's basic problem.

3. Duration of therapy or hospital stay, readmission, and relapse rates; recidivism in delinquents. These are 'chancy', i.e. unreliable, or apt to be affected by administrative policies.

4. Observations of the person's adjustment to work or to people. The use of different informants for different patients produces unreliability, though this can be reduced by well-constructed rating scales, e.g. the Haggerty–Olson–Wickman scales or Stott's (1958) Bristol Guides for teachers' rating of children. Different objective criteria, e.g. of job-success, often yield discrepant findings, since they depend on so many other environmental circumstances.

5. The patient's performance on tests of mental efficiency (e.g. Porteus Mazes) or personality (questionnaires or Rorschach). Questionnaires seem particularly subject to what has been called the 'hello-goodbye effect'; that is, the patient draws a miserable picture of himself when first coming for treatment (or when he discusses his symptoms with the inmates of a hospital), but is either polite to the therapist or is more optimistic when the treatment is completed. However, we shall mention some positive results below, together with studies of therapeutic change based on linguistic analyses. Tests

of abilities rarely show much improvement over that of controls, and we shall comment later on projective techniques.

6. More sophisticated measures of insight and other types of therapeutic change, described below.

7. The patient's statement that he has benefited from, or his criticisms of, the treatment; satisfaction in his subsequent career.

8. Case material collected by interviews with the patient, acquaintances, etc., and evaluated independently by trained judges who had nothing to do with the treatment (preferably not knowing which cases were treated or not).

Williamson and Bordin (1941a) have contributed a penetrating analysis of the variety of criteria used in following up vocational and educational counselling, where closely analogous problems arise, and concluded in favour of a composite criterion, i.e. our No. 8.

In the clinical treatment of neurotic conditions, 'success' has usually been thought of in terms of the achievement of 'normal' behaviour in daily life, vocational adjustment or the educational adjustment of pupils – that is, evaluative conceptions which imply the conformity of the person to arbitrary social standards. These might be appropriate if therapy is conceived as reconditioning, but they are clearly inappropriate if its main aim is to understand, and to increase the patient's understanding of, his condition. But that is no reason why such understanding should not be investigated, and criteria developed which do fit what the therapist is trying to do. Deutsch and Murphy (1955) claim that therapy is successful when it brings about a change in 'inner psychic dynamics', for example, growth of the Ego, dropping of defences, and that this can be assessed only by the therapist; it cannot be measured. Scientific psychologists are very pardonably maddened by such statements, for of course there are ways of measuring changes in inner organization. For the most part, however, they have been developed by psychologists who reject many of the tenets of depth psychology. To these we will now turn.

Investigations at Chicago. The work of Rogers and his followers is of outstanding importance. Its development in the 1940's has been described by Seeman and Raskin (1953). During this period it was concerned mainly with the recording and analysis of client-centred counselling interviews. As a result, Rogers was led to reject the notion of 'cure' or 'success' and to look rather for changes or 'movement' in the client's self-concepts. Particularly influential was

Raimy's study (1948), in which he formulated and tested out the theory that therapy brings about changes in the Self-concept – the map in terms of which a person understands himself, and that it should be evidenced by an increasing ratio of favourable to unfavourable self-references as the sessions progress.

A more detailed form of self-description was provided by adapting Stephenson's (1953) Q-sort technique (cf. Mowrer, 1953; Cronbach, 1953; Rogers and Dymond, 1954). Normally, one hundred miscellaneous statements about the Self are employed, collected mainly from therapeutic protocols, and these are sorted by the patient into nine normally distributed piles, according to the degree to which they resemble him (Self-sort). Further, they can be sorted according to what he would like to be (Ideal-sort) or to what he thinks the average person would be; likewise, the therapist can sort them to represent his conception of the patient, or provide a Self-sort. The various sorts, done at various stages in therapy, can be intercorrelated to yield indications of change, of closer approximation of Ego to Super-ego (Self-Ideal), of identification (e.g. Self with therapist) and so on. Wittenborn (1961) adds that a number of other relationships might be explored, such as those between the self-perceptions of children and their parents' perceptions of them and of the ideal child.

As Mowrer points out, Q-technique includes a number of loosely related procedures, which permit quantification of what are essentially idiographic judgments. A matrix of such correlations can be factorized, as in Stephenson's studies of personality types, and in Cattell's more elaborate applications of what he calls 'O' and 'P' techniques to the study of intra-individual personality structure (cf. p. 195).

In Rogers and Dymond's main research (1954) Self and Ideal sorts were obtained from small groups of patients and controls (usually 10 to 20) at the start of a period of client-centred therapy with the former, or when they first applied and then again after waiting 2 months until therapy started, at the conclusion, and again 6 to 12 months later. Self-Ideal correlations averaged around 0·58 in normal controls ($-0·01$ to $+0·86$) and stayed about the same over 6 to 12 months. But among the patients they averaged near zero (ranging from $-0·44$ to $+0·59$), indicating serious disharmony between the Self and what it would like to be. After counselling, the average rose to 0·34 and remained at 0·31 on follow-up, thus showing significant improvement, though usually not up to the normal level. (Very high correlations, however, should not be expected. They would be characteristic of the paranoid rather than of the normal individual.) The group which waited two months before treatment acted as an additional control; it showed no spontaneous improvement over this period. On the other hand, an 'attrition' group who applied for therapy and, after waiting, failed to take it up or soon dropped out, did increase their Self-Ideal correlations. They felt they had improved, though certain tests indicated that this was defensive, and that they had really deteriorated.

Another method of scoring Q-sort data was to ask experts to designate 'good' and 'bad' statements, and to see whether the clients favoured the former to a greater extent after treatment. Some relation between these adjustment scores and therapists' ratings of improvement was found, also a relation to independently scored TAT records. Moreover, when the Ideal sorts were scored for adjustment, these tended to drop with therapy, indicating that the clients' goals were becoming more realistic or nearer to their capabilities. This type of score comes suspiciously close to the ordinary personality questionnaire, or to a measure of 'social desirability' (p. 202). However, another questionnaire, the Willoughby Emotional Maturity Scale, did not show any relation to therapists' ratings of improvement, probably because the unimproved answered it more defensively – i.e. more in the socially desirable direction. On the other hand, assessments of the clients on the same scale by acquaintances did relate to improvement (a correlation of 0·50 between score changes and counsellor's ratings of change). A further investigation of tolerance towards other people, using an adaptation of the California F, and other, scales, showed that this attitude is somewhat prognostic of therapeutic change, but that it does not usually increase with treatment. The indications were, rather, that extreme attitudes in either direction were modified. Possibly the extreme 'liberal' is as irrational as the extreme 'authoritarian'.

Discussion of the Chicago studies. In general, then, Rogers' studies indicate (as Harris puts it, 1956) that with non-directive therapy the client becomes more like the individual he would like to be and more like his conceptions of others; that he shows more self-insight, and confidence in himself. To the counsellor he seems to become more mature and tolerant, and less dependent. However, certain weaknesses in the researches have been pointed out (cf. Crowne and Stephens, 1961; Wylie, 1961; Eysenck, 1960d). The Self-Ideal correlation is a bit too simple to be an altogether satisfactory measure of adjustment; it is likely to be weak in reliability (cf. p. 224). It could be maintained, also, that it is a measure of self-satisfaction rather than of congruence of personality (cf. Loevinger and Ossorio, 1959). Evidence as to its correlates with other indices of maladjustment are often contradictory, though this may be partly because other investigators who have tried to follow up Rogers' work have used a variety of instruments, including check-lists and ratings as well as Q-sorts of miscellaneous sets of statements. No one has laid down a logical basis for selecting such statements though, as Stephenson has advocated, these can be chosen to cover a particular personality theory. Cronbach (1953) suggests that they should represent a wide range of variables within the same general domain; and that they should all be about equally popular to the average client, though differing greatly between individuals.

A more radical criticism, raised by Eysenck (1960d) and Wylie (1961), is that the obtained results merely represent 'verbal conditioning'. Clients may very readily be influenced unwittingly to produce statements that fit in with their therapist's notions of good adjustment and insight (cf. p. 94), though there may have been no real change in their feelings or behaviour. This is difficult to answer, except through the production of further evidence by alternative techniques, as has been done, for example, in the research by Fairweather and his colleagues, described below.

Rosenthal (1955) applied a test of value judgments in the areas of sex, aggression and authority to 12 patients at the beginning and end of therapy, and to their counsellors, and assessed the benefits from therapy by independent interviews. The amount of change in the patients' values in the direction of their counsellors' correlated 0·68 with benefit. However, this figure is of little significance with so few cases. The mean patient-counsellor correlation rose only from 0·29 to 0·31, which hardly justifies Rosenthal's conclusion that counsellors convey their own concepts and values to their clients.

Rogers tends to stress the agreement between Q-sort data and counsellors' judgment of improvement as evidence of the validity of the former. But even apart from Eysenck's objection, the interpretation of such agreement is open to doubt, since obviously the counsellors base their assessments on the kind of self-concepts the clients bring up in the therapeutic sessions (cf. Zax and Klein, 1960). Despite these weaknesses it seems reasonable to assert that the approach to psychotherapy through the study of self-concepts has been more fruitful than have conventional investigations of 'effectiveness'.

In the course of a well-balanced review of the results of psychotherapy and of the difficulties of investigation, Malan (1959) suggests that the main weakness of the Q-sort is that it is not specific enough for each patient. He urges that the therapist should formulate early in treatment a specific prediction of the kind of change in basic adjustment at which he is aiming. Illustrations are given, but no quantitative evaluation of the success of such predictions. The fact that better research has been done on client-centred than on other types of therapy does not, of course, prove that it is more effective, in any sense of the word. A full psychoanalysis might well produce even greater changes of the same kind, but no analyst (to our knowledge) has bothered to inquire. In one follow-up by Forgy and Black (1954) of 77 students who had been counselled either by non-directive or by more 'structured, counsellor-centred' procedures, there were slight differences in responses to certain questions regarding their satisfaction with the treatment, but these disappeared after three years.

Fiedler (1950, 1953) showed rather ingeniously that there may be less difference between the therapeutic schools in practice than in theory. A number of therapists including Freudians, Adlerians, Rogerians and eclectics sorted a series of statements about 'the ideal therapeutic relationship'. All intercorrelations were high and there appeared to be no grouping of opinions according to school. Thus, although policies regarding interventions, and techniques such as free association, etc., may be varied, the crucial factor of forming good interpersonal relations with the patient is pretty universal. Indeed, as Fiedler showed, the relation is much the same as that operating between understanding friends, or that which a good lay interviewer tries to establish.

Other self-report studies. Dorfmann (1958) applied a similar experimental design to that of Rogers and Dymond, working with child guidance cases – i.e. she compared waiting, pre- and post-therapy and follow-up, and control-group scores. She did not attempt Q-sorts (though Staines (1958) has shown that the technique is feasible with children of 10 to 11 years, and that it does reflect teachers' attempts to influence their self-concepts). Small changes attributable to therapy were found on some sections of Rogers' Personality Questionnaire, and more significant ones on a Sentence Completion (projection) test, scored for general adjustment.

Fairweather *et al.* (1960) employed a variety of measures of change with mental hospital patients, including Self-Ideal sorts, the MMPI, TAT, ratings of behaviour in the wards, and follow-up data, e.g. employment. An elaborate design with two-way analyses of variance made it possible to compare the effects of:

1. Ordinary hospital work assignments (control conditions)
2. Ditto + individual therapy
3. Ditto + group therapy in groups of 4 to 8
4. Ditto + 'group-living' – all the patients' activities being planned by them together

on

a) Psychoneurotic patients.
b) Acute or short-term psychotics.
c) Chronic or long-term psychotics.

In general, changes were more marked in the variances of the criterion scores among groups 2, 3 and 4 than in the means; i.e. some patients improved considerably, others worsened, whereas the controls showed relatively little change of any kind. However, despite considerable inconsistencies on the different criteria, the treated short-term patients and non-psychotics (b and a) showed more adaptive changes, the long-term more maladaptive; whereas in the control group the former showed little change and the latter tended to adapt better than with specialized treatment. While there were no overall differences between the three types of therapy, the group procedures were the more economical and only in the Q-sort changes did individual therapy seem more effective.

Research of this kind is extremely elaborate, and it needs a lot of replication, since types of patients and of treatment vary so widely. Yet, unlike the work described at the beginning of this chapter, it does yield positive results. Numerous other studies of various kinds of therapies and counselling are summarized by Harris (1956) and by Zax and Klein (1960). In some of these there was no adequate control group, and in others the differences from controls were too small and irregular, even if statistically significant, to be impressive. We will pick out a few only that offer points of interest.

Schofield (1953) obtained marked changes in average scores on most of the MMPI scales among student neurotics after psychotherapy, and in psychotics treated with ECT. Hospitalized neurotics, whose treatment seemed ineffective, showed less change and student controls remained relatively stable. The author noted that the more 'subtle' MMPI items (those less susceptible to social desirability effects) provide better evidence of change. Other writers, however (e.g. Barron and Leary, 1955), have failed to confirm the usefulness of this test in studying therapy, and it is obviously difficult to eliminate the 'hello-goodbye' effect. Cartwright and Vogel (1960) were able to demonstrate some improvement on Q-sorts for students counselled either by experienced or inexperienced therapists. But TAT protocols, assessed for signs of mental health, did reveal the experienced as more effective. Morton (1955) found that brief counselling (4 to 7 hours) with students, based on social learning and the elucidation of the meanings of their conflicts rather than on tracing dynamic causes, produced significant improvements both according to independent interviews and to a Sentence Completion test.

Verbal indices of change. Raimy's work on positive Self-concepts was followed up in another direction by Mowrer (1953) and his colleagues, namely by analysing linguistic aspects of therapeutic sessions. He showed that either words, sentences or clauses (thought-units) could be classified reasonably reliably for tension or discomfort as against relief. The DRQ, or Discomfort-Relief Quotient,

$$\left(\frac{\text{Discomfort words, etc.}}{\text{Discomfort} + \text{Relief words}} \right)$$

closely paralleled Raimy's index, and it showed meaningful changes with progress in therapy, although it cannot be regarded as an effective criterion of therapeutic success. Its advantage is that it is objective and quantitative, its disadvantage that it cannot discriminate between different kinds and sources of tension.

Mowrer further shows that progress in therapy is related to:

the Type/Token ratio – the proportion of *different* words used, which tends to be constricted in disturbed persons;

the Adjective/Verb quotient, which likewise increases, as does the use of longer speech clauses;

the proportion of self-referential words, which decreases as the patient becomes less egocentric; and

the use of verbs referring to the future, which increases as he allows himself to plan more.

There is evidence, too, of reduced palmar-sweating, as a measure of autonomic tensions.

Another breakdown of Raimy's positive, negative and ambivalent statements was explored by Bugental (1952). He separated off references to Self as influencing Others, Others influencing Self, One part of Self influencing another part, etc.; and found that the proportions within these categories tend to shift as treatment progresses. More recently, Dollard and Auld (1959) have developed a fairly reliable technique of making a complete content analysis of therapeutic interviews. The scorer attempts to determine the underlying meaning of each sentence-unit from the client's point of view, taking account of dynamic features (intonation, pauses, grammatical structure, etc.), yet avoiding subjective inferences. Examples of the categories are:

A = manifest anxiety, avoidance, guilt   S = sex
S-a = sex wish inhibited by anxiety   Res = resistance
Conf = confirmation by client of therapist's interpretation
N = negation, etc.*

Here too the patterns of category scores are expected to alter with treatment, though little data are yet available. Such techniques are obviously too elaborate to apply to large numbers of counselling interviews, though they may have considerable interest as research tools.

Probably a more productive approach is that of Osgood (1957), who would maintain that the abnormal individual is one who perceives significant persons and situations in unusual ways. Thus, when tested by the

---

* The coincidental resemblance of this scheme to Stott's method (p. 259) of categorizing observations of children's behaviours is worth noting.

Semantic Differential (p. 40) he should express peculiar attitudes to key concepts like 'Myself', 'Father', 'Sex', etc. Osgood and Mowrer have demonstrated changes in meanings as therapy proceeds, which are congruent with the therapist's observations, and Osgood and Luria (1954) present a dramatic illustration of the discrepant concept structures of a case of multiple personality.

Studies of vocational guidance in England. An entirely different kind of demonstration that a clinical approach, leaning heavily on interview judgments, can help the adjustment of the clients, is provided by the vocational guidance work of the National Institute of Industrial Psychology. Such guidance is, of course, not aimed at personality change or therapy (it has to be completed in one or two days); yet the fact that the help of psychologists is sought in what is normally regarded as a family or school matter, and the considerable expense involved, means that most cases seeking vocational advice are to some degree personality problems. The psychologists certainly try to discover the motivations underlying the clients' careers up to that point and their expressed interests and goals, but they make very little use of depth concepts (cf. Wilson, 1945). Nor do they follow Rogers' non-directive approach, since they unashamedly offer general advice, while avoiding telling the client, 'This is the best occupation for you.' The writer has summarized elsewhere (Vernon and Parry, 1949) the extensive evidence from control group investigations of the effectiveness of these methods in inducing greater job-satisfaction, greater satisfaction to employers and more stability of employment. When clients are traced after 5 years or so, roughly 90% of those who followed the advice are adjudged as 'successful', whereas for those who went against it the usual figure is nearer 50%. No published study of the effectiveness of therapy on emotional adjustment has ever approached figures of this order.

Studies of counselling in America. Super (1951) criticizes the view that vocational counselling can be based largely on finding out the client's aptitudes and interests and giving him information about the requirements of the job. He follows Rogers in suggesting that the client needs to discover what sort of person he is, to reconcile this with what he wants to be, and on this basis to choose for himself a career through which he can implement his Self-concept. Facts are important, but he cannot face them and deal with them rationally until he has solved his feelings of uncertainty about himself. This type of non-directive counselling, aimed at helping the client to make his own decisions, is

K

favoured by what is probably the great majority of American psychologists.

A large-scale follow-up of such a system, operating at the University of Minnesota, has been described by Williamson and Bordin (1941b).

> Students were reinterviewed and an overall assessment was made of their present status, adjustment and satisfaction by persons *other than* the original counsellor (a precaution not always taken in NIIP follow-up studies). The case-notes were also scrutinized independently to judge whether or not the student had, on the whole, followed the course which he, or she, and the counsellor had agreed upon. Of a total of 987 students, it was adjudged that 84% had adjusted satisfactorily or partially. 94% of those following the recommendations were adjusted, which suggests (though it is not stated) that of those who did not follow the recommendations some 60% were adjusted. The results were best for those cases where the problem was mainly educational or vocational, less good for those where social and emotional problems were dominant. The 'satisfactory' cases did not necessarily achieve higher college grades; but sometimes their problem had been over-high aspirations, and one of the components of successful adjustment was that their grades appeared commensurate with their aptitudes and interests.

Clearly, the results of this investigation closely parallel those obtained in British studies, which suggests again that the actual technique of counselling is of relatively minor consequence.

Summing up, then, we see that it is quite untrue to conclude that psychotherapy and counselling have no effects, though they may measure up poorly against conventional criteria. The nature of the effects to be expected needs to be analysed, and great care devoted to the development of appropriate measures and the design of valid experiments. Except in some fairly straightforward instances such as vocational counselling, the effects so far isolated are still often small or inconsistent, indicating that expert diagnosis and treatment may not, as one would have expected, have much more to offer than naïve methods. Particularly important, from the point of view of this book, is the lack of any demonstrated superiority for depth-oriented methods. Actually, there is much better evidence for the success of methods based on an approach through self-psychology, though, in all probability, this is attributable merely to better research having been carried out.

Chapter 9

THE SCIENTIFIC STATUS OF CLINICAL METHODS AND DEPTH PSYCHOLOGY

Our discussion of depth psychology and psychotherapy has taken us far afield, and we still have to consider certain general questions as to what constitutes a scientific theory and scientific method. Only then can we decide whether it is fair to dismiss clinical interviewing (in the manner of some critics) as being so subjective or unscientific that its results are naturally valueless. If we reject this view we must still ask, what are the peculiar features of the clinical approach? And is it capable of providing the kind of material upon which worthwhile psychological generalizations can be founded?

The nature of a theory. There is a grave danger in all discussions of depth or clinical psychology of lapsing into what are merely semantic arguments that boil down to differing interpretations of words. This tends to happen, when, for example, we try to decide what personality 'really' is, whether unconscious motives are more powerful than conscious, whether the Oedipus or other complexes 'exist', whether love or aggression are primary drives or secondary reactions, and so forth. These are pseudo-problems of a kind which are particularly apt to bother the psychologist when he takes terms which have traditional, yet ambiguous, connotations – such as instinct, intelligence, personality, etc. – and tries to use them for technical description. All too frequently, also, such arguments resort to emotive words, which may prejudice the reader, but do nothing to advance scientific precision. Thus, theories with which we disagree are called metaphysical, intuitive, or mechanical and elementaristic; 'good' theories are dynamic, holistic, etc. (cf. Meehl, 1954).

Another illustration of the fruitlessness of verbal arguments is provided by the large number of conflicting clinical theories. Freud,

137

Jung, Adler, Horney, Rogers and others start by observing much the same kinds of patients by fairly similar methods, and yet they arrive at irreconcilable explanations. It follows then that we cannot evaluate a theory by logical discussion, by 'commonsense', by its apparent convincingness or persuasiveness, or by clinical observation alone.

A theory is a set of concepts and principles which is logically consistent, and which serves to co-ordinate or link observed facts and relationships, to suggest further relationships, not previously explored, and to yield predictions which can be tested out empirically (cf. Thouless, 1949, 1950, 1951; Woodger, 1956; Toulmin, 1961). Hence a theory should not be thought of in terms of true or false; indeed no theory can be established as completely true (though it may be falsified). It can be superseded by more useful theories, and yet continue to be applicable to certain phenomena. Thus we still employ Newtonian mechanics, though they fail to cover important aspects of the physical universe. It is quite possible, even advantageous, to have more than one theory in the same area; for example, psychoanalytic, learning and self-theories, so long as each brings order into some part of the area, and each stimulates further observation. Hall and Lindzey (1957), in surveying a number of current theories of personality, agree substantially with this view, but chiefly regard theories as effective in so far as they tend to generate research. On this ground, Freud's theories are among the most fruitful – far more so, say, than Jung's. However, we must disagree with the implication that theories can be evaluated on a kind of quantitative basis; for much research can be sterile. The criterion must be more subjective; whether the theory makes sense of the known facts and yields better insights.

One should not, then, reject the naïve theories in terms of which people 'explain human nature' in everyday life. They carry us quite a long way, even though their inadequacy is demonstrated by the evidence from interviews, ratings, etc. They are useful fictions or constructs which enable us to get along with people, just as our theories of the world as consisting of solid, coloured, discrete objects enable us to adjust quite well to our physical environment. Equally, the depth psychologist's constructs are useful if they enable him even better to understand, control and make predictions about people. 'Anal fixations', 'castration complexes' and the like may be unobservable and seem implausible, but they are not unscientific. The devotee of the older sciences tends to criticize the Super-ego, Ego and Id because they seem to imply little manikins in the mind. This objection does not rule them out so long as they are useful constructs in dealing with patients, though it would, of course, be preferable if we could account for the phenomena more economically, by constructs which were more consonant with the findings of neurophysiology and experimental psychology. Similarly, the concept of an aether has played a useful part in the history of science, though physicists generally do without it nowadays. But it is fruitless to argue whether or not it 'exists'.

Where theories do become unsatisfactory is that they may be too vague to lead to specific expectations and hypotheses. For example, the depth-psychological conception of reaction-formation is particularly weak in that it seems to suggest that the same set of circumstances can lead to a certain psychological trait (hating one's father), or to its opposite (loving him). And although the psychoanalyst would doubtless argue that these are distinguishable and predictable patterns, that he is not guilty of 'trying to have it both ways', there is more than a suspicion that *ad hoc* hypotheses are being fabricated to plug the gaps whenever the initial theory is not borne out. Theories which are 'indefinitely flexible' are scientifically useless. In other words theories should be falsifiable. Normally, in psychology, it is impossible to prove a hypothesis, for though experiments may confirm certain predictions, there are always likely to be other implications which have not been explored. That is, the experiments merely show that the hypothesis works under these particular circumstances.

Our naïve theory that most plates are round (although they more often stimulate us as ellipses) is an excellent one, since it could readily be disproved by objective measurement. In contrast, it is hardly possible to conceive of any way of disproving the existence of aggressive fantasies in young babies and, as shown in Chapter 6, most of the developmental propositions of psychoanalysis are equally difficult to pin down. On the other hand, our survey of the evidence indicated that some of the dynamic and therapeutic propositions could be more explicitly stated – i.e. reduced to falsifiable form – and that these tended to be confirmed.

The hypothetico-deductive model. A rather narrower conception of science is espoused by some critics of depth psychology, notably Eysenck (1952b). He argues that the physical and biological sciences have progressed mainly through induction and the hypothetico-deductive method. That is, the scientist observes certain phenomena and reaches a tentative generalization or law which both explains the particular data and makes possible the deduction of further corollaries or expectations. He then carries out experiments to test these expectations, or to decide between alternative hypotheses. The conditions under which the data are obtained are fully specified and controlled, so that other scientists can repeat the process and obtain the same results; likewise the inductive and deductive processes are explicit and logical and therefore replicable. Now the clinical psychologist fails in various ways to live up to these prescriptions, as we shall admit below, and Eysenck suggests that he should be regarded merely as a kind of technician who sometimes achieves practically useful results by rule of thumb, and 'know-how', or by personal wisdom or artistic skill. Like the trusted amateur judge of character, he works by *Verstehen* rather than by science. The scientist, by contrast, eschews technical applications in his concern to establish the underlying abstract principles.

For several reasons we are unable to accept this view. First, we have seen that depth psychology is a science as well as a technology, and that some of its scientific predictions are at least as well substantiated as the practical ones. Secondly, there is no reason to expect all sciences to follow the same model; psychology is not reducible to physiology any more than physiology is to physics and chemistry. And the fact that depth or clinical psychology depend intrinsically upon personal relationships between patient and therapist does not necessarily mean that they can never achieve scientific status. Most sciences, indeed, make considerable use of non-hypothetico-deductive approaches; particularly in their exploratory stages, thinking tends to be imprecise and qualitative, later becoming more rigorous and quantitative. The physicist, biologist and experimental psychologist resort freely to 'hunches' and other loose forms of inference; the astronomer does not conduct any experiments, the anthropologist seldom. Thirdly, to a remarkable extent, the clinical psychologist does follow the scientific paradigm, although the nature of his material inevitably involves some deviations. He does his best to *observe* the patient's speech and actions impartially and objectively, to draw *logical inferences*, and to put forward *hypotheses* about him and to *test these out* (cf. Colby, 1958, 1960).

Clinical thinking. Such therapeutic hypotheses are not, of course, comparable to the scientist's abstract propositions. They are procedural interpretations which have clinical utility and which help to make the case intelligible. It would be fair to say that the therapist's method is an extension of what we do in everyday life, that is, trying to find the intention or motive underlying the patient's behaviour and utterances which seem to explain them, or which make the apparently irrational cues 'seem natural'. Usually he finds that he wants to go further and further back into the patient's life-history to reach the underlying causes (cf. French, 1944). Farrell (1961) points out that when the therapist hypothesizes that the patient's behaviour arises from a certain source, he is not making a scientific statement that all cases of x-behaviour are associated with y: that is, the kind of hypothesis which could be verified experimentally on large numbers of cases. Nevertheless he follows scientific canons in that he tries to verify the hypothesis in a number of ways. The kind of criteria he uses include:

1. The congruence of the hypothesis with everything else he knows about the person. The clinician who sees a patient over many hours elicits an enormous amount of material about his thoughts, feelings and behaviour, past and present. Sometimes he can get indications of the same mechanisms by applying other methods, e.g. projective techniques. He checks the internal consistency of this data in much the same way as does the detective or lawyer or historian, none of whom can apply scientific experimentation, but who are surely comparable to the scientist in intellectual respectability.

2. The consistency of the hypothesis with the whole corpus of depth psychology, that is, with more general theories that he accepts.

3. When his interpretation is communicated to the patient, or the patient discovers it for himself, he accepts it as meaningful, or – more convincing – there may be an emotional release, even just a change in posture or manner of speech, which shows that it has 'touched off' something that is not just suggestion. From Freud onwards, analysts have described 'clever hits', when some apparently chance phrase, a slip of the tongue, an action such as unpunctual attendance, has suddenly revealed a hidden motive which seems almost as plausible to the reader as it did to the analyst and patient.

4. The clinician can and does carry out 'experiments'. If his hypothesis is correct he can predict that other characteristic reactions to relatives, school, job, or to himself should spring from the same mechanisms, and he can follow up, or follow back, to confirm these. He can plan and observe the results of appropriate therapeutic

measures, and he can immediately generate evidence by steering the conversation in some direction and forecasting what resistances or other responses will result. Meehl (1956) suggests that the clinician's forte is 'interpreting episodes during therapy', and that his validatory criteria are specific events rather than the long-term normative dimensions like vocational or education success, or satisfactory overall adjustment, etc., which the actuarialist works to.

Clinical intuition. Is this procedure justly described as 'intuitive' in the sense of irrational? Granted that it is in essence scientific, it is nevertheless idiographic. The clinician has to employ his creative imagination in order to form a conception of an internally consistent, whole person, motivated by needs and other internal variables which cannot be directly observed. No computing machine could form such a 'conception of a person' – a depth-determined homunculus.* Certainly, rational inferences are made, and the clinician draws on his large stock-in-trade of postulates – generalizations regarding the significance of symbols and symptoms, etc., much as Sarbin *et al.* describe. But his processing also involves what has been called *Verstehen* or understanding. Hence we agreed with Meehl earlier (p. 51) that Sarbin's logical model is too restrictive to cover the variety of inferences that enter into naïve or into clinical interpretation. Indeed, the difference between clinical judgment and the interpretations of the unscientific man-in-the-street lies less in the processes used than in the nature of the constructs or dispositions assumed to underly personality, and in the 'daringness' (cf. p. 63) of the hypotheses. Note too, that the procedure is 'clinical' in the same sense as that of the doctor who weighs up the significance of a patient's symptoms in the light of his knowledge of the patient and all his circumstances. Similarly, the prime obligation of both doctor and psychiatrist or clinical psychologist is the patient's benefit rather than abstract ideals of research. However, there is the difference that the doctor has access to a much more firmly established corpus of physiological knowledge to guide his interpretations, and also to diagnostic tools of proven reliability and validity. There is also a closer interplay between medical technology and scientific research than is the case with clinical psychology.

* Rickman (1951) talks of the analyst's picture of the individual in his social setting as 'coming to life spontaneously' in his mind. Perhaps he is somewhat of a visualizer, whereas others incline more to verbal constructs. Yet part of the difficulty in accepting Freud's theories lies in his penchant for spatio-visual representations of the Unconscious.

Another interesting description of clinical diagnosis and prediction is given by McArthur (1954) indicating that the clinician synthesizes his observations into a conception: 'He seems to be the kind of person who –,' and makes his predictions from this overall pattern. McArthur claims, on rather impressionistic evidence, that diagnosticians who try to follow actuarial-type procedures, based on their generalizations from previous cases, or on applying specific theories, are the least successful.

One bit of experimental support is provided by Taylor (1947), who got three judges to study the case records of 141 youths in the Cambridge-Somerville investigation (cf. p. 123). The judges then gave predictions of the likelihood of future delinquency, together with a list of reasons for their judgments. There were high correlations between the judges' overall predictions, and in the choice of reasons, but no relation between concordance of predictions and concordance of reasons. In other words, the predictions derived more from the perceived pattern or structure of the boys' personalities, than from significant symptoms.

While McArthur's and Taylor's studies (together with the present writer's work on the matching method, p. 56) contradict Sarbin's attempt to reduce clinical judgment to actuarial inference, they do not, of course, answer Meehl's demonstrations of the weak validity of such judgment.

Other features of clinical procedure. There is obviously some danger of doing injustice to clinical approaches by lumping together such widely diverse procedures as full-scale psychoanalysis, client-centred, 'eclectic' and other types of therapy, psychiatric interviewing, the clinical psychologist's diagnostic survey of a child's or adult's personality and abilities, and professional counselling – educational, marital, vocational, etc. Nevertheless, these would all seem to have in common the search for insight into the underlying dynamics of the particular individual, and the techniques of verification of evidence that have just been described. Moreover the varying emphasis on diagnosis or therapy is relatively unimportant; to many clinicians, the achievement of full insight by the therapist and patient implies integrating the repressed forces with the Ego, and is thus equivalent to 'cure' (cf. Deutsch and Murphy, 1955).

In all these contexts, again, the clinician is alert to a good deal more than the manifest content of what the patient says. Some may resort more than others to Freudian symbolism in making their interpretations; but most or all would agree that material of latent significance is revealed by choice of topics or phraseology, by the sequences of ideas (what leads on to what), by silences and intonations, and by non-verbal cues such as gestures and displays of emotion. A 'somatic language' tends to accompany the verbal communications; expressions of discomfort or embarrassment, excitement, sex-feeling, etc. are important, particularly when they seem inappropriate. Some clinicians recognize that they are using themselves as 'sensitive resonators', i.e. they observe their own empathic responses. At all times, also, the clinician is guided in his interviews and interpretations by his assessments of the patient's current level of anxiety, of self-insight, and of their interpersonal relationship. There may be a considerable range of variation among clinicians, not only in their favoured diagnostic devices and their policies regarding the giving of interpretations or their choice of therapies (cf. Brammer and Shostrom, 1960), but also in their relative stress on intellectual categorization on the one hand and more emotional intuition or hunches on the other. However, we have already described (p. 132) Fiedler's work indicating that all schools tend to aim at the same kind of patient-therapist relationship. Rogers (1960) likewise claims that the dissensions between different schools are breaking down with increasing recognition of the vital part played by this affective relationship.

The scientific status of depth-psychological theories. We have tried to give as fair as possible a description of how the clinician carries out his primary job in the preceding paragraphs, and it has been shown that the methods tend to be justified by their results despite the difficulties of evaluating 'cures'. Yet at the same time, they are decidedly ineffective in providing reliable and valid diagnoses of practical outcomes. Now this same type of material constitutes the main basis of the more general propositions or theories of depth psychology, and its suitability for this scientific purpose is naturally more open to doubt. We do not wish merely to reiterate the objections of psychologists who are entirely out of sympathy with psychoanalysis, but will list some of the weaknesses which have been admitted by a number of analytic writers themselves (cf. French, 1944; Benjamin, 1950; Colby, 1958, 1960).

1. Given that the 'raw' material must be collected under very different conditions from those of the laboratory, it should still be possible to control some of these conditions for experimental purposes and to make more accurate records. The claim that an

analyst can recall all the significant material of an interview by making notes shortly after, or the same evening, cannot be sustained. Considerable use is indeed now being made of tape-recordings (supplemented by full notes of non-verbal behaviour), and there is no reason why we should not determine the effects of varying the frequency, length and other characteristics of clinical sessions, and the tactics employed. At the same time, the clinician has much justification in replying that his methods are better controlled than those of some experimental psychologists and testers who simply apply stimuli or questions to their subjects regardless of their state of mind. The clinical situation is often more realistic in allowing relevant fantasies, introspections and emotions to have free expression.

2. Not only do the clinician's observations tend to be unsystematic, but they are only too likely to be selective, to be biased by the clinician's pet theories and training, and by his emotional involvement with the patient. Particularly does this seem likely to happen in the application of psychoanalysis to young children, where little regard is paid to environmental factors at home or at school (cf. Rogers, 1939). Psychoanalysts are, of course, insistent that the clinician should be analysed so that he will become aware of, and be able to avoid, these dangers; and even the less intensively trained psychiatrist or clinical psychologist can be conversant with the signs of transference and counter-transference. Deutsch and Murphy (1955) go so far as to claim that analysis frees his creative imagination. Surely this is answered by the fact that those trained by Anna Freud, Klein, Horney, Jung, etc., tend to find, in their patients, material which confirms their own trainer's hypotheses. That large numbers of Freudians are collecting similar material and arriving at similar conclusions in no way assures us that they are more impartial than other clinicians.

3. There is an absence of clear rules for dealing with observations, and, as we have suggested, a good deal of variation and subjectivity in interpretation. This is certainly bound up with what Benjamin (1950) admits to be a lack of semantic clarity in depth-psychological theory. It includes good concepts and inferences, but these are mixed up with metaphors, similes and allegories (which are legitimate if they are realized to be such), and with idiosyncratic speculations. Again, the verification procedures which are outlined above provide little guarantee of objectivity; indeed the lay selection interviewer who arrives at highly biased judgments of a candidate finds just as

great congruence as does the trained analyst among the items of evidence which they regard as most significant.

4. When any new generalization is put forward, the psycho-analyst is apt to think that it can be proved by citing one or two illustrative cases, though the trained clinical psychologist is usually more aware that it should be tested by observing matched experi-mental and control groups or by systematic follow-up. Some psychoanalysts and psychiatrists – Benjamin says only a minority nowadays – are not only uninterested in experiment, but are opposed to it, preferring to accept the authority of Freudian dogma. At the same time it should be remembered that their overriding sense of duty to the patient does often make it extremely difficult to impose experimental controls. Moreover, the multiplicity of variables that enter into the causation of some personality disposition or patho-logical state is so great that it is not surprising that progress is slow. Indeed, we have already had occasion to criticize depth-psychological theories because they do not take account of *enough* relevant variables – namely constitutional influences and cultural factors – but concentrate unduly on developmental 'residues'. Hence it has proved almost impossible to formulate water-tight hypotheses regarding the effects of breast-feeding or other childhood conditions which would allow for all the relevant factors. It is difficult, again, to classify clinical observations into communicable and replicable categories. Nevertheless, many more quantitative analyses of such data could fairly easily be carried out by clinical psychologists and psychiatrists if they were more conversant with principles of experi-mentation and simple statistical treatment. Fortunately there are many indications now of rapid growth in experimental studies of psychotherapy (cf. Seeman, 1961).

Clinical assessments. Returning at last to our main theme, what is the bearing of this discussion on the clinical vs. actuarial dispute, and what are we to conclude regarding the use of depth-psychological concepts in assessing people? Holt (1958) makes the good point that there has been too much emotional controversy and that the distinction between actuarial and clinical approaches has been overstressed. He would prefer to contrast the more naïve with the more sophisticated clinical procedures. The former is wholly qualita-tive, impressionistic; it makes use of observations whose significance is unknown, and processes the data in the light of unvalidated hypotheses, i.e. intuitively. The latter makes a proper 'job analysis' of the outcome that the clinician is trying to predict, and tries to find the precise relevance of material from life-history, projective and other tests. Thus the procedure approaches more nearly to an actuarial model, though clinical synthesis is still involved in building up a picture of the individual case and finally matching him to the criterion. The Menninger experiments are said to bear this out, although, as we have seen, Holt's (1958) evidence for the success of 'sophisticated clinical' is somewhat uncertain. At least we agree that some of the weak validities reported for clinical predictions arise because the psychiatrists, or others concerned, did not know enough about what they were predicting for, or perhaps about the kind of people they were studying. Somewhat similarly Hunt (1959) thinks in terms of a continuum from qualitative judgment to the rigorous laboratory experiment, characterized by increasing clarity and definition of stimuli, standardization of setting and reporting, and replicability. In the field of selection, the work of the psychiatrist or clinical psychologist can move some way up this scale, and in other areas it can approximate quite closely to the upper end.

'Wide vs. narrow band' assessment. Cronbach and Gleser (1957) formulate the issue rather differently, adopting some of the concepts of Information Theory. Information about traits and abilities can be collected either on a narrow front by accurately focused and validated instruments such as objective tests, or more broadly by instruments such as the interview and projective tests which have poorer 'fidelity'. The former approach is more efficient when the outcome to be predicted is a well-defined and relatively precise one, particularly where final, irreversible decisions have to be made, as in educational or vocational selection. Whereas the latter is more appropriate when the criterion is more 'divergent'; for example, there are various ways in which a person's career, or therapeutic treatment, might develop, and incorrect decisions can be corrected or modified both in vocational or educational guidance and psychotherapy. The psychometrist can contribute little to these flexible, exploratory situations; the need is, rather, to make hypotheses about the individual and try them out. Likewise the clinician gets into trouble if he employs his wide-band approach for reaching final conclusions. The psychometrist predicts from scientifically chosen samples of behaviour to performance in a specified class of situations, and applies this uniformly to all individuals, but the clinician considers a much

larger number of varied cues and answers different questions for
different individuals. Thus the approaches should be regarded as
complementary rather than opposed.

Now this is an attractive and illuminating analysis, particularly in
its distinction between final and exploratory-reversible outcomes,
and in its realization of the inflexibility of actuarial approaches. But
it does not really cover the problems that concern us, and it is even
misleading in stating that narrow-band procedures (such as psychometric tests) reveal more 'complex' information, with the implication
that clinical procedures are more 'superficial' because they range
more widely. At least we must add another dimension to Cronbach's
scheme, that of 'depth'.

Conclusions. It is frequently necessary to employ 'wide-band' procedures such as the interview for final decisions. Admittedly, the
results are chancy, yet we do know that some kinds of interviewing
and some interviewers are better than others. A noticeable trend in
a good deal of the research summarized in other chapters is that
more 'surface' methods, which make straightforward inferences from
previous career, abilities, consciously expressed attitudes, and impressionistic tests of the situational type (cf. p. 261) do better than
methods which essay to penetrate the deeper layers of personality,
at least with the majority of reasonably normal individuals (in other
words, those methods which explore the Self rather than the Unconscious). Elsewhere, Cronbach (1960) points out another reason
for this: that the chain of interpretative processes is much more
elaborate in the former than in the latter; hence there are more
opportunities for error. The one matches the behaviour, skills, likes
and dislikes of the person fairly directly with those needed for the
job (or other outcome); the other introduces many 'intervening'
variables which, while doubtless important, are more hypothetical.
Both the surface and the deeper methods are inefficient in weighting
the information relevant to a decision, and yet have other advantages
such as flexibility and acceptability to candidates and employers.
They can pick out particular and unique facts which may be crucial
in the individual case, but which would be ignored by the actuarial
method; that is, they work admirably in one case, but may be (as
Thorne shows, 1961) glaringly in error in another. True, the number
of misjudgments and mistreatments may be small relative to the
hundreds of decisions the clinician has to make in dealing with only
a few patients. Yet the fact that therapy is 'successful', by any

criterion, only in a limited proportion of cases must mean that sometimes it definitely makes people worse.

Similarly, the advice of a counsellor, or of a lay person such as the family doctor or probation officer, or so called mother's instinct, may be effective with some delinquent or problem children, ineffective with others. However, the evidence suggests that both lay and clinical judges (whether depth-, Self- or otherwise oriented) are apt to overstress these unique features, since actuarial methods, whenever they can be applied, are more accurate for the majority. We noted also that successful judgment tends to make more use of stereotypes than clinical psychologists would expect. It may well be, although there is no adequate proof, that the deeper approach to our fourth level of the Self (cf. Chap. 7) is valuable for discovering those individuals who are superficially adjusted, but who may become incapacitated through neurotic illness. Thus there is a case for continuing to employ psychiatric interviews and projective testing in selection procedures, for eliminating a small proportion of candidates. However, such judgments should be followed up, like other selection devices, and accorded the weighting that they can be shown, empirically, to deserve.

Our general conclusion should be, then, that depth psychology has little contribution to make to assessment for most purposes of daily life. Its main value lies in two quite different directions. First, there is its clinical utility in the handling of disturbed patients, where the approach is exploratory and decisions can be sequential and modifiable rather than irreversible. (We should note, however, that there is still a serious lack of evidence as to what kinds of effects it has in these cases.) Secondly, there is the tremendous stimulus that depth-psychological constructs have given to the whole psychology of motivation, development and learning, and the prospect of further cross-fertilization with experimental psychology.

Chapter 10

PROJECTIVE TECHNIQUES

Projective techniques have been, and still are, one of the major issues that divide the clinically oriented from the psychometric psychologist. To many of the former they are the only kind of test of any value for supplementing clinical observation and interviewing and the case-study approach; they are the psychologist's X-ray apparatus for penetrating beneath the façades and barriers to the deeper needs and dynamic forces in the personality. To their opponents, such as Eysenck (1960a), they are little more than a vehicle for the clinician's imagination and intuition to run riot. They are based on muddled theorizing, and all scientifically conducted attempts to demonstrate their validity have yielded almost completely negative results (cf. also Jensen, 1958). Hathaway (1959) attributes their popularity partly to their giving the clinical psychologist moral support; they shift the burden of decisions about a patient from him to the test, and suggest that he is being more scientific than when he relies on interview methods only.

However, extreme condemnation of projective testing is exceptional. Cronbach (1960) and Anastasi (1961), for example, while critical of its shortcomings, express a sympathetic understanding of the clinician's aims. Likewise a number of clinical writers such as Macfarlane and Tuddenham (1951), Ainsworth (1954) and J. G. Harris (1960) have paid serious attention to the psychometrist's objections, though remaining convinced of the usefulness of the techniques. As Rabin and Haworth (1960) point out, the techniques have not only survived repeated attacks, but are being used more and more, not only by clinical psychologists, but by experimental and developmental psychologists, anthropologists (Lindzey, 1961), consumer researchers and others. An enormous amount has been written – on the Rorschach alone there were 2,685 publications up to 1955 (Klopfer *et al.*, 1956) – and we cannot attempt to evaluate all the evidence, let alone describe the many techniques.* However,

* The most convenient all-round accounts are those of Bell (1948), Lindzey (1961), and Henry's chapter on testing children (1960); also cf. Vernon

we will survey some of the major issues, chiefly with reference to the Rorschach Inkblots, Thematic Apperception and Sentence Completion (the most widely used), illustrating with summaries of some of the better designed investigations. For it is vital to make up our minds whether to encourage or discourage their application in practical, decision-making situations such as those listed in Chapter 1.

Main characteristics of projective testing. 1. A wide range of materials can be used to stimulate projective responses: single words, part-sentences or incomplete stories; inkblots, unstructured and structured pictures; play materials and puppets; drawing and painting, etc. Lindzey (1959) classifies these under five main types of response – *associations* to words or inkblots, *construction* of stories, *completion* of sentences or stories, *arranging* or choosing among pictures or verbal alternatives, and *expression* through drawing or play. In so far as different tests reveal somewhat different, though overlapping, facets of personality, it is an advantage to give two or more to the same person.

2. The stimuli and/or the setting and instructions are unstructured or ambiguous so as to encourage freedom and diversity of response. In some techniques, such as the Worlds test, the stimuli may be highly definite or structured, but the Subject can organize them in any way he wishes. In others – notably Sentence Completion and Rosenzweig's Picture-Frustration – the range of responses is considerably narrowed.

3. The Subject is usually unaware how his responses will be interpreted and is much less on his guard to display an acceptable personality than in self-report or behavioural tests. The techniques are valuable in gaining rapport, e.g. when verbal communication is blocked, since they direct attention away from the Self. At the same time, however, they may strike the adult Subject as artificial, and as lacking in face validity (p. 213); and we shall see below that people's conceptions of them both vary widely and have a marked influence upon their responses.

4. There are no right and wrong, or pre-determined responses (except in some multiple-choice adaptations, which are not generally accepted by clinical psychologists). Responses are considered as

(1953). Abt and Bellak's (1950), Anderson's (1951) and Rabin and Haworth's (1960) composite volumes are essential reading for the specialist, but are uneven in that many of their chapters are written by uncritical enthusiasts.

L

fantasy material which can be interpreted qualitatively, or classified in various ways. With some techniques, major emphasis is laid on the formal characteristics (e.g. Rorschach and graphic expressions), in others more on the content (e.g. TAT, Sentence Completion); though normally both are involved.

5. The basic assumption is that the ways the Subject structures or reacts to these materials is a function of his conceptual and personality dispositions, in particular of non-verbalized or un-conscious strivings and mechanisms. They therefore reveal, not so much how he will behave overtly in any concrete situation, as the underlying organization – or as Rosenzweig (1951) puts it – the idiodynamics of the person. Rosenzweig contrasts the viewpoint of the experimentalist who is interested in the universal characteristics of the typical individual, and the psychometrist concerned with statistical distributions of differences between individuals, with that of the projectivist who conceives the individual as 'a world of events'. Both of the former think in terms of stimuli leading to responses, whereas the projectivist intentionally minimizes stimulus-bound responses, while yet providing a standard set of materials in order to highlight individual variations. These stimuli are merely triggers (indeed the individual himself largely selects those aspects of the stimulus that most concern him), and the psychologist infers from the relations between successive responses. Rosenzweig implies that this is a more up-to-date or fully evolved psychological approach, though obviously it has been characteristic of clinical psychology generally throughout the period of growth of experimental psycho-logy and psychometrics.

6. Every response is an epitome of the individual; in so far as it is not stimulus-dominated it reflects central and enduring factors within him. Hence the accumulation of his responses to a set of test materials provides a sample of his total personality. The recurrence of themes in the TAT, or the piling up of signs in Rorschach and other tech-niques, indicate which trends are dominant. This is very different from the psychometric approach which regards any test response as partly a 'true' measure of a variable, partly error, and tries to cancel out the latter component by summing responses to numerous items (cf. Chap. 11). Beck (1953) maintains that these individual features of a response are the ones which are most useful to the clinician – not the tendencies or variables which the Subject shares with people in general.

7. Typically, the classification, scoring and interpretation of

responses takes far longer than with psychometric tests – indeed usually much longer than giving the test itself. For not only must the general trends be isolated, but the significance of each response and its relation to the overall picture must be considered. The categorization or scoring of responses needs considerable training but, with any well-developed test such as Rorschach, Sentence Completion and McClelland's versions of TAT, it has been brought to a point where independent scorers show little discrepancy (it is much less satisfactory in other instances such as Machover's version of the Draw-a-Person test (cf. Swenson, 1957)). Interpretation is inevitably far more subjective and difficult to communicate, since no particular score or other sign is expected to have an invariant significance. Its meaning depends on its place in the overall personality picture. True, many Rorschach workers appear to pay mainly lip service to holism and assume in practice that Movement responses always show inner creativity or imagination, Colour shows affective lability, and so on (cf. Hertz, 1960); similarly with other techniques. But Klopfer denies that these are 'signs'; they are 'working hypotheses'.

8. The techniques were developed by 'creative artists' (Macfarlane, 1951), to yield short-cuts to the traditional verbal interview or free association techniques of studying personality. Such people had little regard for the traditional standards of the psychometrist. Most writers on both sides agree, indeed, that they should not be labelled tests, since they cannot be standardized, nor their reliability and validity determined by the techniques appropriate to tests. This is the main theme of our Chapter.

9. The projective movement is generally considered to have originated as a kind of protest by depth- and Gestalt-oriented psychologists against the Behaviouristic and statistical emphasis of personality studies in the 1920's. However, the principles of interpretation of projective responses are not necessarily psychoanalytic, and owe little or nothing to Gestalt psychology. Not only do they differ considerably from one technique to another, but also any one technique may embody diverse theoretical approaches.

Interpretative theories. The processes involved in responding to projective stimuli are highly complex and varied, and certainly do not all fall under Freud's conception of projection (cf. Cattell, 1951; Murstein and Pryer, 1959; Lindzey, 1961). Thus there is no clear or agreed theory as to why unconscious personality trends should result in a Subject producing Movement, Shading or other inkblot responses. Rorschach himself was more Jungian than Freudian, while Holt (1954) suggests that the inkblot interpreter should draw on the personality theories of Allport, Lewin, Murray and Murphy, as well as Freud (cf. also Schafer, 1954). Klopfer (1954) considers analytic Ego psychology to be the most useful framework, and puts forward a Prognostic Rating Scale for Ego Strength, based on specified Rorschach signs. This seems curious in view of the widespread recognition that the Rorschach underestimates positive personality forces and, more than any other instrument, emphasizes maladjustive tendencies (cf. Grant *et al.*, 1952; Smith, Bruner and White, 1956). Incidentally there is no correlation between Klopfer's scale and Barron's rather well-validated MMPI scale for Ego strength (Adams and Cooper, 1961).

A more hopeful suggestion is that of Bruner (1948) and Abt and Bellak (1950) – that projective reactions should be brought within the orbit of modern perceptual and Self theories. A person's percep-tions represent the ways in which he constructs the world and defends himself against threatening and disruptive stimuli. In so far, then, as he deviates from the norm, his subjective distortions of the projective material arise from the differentiations (Snygg and Combs) or constructs (Kelly, Harvey) he has built up. However, it remains to be proved how far this inkblot 'perceptual space' overlaps with the more central structures, i.e. with what we have called the third level of the Self, or whether the Rorschachist – like other depth psycholo-gists – has not fabricated a fourth level of interpretation which has some clinical, but little predictive, value.

The Thematic Apperception Test was initially based on Murray's theory of needs and presses, but at least six other approaches to scoring and interpretation have been proposed (cf. Tomkins, 1947; Holt, 1951). Bellak's Children's Test and Blum's Blacky Pictures (using animal figures) are both frankly psychoanalytic. But the versions which seem to offer the best evidence of practical usefulness are those which McClelland (1953) and Atkinson (1958) employ for studies of the Achievement, Affiliation and other needs, whose theoretical interpretation is couched in terms of learning theory. A *motive* such as *n* Achievement (need for achievement) is an acquired disposition that has become part of the stable core of personality; but the person's *motivation*, as expressed in the imaginative stories which he produces about TAT pictures, reflects not only the latent needs but also his expectancies that certain acts will lead to success or failure in attaining certain goals, and the momentary incentives that the testing situation arouses.

While we welcomed, in the previous Chapter, the stimulus of a variety of theories, it seems unlikely that closer agreement between clinical psychologists in interpreting the same projective responses will be reached until there is a clearer consensus of basic theoretical positions. As Dailey (1951) suggests, the projective tester seems to assume that he is functioning like a scoring key; whereas what we really need to know is why one tester interprets relatively well, another badly.

Situational determinants. A point which has clearly emerged from research, mainly during the 1950's, is that projective responses depend greatly on methods of administration, the personality of the tester, and the Subject's moods and attitudes, and therefore cannot possibly be accepted as pure expressions of deeper dispositions. Masling (1960) has summarized over one hundred investigations in this area; and though he criticizes the weakness of design of many of these, and their undue reliance on college students as Subjects, he believes that they justify the conclusion that the Subject, when faced with unstructured projective stimuli, makes use of all sorts of cues from the tester and the testing situation in order to formulate what he considers acceptable responses.

This does not mean that Subjects can readily fake a 'good' personality, or that they are much influenced by social desirability, as they are in answering personality questionnaires or self-report tests (cf. Chap. 12), since they do not usually know how their responses will be interpreted. Instructions to fake a certain personality type on the Rorschach do indeed lead to alterations, but the direction of these varies with different Subjects, and they occur more in the content than in the formal scores. If Subjects are instructed to increase the number of Movement or other responses, they can readily do so, and even if one type of response is reinforced without their being aware of it, a marked effect may be found (cf. Gross, 1959).

Pena (1959) showed that it was possible for judges to sort Rorschach responses fairly consistently for acceptability or social desirability. But when Subjects were scored for their choice of acceptable responses, there was a negative correlation with their social desirability tendency in answering the MMPI. Neurotic patients tended to show low desirability effects on MMPI, high on Rorschach, whereas character disorder patients did the reverse. Dollin and Reznikoff (1961) likewise report no correlation between TAT and self-report test distortions.

More important is the manner in which the Subject conceives the object of the test. Describing the TAT as a test of intelligence or as a projection test produces differently toned stories from those elicited by Murray's, or by neutral, instructions (Summerwell et al., 1958).

Henry and Rotter (1956) told one of two groups of women students that the Rorschach is a test for discovering emotional disturbances of a serious nature among mental patients. Though mostly unaware that they were influenced, they produced many fewer responses than a control group (an average of 16 vs. 23½), and showed that they were 'playing safe' by giving more Popular and Animal, and a better percentage of good form, responses. Schactel has advised that Subjects be questioned at the end of testing regarding their conceptions of the test and tester.

Effects of moods and temporary motivations. The effects of previously induced frustration, stress or other moods on Rorschach responses are somewhat inconsistent, and probably small. But they are very marked on TAT, provided pictures are chosen of situations related to the need that is experimentally aroused. McClelland and his colleagues have used this technique to measure hunger, sleep deprivation, sex, and aggressive and fear drives in addition to the needs already mentioned (cf. Atkinson, 1958; also Miller and Swanson, 1960). Attempts have been made to induce personality changes during hypnosis which might be reflected in Rorschach performance; the results are equivocal, but hypnotically suggested moods seem to have more definite effects.

That there is little to choose between projective devices and self-report tests when there is an incentive to fake was shown in an investigation by Davids and Pildner (1959).

They used Sentence Completion (Third Person items), TAT, Word Association and an auditory projection test, together with a battery of five personality questionnaires, including the Taylor Manifest Anxiety Scale. These were given to two groups of 23 and 20 students, the first group believing them to be selection instruments for an assistantship job in clinical psychology, which they badly wanted, the second group regarding them as part of a research project for which they had freely volunteered. All students were interviewed by a clinical psychologist, who assessed them on 'alienation syndrome', i.e. neuroticism or ego weakness; and all tests were scored for the same syndrome and correlated with the psychologist's ratings as criterion, with the following results:

	Mean correlations			Mean validities	
	Among 5 question-naires	Among 4 projec-tion tests	Between question-naires and projection tests	Question-naires	Projec-tion tests
Job-motivated Group	0·472	0·147	0·101	0·234	0·148
Research Control Group	0·538	0·585	0·550	0·650	0·450

In the group with good rapport, both types of test showed consider-able intercorrelations and correlations with the criterion; whereas in the group with strong incentives the questionnaires showed high consistency but low validity, and the projective tests gave scarcely any correlation with one another, with the questionnaires or the criterion. Incidentally the TAT obtained poorer validities as a measure of neuroticism than Sentence Completion and Word Association under both conditions.

This research was carried out on far too few Subjects, and with too restricted a criterion, for its results to be generalized. But it suggests that projection test responses are even less trustworthy than self-report when the Subjects are suspicious; not that the techniques can penetrate to a 'core' level of personality, regardless of such barriers.

The personality of the examiner. This too can markedly affect the results, and Guilford and Lacey (1947) report significant differences in the numbers of responses obtained by nine examiners of large groups of recruits in the USAAF during the Second World War.

Bernstein (1956) found that the mere presence of an examiner in group or individual administration of the TAT tended to lower the emotional tone and level of response. Particularly striking is Lord's (1950) study of three female testers who each gave the Rorschach three times to dif-ferent sets of students, using positive (encouraging), neutral, or negative (authoritarian, cold) instructions and manner. By rotating the groups of Subjects it was possible to show that the tester's personality, the type of instructions, and the order of administration (first, second or third time) all produce significant changes, though the first of these variables has the most marked effects. Thus the three testers obtained averages of 24, 27 and 33 responses over all conditions. One tester produced results similar to those following negative instructions, and she was described by ac-quaintances as forbidding and inflexible; a second was softer, more feminine and protective, and her results resembled the neutral instruc-tions; while the third who was more exuberant and stimulating tended to elicit positive effects. Not all scoring categories were affected, and some of the differences may have been due largely to greater produc-tivity with a positive tester or positive instructions.

Strauss (1961) suggests that in all cognitive and projective testing, psychiatric patients are particularly apt to cast the tester in the role of an encouraging or criticizing father. They are very well aware that they are producing emotional material in their reactions to TAT or MAPS stimuli, and are fearful of revealing their fantasies, lest father disapproves. Miller (1953) cites further confirmatory experiments with the Rorschach and advocates that testers should keep a running check on their Subjects' scores and compare them with those of other testers. This might help them to discover their own biases.

Less is known of the effects of the tester's personality on the way he interprets projective responses, but these have been shown to occur with the TAT by Young (cf. Holtzman, 1959) and with the House-Tree-Person drawing test (Hammer and Piotrowski, 1953). Masling (1960) further draws attention to the effects of the Subject on the tester, having found that those who act warmly towards the administrator and scorer of a Sentence Completion test are, unwittingly, accorded more favourable scores.

Implications for test reliability. Rickers-Ovsiankina (1960) tries to argue that it is an advantage of the Rorschach that it reflects temporary motivations in addition to deeper trends; a Subject will vary around his own mode, hence the answer is to test him several times. Others have suggested that the skilled tester is aware of the effects he may have and can allow for them. But these arguments seem specious, since the responses provide little means of distinguishing tester effects, nor superficial from basic personality changes. A considerable defect of most of the techniques is that methods of administration and the subsequent inquiry, and scoring, are far from standardized, hence there is ample opportunity for examiner differences. Harris (1960) admits that Rorschach responses are affected not only by the conditions we have discussed but by lighting, the edition of the blots, the tester's training and his diagnostic idiosyncrasies.

Rorschach workers have generally denied the applicability of the psychometrist's criteria of statistical reliability, on the grounds that a second testing with the same, or a parallel set of, blots constitutes a new experience; and equally that the one set cannot be split into equivalent halves. However, the fact remains that all attempts to assess reliability have given such poor results for most of the smaller scoring categories that the numbers of the various Shading, Colour, Movement, etc. responses produced on a single testing must be extremely chancy. Yet these numbers play a crucial part in the diagnosis (cf. Holzberg, 1960). In 1954 Ainsworth argued, reasonably enough, that the conventional concept of reliability is not very meaningful in the projective field (apart from reliability of scoring), and that we should instead investigate what factors produce instability in responses. We might claim that this has now been done and that, while the influence of any one situational, tester, mood or other factor may be fairly small, cumulatively they may produce serious distortions in a Subject's Rorschach or TAT results.

The new version of the inkblot test produced by Holtzman and his colleagues (1961) should be greatly superior in that the 45 blots, to each of which only one response is given, provide adequate opportunities for all the main varieties of response-determinants to emerge and to achieve reasonably reliable scores. It also gets over the difficulty that has plagued all attempts to study the significance of response categories in Rorschach's version, namely that every score is affected in a complex manner by the Subject's productivity, i.e. his total number of responses. Many Rorschach workers will doubtless argue that this standardization reduces the value of the technique, but we would prefer to wait for some evidence that the older, psychometrically unsatisfactory, instrument is capable of yielding any information which is not provided by the new.

The TAT is likely to be at least as unstable as the Rorschach. There is evidence that the application of two sets of pictures under the same conditions tends to give a fairly consistent picture of the Subjects. But Krumholtz and Farquhar (1957) found that the correlation between n Achievement scores based on two applications of 4 pictures, 9 weeks apart, was only 0·26. True, changes in motivation might have occurred. But a major difficulty in all TAT testing is that there is no clear policy for distinguishing situational from deeper determinants. Atkinson appears to imply that latent needs should be measured by stories produced under neutral testing conditions. But actually most of the positive results claimed for McClelland's tests were obtained when special steps had been taken to arouse the need. In some instances, indeed, the measure of an internal disposition was based on the differences between stories produced under neutral and under motivating conditions.

While it is an advantage of TAT that it can be adapted to investigate particular motives, a standard method of administration and scoring for all versions is badly needed. Moreover a new standard series of cards might cover all the main needs or other dispositions with which the clinician or counsellor is concerned (and which the technique is capable of eliciting) a good deal more evenly than

Murray's or other current series – in much the same manner as the Holtzman inkblots. The Michigan Picture test for children has gone furthest in this direction (Andrew, Hartwell *et al.*, 1953). Variations in productivity and in the mere verbal fluency of the Subjects create serious problems here also.

An additional reason for desiring greater standardization of materials, administration and scoring of projective techniques is that it would make possible the collection of better norms, wherewith to evaluate individual peculiarities of response. Despite the valuable compilations by Beck and Klopfer of data on detail, form, popular and original Rorschach responses, and by Rosenzweig on TAT themes, together with the many published sets of scores for children of different ages, etc., the clinician still has to rely far too much on his own (probably biased) experience of what is typical for a given type of Subject.

Clinical validity. Most inventors of projective devices have been satisfied that the responses help to provide insights into their Subjects' personalities which seem to fit in well with information from other sources, such as clinical interviewing. It has been pointed out *ad nauseam* that this does not constitute evidence that the device is valid, i.e. that it really reveals what it alleges to do. Even if the device is interpreted by one clinician, and his blind diagnosis is compared point by point with an independent clinician's account of the person (as in Oberholzer's and Hertz's well-known studies), no reliable inferences can be drawn. Nevertheless the same justification holds for clinical applications of the techniques as for clinical diagnosis in general (Chap. 9), namely that they provide useful exploratory leads or hypotheses regarding a patient's or counsellee's personality. We shall see also in Chapter 13 that the conventional criteria of validity may be inappropriate when techniques are used in exploratory and 'adaptive' situations. However, the projectivist is unlikely to be satisfied with this legitimate but restricted role for his instruments. Clearly he regards them as indicating definite psychological qualities, and therefore as suitable for making once-for-all decisions or predictions. In that case he must submit to normal psychometric standards of evaluation.

Correlational evidence. Innumerable investigations have shown little or no correlation between Rorschach scores and other tests or ratings of traits similar to those that the test is supposed to diagnose.

For example the Movement-Colour balance, interpreted by Rorschach as 'introversiveness-extratensiveness' sounds quite close to Jung's introversion-extraversion, but does not correlate with self-report or other measures. Good form, Movement, Original and Whole responses usually show only slight relations to measured intelligence, and even scores for organizing ability, such as Beck's z – though higher among able students than among children or average adults – cannot be regarded as measuring intelligence; and they fail to correlate with organizing ability as displayed in complex verbal tasks (cf. Sinnett and Roberts, 1956).

Eschenbach and Borgatta (1955) collected a considerable amount of information on 125 Air Force recruits from ability tests, ratings, background data, and performance in small groups. They hypothesized 49 relations between these variables and Rorschach scores, and obtained almost as many negative as positive coefficients. Only the productivity or R score yielded mostly positive results.

It is very easy to discount such results on the grounds that the projectivist does not consider scores in isolation, and that his interpretative constructs are not the same as the psychometrist's or the lay rater's. At the same time, Rorschach diagnostic reports often do contain such phrases as 'organizing ability', 'lack of emotional control', 'oppositional tendencies', etc., and it seems highly probable that these statements are based very largely on particular scores. Thus it is incumbent on the tester to prove that what he calls oppositional tendency means much the same as what the layman means; and that it does not merely represent the Subject's tendency to reject conventional black inkblot stimuli in favour of white spaces. If he insists that his statements are based on combinations or patterns of scores rather than single signs, then he should make some effort to exploit the various statistical techniques which Cronbach (1949) and Mensh (1950) have outlined for the purpose. Actually there has been a fair amount of consistency in several factorial studies of the Rorschach, despite the statistical problems raised by non-normal distributions and the pervasive effects of numbers of responses. Thus there is some hope of establishing correlations between stable clusters of scores and external criteria (cf. Sen, 1950; Eysenck, 1960b).

Clinical estimates of traits. More appropriate evidence should be forthcoming if the tester judges the traits or abilities of his Subjects, using any score combinations or aspects of the responses that he thinks relevant. This works reasonably well in estimating intelligence from the Rorschach.

Grebstein (1961) obtained a correlation of 0·66 with Wechsler–Bellevue IQs of mental patients, where a multiple correlation for the most predictive Rorschach *scores* was only 0·55 (and we can be certain that the latter figure would drop in a fresh sample; cf. p. 223).

However, the evidence that affective and motivational qualities can be similarly diagnosed is much less favourable.

Grant *et al.* (1952) obtained judgments of overall adjustment of 146 late adolescents from their Rorschach records by three expert and two non-expert Rorschach workers. There was a fair consensus among them (a mean correlation of 0·64), the novices doing about as well as the experts. The judgments, however, showed scarcely any agreement with careful assessments by social case workers of the Subjects' current adjustment; nor did the experts do any better when using the complete Rorschach records than when judging from the scores alone. Clearly the Rorschachist and the case worker mean quite different things by 'adjustment', though both using the same term.

Hartman (1949) obtained ratings of 35 adolescents on 40 qualities, based on interview and case material, from a psychologist and a psychiatrist. The median intercorrelation of their ratings was 0·44. An experienced TAT interpreter, using only the test responses, attempted to rate the same traits, and his median agreement with the criterion was only 0·16. It was noted that he was least successful with the least fluent Subjects. In addition the TAT records were scored as objectively as possible for some 56 categories, and many of these scores did give plausible and significant correlations of 0·40 upwards with the criterion ratings (e.g. Degree of Self-Reference in the Stories with clinical rating for Self-conscious). However, the relationships established in so small a group would, of course, be highly unstable.

Child *et al.* (1956) found little correlation between student TAT records for ten of Murray's needs or for *n* Achievement, and either good achievement in college or self-ratings on these needs. Whereas the self-rated needs did yield moderate correlations with the achievement criterion. However, McClelland does not expect to get predictions of measured achievement except from special cards, given under appropriate conditions, and agrees that his need measures do not correlate with self-report measures (such as the Edwards Personal Preference Schedule of needs).

Score differences between diagnostic groups. Rorschach himself published a table showing typical score ranges for various normal and nosological groups, and many later workers have claimed characteristic patterns for schizophrenics, epileptics, etc. However, more thorough studies seldom confirm these, and Ainsworth (1954) agrees that objective diagnostic signs of pathology are 'rare'. Knopf (1956), for example, obtained a few significant differences between carefully diagnosed groups of psychoneurotics, psychopaths and schizophrenics, but insufficient to offer any promise for differential diagnosis (cf. also Wittenborn and Holzberg, 1951b). The contradictoriness of some of the findings may be partly due to the unreliability of diagnoses, but not the preponderantly negative results.

Windle (1952) surveys the use of the Rorschach and other tests for prognosis of therapeutic outcomes among mental patients, suggesting that the inkblots are particularly popular in this area because they yield so many scores, whose true diagnostic significance is so obscure, that a few of them are almost certain to show some differences between smallish patient groups. He concludes that none of these has stood up well to cross-validation (cf. p. 223), and that most of the claims made are either contradictory, or attributable to the investigator's lack of objectivity, or to chance. Perhaps the best that can be said is that a combination of certain signs such as Munroe's, or Buhler's* measures something in the nature of personality disorganization or poor prognosis, and that this is probably better than Piotrowski's or Klopfer's indices.

Global diagnoses and matching. The objection to validating separate scores, or additive combinations of scores, can be overcome by the matching method (cf. p. 56), and several studies besides those reported by the present writer in the 1930's have shown that Rorschach or TAT interpretations can be matched with personality descriptions, or nosological categories, with a high degree of success.

In Glueck's (1950) investigation of nearly 500 delinquent and 500 nondelinquent boys, Schactel was able to identify 67% correctly and only 7½% incorrectly (the remainder being judged 'neutral'); and this occurred despite the finding that actual score differences between the two groups were very small. Even allowing for the spurious base-rate (i.e. for the fact that delinquents constitute much less than 50% of the general population, cf. p 229.), this represents a validity coefficient of around 0·70.

Chambers and Hamlin (1957) collected 20 sets of Rorschach records, each set containing one involutional depressive, one anxiety neurosis, a paranoid schizophrenic, a brain damage case, and an adult defective. Twenty psychologists correctly identified 58% of the cases, and although the authors point out that this implies considerable uncertainty of diagnosis, it represents quite a high validity – probably approximating to the reliability of the criterion (cf. p. 80).

* Note, however, Eysenck's (1960b) criticism of this 'Basic Rorschach score'.

Palmer (1951) prepared agreed reports on 28 patients by Rorschach testers, together with 34 multiple-choice items describing their detailed characteristics, as diagnosed by the inkblots. The patients' own therapists were unable to identify the correct multiple-choice answers much better than chance, but they were able to pick out the correct personality report from a group of five reports with significant success. A matching coefficient of 0·43 was obtained, which is a good deal lower than that claimed by earlier writers, probably because greater care was taken to insert each patient's report among a group of four other fairly similar ones.

Criticisms of matching studies. Some of the weaknesses of the matching approach, together with Cronbach's modification of it, have been mentioned above (p. 56). Other writers have pointed out that 'blind' diagnoses and matching, where an interpreter works from the Rorschach protocols without seeing the Subject, underestimate validity, since in practice the clinician makes considerable use of observations of the Subject's behaviour while being tested, and of the manner in which he volunteers each response. Indeed Klopfer stigmatizes blind diagnosis as a stunt, which is unethical if used for making practical decisions about a patient. But it is undeniably valuable in controlled scientific research. Perhaps the most telling objection to judging the value of projective techniques from matching investigations emerges from Henry and Farley's (1959) study of the TAT.

Here the criterion data on each of 36 children, based on objective tests, observation + interview, and Rorschach tests, were broken down into 27 statements, and comparable statements about three persons at a time were submitted to nine psychologists, who tried to match them with personality descriptions derived from the TAT. The average success in identifying correct statements was well above the chance level, and this held both for different sources of data (objective, subjective and projective) and for different areas of personality (though statements regarding Emotional Adjustment and Peer Group Relations were better judged than those concerning Family Relations and Mental Functioning). The authors' major point, though, is that different judges, as often as not, get *different* statements right, i.e. the consistency of their judgments was poor.

This suggests, in other words, that a global interpretation of projective responses does not really yield a fairly valid picture of the Subject's overall personality; rather it reveals some valid points about one Subject, other points about another, and thus allows of a fairly high overall success in matching. Such a conclusion once again justifies the use of the techniques as wide-band clinical procedures, but shows that no particular diagnostic statement based on them can be accepted with much confidence.

Silverman's (1959) study using Q-sorts – another way of providing more detailed results than global matching – is also outstanding in several respects. The criterion was provided by psychiatrists who had been treating 10 young adult criminal patients for at least 35 sessions. They sorted sets of 30 statements in six different personality areas. The judges were 30 clinical psychologists with varying levels of experience and training, each of whom studied the projective responses of two patients to the Rorschach, TAT, HTP drawing and another technique. They then drew up their own Q-sorts. The mean correlation with the criterion was 0·28 (lower for statements about Defence Mechanisms and Interpersonal Behaviour, but higher for Character Traits, Diagnosis and Symptoms); and even this figure was shown to be partially attributable to Stereotype Accuracy (cf. p. 65). Again, the mean consistency among six psychologists judging each Subject was only 0·34. Some psychologists were considerably better than others; those who had themselves had a Freudian analysis obtained an average validity of 0·33, the non-analysed 0·26. But the more experienced (10 years +) showed insignificantly different validities and consistencies from the least experienced (3 years and under). True the Q-sort is an awkward vehicle for expressing diagnostic judgments, and the criteria – provided by single psychiatrists – cannot have been highly reliable. But there is no gainsaying that discrepancies between the conclusions of different clinical testers, even when using multiple instruments, are so large that the validity of blind diagnosis must be low.

Other multiple-instrument studies. In Little and Shneidman's (1959) even more elaborate study of 12 adult males (3 normals, 3 neurotics, 3 psychosomatics, 3 psychotics), more reliable criterion data were obtained from interview and case-study material by having them evaluated by 24 psychiatrists. These judges provided a rating of degree of maladjustment, a 76-item Q-sort, and sets of True-False statements describing each patient. Twelve expert clinical psychologists attempted to predict the diagnosis and these criteria from studying *either* the Rorschach, *or* TAT, MAPS (Make-a-Picture-Story test), *or* MMPI results. Their blind diagnoses contained many gross disagreements; only those based on Rorschach and MMPI showed better than chance consistency. The ratings of maladjustment generally picked out the psychotics as most disturbed, but the projective test interpreters (unlike the MMPI ones) failed to distinguish correctly between the normals and the other two abnormal groups. In the Q-sort the mean correlation between psychologists was 0·33 (much the same for each technique, though MMPI judges did better than TAT), and the mean validities against the criterion sorts were: Rorschach 0·17, TAT 0·10, MAPS 0·13, MMPI 0·27; with different Subjects the validities ranged from about −0·4 to +0·5. The True-False statements were answered fairly effectively for abnormal Subjects, but not for normals except by psychologists interpreting the MMPI. There is much additional data in the original report; for example, when the psychologists repeated their diagnoses after 10 days, the Q-sort judgments changed much more for TAT than for the other three instruments. Also there were marked differences in the success of different judges. Here again, then, there is some – but very low – overall consistency and validity, and the interpreters of the non-projective instrument clearly did distinctly better.

In view of these findings with clinical criteria, it is hardly surprising that projective diagnoses show poor agreement with vocational or real-life criteria, where the tester cannot know much about the circumstances in which the Subject will be working. Guilford and Lacey (1947) report the failure of Rorschach and other experts to predict pilot success in the USAAF; and though Abt (1950) claims much better success in detecting unstable Marines, his judgments were based on a brief scrutiny of an aptitude battery and a self-descriptive inventory as well as Group Rorschach.

Holtzman and Sells (1954) had 19 expert clinical psychologists sort the combined material from a Biographical Inventory, Group Rorschach, Psychosomatic questionnaire, Sentence Completion, Group Szondi and Draw-a-Person for sets of 20 airmen. In all, 100 Subjects were involved – 50 well-adjusted and 50 whose personalities had been found unsuitable for flight training. The judges' mean success was 10·2/20, i.e. just about the chance level, though two of them were correct in 14 cases. If anything, then, the combination of non-projective with projective material confused the experts' assessments. Maybe the task was a particularly difficult one, since all hundred recruits were highly selected and had passed numerous screenings before some broke down. But the results are confirmed by a large-scale investigation at the California Institute for Personality Assessment and Research (MacKinnon, 1958) into assessing the effectiveness of Air Force officers, where neither Rorschach or TAT (nor indeed most other tests) showed any useful validity. Again in MacKinnon's (1962) extensive studies of creative individuals (writers, research scientists, architects), it was found possible to judge TAT stories for 'originality' with some validity, but neither Rorschach scores nor interpretations showed any promise.

As part of the Kelly–Fiske study (p. 84), Samuels (1952) analysed the relation of projective-test judgments to ratings given by combined staff members, based on seven days' observation and interviewing. Independent testers applied and interpreted the TAT, Bender–Gestalt, Sentence Completion, and rated the same traits; and a fourth man gave the Rorschach and tried to integrate the evidence from all these techniques. The mean validity correlations were much the same as in other studies we have cited: Rorschach 0·27; TAT 0·27; Bender 0·19; Sentence Completion 0·28. The figures were somewhat poorer for 'covert' traits (Inner Tension, Insight, etc.) than for more 'overt' ones (Cheerful, Conscientious, etc.). There was virtually no correlation between testers using different techniques.

Covert vs. overt tendencies. When Murray introduced the TAT, he never expected it to reflect overt behaviour tendencies, nor to accord closely with self-reported motives. Often fantasy may be compensatory to behaviour, since it provides a safety-valve for repressed impulses. Hence he anticipated negative correlations between TAT measures of some needs and behaviour, though there might be positive correlations in the case of other needs whose expression is encouraged rather than inhibited by cultural norms. Sanford's (1943) study of children indeed confirmed the existence of negative correlations with overt criteria for some fantasy needs, positive for others; and he attempted to account for these in terms of the interplay of motives, cultural and Ego controls, and opportunities for direct gratification. However, no regular pattern of relationships seems to have emerged from subsequent studies. The matter is further complicated because there are internal defences or barriers which often result in a need reaching fantasy expression in disguised or symbolic form; while at other times the absence, rather than the presence, of some common type of fantasy is supposed to signify that this need is repressed.

These arguments may sound speculative, even casuistical, as answers to the weak validities that we have described above. But they derive considerable support from observation of the play of young children. Quite obviously in their dramatic play children are acting out their emotional problems, their conflicts between impulses, and their difficulties of socialization. Thus it is but a small step to infer that older children and adults are doing the same kind of thing in their fantasies which are stimulated by picture or other projective materials. Equally obviously, though, children's play largely reflects their recent experiences of the real world, and is affected by their current moods or the particular social context. Similarly, as Lindzey (1952, 1961) points out, TAT responses depend not only on central personal motives and defences but on situational factors, temporary motivations and on trivial observations or recollections (e.g. recently read stories, etc.). Holt (1951) has attempted to analyse nine classes of determinants in the TAT, and admits the difficulty of weighing up

M

the relative contributions of each in any particular theme or response:

1. Situational context, the nature of the occasion, the personality of the tester.
2. Directing sets – the Subject's interpretation of the instructions.
3. Realistic perception of details of the pictures; significant omissions.
4. Needs and affects, usually expressing themselves through his identifications with certain characters, through emotional displays, etc.
5. Defensive transformations of fantasies.
6. Associative elaborations which may reflect cultural stereotypes, or the Subject's information, sentiments or attitudes.
7. Abilities – to observe, imagine, organize.
8. The 'internal milieu' – general traits such as optimism, anxiety, etc.
9. Personal style in choice of words, tempo, etc.

Under these circumstances, it is reasonable for the projectivist to maintain that direct correlations between TAT themes or Rorschach scores and external criteria are not very relevant to the validity of the tests, though one might have supposed that criteria supplied by psychiatrists (as in Silverman's and other studies) would be more appropriate. If the variables or constructs in terms of which projective tests are interpreted are by definition non-observable, then the only satisfactory approaches to validation (apart from congruence with clinical exploration) must be indirect. This conception of indirect or construct validation is discussed in Chapter 13. It suffices here to say that – if a construct is a sound and useful one, various corollaries should follow from it which can be tested out experimentally. A tremendous amount of evidence of this kind is available, and we shall see that it does indeed tend to confirm the theories underlying the TAT, Rorschach and other tests, more consistently than do direct or criterion-oriented approaches to validation.

Levy and Orr (1959) point out that not only the type of approach but also the institutional setting in which investigations are carried out seem to affect their outcome. They classified 168 articles on the Rorschach published between 1951 and 1955 according to method of approach, by favourable or unfavourable outcome, and by whether the authors had academic or non-academic affiliations (university vs. clinical or similar posts). The results are worth quoting:

	Academic		Non-academic	
	Construct	Criterion	Construct	Criterion
Favourable	51	12	14	19
Unfavourable	22	23	14	13

Clearly the academics favour the construct approach and get very much better results with it, whereas the non-academics claim if anything better results from criterion studies.

Construct-validity studies of the TAT. Kagan (1960) has surveyed a number of studies of children and concludes that there is no consistent relation between aggressive themes and aggressive behaviour, nor between themes indicative of anxiety or conflict and observable maladjustment. But if cultural prohibitions and expectations of punishment for overt aggression must also be taken into account, we would anticipate different relationships according to the strength of these inhibitory forces. For example there should be a negative relation among middle-class children whose upbringing tends to repress direct expression, and a more positive one among lower-class ones whose families are more apt to permit and encourage it; and this is borne out by Mussen and Naylor's (1954) and Lesser's (1957) experiments (cf. also Sears, p. 100).

The work of McClelland, Atkinson and their colleagues reveals a wealth of associations between *n* Achievement and other data that might be deduced as being affected by this motive, both among children and adults; though the correlations are mostly small and highly irregular with slight differences in testing conditions: for example – with school or college over- vs. under-achievement; with persistence in tackling a difficult intellectual problem; with preferences for occupations (or games) involving risks, negatively with anxiety over taking tests and with resemblance between Self and Ideal Q-sorts (the more achievement-motivated show greater discrepancies); with discreteness or definiteness vs. fuzziness in reproducing doodle drawings. In the Kelly–Fiske study, the candidates high in *n* Achievement were rated by staff members as more responsible and well adjusted; on the other hand ratings by peers (other candidates) were more closely related to *n* Affiliation scores. Even different cultures such as the competitive-Puritan as against the Latin, and ancient Greece during its rise and decline, have been shown to express differences in *n* Achievement in their literary productions. Differences in upbringing, such as the age at which parents make demands for independent behaviour, also fit in with the picture.

> Veroff *et al.* (1960) adapted the McClelland pictures for use in public opinion surveys by doorstep interviewers, and found that it was possible to obtain scorable results from some 85% of the general population, and to eliminate differences arising from variations in verbal fluency. Differences were shown in *n* Achievement, *n* Affiliation and *n* Power between the more and less educated, socio-economic and other groups.

It is not clear, however, that any of these studies definitely demonstrates the operation of depth-psychological constructs such as unconscious defence mechanisms; though they do suggest that poorly formulated attitudes, built up in childhood, in addition to fully conscious motivations, to some extent influence the fantasy content. To a large extent, indeed, they might be attributed to social-class differences, which are known to have pervasive effects on educational and vocational achievements, as well as on attitudes and modes of thought. In other words they may be explicable in terms of rather straight-forward learning theory.

> Both the Rorschach and some TAT cards were used by Kagan (1958) in exploring personality differences between 33 children who had shown marked increases in IQ from 6 to 10 years, and 30 who had declined. The TAT showed more achievement, curiosity, and fewer passivity, themes among the 'ascenders'. Responses with aggressive and curiosity content on the Rorschach pointed in the same direction among the boys, though not for girls. This result too does not necessarily imply psychoanalytic concepts of motivation.

Blacky and DAP tests. That a psychoanalytically based device can also yield fruitful hypotheses is perhaps best demonstrated by the Blacky Pictures. Blum and Hunt (1952; also Blum, 1960) cite the following types of indirect evidence of validity: (*a*) plausible correlations among the various scores; (*b*) sex differences in the predicted directions; (*c*) differences between normals and paranoids, stutterers, sex offenders and peptic ulcer cases as predicted; (*d*) correlations or matching with clinical diagnoses of patients supplied by psychoanalysts; (*e*) correlations of around 0·50 between Blacky variables and measures of group participation in two small groups of adult students. It is possible, of course, that a different theoretical framework might have provided equally effective predictions.

Contrasting with the Blacky is Machover's Draw-a-Person test, in which each feature of the drawing is assigned a Freudian interpretation. No evidence for the validity of these signs is offered, whether of the construct or criterion types; and most of the evidence collected by others is negative (cf. Swenson, 1957). At the same time it would be only fair to say that no experiment has been properly designed to test the author's hypotheses.

The Rorschach test. Many types of evidence could be cited which, as Levy and Orr point out, are generally confirmatory. Stress situations, drugs, mood and motivational changes usually affect certain scores in the expected directions although, as already pointed out, these tend to demonstrate the dependence of responses on the Subject's current state of mind rather than on his more enduring or deeper motivations.

The greatest amount of experimental investigation of Rorschach has centred on the significance of Colour responses. Baughman (1958) surveys 20 studies in most of which differences were sought in the responses to achromatic and to the normal coloured blots; and though he criticizes the methodology of many of these, he concludes that the evidence does not support the far-reaching effects which Rorschach attributes to colour. Klopfer (1956) describes a study in which Rorschach testers discerned the lack of reaction to colour in protocols based (unknown to them) on achromatic cards; but it is difficult to see what this proves. Better support has been obtained for some associations between the production of Movement responses and motor inhibition.

Perhaps some of the most striking evidence comes from studies of differences between rather narrowly specified groups. Heterogeneous categories such as schizophrenia may not show any characteristic patterns; yet a controlled investigation like McGhie's (1961) reports highly plausible differences between the mothers of two contrasted groups of mental patients, which fit in with the picture derived from observing and interviewing them. Similarly Frenkel Brunswik and Sanford (1945) claim differences between anti-semitic and non-prejudiced individuals, which accord with other data on the authoritarian personality. The inkblots have been widely employed in anthropological research, and though Lindzey's balanced survey (1961) raises many methodological criticisms, he concludes that the test does reveal personality differences between different cultures which are congruent with, and help to enrich, deductions based on observational and interview methods. Unfortunately it is still true that studies such as these, being mostly based on quite small numbers, often fail to stand up to repetition by other investigators; also that we still have no satisfactory technique of determining the amount of congruence of Rorschach with independent evidence.

Ainsworth (1954) has suggested that the best method of validating the Rorschach is through the interplay between clinically based hypotheses and experimental testing out of their implications. But Harris (1960) admits that this has been going on for several decades without notably advancing our precise knowledge of the significance of the various response determinants. Indeed there are good grounds for questioning the basic tenet of the Rorschach school, namely that the formal scores are the most diagnostic of personality organization, and for laying more stress on the content of responses. Zubin *et al.* (1956) found that it was possible to score content categories more objectively and reliably than the classical formal categories, and he queries whether the clinician does not, in practice, get a lot more useful information from the content of particular responses than from whether they are details or wholes, movement or shading, etc. This would explain why the elimination of colour makes little apparent difference. In 1951 Sandler and Ackner carried out a factor analysis of content categories and obtained rather striking evidence of validity in the form of correlations between these factors and psychiatric diagnoses. This approach would seem well worth following up.

Sentence Completion. The Sentence Completion technique is one of the most flexible and most easily administered, and its numerous items facilitate quantitative reliability and validity studies (Rotter, 1951; Rohde, 1957). While most commonly scored, by Rotter's method, for general adjustment, it has been used to measure a variety of needs, traits and attitudes (Sacks and Levy, 1950; Trites – cf. Holtzman, 1959), though there is less convincing evidence of its validity for these purposes. It can even be adapted as a creative-response intelligence test (Copple, 1956). In addition it is a fruitful source of material for clinical exploration in counselling interviews. Most writers admit that it does not penetrate as 'deeply' as other projective devices, and is more 'obvious' to the Subjects. However, there is some evidence that, when Third-Person items are used, and it is given as a speeded test, the responses are less censored.

Getzels and Walsh (1958) devised a Paired Direct and Projective Questionnaire (PDPQ) containing items such as:
    When they asked me to be in charge I.........................
and, When they asked Frank to be in charge he.....................

The answers were scored simply as positive (e.g. accepted, did (my) (his) best), or negative (e.g. declined, worried). Some items were relevant to areas of social conflict; e.g. negroes, religion, personal competence, parents; others to neutral areas such as politics, where the college environment of the Subjects encouraged a wide range of opinion. The authors hypothesized that First- and Third-person items in 'touchy' areas would show considerable discrepancies of response, First-person responses tending to give J-curve distributions and Third-person more normal distributions; whereas there would be little discrepancy in neutral areas. This was borne out: 60% of Third-person, but only 19% of First-person 'touchy' items received negative responses, 48 and 41% of neutral items. A similar test devised for children showed that the tendency to disguise First-person responses increases with age from 8 to 13, and is greater among girls than boys.

This study seems to have little relevance to the question of overt and repressed attitudes; rather it supports the distinction, drawn in Chapter 7, between the top and second level of the Self. Similarly Davids and Pildner's study cited above (p. 156) indicates that there is less difference between projective and self-report tests in the level and validity of information they yield than is generally alleged. Admittedly their results were based largely on the verbal-response Sentence Completion and Word Association techniques; but they did also include TAT.

Discussion and conclusions. Our survey of the evidence has provided considerable justification for the distrust of projective techniques in diagnostic testing expressed, for example, by Eysenck (1960a) and Payne (1955). At the same time it would be foolish to reject them as useless in view of their obvious value as exploratory instruments in therapy, and their many applications in developmental and other branches of psychology. The various types of evidence of construct validity, together with the results from global matching, and even the positive (though weak) validities shown by correlations with clinical criteria, all indicate – to use Lindzey's (1961) phrase – that. they are neither infallible nor devoid of any utility.

Even if the experimental, group difference and other construct validity studies were more unanimously favourable, they would still not prove that the techniques are efficient instruments for diagnostic purposes. After all, it is very easy to demonstrate the existence of group differences on most intellectual tasks between different social classes, but this does not justify using social class as an adequate measure of a person's intelligence (cf. also the discussion of construct validity in Chap. 13). Hence it is perfectly possible to achieve logical results through these indirect approaches and yet to obtain the poor validities in practical diagnostic situations that have been described in Grant's, Silverman's, Little and Shneidman's and other researches above.

Clearly the findings do not support the projectivist's view that every response derives from basic personality variables; it would be better to admit, with Macfarlane and Tuddenham, that the Rorschach 'measures a little bit of everything and not enough of anything to give dependable and quantifiable samples' of the personality. Both in this test, TAT and other devices, it seems probable that many responses arise primarily from quite superficial or peripheral associations with recent or past experience, and have only a rather tenuous connection with motivational factors. Furthermore such significant motivational factors as do find expression may arise as much from reactions to the tester's personality and testing situation, or from conscious attitudes, interests and temporary moods as from deeper causes. Indeed perhaps the most useful application of the techniques outside the therapeutic session is that they provide indirect approaches to attitudes which circumvent some of the difficulties of questionnaire and oral interview surveys, particularly in studies with children. Both Maccoby (1954) and Kahn and Cannell (1947) point out the value of picture material as an interviewing aid, and this – together with doll play, incomplete stories and sentences – have become accepted tools for studying child and adolescent attitudes.

Note however that in research of this kind, better results are generally obtained when the instrument is specifically tailored to the ojbect of the inquiry, i.e. when it is designed and revised through experimental trials to cover some particular attitude, motive or ability. General instruments like Rorschach and the standard TAT pictures tend to cover too much ground too thinly to provide precise answers to any concrete problem, and are therefore less effective than what Cronbach (1960) calls focused tests. A further important point is that such research does not necessarily support the view that projective devices are valid indicators of unconscious motives and mechanisms; most of the results seem explicable in terms of the kind of concepts and attitudes which we located at the second and third levels of the Self.

True, the psychologists who employ projective techniques in developmental and motivational studies often draw extensively on depth constructs in formulating their hypotheses and designing their instruments. Not only is this legitimate, but also their insights are often enriched thereby. But unless they can show that explanations in terms of simpler constructs would not be equally effective, their investigations cannot be considered as evidence that projective techniques penetrate to a core level of personality which cannot be gauged from behaviour and introspection. Until more convincing experiments are forthcoming, we have to regard as non-proven the projectivist's major assumption – that an individual's personality dynamics can be fully specified only by studying him both at the overt and covert levels, and that the latter level of repressed impulses and deep defences can be revealed through their expression in fantasy or in Rorschach responses. If this were so, an experiment such as Little and Shneidman's would have yielded *better* diagnoses from Rorschach and TAT than from MMPI, instead of poorer ones; and more experienced testers would have been able to prove their superiority over less experienced.

At the moment there are no clear rules for determining the source of either the formal or content aspects of any response, or the level they represent. The interpretation of their significance in the personality picture depends far too much on the whim and the theoretical orientation of the tester, except when the instrument is specifically focused on some defined motive or concept. The crucial test of their value for general diagnostic purposes would be their *incremental* validity, i.e. what they add to other diagnostic techniques. In view of the length of time required to give, score and interpret them (some 6-8 hours for Rorschach and TAT together), they are not worth using unless they yield information which cannot be obtained by ordinary case-history methods and tests such as MMPI. The evidence at present available suggests that they detract from, rather than add to, such methods.

Part III

Objective Approaches to Personality

Chapter 11

MEASUREMENT OF TRAITS AND FACTORS

We turn now to the approaches to personality which attempt to follow most closely the recognized methods of the biological sciences. They vary quite widely in their underlying assumptions: thus Allport (1961a) and Cattell (1957) agree in their desire to measure the major traits that differentiate people – traits which they conceive as determining factors or entities within the person. However, they disagree in that Allport regards this nomothetic approach as inadequate by itself – it must be supplemented by idiographic understanding of the unique organization of each individual person, whereas Cattell argues that this structure or organization can itself be measured with the aid of modern statistical techniques. At the other extreme the followers of Skinner dispense with any notion of dispositions, and are concerned simply to study the ways human beings build up their responses to stimuli. If we knew enough about the laws underlying learning, we would be able completely to control personal and social behaviour. Other psychologists think of differences between personalities in terms of groups of habitual reactions, which impress the outside observer as showing common features, rather than in terms of inner traits. Shyness, for example, is a set of withdrawing behaviours which the naïve or clinical observer – not the scientific psychologist – attributes to some personal need or disposition that cannot itself be observed. Nevertheless the different writers in this field are united in that they record and measure the characteristics of a personality in the same objective way as the physicist studies natural phenomena or the biologist lower organisms. In this sense the clinician's approach, though it can also claim to be essentially scientific, is certainly more subjective. In the light of his own subjective experience, he conceives the person as a living being who thinks and strives, not like an object or a rat.

179

The development of personality testing. This development has naturally been 'messy' rather than logical, more often wedded to practical needs than to scientific purposes, and subject to the influences of changing fashions. Tests have often been based on adaptations of techniques in common use by other branches of psychology. Thus the success of the Binet and Stanford individual intelligence tests led many workers to think of a personality trait as they thought of intelligence – namely an entity which could be measured by sample tasks or 'miniature situations' that appeared to invoke it. The June Downey Will-Temperament tests based on research in graphology, Fernald's test for measuring endurance by the time a subject would keep his leg raised above a support, and Moore and Gilliland's battery of tests for aggressiveness were some examples. In the 1920's, also, considerable effort was devoted to 'debunking' some of the methods of assessment popular with business employers or the man in the street – the interview and testimonial, phrenology, physiognomy and graphology.

Stock laboratory experiments in psychophysics, attention and word association showed their influence in the scaling of attitudes, in tests of perseveration and oscillation devised by Spearman and his followers, and in the free association and psychogalvanic reflex tests, respectively.

Later, the rise of group tests of ability and attainment, and the attraction of testing large numbers, resulted in a concentration on paper-and-pencil tests of interests, attitudes and personality traits, where the score is simply the sum of responses to numerous short items. These were aimed first at concrete criteria like emotional adjustment in the army (Woodworth's Personal Data Sheet), in school or college, or interests in specific occupations (Strong's Vocational Interest Blank); then at traits of more general importance – introversion-extraversion, ascendance-submission, radicalism-conservatism, etc. Next there was a trend towards the measurement of purer or more homogeneous traits and social attitudes, claimed by factor analysts to be independent of one another (Thurstone and Guilford), and attempts to reduce the obvious deficiencies of personality inventories by external validation of items (as in MMPI), or by 'forced choice' and other devices. And now, as Cronbach (1960) points out, the emphasis is on tests of constructs which derive from psychological theorizing, such as the Taylor Manifest Anxiety scale, the F-Scale of fascist attitudes, the Edwards Personal Preference Schedule for measuring some of Murray's list of needs, and the

Myers–Briggs inventory based on Jungian typology. At the same time, other kinds of testing and measurement have certainly not been neglected in the 1930's to 50's. Apart from rating methods and the rise of projective techniques, discussed in previous chapters, a wide range of objective tests of performance, at all levels from the physiological, sensory-motor and perceptual, up to tests involving complex social behaviour, have been tried out.* However, none of them seem to have achieved the same popularity as the self-report or questionnaire type of test.

Rationale of personality testing. The outstanding exponents of testing and of the application of factorial analysis to the mapping out of personality are H. J. Eysenck in Britain and R. B. Cattell in America. We will discuss their work later but will first describe the more eclectic viewpoint represented by Guilford (1959) and, at one time, by the present writer. This recognizes that personality is so complex that we are unlikely to be able to subject all its aspects to objective measurement. There are a number of ways of studying it – through theoretical analysis, observation, experiment and developmental investigations: and very likely clinical or idiographic methods will continue to be the most widely employed for practical purposes. Yet each of these has its weaknesses; and subjective biases are so ubiquitous, particularly in our daily life assessments, that we should certainly exploit any valid testing technique. The psychometric approach is complementary to these other approaches. Tests may be far from perfect, but that is no reason for rejecting them if they can be proved to yield useful predictions.

Personality traits. Now a person's behaviour in any situation depends, of course, on specific features of that situation and on his temporary feelings or state of mind; but it depends also on his more enduring characteristics – abilities, habits and more general dispositions which may be called traits. Even though we cannot fully control the situational and mood variations, we could go a long way towards predicting behaviour if we could assess these stable features in which people differ from one another. Traits can range from quite narrow habits to broad dispositions; yet even the former show some generality – they are not merely specific responses to specific stimuli.

* A fairly full description may be found in the writer's previous book (Vernon 1953). Cf. also Allen (1958), Anastasi (1961), Cronbach (1960), Freeman (1955), Guilford (1959).

A tic – say screwing up one's nose when talking to strangers – may be elicited by other embarrassing situations. However, the traits we chiefly use for describing people in daily life, and which we would most like to measure, are not so much observable habits as inferred factors, intervening variables or constructs. Traits such as sociability, honesty, assertiveness and so forth underlie a wide variety of behaviours.

Carr and Kingsbury (1938) point out that traits are initially adverbs of actions ('He behaves cautiously'), then generalized to adjectives which describe individuals ('He is of a cautious disposition'), and finally abstracted as nouns ('He has a trait of caution'). But it is as legitimate to name them as it is to refer to 'speed of walking' and the like, provided we are aware of the danger of over-generalizing – of regarding them as entities which make a person always behave cautiously or incautiously, etc.

Most traits of social importance can be regarded as bi-polar, and probably as normally distributed: that is, people can range from one extreme to its opposite, the majority falling near the middle. However, there is often some doubt as to this oppositeness: for example, 'emotional instability' might be contrasted with 'mature, controlled emotions' or with 'apathy' or perhaps with 'inhibited, repressed'. And there are other characteristics which cannot so readily be thought of as lying along a scale or continuum, for instance the combination of characteristics which we recognize as a pathological syndrome. With most traits, though, each individual can be considered as falling at some point on the continuum, depending on the frequency and intensity of his trait-behaviour, and the range of situations to which he responds in this fashion, i.e. on his deviation from normal expectation. Thus he would not be regarded as strong in irritability if he reacted angrily to frustrating situations that annoy most people, or only when he was under strain. At the same time, Guilford suggests, he may vary widely, or narrowly, around his own mode: e.g. he may be more irritable than average at some times, more even-tempered at other times, whereas other individuals show greater consistency. Although we consider traits as enduring, we recognize also that they can and do change with growing older, or with altered circumstances, e.g. getting married (cf. Carr and Kingsbury, also Vernon, 1933b).

The content of most traits is too vague and general for us to be able to place people on them with any great accuracy, and we can hardly expect to find any certain means of so placing them. Their behaviour in specified situations, the impressions that independent observers get and their own reports of their typical behaviour and feelings all contribute, but no one of these is necessarily more accurate than another. Thus the best measurement of their standing is likely to be based on a combination of many kinds of data. In daily life we assess a person as very sociable from observable samples of his behaviour in numerous situations, and the tester can follow the same plan, much as he does in measuring abilities. This was the approach which the present writer employed in one of the earliest attempts to make a comprehensive psychometric study of personality.*

Measurement of 'trait-composites'. Over a period of some 20 weeks in 1929–30, for an hour a week, he applied most of the currently available tests to a small group of 25 college freshmen, including records of behaviour in situations designed to elicit assertiveness, persistence, impulsiveness, etc.; the psychogalvanic reflex, word association, Rorschach inkblots and other projective devices, questionnaires on interests, social attitudes and personality traits, and ratings of self and others. The students' scores on over a hundred variables were ranked, and those which appeared to cluster together were intercorrelated. Wherever five or more scores from different tests or ratings correlated positively, yielding an overall internal consistency of 0·7 or more, it was argued that this composite provided a usable measure of some underlying trait. The composite score is a predicter of the score on an infinite sample of similar behaviours. In this way, composites were established for:
Sociability, Dominance, Emotionality, Dependability, Intelligence, Cultural Level, Impulsiveness, Radicalism, and a number of other traits.

Though the results of a research on so small a group could be accepted only as tentative, they appeared to indicate greater promise for trait-measurement than did other researches of that period. For example, May and Hartshorne's monumental study of character traits in children (honesty, altruism, self-control, integration) suggested that their responses to different tests of, nominally, the same trait were almost wholly inconsistent.† Good character seemed to consist of a set of independent habits rather than a general disposition. However, the field of character may be particularly difficult to cover, especially among children, by means of objective group tests; and in any case there was *some* positive overlapping. In the writer's investigation it was found possible to measure several important

* The work was carried out with the advice of Prof. Mark May at the Department of Education, Yale University.
† Cf. also Brown's (1916) study of suggestibility.

N

traits, even if at considerable cost in technical effort, and in the students' and tester's time. Note that there was no way of validating any test against an external criterion, in the manner that vocational aptitude tests are conventionally validated. But the correlation of a test with a relevant composite or composites could be obtained, thus providing a basis for purifying and improving, or arriving at new and better, tests in further research.

Factor analysis. Another defect of this study was that a fair amount of overlapping remained among the several composites – which is uneconomical. Allport and Odbert (1936) have shown that there are thousands of trait-names for describing people, and obviously many of these are near-synonyms or opposites. Hence it would be an advantage to reduce them to a smaller number of relatively independent categories or major dimensions and to concentrate on measuring these. A few years later, Thurstone provided the tool for doing just this job – multiple factor analysis – and showed that it could be applied to sets of trait ratings and social attitudes.

Other psychologists, notably Guilford, realized that the popular personality inventories were likely to be very heterogeneous in content, i.e. that their items might refer to a number of different traits. By means of factor analysis they were able to break down such complex concepts as extraversion-introversion or emotional stability and arrive at more homogeneous measures. Thus in successive studies Guilford claimed to isolate thirteen components of introversion and emotionality from questionnaire items, though he admitted considerable overlapping among some of them. Unfortunately, the same correlations can be factorized and rotated in many different ways, and subsequent writers (Lovell, 1945; Thurstone, 1951; Eysenck, 1960b) have indeed arrived at quite different interpretations of the traits underlying Guilford's scales. Similar confusions are characteristic of most factorial work in the personality area, to an even greater extent than in factorizing abilities, though French (1953) has made a notable attempt to reconcile the personality factors claimed in most of the major published investigations up to 1952. Both Guilford (1959) and Eysenck (1960b) provide rather exhaustive surveys; but their conclusions are often at variance, the former trying to demonstrate the diversity of human traits as indicated by factorial studies, the latter being more concerned to simplify the picture and to show that different studies point to only a few major factors or types. Certainly there is far too little consensus between them and other factorial writers to justify the hope of arriving at an agreed list of all the major factors that require to be measured for a fairly complete map of human personality.

THE WORK OF H. J. EYSENCK

Despite their disagreements, Guilford and Eysenck concur on many points, notably on the desirability of using factor analysis to arrive at a satisfactory taxonomy of personality, and on the hierarchical structure of such a taxonomy. Eysenck (1952b, 1960b) insists that measurement is essential to scientific advance and that, at the moment, we do not know what to measure in psychology. Constructs such as perseveration, rigidity, dissociative ability (Kretschmer) are employed without any proof that they represent functional unities; and correlational analysis clearly shows that they are not homogeneous traits. Hence the identification of what to measure is an essential first step towards a science of personality. Personality, Eysenck maintains, *is* behaviour, provided we include verbal and autonomic reactions as well as observable performances as behaviour; and it clearly does show consistencies – it is not just a set of specific Stimulus-Response mechanisms. But these consistencies can be found at various levels. Specific reactions group together under more general habits, and numerous habits group together to yield what we call a trait. Over and above this several traits often overlap; in factorial terms they yield a 'second-order' factor, which Eysenck denotes as a 'type'. Thus introversion-extraversion is a general type which enters to some extent into such different traits as shyness, subjectivity, irritability, persistence, etc. One of the reasons for discrepancies between the results of different factorists is their failure to recognize that their factors represent various levels in this hierarchical organization. Another reason is that statistical analysis alone cannot reveal which traits or types are causal entities; behaviour can be classified in all sorts of ways – though these are mathematically inter-convertible, i.e. they are not really contradictory. Far too many factorial studies consist in analysing some randomly assembled battery of test scores or ratings without any clear hypotheses regarding the underlying components, and these merely add to the confusion.

Taxonomy of mental disorders. As an illustration of the fruitful application of factor analysis to the testing of hypotheses we may take the field of abnormal psychology. The various neuroses and psychoses have traditionally been conceived – like physical diseases – as qualitatively distinct categories or syndromes. Obviously they overlap in all kinds of ways, and there is little agreement among the systems of classification proposed by different psychopathologists. Thus Kretschmer envisaged a continuum from manic-depressive psychosis to schizophrenia, with the normal temperamental variations of cyclothymia and schizothymia falling in between; and he grouped hysterics with schizothymics. Jung, on the other hand, contrasted hysterics as extreme extraverts with anxiety and obsessional (dysthymic) neuroses as introverted: while Freud appeared to regard all the neuroses as lying along the same continuum as the psychoses, differing mainly in degree of regression.

Eysenck pointed out that these questions could be settled definitively by applying batteries of tests which discriminate among the various neuroses and psychoses, to normals as well as to pathological groups. Valid pathological distinctions should then correspond with the factors that can be established among the normals. Thus he was able to show that both the extreme groups of psychotics differed from normals on one factor, but that neurotics lay along a different one: also that a factor in normals which might well be termed extraversion-introversion did indeed separate hysterics from dysthymics as Jung hypothesized, but that there was no empirical justification for Kretschmer's manic-depressive-cyclothyme-normal-schizothyme-schizophrenic dimension. The uncertainties of diagnosing qualitative syndromes should therefore be replaced by a three-dimensional scheme.* Each patient, that is to say, should be measured for his *degree* of (*a*) Neuroticism, (*b*) Introversion-extraversion, (*c*) Psychoticism. Most of the available tests may be too unreliable and too time-consuming for routine use at the moment, but they could be greatly improved by analysis against objective, factorial criteria rather than by comparing them merely with subjective nosological classifications. Presumably, if this threefold scheme seems too narrow, it could readily be extended to provide further subsidiary factors, e.g. one that helped to differentiate the obsessional from the anxiety groups of dysthymics. Eysenck (1960c) also argues that the effects of particular treatments, such as leucotomy or drugs, can be better expressed as measurable changes along these dimensions, than in terms of subjective impressions of 'improvement'.

---

* An alternative technique of studying the differentiation between syndromes is canonical variate (or discriminant function) analysis. Eysenck shows that this tends to confirm the findings of factorial studies (S. B. Eysenck *et al.*, 1960).

Eysenck holds that meaningful factors are unlikely to be obtained from the internal evidence of test intercorrelations alone. They should be linked, in the manner just described – known as Criterion Analysis, to widely recognized group differences, and they should derive from sound psychological theorizing. At the same time, many of the factors claimed by other writers who have analysed either ratings, inventories, performance tests, delinquent symptoms, and even measures of autonomic functions, appear to correspond closely with his neurotic vs. integrated or extravert-introvert factors. Eysenck's survey of the field suggests that there is considerable agreement on the major personality dimensions, although of course a large number of additional dimensions (at the 'trait' rather than the 'type' level) have been claimed. How far he is justified in fitting other workers' factors into his two-dimensional scheme seems more doubtful. Factors which have been variously labelled anxiety, integration, ego-strength, will-character, persistence, stability, emotionality, etc., may appear to be similar in content to his neuroticism. But there is little evidence that the tests on which they are based really measure the same thing.

Extraversion-introversion. Eysenck's interpretation of extraversion-introversion differs somewhat from that of most American writers, who conceive it largely in terms of gregariousness + popularity vs. shy, withdrawn, introspective. However, when Guilford broke down this concept into five sub-factors by analysing inventory items, one of the factors, which he called Rhathymia, was mainly centred around carefreeness, spontaneity, outer expression vs. inhibited, scrupulous, self-controlled, serious; and this, Eysenck considers, is nearer to Jung's concept and to the hysteric-dysthymic dichotomy. The notion of social introversion overlaps with neuroticism, and indeed American introversion and emotional instability or neuroticism scales have always tended to intercorrelate closely.* Recently Carrigan (1960) has surveyed factorial studies of extraversion and agrees that these two interpretations should be distinguished.

Much effort has also been devoted to linking extraversion-introversion, not only with neurotic syndromes, but also with concepts derived from experimental psychology, namely with Pavlovian and

---

* The present writer has suggested that, alternatively, the social introversion factor might be retained, as corresponding closely with common usage, and that in this case the main dimension orthogonal to it would be dependability, purposefulness and strong vs. weak character rather than normality-stability vs. neuroticism (1953, p. 137.

Hullian learning theory. In the history of psychology many attempts have been made to attribute this dimension to endocrine or autonomic differences, to characteristics of neural functioning (perseveration, primary vs. secondary function, etc.) even to the predominance of the Id over the Super-ego or vice versa. Eysenck considers that there are neural differences in the speed of production and strength of excitation and inhibition. In the extravert, excitatory potentials are slow and weak, inhibitory potentials strong and slowly dissipated, in the introvert the opposite. He deduces that introverts should be conditioned more readily and forget more slowly, also that differences should be shown in a wide range of sensory, perceptual and learning functions such as reminiscence, figural after-effects, apparent movement, dark adaptation, etc. Moreover depressant drugs such as alcohol and sodium amytal should produce extraverting effects, while stimulant ones which decrease inhibition and increase excitation should have the opposite effects. A large number of experiments designed to test these predictions, both among hysterics contrasted with dysthymics, and among normals scoring high or low on his introversion (rhathymia) scale, are claimed for the most part to confirm them.

Work in other areas. Eysenck differs from most American factorists, as also from clinical psychologists generally, in stressing hereditary determination of his major factors. We have already seen that he casts doubt on the effectiveness of psychotherapies which attribute neurotic traits wholly to conditions of upbringing, and in an experimental study with Prell (1951) of identical and non-identical twins, he claimed to find as substantial an hereditary component in measured neuroticism as is commonly found with intelligence. However, this finding has not been confirmed, and a later twin-study by Shields (1954) of maladjusted children indicated that it was not so much their stability or neurotic potential that was innately determined as their emotional responsiveness and motility, and their performance on tests of extraversion-introversion. The excitation-inhibition theory would, of course, imply a constitutional origin for this latter dimension, and other studies by Blewett and McLeod (Eysenck, 1960b) provide some support.

Social attitudes. Eysenck's approach to social attitudes has paralleled that to personality traits: that is, he shows that the conflicting results of numerous investigations of the organization of attitudes can be reconciled by referring them to two major dimensions which he calls radicalism-conservatism and tough vs. tender-mindedness. Thus the dimension which is favoured by many American social psychologists – namely authoritarianism or fascism vs. democratic, humanitarianism may be clarified by resolving it into conservatism + tough-mindedness. But a more important reason for accepting these factors is that they provide an intelligible scheme of classification of the major political parties: they are not merely interpretations of statistical consistencies. In this area also the hierarchical conceptions of a series of levels ranging from specific opinions to more general attitudes is useful, the most inclusive being an 'ideology' such as conservatism.

Evaluation. In general Eysenck's approach has been invigorating, particularly in Britain where objective studies of personality have been slow to win acceptance. To many clinical psychologists and others, his views seem far-fetched, dogmatic and arrogant. But as pointed out earlier, 'commonsense' has little bearing on the value of a theory, and there can be no doubt that these views engender a great many testable hypotheses and thus stimulate a large amount of research. Eysenck, of course, has no room for clinical and projective approaches, or for understanding the total personality as an unique organization. Each person is unique simply because he would fall at a particular point in factor space – were we able to measure all his factors. However, he tends to ignore a good deal of the evidence that we have cited on the value of idiographic approaches; and the convincingness of his own evidence is often open to dispute.

For example, Storms and Sigal (1958) claim to have discovered flaws in many of the experiments designed to test the hypothesized relation between introversion-extraversion and excitation-inhibition phenomena. We cannot attempt to adjudge between the contestants (cf. Eysenck 1959): the answers can come only from repetitions of the experiments with more careful control of conditions. Eysenck is entirely frank in admitting that tests – whether of personality traits or of conditioning or after-effects and similar phenomena – tend to be highly unstable, being affected by slight changes in the conditions, by the person who applies the test and by the characteristics and attitudes of the population tested.* But this, of course, cuts the

* J. A. C. Brown (1961) ridicules Eysenck's notion that suggestibility, for example, can be measured as a stable trait independently of who does the suggesting and what is suggested. But the facts remain that clinical psychologists and psychiatrists, as well as laymen, often talk o fsome individuals as being suggestible,

ground from under the main foundations of his edifice if he is unable to specify a satisfactory battery of tests which will always provide a reliable and highly saturated measure of a factor in any one type of population. In measuring intelligence the same sort of tests always do work under a wide range of conditions with quite widely varying populations; similarly attitude tests and interest inventories are reasonably stable, even if more limited, instruments; and we know a good deal about the conditions that distort them (faking, response sets, etc. – cf. Chap. 12). But there is much greater variability in the results of personality tests.

This may be illustrated by the following extracts from Eysenck's investigations. In 1947 he found excellent differentiation between Army personnel who had been diagnosed as neurotics and normal controls on several tests, including:

> The Maudsley Medical Questionnaire (no. of neurotic symptoms admitted)
> Dark Vision – Livingston Rotating Hexagon (poor photopic and scotopic sensitivity over a 35-minute test)
> Body Sway – Static Ataxia and suggestibility (maximum sway some 3 to 4 times greater in neurotics)

Next, a battery of 18 tests was applied to 198 male patients and to 93 controls (surgical cases), and the following correlations were obtained. Already the correlations of the first two tests are lower than expected, but it is suggested that the surgical controls may have contained several neurotics, and that the neurotics were less extreme than in the original studies.

	Correlation with normal-neurotic dichotomy	General factor loadings	
		in total population	in normal population
Maudsley Medical Questionnaire	0·23	0·29	0·14
Dark Vision	0·27	0·25	0·39
Static Ataxia	0·54	0·64	0·64
Body Sway suggestibility	0·51	0·69	0·62

Normal-neurotic dichotomy 0·71

In 1952 a further investigation was published of some 200 normal soldiers and some 120 neuropsychiatric discharges. Crown's Word Connection – a group word-association test – was included.

---

others as negativistic; and that a good deal of consistency has been demonstrated among controlled measurements of two types of suggestibility. The effects of the suggester on such tests is a matter for experiment, not for hunches.

	Correlation with normal-neurotic dichotomy	Neuroticism factor loading in normals
MMQ	0·60	0·32
Dark Vision	0·25	−0·02
Static Ataxia	0·26	−0·12
Suggestibility	0·16	−0·15
Word Connection	0·30	0·30

Here the questionnaire gives quite good, and the other tests rather weak, differentiation. But when the battery is factorized among normals, several of the tests show no saturation at all on the factor believed to represent neuroticism. Partly this may be due to using different numbers of cases for different tests, partly to the interference of intelligence differences between the samples.

Heron (1954) applied a battery of tests largely derived from Eysenck's work to 80 industrial workers (grid-casters) and, on factorizing and rotating, identified one factor as a neurotic dimension. The MMQ was not used, but other questionnaires dealing with Worries and Annoyances obtained loadings around 0·45; Static Ataxia also had a saturation of 0·45, but Word Connection one of 0·12 only.

More recently Eysenck, Granger and Brengelmann (1957) tried out a variety of sensory and perceptual tests, along with some of the standard ones, on 20 neurotic and 20 psychotic patients, and 106 'normal' soldiers, though the latter were again considered to be a somewhat inferior sample in intelligence and adjustment, so that normal-neurotic differences are likely to be reduced. Correlations for normal-neurotic dichotomy are not given, but the second column in the following Table lists an approximate indication of the degree of differentiation, from xxx = good, to zero.

	Normal-neurotic differentiation	Factorization in normals	
		Factor I	Factor III
MMQ	xxx	0·41	−0·09
Worries Questionnaire	xxx	0·30	−0·03
Annoyances	0	0·37	0·02
Likes and interests (reversed)	xx	0·27	0·19
Dark Vision – 5 mins.	0	0·17	0·18
Dark Vision – 30 mins.	x	0·25	0·15
Static Ataxia	0	0·27	−0·12
Suggestibility	x	0·15	−0·01
Word Connection	?	0·39	−0·15

Seventy-six sets of test scores were factorized in the normal group, and among the factors identified the first is called 'introspective abnormality', the third 'perceptual abnormality'. Eysenck clearly lays more stress on the latter as the basis of a scientific approach to psychiatric diagnosis, since the former – largely based on questionnaire responses – is more likely to be affected by the patients talking about their symptoms after hospitalization. Yet none of the tests which he had previously advocated show appreciable loadings on this factor and it seems to approximate more closely to 'psychoticism' than 'neuroticism'. Some of the questionnaires differentiated the neurotics fairly effectively; but Dark Vision, Body Sway and Word Connection show very little, or no, differentiation.*

There would seem then to be an entire lack of consistency between different investigations, using somewhat different samples, both in the tests that come out as the best measures of a neuroticism factor, and in those which effectively differentiate patients from non-neurotics. These results have not been picked out as extreme ones. They are fairly typical of what happens in the personality field. Variations between the results of different authors are likely to be greater still.

In his earlier writings, Eysenck assumed that further investigation of the more promising tests would iron out their weaknesses, but there is little sign in his later writings that we are any nearer to having really trustworthy batteries. At the same time, it should be noted that Eysenck has not, like many factorists, taken the easy way out – namely, falling back on personality questionnaires and/or ratings, which much more readily yield stable patterns. He realizes, as will be pointed out below, that they are stable for the wrong reasons, and therefore prefers to search for more objective measures of performance, such as sensory-motor, perceptual and autonomic tests.

Other criticisms. The diagnosis of psychoticism as a unitary trait by means of tests seems even more questionable than that of neuroticism. True, certain differences in speed of response and in types of concept formation between psychotics and normals have been fairly consistently replicated, though their loadings are usually very small. But the usefulness of this dimension is open to doubt because of the difficulty in interpreting the meaning of a normal distribution. What are the characteristics of the extreme non-psychotic, and in what sense can the average normal individual be thought of as half-psychotic?

* Ingham *et al.* (1961) have briefly reported an attempt to assess neuroticism in representative samples of normals and of neurotic patients under identical conditions in their own homes. Significant differences were obtained on the Maudsley Personality Inventory and other questionnaire tests of worries, annoyances and food aversions, but not on such behavioural tests as body sway and manual dexterity.

Extraversion-introversion too has run into difficulties, since the initial linking of extreme extraversion to hysteria has not stood up: both on questionnaires and on some more objective tests of learning and perceptual functions, hysterics tend to differ little from normals or even to score slightly to the introverted side (though they do remain significantly different from dysthymics). More consistent extravert characteristics are usually found among psychopathic patients – a fact which can be reconciled with, but had not been envisaged by the basic theory.*

Despite the factorist's rigorous methodology, he seems apt to indulge in theoretical speculations which merit at least as severe criticism as he himself applies to clinical theories. He sets out, in praiseworthy fashion, to employ operationally defined constructs: for example, extraversion-introversion (or any other factor) *is* the score on a properly weighted cluster of intercorrelated tests. But he soon begins to reify his factor in much the same way as the layman or non-factorist reify their traits, complexes, etc., and to assume that it determines behaviour in all kinds of daily-life situations, on very little or no evidence.† Thus Eysenck hypothesizes that introverts, because of their ready conditionability, are more likely to be social conformists who build up strong Super-egos, whereas extraverts will be more uninhibited and delinquent. Now it is reasonable to expect some linkage between extraversion-introversion and attitudes to authority. But it is doubtful whether 'condition-ability' can be accepted as a unitary trait (i.e. individuals do not consistently acquire different sorts of conditioned reflexes easily or the reverse), and still more doubtful whether ease of sensory conditioning has anything whatever to do with social learning.

Work on the neuroticism factor seems to have led to equally wild speculations. According to Hullian theory, the anxiety aroused by conflict between primary drives and social training in infancy itself becomes an important secondary drive, reduction in which underlies a good deal of learning. Strong anxiety would be expected to facilitate the acquisition of simple responses, as in conditioning, and to disturb the learning of complex ones; and according to Taylor and Spence, anxiety can be assessed as a personality trait by an inventory (the

* Some writers have raised objections, also, to Eysenck's work in the field of social attitudes. Mention is made of these later (p. 275).

† The writer (Vernon, 1961) has drawn attention to the same tendency, though perhaps less egregious, in factorial work on abilities, for example in interpreting Thurstone's rote memory factor.

Manifest Anxiety Scale) almost identical in content with those used for measuring neuroticism. Though Eysenck is critical of this theory, he nevertheless claims that neuroticism or anxiety can act as a drive, and his followers (Lynn, 1959; Furneaux, 1962) even go so far as to interpret neuroticism as motivating intellectual achievement. This is the more ironic in so far as many educational psychologists have tried to explain intellectual *non*-achievement as due to neurotic disturbance. The actual fact is that neuroticism questionnaires normally give small positive correlations with achievement among college students. But since such questionnaires always overlap with measures of social introversion, and social introverts are less gregarious, more studious than extraverts, the correlation is much more easily explained without any resort to a hypothetical drive – particularly a drive which has been found to inhibit complex learning!

Future experimental work may, one hopes, help to clarify the concepts of an exuberant young science. But if one were asked whether progress in factorial studies over the quarter of a century since Thurstone provided the tools, or progress in clinical psychology, had contributed more to our knowledge of personality factors in school achievement or delinquency, it would be very difficult to answer. Very possibly a majority of psychologists would vote for the latter and would add that experimental, developmental and socio-psychological investigations have helped more than either.

We have devoted considerable space to describing and criticizing Eysenck's work, not because he is the only exponent of this approach, nor the most vulnerable. On the contrary, hundreds of other studies have in various ways contributed to our understanding of tests and ratings, while apparently telling us little about people; and many of these have shown at least as serious weaknesses. Few writers, however, have applied factor analysis as energetically and systematically, with the exception of R. B. Cattell (1957), to whose work we now turn.

THE WORK OF R. B. CATTELL

Cattell, like Eysenck, shows the influence of the British psychology of McDougall, Spearman and Burt. But, having worked in America since the late '30's, he has concerned himself with a far wider range of factors than Eysenck's main types. He is equally scornful of clinical approaches to personality, and insistent that the only hope for a science of personality lies in the establishment of 'functional unities' through factor analysis and in their measurement by objective methods. Indeed he goes much further than most factorists in advocating that all psychological problems should be thought of in terms of multi-variate analysis, and that each concept or variable that is investigated should be established as a unitary factor. At the moment psychologists who study the effects of, say, protected home environment, fluctuation of attention, anxiety, fatigue, moods, attitudes, etc., are seldom clear as to what they are talking about, and employ far too restricted observations and measurements of these conditions. Factor analysis can cope with many kinds of relationship besides just correlations between test scores of individuals – with the structure of attitudes within the individual by using correlations between persons (Q-technique), with dynamic relations and changes over time by correlating scores on numerous occasions (P-technique) or score-changes (incremental analysis), also with situational and cultural influences. It would take us too far afield to discuss the revolutionary implications of this viewpoint in clinical or experimental psychology, since in any case there is little prospect of their realization for a long time to come. But we should outline the main features of Cattell's taxonomy of personality.

Source traits and their measurement. Unlike Eysenck, Cattell clearly looks to factor analysis to reveal the major causal entities – the 'source traits' – which lie behind the more superficial clusters of associated personality variables. For example, even the instincts or ergs and the Freudian Super-ego, Id and defence mechanisms, which combine in innumerable complex chains or lattices to determine any piece of behaviour, should reveal themselves as factors, provided their manifestations are measured by sufficiently varied techniques and replicated in sufficient different studies. The main key to the discovery of invariant (stable) source traits is blind rotation of the obtained factors to oblique simple structure. Thus Cattell relies on the internal evidence of consistent clustering, rather than on correlations with an external criterion such as Eysenck favours. He makes much use of demonstrable associations with occupations, pathological syndromes, etc., as well as of depth-psychological theories, in interpreting the nature of his factors, but sees no reason to suppose that such criteria reveal pure factors. The principle of obliquity is important, since the amount of overlapping among source traits may vary considerably in different samples of the population, or in different contexts. Indeed, he attributes much of the confusion in the factorial results of other writers to their demand for orthogonal or uncorrelated factors. Overlapping of factors should be expected, not avoided: for example, people who are well integrated or high in ego-strength tend to be above average in intelligence; but it is much more plausible to treat ego-strength and intelligence as distinct, yet correlated, dimensions of personality.

Cattell recognizes three media of expression of source traits, which yield three approaches to measurement:

1. L-R life-record data. In practice these consist mainly of ratings by trained observers which, provided they are carefully and systematically collected, he accepts as objective measures of typical behaviour.

2. Q – questionnaires or self-report data, including interview responses. The items in questionnaire tests should not merely appear relevant to some trait or attitude, but should be validated against a factorial criterion. Even then such tests are particularly liable to 'motivational lability', i.e. intentional faking or unintentional distortions. However, they provide a useful short-cut to factor measurement. His own 16 PF test for assessing 16 personality factors is an example; and he has published several other such tests for children of different ages, and for clinical and occupational diagnostic purposes.

3. T – performance tests. Though the ultimate goal is to measure all factors through this medium, it is far more difficult than with L-R or Q data. Great creative ingenuity is needed to devise short, easily administered, yet reliable tests which adequately sample important personality traits. Both motor and perceptual tests tend to be too peripheral (under the latter heading Cattell includes projection tests which he considers useful only if their application and scoring are standardized, and they are conceived as tests of 'misperception' attributable to motivational factors). Nevertheless he has published Objective Analytic Batteries of tests, which claim to measure some dozen factors in five hours testing time.

Results. As is generally known, Cattell's basic personality factors were extracted from L-R data, provided by successively reducing the complete list of personality trait-names given by Allport and Odbert (1936). By this method he hoped to ensure comprehensive coverage of the whole 'sphere' of personality. The first half-dozen in the following list have been established repeatedly, and the other nine, though possessing smaller variance, have been replicated in several studies either by Cattell or other factorists.* Neologistic names have been assigned to many of the latter, since they necessarily represent qualities which have not been widely recognized in clinical or lay usage. Their meaning cannot be conveyed fully without Cattell's detailed presentation of their component traits, their origins (including hereditary and environmental influences), their psychopathological implications and their correlates with external criteria.

A. Schizothyme-cyclothyme (easygoing, warm-hearted, frank vs. reserved, obstructive).
B. Intelligence, not simply the cognitive ability but the complex of associated intellectual and personality qualities.
C. Ego-strength vs. neuroticism (stable, mature vs. emotional, undependable).
D. Excitability vs. security (nervous, demanding vs. self-controlled). This does not always separate off clearly.
E. Dominance vs. submissiveness (forceful, assertive vs. timid).
F. Surgency-desurgency (cheerful vs. depressed). Note that this is distinguished from cyclothyme-schizothyme.
G. Super-ego strength (conscientious, persevering vs. frivolous, indolent).
H. Parmia vs. Threctia (gregarious, bold vs. shy, withdrawn).
I. Premsia vs. Harria (dependent, feminine, hysterical vs. hard, practical, self-sufficient).
J. Coasthenia vs. Zeppia (neurasthenic, obsessional vs. vigorous).
K. Comention vs. Abcultion (refined, cultured vs. philistine).
L. Protension vs. Inner Relaxation (paranoid vs. trustful).
M. Autia vs. Praxernia (unconventional, ideational vs. conformist, sensational).
N. Shrewdness vs. naïveté.
O. Guilt proneness vs. confidence.

Since these factors overlap to varying extents, it is possible to factorize their intercorrelations. In this way Cattell arrives at half a dozen second-order factors, the first two of which bear an unmistakable resemblance to Eysenck's types. Thus the first corresponds to the general conception of extraversion-introversion, being based mainly on a combination of factors, F, M-†, E, A- and H;

---

* Cattell has drawn up a 'Universal Index' of the personality, motivational and ability traits which he considers to be established by the consensus of factorial investigations.

† i.e., M reversed = Praxernia.

while the second is identified as integration or adjustment vs. anxiety, combining factors, C, L–, H, E and F– (though not factor G).

In a series of researches with Q data, the intercorrelations of questionnaire items have been factorized. Cattell has indeed worked with more huge matrices than any other factorist; he habitually includes around a hundred variables, and he has shown that it is possible to cope with double this number by splitting the matrix in two and including key-items or 'markers' from the first half in the second half. In this way he arrives at 19 Q factors, at least a dozen of which are claimed to duplicate very closely 12 of the L factors listed above (together with four of the second-order factors). However, another four are peculiar to Q material alone. In most of these factors the item-loadings are small, hence the interpretation offered appears somewhat subjective. Cattell devotes considerable attention to the principles of matching factors from different studies, or in different media, insisting that this cannot be done on an impressionistic basis. In three investigations he has tried to determine the overlapping between L, Q and T factors by applying all three types of measure to the same population. However, the actual extent of correspondence has not been clearly demonstrated (cf. Becker, 1960).

Even more elaborate is the work with T data, and over 200 objective test scores have been analysed in a series of studies, to yield 18 named factors. Owing to limitations of time the tests were mostly short and weak in reliability, hence the loadings listed for any one factor are mostly low and irregular. One would of course expect some irregularities attributable to differences in age, sex or other characteristics of the populations studied; but the instability is if anything more marked than that noted above for Eysenck's tests. Hence it is extremely difficult to perceive the common features in Cattell's groups of test variables, or to follow their connections with the source traits that he postulates.

Though Cattell admits that the aim of covering all the L factors by objective tests has been only partially achieved, he reiterates his optimistic belief that the future lies with objective testing. It is noteworthy that other American and British psychologists have often used Cattell's personality questionnaires (while complaining of the low reliability and high overlapping of many of the factor scores); but that none appears to have accepted his objective batteries. Maybe they are obtuse in looking for good 'face validity', when Cattell's object is to provide indirect tests whose 'meaning' is *not* visible to the testees. But they are entitled to request more convincing evidence that the batteries will yield valid and stable measures of L factors, before they commit themselves.

The measurement of motives. Very remarkable work has been done too in factorizing motives, though here too most psychologists appear suspicious – probably because of Cattell's attachment to McDougallian instincts and sentiments. Moreover, he strongly criticizes their almost exclusive reliance on questionnaires whose items ask merely if one is 'for' or 'against' some object or activity; and prefers indirect tests which reveal interests, attitudes or drives through their effects on memory, attention, beliefs, misperception, speed of decision, autonomic functions, information, etc.

By factorizing these *techniques*, as applied to the measurement of several motives, he claims to have shown that they penetrate to five different levels or components which he identifies with the Id, the conscious Ego, the Ideal Self, the unconscious physiological level and repressed complexes. However, it is possible to reduce these to two major levels – the conscious (integrated) and unconscious (non-integrated). Tests at both levels have been constructed for measuring a large variety of drives and interests. The following factors were obtained (together with several other less clear-cut ones). The first seven are considered to represent 'ergs', largely innately determined, and the other five are major sentiments.

1. Sex. 2. Gregariousness. 3. Parental and protective. 4. Exploration and curiosity. 5. Escape, security. 6. Self-assertion. 7. Narcissistic sex vs. Super-ego. 8. Sentiment to one's vocation. 9. Sports and games. 10. Religion + appeal. 11. Mechanical, constructive, material. 12. Self-reputation.

As an illustration of the clinical usefulness of such factors, seven of them were measured twice daily in one subject over 40 days, and analysed by P-technique (cf. also Luborsky, 1953). A plot of their fluctuations throughout the period appeared to accord closely with changes in circumstances, mood, etc.* Two batteries of 'Dynamic Diagnostic' tests have been constructed for assessing some two dozen drives and interests in the clinical and occupational settings. Cattell envisages the clinical psychologist of the future as measuring 50 to 60 personality and motivational factors in each of his patients or counsellees on 60 or more occasions, feeding the results into a computer, and thus analysing objectively the dynamic structure or

---

* Holtzman (1962) points out a number of statistical difficulties which limit the applications or further development of this technique.

unique traits as well as the major common traits and motives of his personality.

Concluding comment. The very breadth and boldness of Cattell's factorial conceptions gives one pause. His work has not invited specific criticisms to the same extent as Eysenck's. Rather, the reaction of most psychologists would seem to be one of incredulity regarding the possibility of expressing all aspects of personality in factorial terms, and bewilderment regarding the huge number of factors he claims to have isolated. We have already drawn attention to two major weaknesses – the instability of the make-up of factors based on tests, and the lack of evidence for the validity of these tests. Other reasons for doubting the feasibility of his approach will appear in the following chapters when we discuss response sets and spurious factors, the nature of validity and the concept of traits. We can indeed acknowledge the value of Cattell's theoretical and methodological contributions; he has broken through many of the limitations of psychometric work in the past, and evolved techniques which can be applied to a wide range of problems in abnormal, social and general, as well as applied psychology. Yet the results so far hardly justify the belief that this is the most fruitful avenue of progress towards the practical assessment and understanding of people's personalities.

Chapter 12

TEST-TAKING ATTITUDES
AND SPURIOUS FACTORS

To survey the results of studies with objective tests, including performance and self-report, would be a Herculean task. Ellis (1946), and Ellis and Conrad (1948) published valuable critical surveys of personality questionnaires, showing how frequently they fail to agree with external criteria of the traits they are supposed to measure. Some of the weaker instruments may have dropped out of use since then, and some better ones have been constructed. But the trend of innumerable subsequent investigations is that they cannot be trusted. The median validity coefficient – probably around 0·4 – is by no means negligible, though hardly sufficient to justify using the tests for individual diagnosis. But the trouble is rather the variability – tests working fairly well in one investigation, not in another. The validities and stabilities of performance tests are, if anything, even poorer. Considering all the effort and skill that has gone into producing better tests, from the late 1920's onwards, it is surprising how little progress has been made. The object of this chapter is to bring out one of the main reasons why.

Social desirability. In a survey of self-report tests in 1938, the present writer drew attention to a number of weaknesses which were especially characteristic of psychoneurotic and introversion-extraversion inventories, and to a lesser extent of interest tests and attitude scales.

1. It is extremely easy to falsify the answers in such a way as to convey a picture of a 'good' personality, and Subjects will always tend to do this if there is any incentive, e.g. if tests are used for selection, or if they are to be seen by a lecturer upon whom students wish to make a good impression. Hence many more 'unpleasant' symptoms are admitted when they are answered anonymously, or are to be used for counselling purposes where the subject is motivated to be candid.

201

2. More Subjects answer 'No' to an unpleasant item than say 'Yes' to the same item reversed (so that it describes pleasant or socially acceptable behaviour). This suggests that most Subjects are defensive, and that personality questionnaires generally show quite high reliability or consistency of response, more because of this pervasive attitude than because the Subjects are really consistent in their neurotic, introverted or other behaviour.

3. This explains too why there is always considerable overlapping between tests of different traits; the correlations are about as high as between different tests of nominally the same trait. This phenomenon is the same as the halo effect in ratings. Raters tend to judge some people high in all desirable traits, others low, and are particularly apt to exaggerate their own desirable qualities. Even when the test attempts to describe objective behaviour symptoms, Subjects answer it very largely in terms of their self-halos.

4. Quite apart from intentional faking, people do not know themselves well enough to answer factually: they are likely to produce unwitting self-deceptions or rationalizations.

5. However, not everyone aims merely to display a favourable self-picture. Some are more suggestible and thus tend to exaggerate their defects, e.g. neurotic patients. Highly educated persons such as students are very often self-analytic and introspective, more self-depreciatory than non-academics.

6. In any test where a range of answers is provided, e.g. from Strongly Agree, through Agree and Doubtful to Strongly Disagree, some subjects give many more extreme responses, fewer middling ones, than others. Similarly in interest tests such as Strong's, where the responses are Like, Indifferent, or Dislike, some people are universal 'likers', others more guarded. The same kind of differences in interpreting scales of response occur in ratings of others, and indeed in examination marking. It is doubtful whether they have much significance for personality. Thus the writer found little connection between extremeness of response and Emotional Stability or Impulsiveness composites. Yet they are clearly liable to distort the Subjects' scores on the variables at which the tests are aimed.

A. L. Edwards's contributions. Subsequent work has amply confirmed the susceptibility of self-report tests to faking, and their greater usefulness in counselling, screening or research situations when motivation is favourable. A. L. Edwards (1957, 1959) has formulated the hypothesis that, to a large extent, any such test is answered in terms of the Social Desirability of the items, as perceived by the Subjects, and this (as suggested above) accounts for high reliabilities and intercorrelations. If a group of independent *judges* assess each item according to its probable social desirability or acceptability, Edwards showed that there is extremely close correspondence with the actual frequency of endorsement of the items by a group of *subjects*. However, he does not appear to offer any clear explanation for the big individual differences that exist in the influence of social desirability; nor does he commit himself regarding the significance of such differences for personality. When a subject scores highly on socially desirable items, does this merely represent his faking, or self-deceiving attitude, or does it show that he is genuinely above average in socially desirable traits? Or is it, as the writer believes, a mixture of the two?

Some further light is thrown by the common finding that college students – who are hardly likely to be below average in 'good' traits – nevertheless seem rather more neurotic and introverted than the less educated; and small but rather consistent correlations are found between these 'bad' traits and academic achievement (cf. p. 194). Loevinger and Ossorio (1959) suggest that, to a large extent, the tests measure cultural sophistication vs. conventionality. The ordinary man who is not highly educated is stereotyped, intolerant, self-satisfied, non psychologically minded, and rejects any imputation of psychological weaknesses: whereas the better-educated man takes a more detached view of himself and is more aware of his conflicts and anxieties.

An interesting confirmation comes from a research by M. Gulutson,* who set out to find whether mental health instruction in schools, with group discussions of emotional problems, would reduce anxieties and improve pupil adjustment. In fact the opposite occurred: the instructed pupils' scores on the Taylor Anxiety Scale rose significantly, presumably because they became more psychologically minded.

However, this sophistication factor would account only for a limited proportion of test variance. No doubt the more emotionally disturbed do reveal their problems when they feel it is safe to do so – i.e. their responses represent the second rather than the top or the deeper levels of the Self-concept (Chap. 7), and thus can be of considerable value to the psychological counsellor, at least as a starting point. Guilford (1959) objects to criticisms of questionnaires on the grounds that it is inconsistent to say (a) that Subjects do not know

* Unpublished Ph.D. thesis, University of Utah, 1962.

themselves well enough to answer truthfully, and (b) that they are apt to falsify. But this is precisely what our theory of the Self would lead us to expect.

Corrections for falsification or social desirability. Some tests incorporate devices for revealing dissimulation and even for correcting it. The K and Lie Scales in the MMPI indeed show the expected relationships with the social desirability variable, but – as Sarason *et al.* (1960) point out, they do not provide an adequate means of freeing the scores on other scales from distortions.

Rather more effective is the Forced Choice technique, introduced in some of the World War II inventories, and adopted by Edwards in his Personal Preference Schedule. Here the alternative answers to each item have been equated for social desirability or frequency of endorsement, but are known to differ in their validity, i.e. their correlation with whatever trait the test is designed to measure.

Yet another solution, found in the MMPI, the Strong Interest Blank and other tests, is to insist on external validation of each item, and to disregard the apparent meanings of the items. This is known as empirical keying. For example, certain items are keyed to yield a score for Hysteria (or other syndrome), because they have been found to differentiate hysteric patients from other patients, and from normals, not because they look like characteristic hysteric symptoms. It is assumed that this technique will adequately take care of social desirability or other distortion tendencies. However, for statistical reasons which will be brought out in the next chapter, it is far from satisfactory.

Cattell and Guilford also stress item-validation. But as they use internal or factorial criteria, it is obvious that social desirability is in no way eliminated. It is merely partitioned out, in varying amounts, among the various factors. For example, it probably loads Guilford's Depression and Sociability scales more than it does Rhathymia, since self-restraint (vs. happy-go-lucky) is much more socially acceptable than moodiness and seclusiveness.

Test-taking attitudes. Sarason (1950) suggests that the predictive value of personality (and ability) tests has been disappointing because we have neglected the many factors that influence the Subject over and above the actual content of the test – the nature of the instructions, his idea of the purpose of the test, time of day, the personality of the tester, what he has learned from previous testings, etc. (cf. also

Vernon, 1958). Sarason's own investigations (1960) have brought out the extent to which children feel threatened by, or anxious about, tests of any kind. Many researches in the area of personality are carried out with paid students or with psychology classes, who are unlikely to identify closely with the investigator's aims and may therefore perform defensively or facetiously. None the less, much work published in the 1950's–60's has shown careful attention to, and great ingenuity in manipulating, the motivation of the Subjects.

Eysenck, Cattell, Cronbach and other writers admit these difficulties with self-report tests. Eysenck, for example, has largely given up using them in his work with mental patients because he considers that hospitalized patients tend to acquire stereotyped notions of what symptoms they ought to show, after discussions with other patients or with the hospital staff. Hence these authors stress the desirability of substituting performance tests. But we cannot see the slightest reason why performance tests should not also be 'motivationally labile', to use Cattell's term. In the light of Chapter 2, we would expect a Subject to react to any kind of testing according to his impersonation – what he thinks the tester is after, what sort of personality seems to him appropriate to the occasion.* As J. A. C. Brown (1961) points out, the psychologist tends to forget that, when he is experimenting with people, he is an additional factor in the situation: hence the unexpected results of the famous Hawthorne experiment. His criticism could not fairly be applied to child psychologists, engaged in observational or experimental studies of young children (cf. Mussen, 1960). But a contributor to Mussen's Handbook – D. R. Miller – warns us of the 'grapevine effect': when a psychologist starts to apply a battery of tests to a group of subjects who know one another, e.g. a school class, they soon build up myths regarding the object of the tester, and react accordingly.

Cronbach makes the useful distinction between 'maximal performance' and 'typical performance' tests, the former being employed in testing aptitudes and achievements, the latter in personality and attitude testing. Neither term is really satisfactory, for we know that Subjects who are trying too hard in ability tests tend to perform somewhat erratically. But 'typical' or 'normal' is still more ambiguous, since the 'normal' response of any person is to 'put across' a 'suitable' personality and *not* to display his 'real' Self if he can possibly help it. Cronbach goes on to say that the tester must give the Subjects the fullest possible instructions in ability testing as to what he wants,

---

* Masling's criticism of projective techniques (cf. p. 155) applies here also.

but in personality testing he must conceal his aims. Thus he should in general avoid performance tests which constitute direct samples of a trait, such as May and Hartshorne used in studying honesty. But the tester who conceals his object is in danger of becoming so deceptive as to transgress ethical principles; or his evasions may merely encourage the Subjects to build up more distorted myths. Cronbach therefore favours more indirect tests, as do Cattell and Eysenck, e.g. tests at the perceptual, motor or autonomic levels, which appear to have no social desirability implications. If there is no incentive to distort one's performance in any acceptable direction, it is more feasible to standardize motivation or keep it constant. But in view of all the work that has been done on sets and attitudes in psychophysical, perceptual and reaction time experiments, this seems open to doubt; and the more true it is, the less relevance – one suspects – do such indirect tests bear to any important personality variable. Just because distortions are more complex and varied, or less obvious, than social desirability, it does not mean that they are negligible.

Response sets. This is Cronbach's term for another type of extraneous influence on test scores, namely stylistic consistencies, stimulated by the form of response. The present writer drew attention to this in personality inventories (cf. (6) on p. 202), but Cronbach showed that similar individual differences in response styles occur in many types of test, including tests of abilities. He also demonstrated that Subjects tend to display the same styles in different tests. Frederiksen and Messick (1959) classify some of the commonly occurring sets as follows:

    1. Acquiescence, tending to accept any personality statement as applying to oneself, or alternatively to reject all items. This may or may not be the same as preference for Trues, or for Falses, in the True-False achievement test.

    2. Evasiveness – giving many Doubtful or Indifferent responses.

    3. Extremeness – giving a preponderance of Strongly Agree or Disagree rather than intermediate responses.

    4. Inclusiveness – when the number of responses (e.g. 'Likes') is unspecified, giving a large proportion of these. Its opposite may be Criticalness in accepting words, phrases, etc., as adequate or as equivalent.

    5. Answering in terms of social desirability.

    6. Other tendencies to fake or distort, wittingly or not.

    7. Cautiousness, e.g. omitting difficult items in an ability test, vs. guessing.

    8. Preference for working at speed, or slowly.

    9. Tendency to be consistent or inconsistent where two or more re-

sponses in the same tests have practically the same content. Perhaps the authors would include such measures as Binet or Wechsler scatter under this heading, though they do not say so.

Actually there is no clear dividing line between form and content, or between extraneous or stylistic and intrinsic components of a test. Thus in testing achievement, some students do relatively better at new-type items, others at essay-examinations. These differences are stylistic, but they are also important abilities. Relative capacities at pictorial or non-verbal as against verbal test items might also be listed, though these are probably linked with spatial vs. verbal ability factors.*

Frederiksen and Messick (1959) investigated No. 4, criticalness in evaluating the similarity or acceptability of words, verbal passages, etc., hoping to bring out its personality correlates. The scores on several subtests gave positive correlations, showing that it is a fairly reliable and generalized tendency, independent of accuracy of discrimination. It overlapped (negatively) with (1) acquiescence, but yielded only tiny correlations with anxiety or other personality self-report scales. One might opine that this response trait would be largely affected by the Subjects' educational histories, i.e. what sort of standards of equivalence they had become habituated to in their own school work. Fillenbaum (1959) provides evidence of some consistency in coarseness vs. fineness of categorizing in perceptual as well as verbal comparisons.

Here however we are concerned with sets that affect personality test responses, and these appear to depend to varying degrees upon: (a) significant personality traits, (b) uninteresting stylistic or expressive habits, (c) temporary moods or reactions to the test content or instructions. Cronbach is inclined to stress the two latter sources; that is, he doubts the permanence of response sets, or their promise as indirect tests of personality.

Acquiescence. The most extensive work has been done on Acquiescence, since it became apparent that all questions in the scales for anti-semitism, authoritarianism, prejudice, conservatism, etc., used by the investigators of *The Authoritarian Personality* were worded in the same direction. This meant that scores for any of these attitudes depended on the number and extremity of acceptance responses (as all questions had to be answered on a $+3$ to -3 scale). It may well be that acquiescence and extremeness are characteristic of the authoritarian person, and rejection of dogmatic opinions or doubtingness

* The writer has presented an extensive discussion of these formal factors in achievement tests elsewhere (1958).

more characteristic of the democratic or liberal person. But it was demonstrated by Messick and Jackson and others that these scales were certainly measuring something other than would appear from their content (cf. Messick and Frederiksen, 1958; Chapman and Bock, 1958; Christie *et al.*, 1958). For when the wording of some items was reversed (so that 'prejudice' depended on a No instead of a Yes response) there was very little correlation between the two sets of items. Apparently Subjects do not realize the inconsistency of answering Yes to both the following, or No to both.

No weakness or difficulty can hold us back if we have enough will-power.

It takes more than will-power to conquer most obstacles.

By including both types of items, it is possible to score Subjects separately for acquiescence and for authoritarianism. Chapman and Bock (1958) list eight such experiments and conclude that, although there is some variation in their results, roughly 35% of the variance in F-scale scores should be attributed to 'content' of the items, about 25% to 'acquiescence', some 20% to the covariation of these components (i.e. to the fact that 'authoritarians' *do* tend to be 'acquiescent'), and the rest to error or unreliability. Note, incidentally, that this correction of attitude scores by holding acquiescence constant is analogous to the correction of personality inventory scores for social desirability by means of forced choice devices.

This does not entirely settle the matter, for it is by no means easy to devise statements with No for a prejudiced answer which are logically equivalent to statements with Yes for an answer. Christie *et al.* (1958) further point out that acquiescence is most likely to arise when statements are difficult and ambiguous: and they were able to show that it was the moderately prejudiced, rather than the extreme authoritarians or extreme liberals, who were most susceptible to saying 'Yes' regardless of content. College students are apt to be in a state of transition or uncertainty; predominantly they are moderate liberals. But if wider ranges of opinion are sampled, and if the reversed or 'No' items are well worded, the correlations between 'Yes' and 'No' prejudice scores rise. In other words the acquiescence variance becomes relatively less important. Though this implies that tests like the F-scale are not so bad as is sometimes thought, we still cannot afford to neglect the operation of response sets.

Acquiescence in personality inventories. Messick and Jackson (1958) have brought out the important influence of acquiescence on such personality inventories as the MMPI. Here the scores for the various scales, Hysteria, Schizophrenia, etc., involve both positive and negative items; i.e. the Subject has to answer Yes to some, No to others, to score highly on most scales. But it happens that a great many items are keyed Yes in some scales, fewer in others, and Messick shows that the same scales that have the largest proportions of Yes's, i.e. those most likely to involve acquiescence, are also the scales that load most highly with the first, general factor obtained by intercorrelating and factorizing (this is confirmed by Barnes, 1956). In other words, a strongly acquiescent Subject who accepts both positively and negatively worded items is likely to score highly on all scales and so to appear generally abnormal or psychotic. The second factor appears to be closely connected with social desirability, since it loads most highly these scales with many items keyed 'No'; i.e. it involves the rejection of socially unacceptable items. Messick concludes that 'three-quarters of the common variance and over half the MMPI variance is attributable to stylistic response consistencies which are apparently independent of specific item content'. However, he admits that acquiescence may to some extent be a genuine trait of the psychotic and of the authoritarian, just as rejection of social desirability is partly a genuine trait of the neurotic. Barnes adds that the 50% of specific variance in MMPI scales *not* accounted for may well be diagnostically useful.

Further light on the personality correlates of acquiescence is thrown by the common finding that the F-scale and other tests of dogmatism and conformity tend to give considerable negative correlations with academic achievement (cf. Stern, Stein and Bloom, 1956). Indeed Hyman and Sheatsley (1954) suggest that many of the differences between authoritarians and democrats claimed by Adorno (1950) are largely due to the better education of the latter. Despite suspicions to the contrary, academic staff seem to prefer, and award good grades to, students who are both tolerant and nonconformist in their opinions. Gough (1953) constructed an academic achievement key for the MMPI by picking out 36 items which most consistently discriminated good from poor college students. Though he does not point out the fact, the 'good achievement' answers to 33 of the 36 items are 'false'. True, the content of these items suggests intolerance, rigidity, irrational fears, intellectual inefficiency and related qualities, but it may be that his scale works effectively because it mostly measures non-acquiescence. Others have shown that acquiescence tends to correlate with extraversion, impulsiveness, low intelligence, and with rigidity at the Einstellung Test (Jackson *et al.*, 1957).

On the basis of a factorial study with neurotic patients, Eysenck (1962) claims that acquiescence and extremeness vs. indecisiveness affect scores on social attitude tests like the F-scale, but not those on personality inventories. However, this runs counter to many other investigations. In particular, Couch and Keniston (1960) derived a highly reliable acquiescence score from 360 positively and negatively worded attitude *and* personality items, which correlated both with the F-scale and with MMPI psychotic-factor scales. By analysing the most highly loaded items, and through intensive study of strongly acquiescent and non-acquiescent individuals, they concluded that acquiescence is by no means a mere stylistic idiosyncrasy – that it arises from important personality trends. The acquiescent person – the 'Yea-sayer' – tends consistently to yield to internal or external pressures, to accept conventional identifications and superficial values. Whereas the 'Nay-sayer' shows more Ego-control and self-determination, inhibition of immediate responses, and repression of libidinal and aggressive impulses. (Note the resemblance of this picture to Harvey, Hunt and Schroder's abstract vs. concrete type (p. 113) and to Miller and Swanson's description of the middle-class, democratically-reared adolescent (p. 101). It is reminiscent too of Jung's Thinking vs. Feeling types, of Cattell's Schizothyme-Cyclo-thyme, and of Guilford and Eysenck's rhathymic type of introversion-extraversion.) Neither pole, however, is strongly linked with neurotic traits – instability, conflict, anxiety, social introversion. Although the 'good student' or sophisticated person is apt to show both lower dogmatism and higher anxiety than the more immature or average person yet, overall, authoritarianism or dogmatism scales tend to give small positive correlations with anxiety scales (Rokeach and Fruchter, 1956). In other words, acquiescence and the social desirability tendency should be regarded as essentially unrelated.

This has been a complex discussion, and it has failed to lead to a satisfactory outcome. It implies that self-report test scores are seriously distorted in two main directions, and yet at the same time we cannot get rid of these distortions without impoverishing the scores. The situation is similar to that with halo in ratings.

Yet another source of confusion may be that some acquiescence or yea-saying scores are more liable than others to be boosted by the extremeness vs. cautiousness response set. The Californian scales, together with Rokeach's and Couch and Keniston's tests, require responses on a 7-point scale; whereas most personality inventories provide only 3 or 2 choices.

Bearings on factorially established traits. Although the findings are not clear-cut, they are very relevant to Eysenck's claim that neuroticism and extraversion-introversion are the major dimensions of personality, and to Cattell's equivalent second-order factors. In part at least these dimensions arise from social desirability and acquiescent sets. We might also recall Osgood's demonstration that people think about almost any concept in terms of the three dimensions – evaluation, strong-weak and active-passive (p. 40). Thus both the stylistic and the content components of Eysenck's and Cattell's major factors may be thought of as arising from people's common conceptual classifications or semantic space. At the moment our research techniques are inadequate for resolving these components, but at least the data presented here justify very grave suspicions of the usefulness of self-report tests. Both personality and attitude questionnaire scores, syndrome scores like those of the MMPI, and factor scores such as Cattell's or Guilford's, are influenced in many complex ways by the Subjects' linguistic and categorizing habits as well as by their varying conceptions or levels of the Self.

Performance tests might appear to escape this criticism, but do not in fact do so in so far as the Subject always guides his voluntary responses in accordance with his conceptualizations. His involuntary responses would not help us much. We can see, also, why both self-report and performance tests tend to give very inconsistent results in different studies, since the influential test-taking attitudes and sets will naturally vary considerably with the circumstances. But the main implication is that, while we can often find composites, factors or other consistencies among scores on performance or self-report tests, we can never be sure that these do not arise from some unsuspected set, or conceptualization, or habit system rather than from the trait that they appear to sample.

Campbell and Fiske (1959) have drawn attention to the prominence of what they call method factors in personality, social and applied psychological research. Psychologists set out to investigate some construct – morale in industry, anxiety, the achievement motive, etc., and appear to discover meaningful relationships so long as they confine themselves to one method or type of instrument, say ratings, *or* attitude scales and questionnaires, *or* interviews, *or* projective devices, *or* behavioural measures, but little or no agreement where the same construct is tackled by different methods. Thus self-report data on industrial *morale* tend to give negligible correlations with output, absenteeism and other objective data (Campbell and Tyler, 1957). Again, satisfaction of an employee with his job and satisfactoriness to his employers seem to be unrelated aspects of vocational *adjustment*. Campbell and Fiske list numerous examples and suggest that the proper procedure should be to study at least two traits or concepts simultaneously by at least two methods, so that the variance attributable to method or apparatus factors can be determined. Similarly McGee (1962) argues that social desirability, acquiescence, etc. can never be satisfactorily isolated or analysed by using only paper-and-pencil tests, all of which are contaminated with these response styles. What is needed is research that employs other kinds of instruments, or external criteria, for determining the nature of the paper-and-pencil styles.

Cattell (1961) is not unaware of these difficulties, and admits that his, or other psychologists', personality factors may be influenced by 'instrument factors' or other kinds of 'perturbations' (e.g. situational factors). An instrument factor is a common element among variables which resemble one another in mode of presentation or of permitted response or of scoring, but which does not extend to tests of the same construct that are couched in other modes. He is of course correct in stating that they will be revealed by properly designed experiments, but seems unduly optimistic in assuming that we know enough about them to measure them and thus effectively to remove their influence from our personality data. Still less can we agree that, with his present instruments, he can successfully disentangle 'source traits', free of all perturbations.

Chapter 13

THE CONCEPT OF VALIDITY
AND OTHER TECHNICAL
CONSIDERATIONS

A complaint frequently voiced in the two previous chapters is that current personality tests are low in validity. Why is this so, and what, indeed, do we mean by validity? Various definitions have been proposed, but they mostly imply, in essence, that a test is valid in so far as it indicates or measures whatever it is supposed to. We intend to argue a somewhat more unorthodox view – that a test measures only itself, but that it is valid in so far as it can be shown to correlate with other observable behaviour. That is, its validity lies in the inferences we are entitled to make from it. Before this position is reached, it is necessary to discuss the several types of validation which are customarily distinguished.

Face and content validity. In some instances the content of the test is sufficient guarantee of what the test measures. Reaction time tests measure reaction time; spelling tests sample the child's spelling; similarly bar-pressing in rats, sociometric choices of children, and so on. While this is quite legitimate, the trouble is that testers are continually tempted to infer beyond the behaviour itself – to regard the spelling test as measuring spelling ability in general, not just ability at that kind of test item, reaction time as a measure of 'quickness of response', sociometric choices as showing popularity or other qualities. Content validity thus shades over easily into the 'face' validity which psychometrists unanimously condemn, that is judging what a test measures by what it 'looks like', or by analysing its content subjectively. This has been the bane of vocational aptitude testing, and it was widely accepted in the early days of personality testing. Thus personality questionnaires were made up of items believed to be characteristic of the neurotic, the extravert or introvert, the liberal or conservative, etc., and were straightaway assumed to measure neuroticism or other traits, or attitudes. Educational psychologists can reasonably argue for what they term *logical validation* – that an achievement test which systematically covers the desired information and skills requires no validation, since in itself it is a better criterion of achievement than, say, teacher's marks. The weakness in this argument is that different tests in the same school subject often correlate only to a moderate degree, showing that their authors were not justified in inferring from the items they selected to all-round achievement in the subject.

At the same time, as Mosier points out (1947), the apparent or face validity of a test is of considerable importance in winning acceptance from test-users and test-takers. Both employers and candidates for employment will complain if the latter are rejected by tests that don't 'look' relevant to the job.

External validation (concurrent or predictive). For many years, then, the orthodox view was that a test must be validated against an external criterion of what it is supposed to measure. Either it should correlate with present evidence, such as ratings of the trait or aptitude concerned, or it must predict future performance, e.g. in school or a job. Insufficient distinction was drawn between 'notional' and 'empirical' criteria, since admittedly they overlap. Empirical or objective criteria are hard to come by even in the occupational field (cf. Vernon and Parry, 1949), and it is often necessary to resort to employers', supervisors' or other assessments, which are obviously open to many kinds of bias. Nevertheless there is a clear difference between such real-life facts as receiving job promotion, committing legal offences, being diagnosed as schizophrenic, benefiting from shock therapy, choosing to enter a particular occupation, etc., and estimates of traits or 'constructs' such as neurotic, intelligent, ascendant, honest, etc. We will deal with empirical validation later. Notional criteria are extremely unsatisfactory because of their inevitable subjectivity, even when they take such forms as school grades, or where, say, a new group intelligence test is validated by correlating with Stanford–Binet. We can never tell how far weak validity is due to the defects of the criterion, or to those of the test.

In a critical discussion of validation, Ebel (1961) objects to 'notional' and 'construct' validation (see below), since both imply the philosophical fallacy that we are measuring some pre-existing trait or entity in the individual, i.e. an abstraction rather than an operationally definable concept such as physical scientists or engineers measure. It suggests too that each test has some single, fixed validity, instead of recognizing that it can be used for various purposes, and that its validity will vary with the circumstances and often with the population studied. For example a mechanical aptitude test would give different correlations with success at different mechanical jobs or training courses.

Factorial validity. Even when we measure a fairly straightforward construct such as general intelligence, external validation is inapplicable. For though intelligence test items have often been selected on a basis of improvement with age, or correlations with teachers' ratings, the test is intended to replace these unsatisfactory criteria of ability. Hence, following Spearman, intelligence was thought of as the *g* factor that runs through any sub-tests or items with good content validity (i.e. any which appear to involve higher intellectual processes); and the best tests were those with the highest loadings. Similarly, many personality questionnaires, attitude scales and educational tests selected their items on a basis of internal consistency (correlations with total score).

Spearman's conception of factorial validity has been followed, in the personality field, by the present writer, by Cattell and others, as shown in the previous chapter, where its inadequacy was also pointed out. The common element running through a set of intercorrelated tests may be a response set, or halo or social desirability, rather than the presumed trait. In other words, factorial validation and internal consistency validation reduce to much the same thing as content or face validation. This is largely true also of ability factors such as Spearman's, Thurstone's or Guilford's. Factorists have presented impressive evidence for a large number of reasoning, creativity, evaluative, memory and other factor-constructs, but have seldom demonstrated that these represent anything more than factors running through particular kinds of psychological test; i.e. they are 'instrument factors' which may or may not be related to the constructs or thinking functions *with the same name* that we observe in everyday life.

Construct validation. In 1954, however, a committee of the American Psychological Association pointed out that factorial evidence could make a valuable contribution to the broader conception of construct validity. The fundamental principles of this approach were formulated by Cronbach and Meehl in 1955. The psychologist is primarily interested in such constructs or 'intervening variables' as anxiety, authoritarianism, intelligence, extraversion-introversion, defence mechanisms, etc. which are not observable, and for which no satisfactory external criterion is conceivable. He cannot do without these theoretical abstractions (cf. Chap. 9), but he can and should test out their implications in as many ways as possible if they are to retain their usefulness as explanatory principles. This is clearly true of clinical and experimental studies of personality where, for example, the investigator wishes to discover the effects of some method of upbringing, or therapeutic treatment, on the child's Super-ego structure. But it holds good also for a great deal of applied or decision-making psychology. The vocational counsellor is not much concerned with the validity of a test for predicting success in a particular occupation. If he applies a mechanical comprehension test he wants it to correlate consistently with a wide variety of indices of 'mechanical-mindedness'. And in the personality area, he requires information on such constructs as the counsellee's main interests and goals, his persistence in pursuing them, his adaptation to different social situations, etc. Even the personnel selector, who is more likely to adopt an empirical approach, tends to think of the job criteria and the selection procedure in terms of underlying personality dispositions and generalized rather than specific abilities.

Construct validation implies testing out the theory underlying the test, or determining the psychological meaning of the test score. For example, if 'sociability' is a measurable construct, there should be factorial consistency. Sociability should manifest itself in several types of test which intercorrelate positively, but which do not correlate with other factors or variables which are hypothesized as distinct. A valid test of sociability would be expected to show some, though not necessarily high, correlations with acquaintances' judgments, sociometric choices, etc. Experimental evidence that people tested as sociable react differently to certain situations from those tested as unsociable would also be of value. Group differences, introspective analysis and longitudinal data can also be incorporated: thus children brought up in one way should be more sociable than those with a different upbringing. Eysenck's work on extraversion-introversion conceived as excitation-inhibition is another good example of construct validation. If the predictions from the theory are not confirmed it must, of course, be abandoned or modified. But one would expect a whole network of relationships with the construct to be elaborated and verified; and it is in terms of these relationships that the construct, and the tests devised for it, are accepted as valid.

Limitations of construct validation. This approach has considerably clarified the work of the personality tester. It has been particularly useful in projective testing, where the classical approach to validation of, e.g., Rorschach scores, was most inadequate (Chap. 10). Yet it is not without its dangers, since theoretical speculation is apt to get out of touch with experimental verification. Thus Adorno *et al.* presented a wide range of supporting evidence for the construct of authoritarianism, but failed to realize that much of what they were measuring with the F-scale was acquiescence. Similarly, Jesser and Hammond (1957) point out that a test such as the Taylor Manifest Anxiety scale, which is supposed to measure the Hullian construct of anxiety as a drive, is based more on convenience of administration than on the properties of the construct (cf. p. 193). The 'naming fallacy' or overgeneralization, so characteristic of content validation, is by no means eliminated. However, the construct validity approach provides a way out, since any psychologist is at liberty to propose an alternative theory, and to devise experiments which demonstrate its superior explanatory value, as Messick and Jackson did with the F-scale. The most valuable feature of this approach is that it calls for statements of explicit hypotheses: these can fairly readily be retested by other workers, or further corollaries can be tried out, so that the evidence is cumulative.

There is a very real difficulty, however, when the evidence is necessarily circumstantial or indirect, in deciding standards of acceptability. When validity was regarded simply as a correlation with a criterion we at least thought we knew how valid for practical predictions was a correlation of say 0·6. But how complete must the confirmation of a construct be? We have already criticized the subjectivity of Eysenck's and Cattell's standards of acceptance of factorial evidence. Many other authors are much less cautious.

An extremely common type of investigation is to devise a test to measure some construct, to pick out the extreme scorers on the test, and to show that the highs and lows differ significantly in their responses to certain hypothesized situations. Having found some small differences in the expected direction, the authors immediately seem to assume that the test is a valid measure of all that is implied by their construct. Such differences may be equivalent to correlations of around 0·2, and although very high figures might not have been anticipated, such low ones obviously tell us scarcely anything. They mean, in fact, that 96% of whatever the test measures is unaccounted for.

Another danger with the extreme-group technique is pointed out by Loevinger (1955), namely that we seldom know whether the construct can reasonably be regarded as a linear continuum. For example, very strongly aggressive children and very non-aggressive ones may both be highly insecure in their personalities. Thus differences found between them may not be true of differences between moderately aggressive and non-aggressive scorers, for whom the test is chiefly required.

Conclusion. While accepting the usefulness of the construct validity approach, we would prefer to formulate validity rather differently, along similar lines to Ebel (1961). We share his distrust of abstract constructs (except as useful guides to research), but would suggest that the difference between these and operational or concrete qualities is merely a matter of degree. Many of the psychologist's measurements, as we have seen, require no more validation than the physicist's – they are direct records of the behaviour in which he is interested. But when he measures, say, reaction time and calls it a test of 'quickness of reaction' he is in fact talking about a construct, albeit not a highly abstract one. It is just as necessary for him as it is for the tester of 'anxiety' and the like, to explore the correlates of his test, what conditions affect it, what other aspects of the generalized ability – quickness of reaction – it does not cover.

Fundamentally, then, a test measures itself, and its further validity rests entirely on its established relations to other behaviours. It is the network of its relations to other variables and to real-life situations that gives its meaning. We can follow the construct validity approach provided we realize the need always to return ultimately to external data of some kind. A valid test must give meaningful results; that is, it must link up with various kinds of observable behaviour which have been predicted from the construct. Thus intelligence tests are acceptable, not merely because they conform to a factorial model (useful as this is), but because they do correlate with educational and other kinds of achievement, and with observers' judgments, in a logical way. Many attitude and interest tests, despite their weaknesses such as fakability and prominent response sets, measure up well to similar real-life criteria, whereas personality inventories, performance and projective tests usually don't – however promising the underlying constructs or the factorial confirmation. Nevertheless the personality inventory is entirely valid if it is accepted as a sample of the person's Self-concept at the topmost or 'public' level. It is only when it is generalized beyond this to some much more abstract construct such as neuroticism that additional evidence is needed.

The value of a test rests not only on the richness of its correlates, but also on their stability. Thus although the construct of intelligence is open to various criticisms, the Terman–Merrill test not only correlates with many kinds of behaviour which we might expect to be affected by intelligence, but succeeds in doing so almost everywhere it is applied to almost any kind of English-speaking children. Mannheim and Wilkins (1955) point out similarly that the indices they find most useful in the actuarial prediction of recidivism are those that have proved predictive in many studies of delinquents in many parts of the world – previous offences, broken home background, unstable employment record, etc. This notion of the stability and range of predictions differs from the psychometrist's classical conceptions of reliability and validity, and there is as yet no accepted means of measuring it.

Cattell (1957) recognizes that, in personality testing, we need to take account not only of repeat reliability (freedom from short-term function fluctuation) and internal consistency or homogeneity (all the component parts of the test measuring the same thing – which he considers often to be overstressed), but also of administrator and scorer reliability (stability with different testers). But even when these sources of error are controlled, instability may result from test-taking attitudes and sets, and there is no guarantee how far the test results are generalizable.

ACTUARIAL OR EMPIRICAL VALIDATION

In view of the apparent vagueness of the construct approach to testing, there is considerable justification for those tough-minded psychometrists who distrust theorizing about the traits or mental processes of testees, and advocate going straight from their responses to an external objective criterion. It does not concern them whether subjects are 'telling the truth' or 'acting naturally', provided the responses can be shown to be predictive. Also, as mentioned earlier, the criterion is not some 'notional' quality, but an observable, objectively recorded, piece of behaviour. The empirical approach to test validation and test construction manifests itself in a number of guises.

1. *Actuarial selection or prediction procedures.* Several tests or indices that may be related to achievement, prognosis or some other outcome are followed up, and those with the highest validities are picked for future use. As pointed out in Chapter 5, the efficiency of prediction can be maximized if the intercorrelations of the predictors are also known, since they can then be appropriately weighted. As in any multiple regression or discriminant function procedure, some variables may have very low validities by themselves and actually receive negative weights, and yet be useful as 'suppressors'. This can

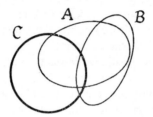

Fig. 4. Hypothetical test correlations.

be illustrated by Figure 4, where the circle C represents the criterion, and the ellipses A and B are two tests. A overlaps the criterion considerably; it has good validity and is likely to receive a high weight or regression coefficient. B has little validity, but it correlates highly with the *invalid* component of A. Hence if some fraction of the B scores is *subtracted* from the A scores, the validity of A will be improved.

A simplified version of this occurs in the MMPI, where the scale scores may be corrected by subtracting some fraction of the K (defensiveness) score, with the object of reducing the tendencies to undue self-depreciation or undue negativism. There is considerable doubt, however, as to its effectiveness. Theoretically, we could similarly adjust any inventory or attitude scale for social desirability, acquiescence, etc., if we had a suitable external criterion.

2. *Criterion analysis.* Eysenck's procedure is essentially similar. A general factor is found running through a battery of tests which – with or without rotation – closely matches the correlations of the tests with the neurotic vs. normal dichotomy, or other criterion. A simple weighting of the tests based on their factor loadings is likely to be almost as effective a predictor as the full regression equation.

3. *Differential and prognostic tests.* A complex test such as the Rorschach yields numerous scores and indices, and those signs which

best differentiate mental patients who benefit under shock therapy from those who do not benefit are picked out. The mere sum of these signs, or a simple weighting, is used for future prognosis. Similarly, a series of perceptual, motor or autonomic tests, which may or may not appear to have meaningful connections with the criterion, may be combined empirically.

The same procedure, in effect, was used by Strong in developing scoring keys for his Vocational Interest Blank and by Hathaway and others in constructing MMPI scales. Here the main features are that multiple criteria are employed, and that the tests contain very large numbers of items. Full regression analysis would not be possible, but simple weightings are calculated for the positive, negative and doubtful responses to every item, based on the extent to which they differentiate any occupational-interest group (or pathological group). Thus some responses are keyed for several of the criteria, others for one or two, and some items are still retained though they have so far shown little or no differential value.

Another type of empirically scored test is the Biographical Inventory. This was almost the only motivational or personality test that was found to be of any use for selecting USAAF pilots in World War II (Guilford and Lacey, 1947). It consists of a large number of multiple-choice items dealing with the candidates' background, educational and vocational career, interests, etc., most of which are formulated initially on the basis of hunches that they might be relevant to the qualities which differentiate a good from a poor pilot. They need, however, to be validated in a very large group – preferably in several comparable groups – before a scoring key is established for the significant items. The technique has had considerable application in the American services, and in other situations involving large populations.

Berg (1959) makes the interesting suggestion that items for any of these differential tests should *not* be chosen for initial face validity. For example interest items might differentiate pathological groups, and pathological items differentiate occupational groups all the better than those where the Subject can see how his responses may be scored. This is much less illogical than it sounds, the point being that, if we want to differentiate one group of people from another, we are likely to do better with items where their responses tend to deviate from the norm than with those where everyone answers pretty much alike. Berg describes tests based on preferences and response sets in judging meaningless drawings, claiming that these differentiate successfully among nosological groups (cf. Barnes, 1955). However, we shall see shortly that there are strong grounds for doubting the effectiveness of this extreme empiricism.

4. *Paired item measures.* McQuitty (1953) has suggested that differences in response patterns to pairs of items within a single inventory would provide an objective approach to personality measurement. For example pairs can be found which most Subjects answer alike (either Yes or No), but abnormal Subjects more frequently answer them differently (one Yes, the other No). He has proposed other techniques for empirical differentiation (1959), but seems to have had little following, presumably because of the tediousness of analysing response patterns.

5. *Forced-choice rating scales or inventories.* These consist of pairs (or blocks) of items, one member of each pair having been proved to have higher empirical validity than the other. The members are, however, equated on Social Desirability, or other variables which the tester desires to eliminate. Clearly this is an alternative to the suppressor procedure shown in Figure 4 for eliminating unwanted sources of variance.

As Edwards (1959) points out, the construct and empirical approaches were combined in the *Study of Values* and in his own *Personal Preference Schedule.* On the basis of psychological theories regarding important human values and needs, respectively, items were constructed, and uniform popularity or desirability for the alternatives within any item was ensured by empirical trials. Then the internal consistency of each response with the total score for the construct was investigated, and the correlates of the scores with a wide range of other, logically related, variables were explored.

6. *Moderating variables.* It has been suggested that the personality variables measured by inventories or other tests, although they fail to correlate consistently with some outcome such as educational or vocational achievement, may nevertheless indirectly affect or 'moderate' the operation of other predictors. In other words, different personality 'types' may apply or use their abilities differently.

For example, Furneaux (1962) has given the Maudsley Personality Inventory to successive batches of engineering students, and classified them into those above and below average on the neuroticism-stability and extraversion-introversion scales. He claims very different correlations between ability measures and subsequent achievement in these different personality groups. Among stable extraverts the predictive value of ability tests is quite high; they are uncomplicated people whose educational success depends mainly on their aptitudes. But among unstable introverts, correlations are around zero, and previous attainment provides a much better prediction. Stable introverts and unstable extraverts tend to be intermediate, and a combination of aptitude and attainment measures gives a better basis for prediction. Similarly, Frederiksen and Melville (1954) used reading speed and comprehension tests to classify students into 'compulsive' and 'non-compulsive' groups, and found higher correlations between interests (as measured by the Strong VIB) and achievement in the latter group. Obsessional students, it was suggested, will work hard at anything, whereas the others are more dependent on interest in a subject if they are to do well at it.

Neither of these claims has yet been confirmed by independent investigations. But clearly such an approach, through patterns of scores, could have important bearings in counselling.

Shrinkage and instability in empirical validity. It has long been realized that the multiple correlation of a battery of tests with a criterion is lower in practice than when it is initially calculated. Both the validity coefficients of the separate tests and their intercorrelations are subject to chance errors, particularly when the group of Subjects is small, and regression analysis capitalizes on these errors. Thus, if test A has an unduly high validity in the initial group, and test B an unduly low coefficient, the former will be overweighted, the latter underweighted, in the regression equation. Applying these weights to a fresh group, the errors are likely to alter, hence the multiple correlation with the criterion drops. Wherry has proposed a formula for estimating the consequent shrinkage. But a better precaution, favoured by most psychometrists, is that of 'cross-validation': the effective validity of a battery of tests is assessed, not from the group on which the weights are calculated, but from a fresh group.*

Just the same difficulty applies to all the procedures mentioned above. Indeed it is all the more serious when test items or Rorschach signs and the like are validated, since their reliabilities are lower than those of most sub-tests, the error component of their validity coefficients larger. In a test such as Strong's, this matters little, both because so many items are keyed and because Strong normally insists on very large groups (500 or so representatives of any occupation) in working out his weights. In many Rorschach sign studies

---

* Various refinements have been suggested, such as splitting the initial group into two halves, applying the weights from each half to calculating the multiple correlation in the other half, and then averaging the two sets of weights, or accepting only those sub-tests (or items) which yield significant weights in both halves (cf. Mosier et al., 1951).

it is fatal, since the number of patients representing any particular syndrome is likely to be small. This was true also for several of the original MMPI standardization groups, hence such keys have failed to stand up to cross-validation.

Unfortunately the stability of validity coefficients and regression weights is even poorer than would be expected from statistical consideration of chance errors. Even in personnel selection on a basis of ability tests, remarkable variations occur between apparently similar groups, presumably because of unanticipated and uncontrollable variations in the conditions of testing or in the criterion (e.g. the selected employees who are followed up may be assessed by different instructors and this alters the relative validities of the selection tests).* Variability is even more marked in the personality field, as pointed out in the previous Chapter, on account of variations in the Subjects' test-taking attitudes, and the unreliability of any criteria based on ratings, psychiatric diagnoses and the like.

Another aspect of this problem is that any difference or ratio scores (or the regression coefficients of suppressor variables) have lower reliabilities than those of the variables from which they are derived. This is simply demonstrated by the formula for the reliability of differences between scores in two tests, A and B, when the reliabilities of the initial tests are r_{AA} and r_{BB}.

$$r_{(A-B)(A-B)} = \frac{r_{AA} + r_{BB} - 2r_{AB}}{2(1 + r_{AB})}$$

Suppose A is an impure test of authoritarianism mixed with acquiescence, whose reliability is 0·85, B a pure measure of acquiescence with a reliability 0·65, and that the two intercorrelate 0·50. Then if we try to correct the A test by subtracting B, the reliability of the A − B score would be only 0·167. Perhaps a less extreme, yet similar, drop would occur if we held acquiescence constant by partial or multiple correlation or by the forced-choice item technique. Psychologically this shows itself in the reluctance of Subjects to answer forced-choice items (or raters to judge people on forced-choice scales); they feel that their choices are unreliable when they are prevented from discriminating in terms of their habitual response sets (social desirability, acquiescence, halo, etc.). In practice, tests of this type with 'built-in' corrections never do retain their purity. Although the Edwards PPS forced-choice items were chosen to be of equal social desirability, the scores still show some social desir-

* An example of this is described by Vernon (1958, p. 30).

ability influence, though less than in ordinary inventories. The reason is, of course, that the correlations of each item with the desired trait and with social desirability, used in item selection, were unstable; chance errors were capitalized, and when the test is applied to a fresh group, trait-correlations tend to drop, social desirability ones to rise.*

The US Army psychologists have unrivalled experience in the construction of forced-choice and other empirical inventories, e.g. for officer selection, though most of their work has not reached the standard journals. Osborn et al. (1954) suggest that forced-choice items should be as valid as, or more valid than, 'straight' items, particularly in a long test, because their intercorrelations are lower (their common social desirability variance having been removed). However, other reports suggest that they are dissatisfied with forced-choice or other types of corrected scores, because they do not retain their validities. 'Straight' inventories at least stand up fairly well to repeated use in fairly varied contexts, even if their scores are often distorted by social desirability.

Why do interests tests such as Strong's and even forced-choice ones like the Study of Values and the Kuder Preference Record retain more stable validities than tests of personality traits? The reason is surely that in these the tester wants to measure self-concepts – the Subject's underlying notions of his own business, artistic or other consistent interests and attitudes; whereas in the personality inventory such self-concepts and attitudes are treated as disturbing response sets; and for the statistical reasons we have outlined, any attempt to remove or control them is likely to be disappointing. Hence we cannot agree that Berg's approach (p. 221), which wilfully disregards self-concepts, is capable of yielding tests with satisfactory stability.† It is noteworthy that in those instances cited by Meehl where actuarial prediction has worked well, the psychometrist's raw material has consisted of surface characteristics, having high face validity, not of indirect, and subtle tests.

Pearson and Swenson (1951) found that an MMPI scoring key based on item-responses of schizophrenics who improved, or failed to improve, with ECT broke down when cross-validated. However, scores derived

---

* The same kind of thing may have happened with the Davis–Eells Games test of intelligence, where the items were chosen to eliminate social class differences, yet the test continues to correlate with social class.

† Barnes's (1955) thorough cross-validation of the Perceptual Reaction test appears to contradict this statement. There seems, however, to be no recent evidence that the scoring keys are standing up to use with other groups.

from some of the relatively stable scales did show significant prognostic value in a new group of patients. It is noteworthy, too, that one of the best cross-validated keys for the MMPI is Barron's (1953a) scale of 68 items which he regards as measuring Ego-strength. The items tend to contrast feelings of well-being, personal adequacy and good reality contacts with broodiness, seclusiveness, repressive feelings and fatigue. We may interpret this as a self-concept which tends to be consistently predictive of good prognosis among abnormals, and of strong resources among normals.

A particularly good example of the failure of the empirical approach is supplied by Ryan's (1960) excellent investigation of teacher-success.

The concept of 'the good teacher' is, of course, complex and vague; and hundreds of studies of teacher-selection and teacher-competence have broken down through inadequacies in the criterion. However, Ryans arrived at well-defined and usable criteria by factorizing observations of their classroom behaviour. Three factors or dimensions of behaviour were obtained, which could be assessed with high reliability:

X. Understanding, friendly vs. aloof, egocentric.
Y. Responsible, business-like, systematic vs. evading, unplanned, slip-shod.
Z. Stimulating, imaginative, enthusiastic vs. dull, routine.

He and his colleagues then set out to construct tests which would correlate with or give useful predictions of these criteria. Extremely varied techniques were exploited, including tests of attitudes, biographical inventory items, word association, sentence completion, pictorial situations, etc., the only restriction being that they should be readily applicable in group form, and objectively scorable. Each sub-test, and all the items within each sub-test, were given repeated trials. Yet the best validation for the combined battery obtained with fresh groups of teachers averaged around 0·37 at the elementary and 0·31 at the secondary levels. And when the tests were applied for predicting success 2 or 3 years ahead (e.g. in student selection), the mean correlations with X, Y and Z ratings dropped to around 0·12.

Maybe teacher-traits are particularly difficult to assess with printed group tests, or they are greatly affected by situational influences, or are very unstable over the years of teacher training. But similar difficulties are likely to arise in predicting personality characteristics in almost any occupational or educational context. And if Ryans, with considerable financial and staff backing, and with great ingenuity in test construction and psychometric sophistication, could do no better, then the prospects for empirical measurement of personality traits in general, along the lines envisaged by Berg, Guilford, or Eysenck, are not very bright.

Actuarial prediction. In Chapter 5 we found that the actuarial approach to prediction was limited to 'recurrent situations' where the type of population, the conditions of testing and the nature of the criterion all remain stable. The above discussion raises the question whether it is not indeed so inflexible that it can only exceptionally be applied in practice. Take the classical example of a weighted battery of aptitude tests for vocational selection purposes. It is no use calculating the weights by following up a group of one or two hundred candidates since, as we have seen, they vary much more from one group to another than would follow from ordinary statistical unreliability. Only occasionally, as in the war-time selection of USAAF pilots, in the selection of pupils for English secondary grammar schools, or of American college students, can large samples be obtained repeatedly, so as to iron out these irregularities. Once the procedure is put into effect, it cannot be altered since only those candidates who pass the tests are accepted; and though we can follow them up to try to ensure that the battery of predictors is still effective, the correlations within a selected group provide rather inaccurate estimates of the correlations among unselected candidates (on which the weightings must be based). If we wish to introduce a new test, or if the kind of candidate alters, or the job for which we are selecting changes, it is necessary to start again from scratch and to follow through hundreds of unselected candidates before fixing the revised weightings. Obviously the difficulties are enhanced when personality variables rather than aptitude test scores are involved, since these tend to be even more unstable.

Maybe this sounds unduly gloomy, and it is true that regression weights can alter over quite wide limits without markedly reducing the multiple correlation of the predictors with the criterion. But if we look at the instances from the literature where actuarial prediction or empirically constructed tests have worked, we will realize that they are decidedly limited.

Conventional tests of educational attainments and intelligence are more often constructed on a basis of face or content validity and internal consistency than by selecting items against an external criterion. However, such tests work well over a considerable range of contexts, with a wide variety of populations, because such abilities possess a relatively high degree of generality and stability. Almost any combination of school grades or attainment tests with almost any intelligence tests gives fairly efficient predictions of all-round educational capacity over the next few years. But educational psychologists have been notably less successful in devising tests or batteries for giving trustworthy predictions of more specific outcomes (e.g. grades in engineering courses), or for differential placement of students.

We have commented already on the good results consistently obtained with certain attitude and interest tests, attributing this to the fact that they measure rather stable and broad self-concepts. Moreover these contain large numbers of items, hence variations in their item validities in somewhat different populations or contexts do not matter much. A rather different principle enters in the actuarial prediction of delinquency and recidivism: relatively few symptoms or indices may be selected, but they tend to be highly objective (not, like test responses, dependent on the Subjects' attitudes). It is usually possible to investigate large numbers so as to stabilize the weights, and the criterion is a well-defined and stable one.

It seems unlikely that actuarialism will have many applications in abnormal psychology in view of the subjectivity of diagnosis and of criteria of 'improvement', and the paucity of stable symptoms and other predictors. Its limitations in vocational psychology, e.g. in making professional and managerial appointments, are no less obvious. Taft (1959) agrees that in most selection or other situations where decisions have to be reached about individuals, the information regarding each person may have to be synthesized by clinical, subjective methods, because no formula for empirical weighting exists. Empirical techniques are likely to find their main application in mass-screening procedures, though even here – Taft notes – validities show an unfortunate susceptibility to 'drift'.

None the less some progress has been made, for example, in isolating consistent patterns of MMPI scale scores (Hathaway and Meehl, 1951; Dahlstrom and Welsh, 1960) which are associated with psychopathological syndromes. But this is very different from purely empirical selection of items to yield a scale for mechanically diagnosing a syndrome: rather it is a type of construct validation. It may be that such patterns, combined with symptom ratings scales such as Wittenborn's, background items, scores on the Wechsler intelligence scales, etc., will enable us to approximate to something like the actuarial tables or cookbooks which Meehl (1956) envisages using in clinical diagnosis. Certainly the search should be continued. Furthermore, almost any actuarial research contributes useful information regarding the correlates of personality tests which contribute to their construct validity. What we must insist, however, is that empirically constructed tests and actuarial procedures show little prospect of providing the answers to all problems of personality assessment, as many contemporary psychometrists would have us believe.

OTHER PROBLEMS OF VALIDATION

Selection ratios and base-rates. The older, rather narrow conception of validation as finding the correlation between a test and some external criterion or outcome is giving way in other directions. In many respects the validity of a test varies with the context in which it is used. Of special importance are the Selection Ratio in personnel studies – that is the proportion of persons to be selected from the given population, and the corresponding conception of the 'base-rate' – the normal frequency of occurrence of a specified type of patient – in the clinical field. Account has to be taken too of the relative seriousness of selecting the wrong individuals on the one hand, or rejecting the wrong ones on the other. The 'pay-off' of the method of selection – its usefulness in any particular set of circumstances – can generally be calculated, but it will alter greatly with different circumstances, as the following illustrations show:

Suppose that 50% of applicants are normally suitable for admission to college, and that we apply a selection test or examination to try to pick them out. An ideal test would give these results:

		College success	Failure	
Test	High	50	0	50
	Low	0	50	50
		50	50	100

All those scoring high on the test, but none of those scoring low, are later found to perform satisfactorily.

Now when the validity coefficient of the test takes various lower values, the numbers correctly selected and rejected are as shown overleaf.

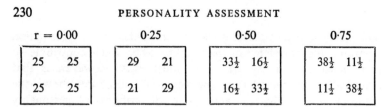

r = 0·00		0·25		0·50		0·75	
25	25	29	21	33½	16½	38½	11½
25	25	21	29	16½	33½	11½	38½

It can be seen that a test with low validity (0·25) brings about little improvement over pure chance selection: only 29 of the high scorers instead of 25 do well; and 21 of the 50 are wrongly selected, 21 others wrongly rejected. As the validity improves, the proportion correctly selected rises from 50 to 58%, then 67% and 77%, though even at r = 0·75 it falls far short of 100%.

Now contrast this situation with one where the Selection Ratio is only 1 in 10, that is only 10% of the general run of candidates are suitable for the work of the college. The corresponding tables are (approximately) as follows:

		r = 0·00			0·25		0·50		0·75		1·00	
Tests	High	1	9	10	2	8	3	7	5	5	10	0
	Low	9	81	90	8	82	7	83	5	85	0	90
		10	100	100								

Here only 20% of those scoring high on the test do well in college if the validity is low; and it is not until the test reaches a validity of 0·75 that half the persons selected are likely to be successful.

A parallel situation occurs in appointing a manager or a professor. Say there are 10 applicants and 1 is chosen, and the validity of our interviewing procedure is only 0·50. Then there are but 3 chances in 10 that we will pick the best man. Again in the clinical diagnostic situation: suppose we know that 10% of cases in a general mental hospital are likely to be brain-damaged, and we apply a test to detect them. We would actually make more erroneous than correct diagnoses of brain damage by using the test, unless we knew that its validity exceeded 0·75. When the base-rate is 10% (and in many diagnostic situations it is lower still), it might be preferable to decide that none of the patients were brain-damaged, for then we would be wrong about 10% of all patients; whereas if our test had a validity of 0·5, we would certainly be wrong in 14% of all cases.* There is an even

* Meehl and Rosen (1955) bring out the importance of considering base-rates and show, by applying Bayes theorem, that the ratio of the proportion of 'false

wider implication: the psychiatrist and clinical psychologist, as we have seen, specialize in making 'rare' judgments, i.e. in diagnosing personality dispositions that seldom if ever occur among other patients. Clearly they are far more apt to be wrong than when they infer commonly occurring characteristics.

Thus when we are considering the interests of the selectee – is the right man chosen – correct selection is more difficult the more the Selection Ratio or base-rate departs from 50%. If however we consider the interests of the selector, who mainly wishes to improve the quality of those selected, the situation is quite different. A small Selection Ratio is an advantage. In our first example, the test with a validity of 0·75 raised the proportion of good students only from 50 to 77%: whereas in the second example the same test raises the proportion from 10 to 50%, and even the test with a validity of 0·25 roughly doubles the number of good selectees. This may well have some bearing on the clinician's (or the layman's) conviction that he is right when he does make a judgment of a unique, or rare, personality pattern.

The 'cut-off' level. So far we have assumed that the test is used to cut off the exact numbers of cases whom we expect to be successful (or who fall within a given diagnostic category). But obviously the cut-off can be raised or lowered. Thus when a screening test with validity 0·5 is used to refer recruits for psychiatric interview, and it is believed that roughly 10% of all recruits are likely to be seriously maladjusted, we know that picking the 10% highest scorers will give us the same table as before:

		Actual maladjusted	Not	
Test	High	3	7	10
	Low	7	83	90
		10	90	100

As the test has caught only 3 out of 10 genuinely maladjusted

positives' to 'true' must be less than the base-rate, for the test to be worthwhile. With a validity of 0·5, our test picks out 3/10 of the 'trues' (those who should receive the treatment) and 7/90 of the 'falses': $\frac{0.078}{0.30} = 0.29$, and the base-rate is only 0·10.

The improvement in quality of selectees by applying tests of different validities, at different selection ratios and cut-offs, is discussed by Arbous (1955).

Q

(along with 7 out of 90 false positives), we try lowering the borderline, with the following results:

Top 20	5	15	40	7½	32½	60	9	51
Test Bottom 80	5	75	60	2½	57½	40	1	39

In order to pick up nine-tenths of the genuinely maladjusted, we have to adopt such a low cut-off that there are now 51 out of 90 false positives. Clearly it is a matter of judgment whether it is worse to misdiagnose a lot of normal individuals than it is to miss out several of those who should have been diagnosed as potential neurotics. The same situation occurs in university selection, where the selectors hope to reduce the numbers of weak students by raising entrance test standards. Though they may succeed in decreasing the failures, they do so only at the cost of rejecting an even larger number of potentially successful students (cf. Parkyn, 1959).

It should be noted that all the above calculations have assumed the validity of our test or procedure to be consistent throughout its range. In practice, however, tests often show non-linear relations with criteria, so that they work better, or worse, at some Selection Ratios and cut-off points than at others. While this may mean that some form of non-parametric statistics should be employed in checking the value of the test, it does not affect our main argument that this value depends greatly on the set-up in which the test is used.

Another statistical condition of the utmost importance in interpreting aptitude and achievement test correlations is the heterogeneity of the population studied (cf. Vernon and Parry, 1949). Its implications in the personality field have received less attention, probably because we seldom have very definite knowledge of restriction of range on personality variables. But we should certainly expect lower reliabilities, validities and factor loadings in, say, a group of neurotics than in an unselected normal group, or among college-student Subjects than in the population at large.

Incremental and differential validities. Cronbach and Gleser (1957) have pointed out that in many decision situations we may be misled by considering only the validity of a test in isolation. Thus in selection, certain information is often very readily accessible to the selectors such as age, education, social class background and vocational experience, and these items by themselves go a long way in making good predictions. Any additional specialized technique should therefore make contributions over and above this information, and this implies that the *non-overlap* of the technique with previous information is as important as, or more important than, its own correlation with the criterion. Thus an intelligence test may show better correlations than Rorschach or interview judgments with vocational suitability. Yet the intelligence test may merely cover much the same ground as the level of education achieved, whereas the Rorschach or the interview may throw light on quite independent qualities and therefore be more useful, provided it is not overweighted in the prediction equation. (We have already touched on this point in connection with the Stereotype and Differential Accuracy of personality judgments.)

This is particularly likely to happen in situations involving differential prediction, i.e. distinguishing candidates suitable for one type of work from those suitable for another, or in differential diagnosis of patients. Here the value of a selection instrument resides as much in the *lowness* of its correlation with one outcome as in the *highness* of its correlation with the other: and its independence from other predictors is crucial. Thus interests tests are generally more useful than ability tests in predicting relative success at different university courses, although their correlations with good grades may be low. For interest in science is likely to be negatively correlated with interest in Arts, and to correlate more strongly with science than with Arts grades. Whereas achievements in the two types of course, and aptitude tests for such courses, are all likely to show substantial positive correlations. Again, then, we might expect the clinical interviewer or projective tester, who can judge complex patterns of personality characteristics, to be at an advantage over the psychometrist with his limited battery of objective predictors. However, this is offset, as we have seen, by the rarity of particular patterns and, of course, by the distortions arising from his 'built-in' personality theories, stereotypes and halo.

Sequential and adaptive treatments. Cronbach and Gleser too are responsible for demonstrating that the worth of tests or other procedures depends on the way their results are applied. In general the traditional irreversible or once-for-all selection is better avoided, since it is more efficient to narrow down a decision progressively or sequentially. This is already common practice in education, employment and elsewhere. Thus students take a variety of courses in school or college to discover their interests and abilities before they finally specialize on a major field. The business or other employees often gain experience of many aspects of the firm's work before their particular job is decided: a man 'tries out' many female acquaintances before proposing marriage; and most psychotherapy is frankly exploratory. Not only is the field of choice reduced by this approach, so that finer discrimination becomes possible, but also predictions based on highly relevant and recent situations, i.e. on 'work samples', are naturally more valid than any based on more distant and more general tests or other data. A. Rodger (1961) has advocated what he calls 'planned procrastination' as a major principle of vocational guidance.

The situation differs once more if the 'treatments' accorded to persons who have been sorted out by tests are adapted to their abilities and personalities. This too has long been realized in education, where the teacher uses a different approach to brighter or duller children in the same class, as well as in employment and clinical practice. Final decisions, based on inadequate evidence, can often be avoided if rethought in terms of training and adaptation rather than selection.

Conclusion. The main concern of this Chapter has been to note the limitations, both of the traditional notion of a personality test as measuring a certain trait more or less validly, and of the actuarial model of constructing tests or using them to predict specific outcomes. We recognize that actuarial prediction still provides the most efficient way of using information about people under certain restricted circumstances, but it has little bearing on the enormous variety of other situations in which some form of personality assessment is involved. Other approaches to assessment are not, then, merely inefficient approximations to the actuarial model. Cronbach and Gleser, Cattell, McQuitty and other statistical writers have pointed the way to a number of alternative models, though too little use has been made of them so far for their implications to be fully realized.

Earlier (p. 86) we admitted that a computer can always sort and synthesize complex information better than the human mind. But this is only true if the computer can be fed with definite instructions on the relevance of each piece of information to specified outcomes. At the moment, personality diagnosis and assessment take place in such varied circumstances and with such varied purposes that we are practically forced to rely on the practitioner to interpret and weigh up the relevance of test, interview and other personality data. This is dangerously subjective, however, and our practitioner would be well advised to make as much use as possible of information which possesses high construct validity, i.e. single tests, factor batteries or other data which have rich and stable correlates or whose psychological meaning is known. Any such instrument helps to provide the counsellor and his client with some relatively fixed points, and to reduce their dependence on more subjective evaluations of the evidence. At the same time the counsellor is entitled to interpret other observational and interview material which we do not yet know how to validate, but which may well prove superior to more objective data in exploratory, adaptive and other non-actuarial types of diagnoses.

Chapter 14

THE PERSONALITY SYSTEM

Trait theory. The difficult problem of defining personality was by-passed in Chapter 1, by phrasing it: 'What sort of a person is so-and-so; what is he like?' However, we cannot shirk the issue any longer. Not only the naïve and the depth-psychological, but also the psycho-metric, approaches to personality rest on the assumption that it consists fundamentally of internal dispositions, functional unities or causal factors within the individual which account for his behaviour. It makes little difference whether we call these traits, interests and attitudes, or talk of factors or dimensions, or employ more theoretical constructs such as a strong Super-ego, defence mechanisms, need for achievement, level of aspiration and the like. All these qualities are thought of as fairly stable and generalized dispositions which are properties or possessions of the person in much the same sense as his skin colour, or his weak heart, or his musical talent.

Trait theory, as we shall call it, derives a good deal of plausibility from its accordance with the way we normally describe and explain people in daily life. In Chapter 2 we saw that descriptions or measurements of behaviour as such do not tell us the personality. It is the intentions or dispositions underlying particular acts that we want to know, and traits or factors seem to provide the explanation. Many psychometrists would not go as far as Cattell in regarding factors as causal entities, nor as basic components analogous to the elements in a chemical compound. But even if they are regarded primarily as useful abstractions or descriptive categories, they are presumed to reflect the underlying dynamic structure of the individual. Usually they are sufficiently similar to the traits the layman talks about for the tester or counsellor to be able to communicate readily with his client (whereas depth constructs, as we have seen, are relatively implausible). Yet at the same time they have the advantage of better definition and distinctiveness than many of the layman's categories. Eysenck is probably justified in his belief that if we could accurately measure half a dozen or so major dimensions, we could do a better

236

job in most personality assessment situations than we can by naïve intuition or clinical methods.

Unique traits. That any system of description in terms of traits or factors is an oversimplification would be generally admitted. No one behaves in accordance with his imputed traits all the time. They give too crude an indication of how he reacts in any particular context and, though they may be useful for comparing one individual with another, they fail to cover the unique, dynamic features of any single individual. Gordon Allport believes that these difficulties can be met by recognizing that 'common traits' (i.e. those present in varying degrees among all persons) are rough approximations only, and that each individual is characterized by certain 'unique traits' or 'personal dispositions' which are the key elements or guiding lines peculiar to himself. Thus although he may appear inconsistent when graded on any one common trait (as did the children in Hartshorne and May's studies of honesty), yet if we knew his personal dispositions we would know why he acted inconsistently, and the true lawfulness of his behaviour would emerge. This conception has not won general acceptance among psychologists, largely because – as Allport admits – we lack objective means of diagnosing unique traits. We have to infer them through observation, from case-study material and personal documents, rather than through testing (cf. also Allport 1961b). Nevertheless Cattell substantially agrees, and insists that unique dispositions can be measured as factors within the individual (p. 199).

Situational determinants. The crucial difficulty is that a trait, in so far as it represents a homogeneous and well-defined dimension, cannot be expected to account for people's behaviour in a wide range of situations. People vary too widely from one situation to another, depending on their current social roles, moods and intentions, the groups or persons they are reacting to, etc., for their position on any trait to be highly predictive. Indeed, one school of thought: the transactionist, would claim that personality must be conceived in terms of interactions between the personal determinants and the demands of the situation. Many counsellors and selectors are sympathetic to this view (cf. Stern, Stein and Bloom, 1956); the employer is less interested in the prospective employee's personality in the abstract than in how he will fit in with the aims and staff of the firm. The psychotherapist must consider the individual in relation to his environment (cf. Leary, 1957).

Allport and Guilford admit this situational variability, but hope to overcome it – somewhat as Spearman overcame specific factors in intelligence tests – by generalizing from, or averaging, behaviour in many different situations. But of course, the broader one's trait-construct the less predictive can it be in any one situation. Cattell thinks that the answer is to categorize or factorize situations in much the same way as people; but he cannot be said to have provided evidence that this is a practicable solution. Allport adds that people do seem to retain the same major personality qualities in spite of situational upheavals such as emigration, marriage or changing a job. Very likely biographers or naïve observers over-estimate this consistency, but it can hardly be denied. Similarly, despite the many roles that people impersonate in different social settings, common features running through them all can usually be discerned. It is these stable traits, common or unique, that we most need to assess in counselling or making practical decisions about a person.

It is well to remember that the problem is one of degree. As Mann (1959) points out, psychologists at one time treated 'leadership' as though it were purely the property of the person, and then veered to the opposite extreme by studying it as a property of the social group or situation. He suggests that it is preferable to think of it, like the nature vs. nurture problem in intelligence, as the product or interaction of both components.

Mann surveyed a very large number of investigations of small groups and noted rather consistent, though small, correlations between leadership behaviour and measured characteristics of the individuals concerned, particularly with their intelligence, non-neuroticism, extraversion, dominance and authoritarianism. But as the median coefficient was around 0·2, it seems unlikely that, even with better tests, we could account for more than a small proportion of variance in leadership (or other such types of behaviour) by means of personality measures. On the other hand, the variance attributable to such group characteristics as have been studied so far appears to be even smaller.

Other criticisms. It is sometimes maintained that any form of trait theory (whether based on psychodynamic forces or on more descriptive categories such as factors) represents an unsophisticated, animistic kind of thinking about human beings. Merely because we do not know enough about the laws or regularities of behaviour, we are apt to ascribe it to entities such as the will, conscience, traits, the Ego, Id, needs or other forces which we envisage as operating independently of the situation.

To the writer, the real argument against the trait and factor approach is not that it is a bad theory; its weaknesses are recognized, and we cannot do without some form of 'intervening variables'. The real trouble is that it has not worked well enough and, despite the huge volume of research it has stimulated, it seems to lead to a dead end. In thirty years or more of trying to measure traits, no one has produced a battery of tests which a majority of other psychologists find sufficiently convincing to be worth using for practical purposes, apart from certain attitude and interest measures (perhaps the MMPI should also be excepted). Many of the available tests make useful research instruments, but then their results are usually interpreted with considerable caution, as dependent on a number of constructs, not as direct measurements of specified traits. One might have hoped also that trait theory could effect some rapprochement between psychometric and clinical psychologists, since both employ the notion of internal drives, albeit at different levels. Yet, the opposition between nomothetic and idiographic approaches remains as strong as ever.

The nature of internal dispositions. Harsh and Schrickel (1950) point out that the current trend in personality theory is to reject the notion of personality as a sort of substance with inherent traits and properties, and to regard it rather as a 'complex of interactive forces'. However, this still involves a belief in the existence of organizations, forces or dispositions *within* the person which underlie both his behaviour and his conceptual structure, and which cannot be directly observed or classified. Many different interpretations or classifications of such forces are put forward by different observers, according to their varied cultural and linguistic stereotypes and theoretical biases. The internal dispositions which we name are abstractions or theories to account for behaviour; in other words, they are fabricated constructs which we use to describe the person, rather than entities inside him. As Kelly maintains, the impasse in personality psychology will continue so long as we persist in believing that these dispositions are *there*, waiting to be discovered, instead of agreeing that we have to invent them.

Nevertheless, some inventions are more fruitful than others. In accordance with the principles of construct validation we can check many of our theories by experimental, comparative, developmental, as well as by clinical and psychometric evidence. Thus, it is reasonable to think of dispositions as organized on a temporal basis, the biogenic forces (primary drives and innate temperamental differences) and earlier acquired components lying at 'deeper' levels than later acquisitions. It is generally agreed too that man is a psychosomatic unity, not a mind *and* a body. Hence, Burdock *et al.* (1958) argue that abnormal personalities should be studied at the neurobiochemical, sensory, psychomotor and perceptual as well as at the conceptual levels; and they describe tests which tend to differentiate the schizophrenic from the normal at all these levels. One may hope then that part of what is now referred to as the Unconscious will eventually be formulated in terms of physiological components which are more accessible to direct observation and measurement. As regards medium-level motivational constructs or intervening variables, it would seem best to retain an eclectic outlook. In Chapter 9 it was shown that psychology can benefit from a wide range of theories, including depth-oriented and Behavioristic. However, the present writer's preference would be for dispositional constructs which can be defined largely in terms of common behaviour patterns, concepts and attitudes, or what are referred to as 'trends' later in this Chapter.

Approaches to personality. Without listing precise definitions, we can distinguish a number of points of view regarding personality. Each of them is tenable, though each has its weaknesses, as our brief comments will indicate:

1. Personality is behaviour, or consistent reaction patterns. *Objection:* that the consistency becomes apparent only when referred to internal dispositions and intentions.

2. Personality is the roles, behaviour patterns and attitudes, that the person acquires from his culture. True, these should not be neglected; they account for much of the person's behaviour. But his individual deviations from the roles are also important.

3. Personality is an organized structure of traits and other dispositions. *Objection:* Situational determinants are neglected, and such dispositions are necessarily hypothetical.

4. Personality consists of transactions between internal dispositions and situational forces. *Objection:* Apart from the problems raised by dispositions, it is not the situation as such but how the person interprets it which determines his behaviour.

5. Personality is a matter of subjective concepts – the ways a person views himself and his environment. *Objection:* The Self should not be confused with the personality; it is intrinsically 'private' whereas the personality is to some extent observable.

6. Personality is the impressions and evaluations of others; it resides in their concept structures. Presumably the individual himself can also be an intepreter, when he views himself as an object. *Objection:* What is it that supplies the cues which observers interpret?

7. Personality consists of relationships between the individual and his observers. While providing a possible basis for the experimentalist, this seems particularly difficult for the practitioner to conceptualize.*

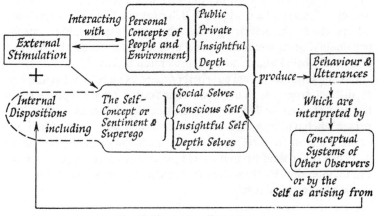

Fig. 5. The personality system.

The personality system. We seem to be going round in circles; and indeed this is the solution that we propose to adopt – to conceive of personality as a kind of chain, which can be arbitrarily broken into and studied at many points. Figure 5 provides a rough diagram, which embodies and extends Figure 3: the inferred Self. It tries to suggest the more objective links by squares, the conceptual by rounded figures, and the hypothetical Internal Dispositions by a dotted figure.† All parts of the system are interactive, though it is difficult to show this by arrows.

The personality with which depth psychologists, together with

* A number of other views, together with potent criticisms of those we have mentioned, are described in the earlier (1937) edition of Allport's book on personality (1961a).

† Tolman's (1951) 'psychological model' is much better spelled out than this attempt. But it appears to involve a greater number of assumptions regarding intervening variables, and is not specifically adapted to personality description. Tolman's 'belief-values matrix' is, of course, the same as our Personal Concepts of People and Environment.

'normal' psychologists such as Allport, are concerned, is the Internal Dispositions, which include the Self-sentiment, the basic drives, the Ego and Super-ego. A caution should be added: that there is no necessary correspondence between Dispositional levels (p. 240) and levels of Self (p. 118); i.e. it must not be assumed that the Depth Self is cognizant of deeper, unconscious dispositions.

Both Internal Dispositions and External Stimulation (which is objective) are activators which impinge upon, and are interpreted by, the Construct System, i.e. the various levels of Self- and outer-concepts. This results in objective Behaviour or Utterances which are interpreted by the Self or by other observers as emanating from the personality. Such a scheme, we believe, incorporates all the views of personality listed above, with the exception of No. 2.

In Chapter 2, it was asked whether there exists a 'real personality' as distinct from the many impersonations a man adopts. Clearly the answer must be No; or else the question is unanswerable. The person's behaviour in different roles is an important part of him just as are the more 'natural' qualities that he might display if he had no audience other than himself or his psychotherapist. In any case we cannot infer directly from Behaviour patterns to Dispositions (except at the physiological level).

The problem of personality description. An obvious implication of Figure 4 is that we need to study a man's behaviour, the situations which affect him, the people he reacts to and who interpret him, as well as his conceptual system, in order to know his personality. But we must ask whether it is possible to 'break into' the system more effectively at some points than at others, in order to diagnose or influence his personality. The study of External Stimulation and Behaviour alone, as advocated by the Stimulus-Response theorist and by the actuarialist is unlikely to be as profitable with humans as it is with rats, because of its neglect of the Personal Conceptual system. (Nevertheless, such phenomena as the conditioning treatment for enuresis show that it is possible to by-pass the Self, to modify dispositions and 'shape' behaviour directly.) Behaviour patterns do indeed reflect all levels of Internal Dispositions, the deeper as well as the more superficial, but the Conceptual System of the observer always intervenes in inferring the Dispositions from the Behaviour.

How far can we get by studying the Personal Conceptual System alone? Theoretically, if we knew all the levels of the Self and of its outer-directed concepts, we could predict how the person would react in any situation. Normally, though, the person will describe himself only at the two top levels of this System, and will do his best to limit his Behaviour to what is congruent with these levels. What he can tell us at Level 2 can be very revealing, though also considerably distorted. By getting down to the third level, through non-directive interviewing, and checking this with observations of behaviour patterns, we are likely to arrive at the most valid account. There is little evidence as yet that penetration to the Depth level will improve our knowledge or control.

Categorization. Bound up with these questions is the problem of what descriptive categories, units or elements we can best employ in order to describe a personality about whom decisions are to be made.

Categorization is most straightforward in the areas of abilities, interests and social attitudes, since all of these are linked to objects, groups or institutions, etc., in the environment. Although we lack any generally agreed set of categories at the moment, considerable progress in sorting them out has been made by means of factor analysis. In effect, we are 'breaking the chain' at the point of External Stimulation, which is permissible so long as we are content to think of an ability as capacity in handling a certain class of stimuli, an attitude as accepting or rejecting such a class. They can be regarded as Internal Dispositions without further ado. This solution becomes unsatisfactory however as soon as we wish to probe more deeply into the significance of the ability or attitude in the person.

Much more serious difficulties arise in handling general emotional qualities or styles of behaviour, and individual motives and organizing tendencies. They cannot be defined by classes of stimuli or of responses. The content of 'mathematical ability' or of 'anti-semitism' is fairly easy to agree upon, though obviously open to some diversities of interpretation; but 'sociability' or 'anxiety', say, are far more equivocal.

No doubt the trait-concept will persist in common discourse, and many psychologists (e.g. counsellors) will continue to find it useful, although it constitutes the most intangible and most uncertain link in our chain. Alternatively, the depth psychologist possesses an extensive vocabulary of personality components; and in so far as these are technical terms they may be better defined than the layman's, or normal psychologist's, traits, though no more objective. The clinician also has some advantage over the trait-psychologist in that he can put his units into a pattern or describe their interaction, thus being better at communicating personality structures and diagnoses. However, the biographer, or the testimonial writer, often succeeds in conveying patterns largely in terms of trait units. But none of these observers is able to provide accurate specifications of the person; no two clinicians, or lay biographers, would describe him identically, and we know that their predictions of his behaviour are often wrong.

At the opposite extreme, the Behaviour theorist employs as his units conditioned reflexes and habit systems, which do not begin to provide a usable description of personality. Alternatively he takes over, or invents, Dispositional constructs, sometimes with dubious consequences (cf. the naming fallacy, p. 217). The strict actuarialist is fortunate in having no need of any such elements: his categories are wholly operational.

How about statistical factors? Clearly they can be established in any of our realms of discourse – in classes of stimuli, in the person's concepts or in those of observers, or in behaviour patterns; or they may combine several of these. We must still dissent from Cattell's direct identification of factors with Internal Dispositions though if, as he hopes, factors from several different sources were found to coincide, they would certainly strengthen the case for a construct. Probably factor analysis will be of most value for mapping out the person's concepts, as in Osgood's and Kelly's work, and it should be applied to the classifications proposed by Harvey, Leary and others. In this area it can be used either nomothetically (for exploring differences between individuals), or idiographically (for delineating patterns within the individual).

Needs and presses. An approach to categorization which appears to gear in rather neatly with our Personality System is H. A. Murray's theory of needs and presses. His list of 20 main needs is eclectic, including viscerogenic and psychogenic, overt and covert, internally and externally aroused, focalized and diffuse or generalized tendencies; i.e. he attempts to cover most of the important determiners (the Internal Dispositions) of the individual. He defines each one, and believes that they can be assessed or diagnosed by observing their end results, and their expression through selective attention, fantasies, satisfactions and other affective responses (that is, they are inferred from Behaviour and Constructs). Complementary to this list, is a categorized list of environmental 'presses' – the chief kinds of situations which affect the person. This is subdivided into *alpha* presses – the forces as elicited by objective inquiry, and *beta* presses – the forces as perceived by the individual. The correspondence with External Stimulation and Outer-directed Constructs is obvious.

In fact, few psychologists have made much use of the press-system, though the need-system has been widely adopted by clinical psychologists, for example, in interpreting TAT and Sentence Completion data. Whether need and press can provide a satisfactory terminology of personality for the practitioner seems rather doubtful, not only because they are still somewhat vague and esoteric, but also because there is no sure way of determining them. Thus the Need for Achievement depends greatly on the method used for assessing it; similarly, it would be rash to assume that the 15 needs assessed by the Edwards PPS represent anything more than second-level self-concepts. Nevertheless, further efforts to apply the need-press approach in counselling should be well worthwhile.

Trends. An alternative proposal by F. H. Allport (1937) is that people should be described in terms of their 'teleonomic trends': that is, the main purposes that they seem to be trying to carry out (cf. Gregory, 1945). Although one of the objects of this theory is to dispense with traits, trends bear a close resemblance to Gordon Allport's unique traits or personal dispositions. They are defined by consistencies in the individual's behaviour rather than by similarities between individuals. They do, however, differ from traits in that they mostly involve interactions with other people or situations, i.e. they are not located so completely *in* the person.* There is no assumption that they are conscious or unconscious, nor necessarily determined by instincts or by early learning. Probably they are often laid down in childhood; for example, the child discerns that scholastic achievement gains attention and is rewarded, hence this purpose becomes reinforced. However, much the same situation may stimulate the growth of different trends, as when parental criticism reinforces *either* trying to escape the notice of others, *or* trying to become

---

* A more extreme form of interactionist theory is represented by Secord and Backman's (1961) attempt to account both for personality stability and for personality change in terms of relations between a person's self-concepts and his perceptions of others. Mention should be made also of Sears' (1951) emphasis on the study of dyadic relationships, i.e. interpersonal reactions, at the behavioural level. While providing fruitful frames of reference for experimentation on personality development, neither of these seem capable of yielding the sort of constructs or units that the practising psychologist requires.

better accepted by others. Often an individual may have little insight into some of his trends (though presumably this is increased by non-directive counselling). They are inferred partly from consistent behaviour over numerous situations, partly from self-report in interviews or autobiographical materials. Two or more trends may conflict and produce tensions; that is, they account for inconsistencies and neurotic tendencies as well as for normal personality qualities.

Gregory provides the following description of the main categories of trends:

1. Securing reactions from others to self, e.g. to attract or escape attention, to gain submission from them. This is apt to be associated with emotional instability and maladjustment.

2. To affect others, e.g. to be honest; to help people.

3. To develop and maintain reciprocal relationships, to co-operate, to make friends.

4. Reacting to the expectancies of others, e.g. to be law-abiding, identifications with church, family, nation.

5. Developing and maintaining evaluative self-attitudes, e.g. compensating, proving oneself superior.

6. To express and actualize oneself, e.g. to gain independence, to learn something.

7. To affect oneself, e.g. improve one's health, secure aesthetic pleasures.

Floyd Allport claims that this approach has proved useful in counselling and in vocational guidance – thus, a person's occupation should be chosen with an eye to his main trends; also that it serves as a basis for predicting things about people. For example, in an experiment by Allport and Frederiksen (1941) it was found that essential trends could be discerned in people's written productions better than either common traits or the overall personality pattern.

This approach might provide a common meeting ground for the depth psychologist, the behaviour theorist and the self-theorist. It allows for repressed mechanisms, and for situational variations, while yet emphasizing present goals. Moreover it offers a *modus vivendi* between the nomothetist and idiographist. Many trends are sufficiently similar among most members of a cultural group to be assessed and compared, and yet they also tend to have an individual flavour; while others may be peculiar to a few or to single individuals. From the applied psychologist's viewpoint, however, the trend system is less satisfactory because it has no taxonomy – no specification of common trends to look for, and no clear indication of how to assess these effectively. In other words, it needs considerable development if it is to become a usable system. Gregory's main suggestion is that the psychologist should ask the person he is studying to write down or report orally as many pleasant and unpleasant experiences and incidents as possible, to expand them in interview inquiries and to say why they were liked or disliked, and then to classify and count the number of items falling under each heading that emerges from the material itself. This can be supplemented by autobiographical material and by observations of behaviour over a period. So far there is no evidence that different psychologists studying the same person would end up with the same list or pattern of trends. Nevertheless, it seems highly probable that such psychologists would reach at least as much agreement, and would make more valid vocational and other inferences by this method than they do at present by studying equally unstructured projective responses. We will return later to further suggestions for putting this into practice.

Part IV

Practicable Methods of Assessment

Chapter 15

TESTS AND OBSERVATIONS
OF BEHAVIOUR

The present position. The reader who has reached this point may be pardoned for feeling somewhat discouraged. Personality, it seems, is so complex that all the efforts psychologists have put into clinical and psychometric research over the past thirty years or so have brought us nowhere. Projective testing and factor analysis are equally blind alleys. We still seem to be able to do little better than the layman, with his naïve, commonsense – yet obviously inaccurate – methods of diagnosing and assessing personalities.

In fact the present writer is by no means so pessimistic. True, he has no 'break-through' to offer, no panacea to solve our difficulties of assessment. Nor is there any likelihood that the perfect test, or other method, will be discovered. But he would certainly not agree that there has been no progress. For one thing, we know a great deal more about what the interviewer, or other assessor, is doing; how he makes his judgments and why they go wrong; what are the resistances to be overcome in penetrating to the third level of the Self. We know that non-directive methods are effective for many purposes; and there is some information on the characteristics of the successful therapist, judge or interviewer. Though the issue is still controversial, we have good grounds for avoiding depth-psychological constructs and methods in the practical counselling and selection of normal adults and children, and for working as far as possible in terms of overt behaviour patterns, trends, and concepts of Self and others.

One would disagree, again, that personality tests are useless. What we should distrust is the notion that they can measure (albeit imperfectly) a person's traits or other motivational dispositions. But it is entirely legitimate to accept them as samples of a Subject's behaviour or concepts. There is no test of, say, aggressiveness in general; but we can investigate the conditions that have led up to

251

specified kinds of aggressive reactions, aggressive fantasies, aggressive attitudes, etc. (cf. Bronfenbrenner and Ricciuti, 1960). Knowledge of personality structure and development is accumulating all the time, and it should be possible eventually to apply much of this in making better practical assessments. True, the results of such research are often highly conflicting, but this means that we are still over-generalizing from limited samples of behaviour, and it should stimulate more precise theories and definitions and more effective methodologies.

A third reason for optimism is that we have arrived at some conclusions as to how tests can be used and interpreted. Any test of a relatively stable behavioural or conceptual pattern, which has been shown to possess rich and consistent correlates, can provide the practitioner with valuable 'fixed points', thus reducing his reliance on more dubious data and on subjective synthesis or weighing up of all the data. His judgment cannot be dispensed with, except in those rare situations where the outcome is sufficiently precise and the predictors sufficiently valid to permit of actuarial or computer prediction. But he will make fewer mistakes if he bases as many inferences as possible on the kinds of tests that we shall outline in this Part, and regards himself, not as a super-computer, but as one fallible link in the chain that we have called the Personality System.

However, both the methods of interviewing and synthesis, and the value of tests, must naturally differ according to whether the main aim is decision-making, counselling, or exploratory-therapeutic. In the pure selection situation (Cases 1 to 3, on p. 2), we must expect the person being evaluated to do his best to prevent the selector from finding out what he most wants to know; hence few tests are likely to be of much use. The less fakable or obvious tests, such as perceptuo-motor and projective techniques, tend to have the weakest validities, and are also the most unacceptable to the persons concerned. Candidates not only distrust them because they cannot see their relevance, but are likely to build up inaccurate notions of what constitutes a 'good' performance, and to react accordingly. Here therefore the interviewer should chiefly try to elicit the person's past trends – his behaviour in specified social, vocational and other situations, and his top and second-level concepts and attitudes. He should then infer from these and from any available test results as directly as possible to future behaviour and concepts in similar situations. He should keep his theories about the person's inner dispositions to a minimum, and should rely more on Stereotype Accuracy than on Differential Accuracy (cf. p. 65).

In less threatening decision situations, also in counselling (e.g. Cases 4–10), there is considerably more scope for the kind of tests we shall describe. Here the interviewer can use their results, along with a more permissive type of interviewing, to help the person reach his third level of the Self and, as far as possible, make his own decisions. Finally, in the therapeutic situation, most clinicians will probably regard the tests that we list as too crude for their purposes, and will prefer to employ their own techniques for formulating a fourth level of the Self.

If certain tests are singled out below as among the most promising for purposes of assessment in counselling and selection, this does not imply decrying all others. There are many which can be given under the relatively controlled motivational and other conditions of a research project, but which would be too readily distorted or apt to vary under somewhat different conditions, or which are otherwise unsuitable for practical use.

Somatotypes. Sheldon's original correlations between body-types and temperamental ratings were so obviously exaggerated (whether through miscalculation or through contamination of the criterion) that psychologists have hardly given them the credit they deserve. Somatotypes are suspect also because they certainly change to some extent with age and other circumstances; i.e. they are not wholly constitutional. Thus it has been suggested that the fat boy becomes easygoing and jolly because he is expected to, or alternatively that easygoing comfort-lovers naturally tend to put on fat. Mental states can affect the endocrines as well as vice versa. Be that as it may, there are certainly some correlations sufficiently high to justify the counsellor inferring that persons with marked endo-, ecto- and mesomorphic physique have a considerable potential inclination towards social-extraverted, intellectual-retiring, and aggressive-independent traits, respectively. Among Glueck's (1950) large groups of delinquent and non-delinquent adolescents (around 14 years), the distributions were:

	Endomorph	Ectomorph	Mesomorph
Delinquent percent	11·8	14·4	60·1
Non-delinquent percent	15·0	39·6	30·7

Davidson and Parnell (1957) developed a simplified technique of somatotyping 7-year-olds and obtained correlations of 0·30 to 0·65 with tests or with ratings based on interviewing the mother, as follows:

Endomorphy with high IQ

Ectomorphy with Verbal/Non-verbal IQ ratio, scholastic attainments, anxiety and emotional instability

Mesomorphy with low Verbal/Non-verbal ratio, low attainments, and (negatively) with submissiveness.

Winthrop's (1957) finding of more logically consistent attitudes in ectomorphic students, more indiscriminate and contradictory ones in endomorphs, also fits in, and goes some way to offset the very low correlations published by other writers between somatotype and self-report test scores.*

Other physical characteristics.† The likelihood that a particular physical abnormality may affect a person's Self-concept was mentioned earlier (p. 55). But it would be rash to regard any such disabilities as reflecting any consistent personality traits. It is possible that general sensory weakness is sufficiently associated with neurotic trends to make it worth measuring dark vision, visual and auditory acuities, though the correlation would certainly be low. Many claims have been made for the diagnostic significance of EEG patterns; and abnormal patterns certainly tend to occur more frequently in delinquent psychopaths. But though certain types of waves are indicative of cerebral dysfunction in epileptics, the brain-injured, and some defectives, they seem to have no clear associations with personality (cf. Kennard, 1953). The trouble may be partly that records are taken from too localized an area of the brain, and are then interpreted too subjectively (cf. Allen, 1958).

The work of Sanford, Wenger and others on autonomic measures stimulated hopes for a physiological approach to temperamental traits such as instability and/or introversion. But the results are so variable that it is now more generally believed that individuals have their own characteristic patterns of autonomic response, e.g. to stress, and that these may bear no more relation to personality than physical features do. The Psychogalvanic Reflex likewise has shown a history of disappointments – considerable correlations with one

---

* Rees (1960) provides a comprehensive survey of the evidence for personality and psychiatric correlates of Sheldon's and other types of body-build.

† Earlier work is summarized by Vernon (1953). More recent publications tend to confirm the lack of any useful or consistent validities for physical and physiological measures, apart from somatotype or analogous indices of build.

set of conative or affective traits being claimed by one investigator, with a different set (or no correlation at all) by another. Possibly it is better regarded as an index of the Subject's present state of vigilance or attentiveness than of any enduring disposition.

Cognitive tests. This has been one of the most active fields of investigation in the 1950's, since Blake and Ramsey's (1951) book urged that perception depends not only on the stimulus characteristics but on the total psychological organization of the individual, including motivational factors and characteristic 'styles' of dealing with incoming data (cf. p. 41). The basic ideas were implicit in Rorschach and other projective testing of the 1940's, but it seemed reasonable to hope that better controlled and more precise measures of perceptual characteristics might yield more trustworthy links with personality. Individual differences in the structural or formal aspects of conceptualization likewise appeared promising, in the light of Kelly's analysis of constructs and Rokeach's (1960) work on dogmatism vs. open-mindedness. If, for example, one could determine a person's level or type on Harvey, Hunt and Schroder's scheme (p. 113) by means of objective cognitive tests, this should have highly significant implications for diagnosing his personality. Much work with pathological groups is suggestive also, e.g. Goldstein and Scheerer's (1941) tests of 'concreteness' of thinking in brain-damaged and schizophrenic patients, and Payne's (1960) more recent studies of 'over-inclusiveness' among psychotics.

Witkin's 'personality through perception'. Perhaps the most ambitious and thorough investigations have been those of Witkin and his colleagues (1954) on field-dependence vs. independence.

They developed several tests of the ability to judge the upright when either the perceptual field, or the Subject himself, is displaced. The 'dependent' person continues to rely passively on the distorted visual cues, whereas the 'independent' is more analytic and judges correctly from body sensations. This ability correlates quite highly with Flexibility of Closure, as measured by the Gottschaldt or Embedded Figures test. Men were found to be more 'independent' than women on most tests; but within both sexes there were strong correlations (of the order of 0·4 to 0·6, though generally lower and less consistent for women) with personality characteristics as assessed in clinical interviews or by Rorschach, TAT and other projective tests. The dependent were more passive in dealing with their environment, lacked insight into and feared their own impulses, were tense and prone to inferiority feelings, and had a more primitive and undifferentiated body image. The independent showed the reverse, active-independent characteristics, together with higher self-esteem and self-direction. Such results gain plausibility since, as we have seen, the body image is an important component of the Self-concept.

There has been some, though not enough, independent confirmation of the construct validity of Perceptual Dependence. Witkin was unable to find consistent differences among different types of psychiatric patients (as would be expected from Harvey's claims); and there is no evidence that the more and less dependent are suited to particular kinds of jobs. However, Linton (1955) obtained correlations of 0·54 and 0·66 between field-dependence and conformity or suggestibility in autokinetic and attitude-change tests (the Embedded Figures likewise gave correlations of 0·43 and 0·32). MacKinnon (1958, 1960) has confirmed a relation between the Witkin tests and self-reported ascendant characteristics, though they were of little value in differentiating outstanding Air Force officers. Likewise Pemberton (1952) found a tendency for high-scorers on Embedded Figures to display self-sufficient characteristics. It may be noted that this Figure test depends largely on S-factor or spatial ability, which is consistently higher among males than females, delinquents than conforming children, mesomorphs than ectomorphs. It is interesting, too, that Harvey *et al.* characterize both extreme dependents and extreme independents as less mature than the abstract type in their scheme of development. Gruen (1957) has attacked Witkin's work, but his only valid criticism seems to be that the orientation tests are considerably affected by the particular conditions of testing and the way the Subject interprets the instructions. It could hardly be claimed that these tests are very practicable for everyday use in counselling or selection, though they should be followed up and their behavioural, rather than their projective, personality correlates better established. Group spatial tests alone are unlikely to have much predictive value, since they depend so largely on intellectual abilities.

Other cognitive variables. The results of other tests have generally been much more unstable. Thus many investigations have shown that rigidity vs. flexibility is not a consistent trait which operates throughout the cognitive, motor and personality areas; also that the well-known water-jar or Einstellung test of intellectual rigidity more often than not fails to correlate with other rigidity phenomena (Levitt, 1956). True, inconsistent results sometimes arise because different experimenters use somewhat different versions of a test; but variations in test-taking attitudes and sets may be even more important.

There is a paucity of evidence, too, for the generality of most of the popular perceptual styles. Thus Kenny and Ginsberg (1958) found scarcely any correlation between 12 measures presumed to involve intolerance of ambiguity, and no such correlations with authoritarian attitudes as Frenkel Brunswik (1949) had suggested. However, they included extremely miscellaneous phenomena, most of which could hardly be called perceptual. Another considerable difficulty is that the more interesting styles generally require individual testing, hence it is seldom possible to accumulate enough cases to demonstrate consistent dimensions. Gardner and Holzman (1960) attempted to find the major factors underlying levelling-sharpening, field-dependence, focusing vs. scanning, equivalence, tolerance for unrealistic experiences, and other perceptual phenomena. They regard these as regulatory structures or controls in perceiving and thinking, which might be traced back to psychoanalytic mechanisms. But as they tested only 30 men and 30 women, their obtained factors are unconvincing.

Thurstone hoped that the perceptual factors established in his large-scale factorial research (1944) would help to differentiate leaders, pathological and other groups, but the promise has not been fulfilled. Other cognitive factors studied by Thurstone and his followers include two or more types of verbal and ideational fluency, and in so far as these indicate speed and richness of mental associations, they should have implications for personality. At one time, indeed, Cattell regarded f (fluency) tests as good measures of surgency. But while oral fluency may well be characteristic of the extravert, and of the manic as against the depressive patient, there is little evidence of the usefulness of written fluency tests in personality diagnosis.

It may be pointed out that cognitive styles or factors are, in a sense, 'response sets'; and we regarded these, in Chapter 12, as psychologically trivial, although we found that they did tend to overlap with personality variables. Again they resemble expressive movements (p. 57) in showing some statistical consistency, but depending on too many other influences to be of much diagnostic value. Doob (1958) noted only slight overlapping between field-dependence measures and stylistic or grammatical characteristics of written documents, concluding that the latter vary too much with the kind of writing (or in the case of oral material – too much with the relations between the speakers) to provide a useful approach to personality. However, he did not analyse more complex stylistic patterns which might have proved more significant than grammatical counts.

Numerous tests have been alleged as relevant to mature, rational, abstract, critical, complex or sophisticated thinking, and are said to measure qualities beyond the conventional intelligence test – the Hanfman–Kasanin, Vigotsky, Shaw and other concept-formation tests, Beck's z score for Rorschach, Bieri and Blacker's (1956) adaptation of Rorschach and the Rep test, Welsh's Art test (cf. Barron, 1953b), etc. In view of the number of different factors found by Guilford in higher intellectual capacities, it seems unlikely that all these measure the same thing, or that they have much connection with maturity or other qualities of personality. However the last of them, the Barron–Welsh test, based on relative preference for complex-asymmetrical as against simple-symmetrical figures, was strikingly successful in MacKinnon's (1962) studies of highly creative artists, architects, writers and scientists. Using self-report tests and staff ratings as criteria, Barron (1953b) found that high scorers on this test tend to be dissatisfied, opinionated, original, nonconformist, and effeminate. In contrast, the ability tests which Guilford devised as measures of creativity showed little or no difference between MacKinnon's creative and non-creative groups. It appeared that tests or assessments of attitudes, interests and motivation were generally more diagnostic than cognitive tests, and we may reasonably conclude that these will provide a more profitable approach to the construct system.

Finally, mention should be made of relatively simple tests such as flicker fusion, after-effect, reversible perspective, and the like, which often give interesting differentiations among pathological groups, though here also the results are remarkably unstable (cf. Granger, 1953; Eysenck *et al.*, 1957). There is little to suggest that they could contribute to assessing normal personalities.

Direct observations of behaviour. We have given sufficient reasons already for doubting the diagnostic value of performance tests designed to evoke particular traits, e.g. tests of persistence, suggestibility, aggressiveness, or of character, such as Hartshorne and May used. But though motivations cannot readily be manipulated and measured, there are various more indirect approaches for observing and recording significant behaviour patterns in everyday or natural situations. The main requisites are to define beforehand just what categories of behaviour are to be looked for, and to record them systematically. Such categories can be 'molar' rather than 'molecular', i.e. observers can interpret with reasonable reliability that a child is showing aggressive, leadership, sympathetic or other behaviours, not merely that he is making such-and-such movements. In studies of child development and of individual differences among young children, the time-sampling technique has proved extremely fruitful.* It is somewhat more difficult to apply to older children and adults, both because their expressions of emotions and intentions are more complex, more disguised, and because they are more likely to be affected by the presence of an observer. Nevertheless it might be adapted to the needs of a school counsellor, or a psychological diagnostician attached to the play groups in a Child Guidance Clinic. Other techniques of systematic sampling can be illustrated by Lewin's work on regression and on social climates, and Anderson and Brewer's researches on teachers' characteristics and their effects on children's classroom behaviour.

Rating methods: Stott's 'Bristol Guides'. The difficulties in using ratings or informal reports on behaviour that has been casually observed by teachers or other acquaintances, were pointed out in Chapter 4. When a group of children, or adults, have lived or worked together over a period, their sociometric judgments of one another can be of considerably greater reliability and predictive value (for example in officer selection in the Services), than the judgments of superiors. However, such material yields generalized indications of rather superficial characteristics of acceptability and competence, and gives little information on individual personality trends.

An interesting approach which represents a compromise between ratings and more detailed short-term behaviour observations is that of Stott's *Social Adjustment Guides* (1958). Though limited to surveying symptoms of maladjustment in children of about 5 to 15 years, the same approach could fairly readily be adapted to any counselling or selection situation where children (or adults) can be observed over a month or so. It could well be combined with Flanagan's (1954) Critical Incidents Technique of isolating significant behaviour patterns.

Stott's aim is to provide a vehicle whereby teachers, or observers of children in residential schools or their own homes, can record disturbed

* Its uses and limitations are well brought out by Wright (1960).

behaviour for the information of clinical psychologists and psychiatrists. (Different instruments are provided for the child at school, in residential care, and in the family.) He has made a determined effort to get away from traits, and to list behavioural items which can be observed as present or absent with a minimum of interpretation, e.g.:

> Likes to be treated as a much younger child
> Continually squabbling
> Shrinks from any affectionate approach
> Tries to get round adults.

He calls these 'situation-attitudes', or patterns of deviant reaction tendencies, that commonly occur among disturbed children. On the basis of extensive trials with normal and disturbed children, a series of syndromes or groupings of items has emerged, by a kind of trial-and-error procedure rather than by formal factor analysis. Thus various sets of items provide indices of Anxiety, Hostility, Estrangement from Parent, Unforthcomingness, Depression, Unconcernedness, and a dozen other categories. The child's form is not scored, but the checked items are transferred to a Diagnostic Chart, which portrays the piling up of symptoms in particular categories. Actually, other psychologists have found part-scores, or the total, to yield useful overall ratings for maladjustment, anxiety, withdrawing, etc. (e.g. Lunzer, 1960), though there are no norms. The instrument should be useful, too, in studying personality change following on various kinds of treatment.

To the psychometrist, Stott's instruments are likely to seem distressingly amateurish; but their virtue lies in their simplicity – that they use terms to describe deviant patterns which lay observers can readily apply, and that the psychologist or psychiatrist is presented with an overview, only roughly categorized, so that he can further explore particular symptoms. No doubt the categories overlap a good deal, and might be purified by more thorough statistical analysis. Doubtless also, despite Stott's claims for high inter-rater agreement, there is a good deal of subjectivity and halo in a typical record as filled in by, say, a teacher. But these should be less marked than in the ordinary rating scale, or in third-person questionnaires designed to measure some named trait or traits.

Qualitative aspects of performance at ability tests. Another approach, surveyed by the writer elsewhere (1953), is the observation of the personality characteristics of testees engaged on a performance test of abilities, where the manner of reacting to difficulties and stresses, together with social reactions to the tester, may be significant. In so far as the person believes that his ability is being measured, he is less likely to put on a personality façade. Moreover there are certain tests such as the Q-score in the Porteus Mazes, the dotting machine and Cattell's CMS (Cursive Miniature Situation) where objective indices of personality differences can be recorded. Though there is some evidence of useful validity when these scores, or the tester's subjective judgments, are compared with ratings, with delinquency vs. non-delinquency, or with pathological diagnoses, other follow-up results have been disappointing. For example, types of reaction to complex psychomotor tests among USAAF pilots gave no useful correlations with pilot success (Guilford and Lacey, 1947). Not only is there the danger of testers jumping to conclusions on too meagre a basis, but also the likelihood that Subjects may not respond to these limited test situations as they would to real-life stresses. However, there is room for further attempts to develop better indirect tests, which might evoke a greater range of reliable personality differences as well as measuring abilities relevant to jobs, training courses or other 'treatments' for which a person is being assessed.

Situational and 'Leaderless Group' tests. In appointing people to high-grade posts, it is common practice to ask the promising candidate out to dinner, or to observe him in other situations outside the interviewing room. The interview itself, indeed, often involves as much inference from behaviour as from what the candidate says, although most interviewers realize that the social situation is far from typical of the situations with which he will have to cope in his job. Thus the so-called Situational test – better termed the Group Observational test – does not represent a fundamentally new departure, except in so far as several candidates are usually observed simultaneously, and the observers try to specify beforehand just what they are looking for.

The development of these tests, first in the pre-war German Army, then in the British Army and Civil Service, and their extension to selection in industry and a host of other jobs (even to selection of children for secondary schooling) is summarized elsewhere, and some of the weaknesses are pointed out (Vernon, 1953; Arbous, 1955). They are now included in the standard vocational guidance procedures of the National Institute of Industrial Psychology. Flanagan *et al.* (1954) have published an excellent review, mainly centred on the Leaderless Group Discussion, where a set of candidates is simply given some controversial topic and told to discuss it among themselves. In other Leaderless Group tests they are instructed to carry out some practical task which roughly resembles some of the problems they might meet in the job. No leader is appointed, and they are observed to see who comes to the fore, who helps to organize or who disrupts their efforts, what is the quality of each one's contributions and his interactions with the others.

To some extent this resembles the indirect tests, mentioned above, in that the candidates should be concerned primarily with getting the job done, or with carrying on a sensible discussion. They can hardly fail, though, to be aware of the sort of thing the observers are looking for, and to play up accordingly. Nevertheless such situations obviously offer scope for observing a wider range of more relevant behaviour than does the usual selection or guidance interview. Moreover the situations are too complex for the participants to be able to guess readily what is 'suitable', though this also means that the observers will have difficulties in agreeing on the most significant features. There is a little evidence to indicate that previous coaching, or strong motivation to shine, do not greatly alter the candidates' behaviour (Bass, 1954).

Another of the dangers of this approach is that it has high 'face validity'; it appeals to selectors as well as to candidates, and the former are tempted to assume that they can make valid judgments without recourse to the careful controls that psychologists would regard as essential. Even the apparent advantage of seeing candidates in a social situation may be a disadvantage, since each particular group of candidates constitutes an unique structure. Thus candidate A might show very different characteristics in a group with G, H, I, J and K from those displayed when he is with B, C, D, E and F.

The validity of situational tests. While Leaderless Group and other situational tests are quite widely employed in American military and industrial selection, they are viewed more critically by American than by British psychologists. On the one hand, it is said, they are poorly controlled and seldom provide enough samples of the kind of behaviour in which the selectors are interested for them to be able to reach reliable judgments. On the other hand the tests cannot readily be made to resemble most jobs very closely. For example, battle stress cannot be reproduced, and when attempts are made to introduce greater realism (as in the OSS procedures, or in so-called stress interviews) they still strike the candidates as artificial, and their responses become unnatural. A further disadvantage of tests that are too much like actual work samples is that it is difficult to compare candidates with different amounts of prior experience of the job. A common verdict is that they do not add sufficiently to other, easier, methods of assessment to justify the time they take and the expense.

This is the conclusion reached by Kelly and Fiske (cf. Flanagan, 1954) as a result of their experience in selecting clinical psychologists.

However, their choice of situations could probably have been improved. Moreover they did obtain *some* additional validity by including such tests, and their argument that single objective tests (e.g. a test of interests or intelligence) obtained as high follow-up validities as judgments based on Situations + other data, cannot be accepted. There is no evidence that these objective tests would have consistently shown as good validities in other groups. One test happened to work well in relation to one criterion, another test with another criterion; but the Situations tests showed fairly stable validities with a wider range of criteria than any objective test except, perhaps, the Miller Analogies.

Bass (1954) summarizes findings with the Leaderless Group Discussion test in a number of independent researches. Correlations with merit ratings reach the very promising median figure of 0·4 (range 0·29 to 0·68), in studies covering 1,495 cases in all. Judgments based on this test overlap to some extent, as might be expected, with intelligence and education, and with ratings on energy, self-esteem, participation, etc. But the median coefficient is only 0·30, and there is little or no consistent overlap with self-report measures of stability, extraversion, dominance and the like. Cronbach (1960) suggests that these impressionistic judgments of surface qualities by laymen whose outlook is similar to that of the candidates are superior to those of professional psychologists and psychiatrists or older officers; in other words, that a main virtue of the technique is that it does not set out to discover underlying motivations. Bass notes a median correlation of 0·60 (range 0·30 to 0·78) with other situational tests of leadership, but points out that this may be spurious in so far as the same judges often observed the different tests. Correlations among experienced observers of the same test average as high as 0·82.

That the test elicits fairly stable qualities is further indicated by the results of several independent factorial studies reported by Carter (cf. Flanagan, 1954). In these, the observers were asked to assess a series of fairly specific behaviours, which were then intercorrelated and analysed. Three factors were usually obtained which indicate the main content or dimensions of behaviour in the leaderless group situation as:

1. Forceful leadership, confidence, initiative, individual prominence.
2. Co-operation, friendliness with others.
3. Competence and adaptability at the task, striving for the group goals.

8

The first factor tends to be the largest, and other evidence indicates that this particular test most effectively brings out initiative and capacity to influence others verbally, rather than considerateness to subordinates.

Further applications. The American Institute for Research (Flanagan, Weislogel, 1954) and the Educational Testing Service (Frederiksen, 1960; Ward, 1959) are both engaged in developing more reliable tests, more closely relevant to particular jobs for which selection is necessary. Such a test should be constructed on the basis of a survey of the critical requirements of the job. It should contain numerous opportunities for the candidates to display relevant behaviour, and the behaviour should be recorded as objectively as possible, e.g. in the form of checklists – 'did so-and-so', or 'did not', rather than in terms of ambiguous traits. The situations are not necessarily social in nature. Flanagan is willing to employ role-playing, where the candidates act out specified features of the job, but he also resorts to movie films where each candidate sees some job incident and records his own judgments of what appropriate action should be taken. (Some attempts have been made to apply the latter technique in selecting clinical psychologists, by showing films of disturbed children in family or school situations. But the writer is unaware of any satisfactory follow-up.)

Investigators at the Educational Testing Service have concentrated on the 'In-basket' test for commercial executives, school administrators, etc. This consists of a series of documents designed to resemble the kind of paper-work problems that people in these jobs would meet in their daily work. After a period of studying information about the firm, or the school, they take appropriate action on the given documents, and are scored on a number of defined features. So far the authors have been more interested in the common factors running through these scores, i.e. in isolating stable patterns of behaviour, than in validation; though Ward has noted marked differences in score patterns between experienced managers and trainees. At the moment, both the administration and scoring of the ETS type of test is exceedingly lengthy, but it seems reasonable to hope for abbreviated procedures which would not occupy more than, say, half a day for a small batch of candidates.

Note that these approaches to Situational testing are highly analytic, whereas the original proponents of the method claimed that it allowed the expression of the total personality, rather than of isolated habits or traits. But there is good reason to doubt the value of intuitive, holistic judgments here, as in the field of clinical diagnosis, and to prefer measurements or assessments that focus on specified behaviour patterns.

The same sort of methods could be extended to a considerable variety of jobs; and more generalized tests, covering behaviour to common groups of jobs, could be of the greatest assistance to the vocational counsellor. However, the development of suitable tests to a point where they yield reasonably objective and reliable indications of job behaviour must necessarily be an elaborate and technically complex business. Thus it is always worth remembering that a period of trial on an actual job is likely to be more predictive of future success at this job than any short-cut method.

Chapter 16

SELF-REPORT TESTS

It would be foolish to discard such a convenient and easily scored instrument as the self-report of personality, attitudes or interests, so long as we recognize its weaknesses and accept it simply as one method of approach to a person's conceptual system. Either skilled interviewing, or some of the techniques discussed in the next chapter, may yield more reliable information, derived from less superficial layers of the self, but the inventory still possesses positive advantages.

First of all, it can be readily normed or standardized, so that the person can be compared with others of his kind. The selector or counsellor who prefers other approaches can evaluate the person's standing, or the strength of his attitudes, only roughly and subjectively. Test scores, again, can be readily treated statistically, correlated with other variables or factorized.

Secondly, self-report tests and inventories typically contain a considerable number of items which have been shown by item analysis to be relevant to the central concept or attitude; hence they tend to give a more reliable indication of this concept than a few random questions in an interview. It is well known, for example, that an adolescent's reply to a question on his vocational choice may reveal little because of his ignorance of the demands of the job; whereas the pattern of his anwers to a large number of interest items gives a truer picture. Similarly, the unreliability of answers to single questions in public opinion polls is notorious. Probably a skilled interviewer could overcome this by intensive questioning; but it is doubtful if he could cover as much ground in, say, half an hour as a well-constructed test, which might yield half a dozen or more reliable scores in the same time.

Thirdly, it might be maintained that some subjects, though not all, will be more candid and objective when answering an impersonal printed questionnaire than when interviewed or, say, asked to write an autobiography.

Our object here is not to describe and evaluate self-report tests exhaustively, but to comment on some of the more widely employed examples in the light of recent research, to point out their legitimate uses in selection or counselling, and then to suggest alternative or additional techniques that accord with the theoretical position taken in Part III.

Personality inventories. The MMPI is likely to continue to be favoured in clinical diagnosis of abnormal patients, although it is generally admitted that the original scales are obsolete. However, so much evidence has been collected on patterns of scale scores and the correction scores (Hathaway and Meehl, 1951; Dahlstrom and Welsh, 1960), and so many additional scoring keys have been worked out for special purposes, that no one likes to scrap it. Most of these scales show considerable intercorrelations, suggesting that it is in-efficient to score so many different ones, and we have seen that they are highly dependent on acquiescence and social desirability. At the same time each separate scale contains very heterogeneous items, i.e. is factorially impure. Another disadvantage is that interpretation of score patterns is a highly skilled matter, and there is no guarantee that inexperienced clinical psychologists can pick it up from the published manuals. Few would dispute, however, that the good ones can arrive at useful diagnostic information by rational inference rather than by intuition.

Unfortunately the test is also widely used in the United States as a general screening device for teachers and other job applicants, and this is to be deplored. It is most unlikely that score patterns have the same significance under these conditions as they do in a mental hospital, and there is no evidence that psychologists can reliably pick out individuals with 'unsuitable' personalities by means of it. How-ever, considerable progress has been made in tracing characteristic score patterns among college students seeking counselling,* delin-quents and criminals in the general population, etc.

Thurstone's Temperament Schedule, Guilford's scales and Temperament Survey, and Cattell's 16 Personality Factor Tests are more logically constructed instruments, and more suitable for use with young adults or older secondary pupils. Each includes items chosen on a factorial basis to provide measures of a number of distinctive factors. A more modest instrument, widely used in Britain, is Eysenck's MPI (Maudsley Personality Inventory) for assessing

* Gough's (1957) California Psychological Inventory is a good alternative to the MMPI for work with the general run of older secondary pupils and young educated adults.

neuroticism-stability and introversion-extraversion only (cf. p. 222). Other inventories provide scores in several arbitrarily selected areas, e.g. adjustment to home, school, health, etc., or, like the Edwards PPS (Personal Preference Schedule) refer to a set of theoretical constructs such as Murray's needs. The Myers–Briggs Type Indicator aims to classify people according to Jungian typology as extravert vs. introvert, sensation vs. intuition, thinking vs. feeling, and judging vs. perceiving (cf. Stricker and Ross, 1962).

None of these is particularly satisfactory, for the reasons pointed out in Chapters 12 and 13. In most of them the sub-scores show considerable overlapping, even when designed to measure independent factors. At the same time the scores on similarly named variables, when assessed by different tests, often show surprisingly low correlations; and when, as in the 16 PF Tests, the number of items contributing to a factor score is small, reliabilities are often inadequate. Such difficulties are inevitable, partly because of the insidious influence of response sets, partly because the constructs or traits aimed at are so equivocal, and so differently interpreted by different test constructors and different groups of Subjects. Thus it is unlikely that we can ever arrive at an instrument which will yield reasonably stable and reliable scores for several clearly defined and distinct traits, among a wide range of populations and under varying motivational conditions. Let us, however, sketch what would appear to be the most sensible steps towards producing an improved test.

Response sets. These, we have seen, cannot be eliminated by forced choice or correction devices without still further reducing the test's stability. However, if we can get strongly saturated measures of acquiescence and social desirability, some allowance can be made for them in interpreting scores on other variables; and whenever scores are correlated with some external criterion or outcome, the acquiescence and desirability measures may operate as suppressors. Our test, then, should have at least 20 items (mixed up among the rest) which invite positive responses to rather extreme and ambiguous statements, and whose content is varied so that the total score yields fairly low correlations with other variables at which the test is aimed. Another 20 or more items could consist of statements with strong social desirability or undesirability implications but of minor diagnostic interest.

The remaining items which are to be scored for diagnostic content should include positively and negatively worded statements (about the same proportion of each for every variable). They should mostly avoid threatening or defensive topics, e.g. personal abnormalities, referring rather to a wide range of daily-life behaviours, which indirectly reflect conceptual differences. For example, depressive-anxious-neurotic trends are known to be measurable by psycho-somatic or health complaints and food aversions at least as effectively as by more introspective items.

Items might allow of three or five grades of response (from 'Strongly Agree' or 'Like me' to strong rejection), but should probably be scored dichotomously only, as near as possible to the median, in order to avoid the extremeness-evasiveness response set. Alternatively, numbers of extreme responses and of doubtfuls (regardless of content) could be totalled as response set measures and included, as before, in any regression equation.

Empirical vs. factorial keying. Loevinger (1955, 1959) suggests that a test consisting largely of statements about everyday experiences and attitudes could be treated empirically, like the MMPI or Strong VIB. That is the items should not be chosen with any particular variable in mind, but should be correlated with a number of external criteria, to yield a series of scoring keys. Academic achievement, sociometric popularity, leadership activities, sex, age, social class background, delinquent or criminal tendencies, seeking psychiatric help, psychopathological diagnoses, are but a few of the criteria that come to mind. However, this plan seems unwise in the light of the instability of empirical keying; and we would prefer to discover what homogeneous variables or clusters the test itself contains. Each variable should be measured by a separate set of items (i.e. no one item would contribute to several scores, and there should be no 'junk' items which are unkeyed), and the external correlates of these total scores would then be established. A tentative list of important self-conceptual and interpersonal variables should be drawn up by clinical psychologists, and sets of items formulated to represent each of these. The items need not all take the Agree-Disagree or Yes-No form; varied types of responses could be tried, as in the old Pressey Cross-Out test (provided they could be objectively scored), and pictorial items might supplement verbal ones, at least for some of the hypothesized variables.

Item-selection. The standard procedure in choosing items for the final form of the test is to retain those which correlate well with total score on the variable which they are supposed to measure. Though this yields acceptable internal consistency coefficients, it is not satisfactory. It may merely show that all the items refer to some very narrow or specific self-concept, or that they all have the same error-component such as a social-desirability set. Good item-validities (so-called) can be obtained even when the total score represents two or more factors – as has happened in the F-scale. Cattell (1957) points out that what is needed are items all of which measure the same general factor or construct, but which do not have other group factors in common. Lumsden (1961) agrees that item factor analysis is the only satisfactory technique for achieving homogeneity. Hitherto this has involved too much calculation for most test-constructors to undertake; but with the wider availability of electronic computers, it is likely to spread. To obtain a test with wide applicability, it is desirable to study the item-intercorrelations in a number of rather different populations, and to pick out clusters of items that consistently hang together, while also showing relative independence of items in other clusters. This approach, used by L. Siegel (1956) in constructing his Biographical Inventory for Students, seems more likely to yield stable variables than a formal factor analysis. By this method we could expect to arrive at some half-dozen factors (plus acquiescence and social desirability scores). These would not necessarily correspond with the originally hypothesized variables, but rather represent some synthesis of them. The writer would not venture to argue for any particular set of dimensions, beyond suggesting that Ego-strength or Inner Resources (as delineated by Barron, 1953a), and Eysenck's extraversion or rhathymia, should be two of them. Correlations between factors could not be eliminated, but should be kept low. Many items which did not fall clearly within any of the chosen factors would be discarded. Finally, the correlates of each scale with external criteria, and the patterns of scores in groups with well-known characteristics – not merely the logical content of sets of items – should be employed in interpreting their meaning.

Much the same principles could be applied in preparing more modest inventories for specific purposes. We would suggest, however, that no test of this kind is suitable for young adolescents or pre-adolescent pupils. Their self-concepts are too vaguely formulated for their responses to represent anything much beyond the top level of the Self.

Attitude and interest tests. It is considerably easier to construct questionnaire-type tests or scales for almost any social attitude, or type of opinion or belief, interest, sentiment or value which (as pointed out on p. 243) is centred around some definable category of external stimuli. The attitude must, however, be reasonably clear-cut or crystallized in the population concerned. Thus there are greater difficulties with pre-adolescent children or adults of low intelligence and education: their attitudes are less verbalized, and it is more difficult to ensure that the items convey the same meaning to them as to the tester. Also such Subjects are less capable of sustained consideration of a long list of items. With other, literate, Subjects, these tests will generally show acceptable reliability, and good construct validity in the form of correlations with other tests that might be expected to overlap, or plausible group differences. True, it is still problematic how far the scores represent 'private' or 'public' attitudes (i.e. from which level of the Self they arise), how far they are affected by response sets, and whether they should be considered as determining overt behaviour or solely as reflecting verbalized thoughts and feelings.

Clinical criticisms. Clinical psychologists can point out, with considerable justification, that scores on such tests are of dubious psychological significance. The social worker or public opinion interviewer take immense trouble to secure good rapport, realizing that an informant's expressed attitudes may be markedly affected by what he thinks is the object of the inquiry, and by his personal relations with the interviewer (cf. Maccoby, 1954; Kahn and Cannell, 1957). The tester usually gives just a general instruction about co-operation and frankness, and ignores the very diverse reactions that the test is likely to stimulate in different testees.

Smith, Bruner and White (1956) have cast serious doubts on the value of any single attitude score, and on studying attitude structure by correlating scores on attitude and personality scales.

On the basis of over 30 hours of testing and interviewing each of 10 mature adult males, they showed that an attitude to such topics as Communist Russia is far more complex than just 'pro' or 'con'. It is embedded in the overall structure of how the person copes with his world, and it may arise from many different sources – internal needs, social pressures, and reality demands. At the same time these authors found that straightforward discussions on, e.g. 'What matters to you most in life?' were more revealing than projective or other tests, or depth-oriented inquiries.

While admitting the force of these arguments, the case for standardized and normed measures (p. 266) still stands. Further, despite the obvious importance of investigating the origins and development of attitudes, values and interests, there is no evidence to show that better predictions in decision-situations can be made from the clinician's understanding of a person's attitude-interest structure than from test scores. Nevertheless we agree that such scores should be supplemented by the methods discussed in the next Chapter.

A novel demonstration of the value of written attitude responses is provided by Newcomb's research (1958) in which 17 students, previously strangers, roomed together for a semester, and observations were made of the development of friendships among them. Newcomb found that it was possible, from initial responses to a 100-item attitude questionnaire, to predict very closely who would become friendly with whom by the end of 4 months. Predictions of their attachments after 2–3 weeks were less accurate. (As pointed out in Part I, interchanges between people meeting for the first time consist largely in 'scanning' each other's attitudes, with a view to assessing mutual congeniality.) One wonders whether a clinical psychologist, who interviewed these students at the start, would have been equally successful in forecasting their attachments.

Cattell's objection to self-report tests. A rather different criticism of self-report tests of attitudes and interests is voiced by Cattell (1957), namely that a person's consciously verbalized opinions and preferences cannot reveal his major dispositions or long-term motives – though this conflicts oddly with his own use of Q-tests like the 16 PF to assess basic personality traits. As we have seen, Cattell prefers more indirect and objective tests which are claimed to measure motives both at the overt and covert levels. But we know of no evidence that these yield as good predictions of external criteria, such as entering and staying in a job, as do the ordinary interest inventories and social attitude scales.

It is true that such tests are much too readily fakable to be trustworthy in most selection situations, though even here candidates tend to be more honest than one might expect. For example, the Minnesota Teacher Attitude Inventory often yields moderate validities against ratings of teacher competence, although the 'right' answers must be pretty obvious to any sophisticated testee. However, there is a good case for trying more diverse and indirect item-types than the straightforward Agree-Disagree or Like-Dislike: for example, preference items as in the Study of Values and Kuder Preference Record, or items involving estimates of 'what most people think' rather than 'what I think', or – as in the Watson Test of Fairmindedness – items based on biased reasoning. In selection situations, where there is definite motivation to fake, it might be safer to resort to information tests, for measuring knowledge about various hobbies or jobs, or to Hammond's 'error-choice' device, where two answers are provided to information questions, both of which are (unknown to the Subject) biased in opposite directions.*

Classification of attitudes and interests. Perhaps our main problem is to decide which attitudes and interests to test in general counselling work. Their number is limitless; but there is so much overlapping that there is a clear case for reduction to a few main types or factors. On the other hand, the more generalized our measures, the less information they provide relevant to specific decisions. The Strong VIB provides keys for some fifty (male) occupations, yet almost every professional or other high-grade occupation contains additional specialities which differ considerably in their interests (for example, the clinical, experimental, psychometric and social species of psychologists). Strong also has keys for 11 main clusters of jobs, and it would seem more efficient to score these and then to proceed to more detailed diagnoses by combining information about characteristic score-patterns with interview or other techniques of probing.

Most writers would distinguish interests in occupations from avocational pursuits, and would separate off both of these from attitudes or opinions about social issues and institutions; general values, philosophies, ideologies and modes of thought – scientific thinking, prejudice, authoritarianism, etc. – would usually be considered as yet another realm of discourse. But there is a great deal of overlapping among all of these, and even between them and what would commonly be called personality traits. For example, the Allport–Vernon–Lindzey Study of Values shows significant correlations not only with Strong and Kuder interest measures, but also with authoritarian prejudice and Eysenck's tough-mindedness (economic + political vs. aesthetic, social and religious), and even with Jungian types.† Thus Saunders (1960) finds that 27% of the variance in Values scores is covered by the Myers–Briggs inventory:

High scores in Theoretical values tend to go with Introverted, Intuitive, Thinking type, while –

* Fuller descriptions and references are given in Vernon (1953).
† Cf. also the resemblance of Couch and Keniston's Yea-sayers and Nay-sayers to the Extraverted-Sensation and Introverted-Thinking types (p. 210).

High scores in Social values tend to go with Extraverted, Sensation, Feeling type.

Stern, Stein and Bloom (1956) tested a large group of students for 'Stereopath Syndrome' or authoritarianism, and found a marked association with their choice of careers on entry to college (cf. also Rokeach, 1960).

> Social service, Teaching, Art and other creative occupations were preferred by 83% of strong non-stereopaths, 31% of stereopaths.
> Accounting, Engineering, Business, Law, Medicine and other more practical occupations were preferred by 17% and 69% respectively.

Conceivably we might determine a man's vocational and leisure interests by measuring his conceptual type, according to Jung's, or Harvey's, models, or vice versa. Darley and Hagenah (1955) report a number of other associations between Strong VIB interests and personality and attitude variables; and Holland (1958) has even constructed a set of personality scales based wholly on likes and dislikes for a long list of occupational titles.

Eysenck regards extraversion-introversion as a major factor determining tough- vs. tender-mindedness. Social introversion is often measured largely by questions which contrast intellectual with gregarious-sporting interests; and both introversion, neuroticism or anxiety, and tolerance (non-authoritarianism) are associated with high educational achievement. On the other hand, a number of studies indicate that personality-inventory and interest-test measures are fairly distinct. Thus Cottle (1950) found scarcely any overlapping between MMPI + Bell Adjustment and Strong + Kuder Preference scores, apart from small negative correlations between social introversion and persuasive, business and social welfare interests.

This should surely be the kind of tangle that factor analysis could sort out. It has failed to do so, partly because it cannot distinguish cause and effect (i.e. whether traits, attitudes or interests are the more basic), and partly because of inconsistent factorial results in different populations or inconsistent formulations and rotations among different factorists.

Tough-mindedness, authoritarianism and dogmatism. These constructs provide a good illustration of the present state of confusion. Eysenck (1956ab) argues that the Californian F and E – fascist and ethnocentric – dimension is better resolved into a combination of Tough-mindedness and Conservatism. Whereas his critics, Rokeach and

Hanley (1956) and Christie (1956), dispute the validity of his evidence and prefer Authoritarian vs. Democratic and Religious-Irreligious as more fundamental variables.

However, the F-scale itself is far from being a pure measure of authoritarian prejudice. In addition to acquiescence it seems to involve dogmatism, conformism, masculinity, and right-wing bias (cf. O'Neil and Levinson, 1954). Rokeach (1956, 1960) argues persuasively for the primacy of dogmatism vs. openmindedness: dogmatism is 'a relatively closed cognitive organization of beliefs and disbeliefs about reality' and about absolute authority. It characterizes the whole structure of a person's attitudes and expectations, and is thus more general than fascism or other political, ethnic or religious prejudices; and it may express itself as intolerance either in right-wing or left-wing opinion.*

Rokeach's 40-item inventory is very broadly based, including statements that deal with egocentricity, insecurity and self-hate, defences against external threats, the need for a stable framework wherewith to face the world, and identification with absolute authority. It shows good construct validity in that it correlates with the F- and E-scales but not, as they do, with conservatism or right-wing opinion; it also overlaps with anxiety or neuroticism. It differentiates communists from liberals, much as does Eysenck's tough-tender-minded scale, and the more from the less dogmatic religious groups. Again it shows some association with difficulties in reorganizing beliefs or assumptions when tackling a complex and unfamiliar intellectual problem. Two factor analyses by Rokeach and Fruchter (1956; Fruchter et al., 1958) indicate that the main 'dimensions' in this area are Radicalism-Conservatism, Rigidity + Authoritarianism, and Anxiety – Dogmatism being a combination of the latter pair. But as most or all of the tests that they analysed would be strongly subject to acquiescent, social desirability or other response sets, no clear interpretation of their factors is possible. Thus Couch and Keniston showed that general acquiescence or 'Yea-saying' correlates 0·37 with the F-scale, 0·40 with Rokeach's dogmatism scale, and 0·64 with Yes responses on MMPI.

'Inner' vs. 'outer' attitudes. Another plausible basis for classification in this area might be to distinguish attitudes that arise from inner needs from those which are organized around environmental objects. Stern, Stein and Bloom (1956) describe an Activities Index, whose items were chosen to refer to Murray's list of needs, and which, they claim, differentiates well between good and poor college students.

---

* Despite Rokeach's opposition to Eysenck's work, his construct bears a decided resemblance to the latter's tough-mindedness, as also to Harvey, Hunt and Schroder's concrete vs. abstract.

However, many of these items are very similar to those that occur in an 'environment-oriented' test such as the Kuder Preference Record. Cattell believes that his factorial investigations enable one to test drives or ergs and objects or sentiments, and he lists some 12 of the former and 27 of the latter which, between them, should cover all the more frequently occurring types of motivation. Few psychological counsellors or selectors, however, would feel happy in applying this formulation, and even if it were possible to measure so many variables with reasonable reliability in a reasonably short time, there would be certain to be a great deal of wasteful overlapping among them.

Guilford, Shneidman and Zimmerman (1954) have probably gone furthest in sorting out this area. In two factor analyses of the responses of male adult groups to 95 'interest' tests, they arrived at 17 factors which include environment-type and need-type variables, viz:

Mechanical interest	Adventure vs. security
Scientific interest	Cultural conformity
Social welfare	Self-reliance vs. dependence
Aesthetic appreciation	Need for Diversion
Aesthetic expression	Autistic thinking
Clerical interest	Need for attention
Business interest	Resistance to restrictions
Outdoor work interest	Physical drive
	Aggression

The GSZ Interest Survey covers nine types of vocational and leisure interests, and the DF Opinion Survey measures ten of the 'Dynamic Factor' components. Guilford further points out that it is most unsafe to infer vocational interests from avocational. These tests probably come as near as any published to measuring the kind of variables which, in our view, would be of assistance to the counsellor. They are, however, suitable only for young American males, and there is much less evidence for the stability or the external correlates of the scores than there is for the Strong VIB, Kuder Preference or Study of Values. Very little is known of the usefulness of the Dynamic Factors; and it is probable that all scores are to some extent affected by acquiescence or inclusiveness sets.

Yet another mixed test is L. Siegel's (1956) Biographical Inventory for Students, whose 388 items have been classified by cluster analysis as measuring the following 10 variables:

Athletic activities	Political activities
Social activities	Socio-economic background

Heterosexual activities	Economic independence
Religious activities	Dependence on the home
Literature, Music, Art	Social conformity

Apparently the only basis for choosing this particular list is that they represent the kind of questions which are normally included in bio-graphical inventories, and which (male) students will answer fairly readily. A briefer multiple test for individual, clinical, use is that of Toman (1955), which assesses the following 12 attitude variables by 5-item, Guttman-type, scales. It makes no attempt to measure vocational or other interests.

Respect or love for parents	Liking for superiors
Respect or love for siblings	Liking for equals or peers
Father-mother preference	Religious tolerance
Brother-sister preference	Political tolerance
Male vs. female prejudice	Racial tolerance
Liking for children	Attitude to rich people

Excellent agreement was found between the test scores and independent clinical interviewers' assessments of the attitudes.

Conclusions. Many other lists could be culled from the literature, and it is likely that every practising psychologist or counsellor would have his own preferences, depending on his particular purposes and theoretical framework. Nevertheless it may be worthwhile summarizing the type of test which would appear most useful in the light of factorial, response set and other research.

1. It should be a group test covering a limited number of variables (say a dozen or less), in order to yield fairly reliable scores in a fairly brief time. The aim should be to provide a well-normed framework of major attitudes and interests, rather than to pin-point specific vocational or other preferences, and it could be used to stimulate interview discussions or supplemented by the free-response tech-niques advocated in the next Chapter. Darley and Hagenah (1955), Super (1957) and others point out the dangers of assuming that counselling can be based simply on matching test scores to the interest + aptitude content of particular jobs.

2. The items should be meaningful to, and give consistent results with, older secondary pupils and young adults of both sexes, say 15 to 24 years. (This might involve the provision of some alternative variables for the two sexes, e.g. domestic interests for women to complement the mechanical interests for men.)

3. The variables should be chosen for general usefulness and the items formulated to cover them, rather than following Strong's

empirical method of construction and standardization. While external criteria for item-selection could be applied to some variables, multiple-keying should be avoided (cf. Christie's objections, 1956). A compromise would be necessary between independence or orthogonality of variables and tieing them to important environmental 'presses' (e.g. to common job-types).

4. Esoteric or highly theoretical constructs should be avoided, for example the Jungian types of the Myers–Briggs inventory, Murray's needs and many of Guilford's Dynamic Factors or Cattell's ergs. The writer would certainly hope to include scales for radicalism-conservatism, and for dogmatism or intolerant, prejudiced thinking; possibly also for dependence vs. negativism, so as to cover the four main stages in Harvey's model. Alternatively such variables could be included in the personality inventory, outlined above, rather than among the interests and attitudes.

5. Like the Strong VIB, the test could be in several parts (each part covering many, or all, of the variables); but there should be a wider variety of item-types. Forced-choice or preference items are useful for eliminating acquiescence sets, though they should not be used exclusively, since some indication of overall level or strength of attitudes and interests is needed, not only the pattern. (Hence the Kuder Preference profile often seems less informative than the Strong, because the Subject has to score low on some interests if he is strong on others.) One part might well consist of items couched in extravagant, cliché form with $+3$ to -3 responses, in order to provide independent measures of acquiescence and of extremeness-indecisiveness, which could be used either to adjust, or to help in interpreting, the other scores. Very high item-discrimination coefficients, or internal consistency correlations for each variable greater than 0.75 to 0.80, are unnecessary since they tend to reduce the breadth and validity of the variables.

6. External correlates and group differences in profiles should be sought. For example a combination of Dogmatism $+$ Right-Wing $+$ Acquiescence $+$ Extremeness might closely duplicate Authoritarianism scales; while other combinations might adequately substitute for measures of the Spranger values, or for the numerous specific occupational scores of the Strong VIB.

Chapter 17

THE STUDY OF PERSONAL CONCEPTS

G. Kelly (1958) writes: 'When the subject is asked to guess what the examiner is thinking, we call it an objective test; when the examiner tries to guess what the subject is thinking we call it a projective device.' The personality inventories, attitude scales and interests tests discussed in the previous chapter can all be thought of as measuring the Subject's self-concepts and concepts of others, but they also require him to translate these concepts into the psychologist's frame of reference; that is, they show how closely his attitudes conform to the psychologist's notions of an extravert, an authoritarian, etc. Projective devices, in Kelly's view, try to show how the Subject himself structures or codifies his experiences, though we would add that such devices are still apt to tell us as much about the psychologist as about his Subject, since the responses have to be interpreted in terms of a depth-oriented or other theory. A number of techniques are considered in this chapter which perhaps allow more direct expression of the personal conceptual system than those described in Chapter 10. They have not been employed to anything like the same extent as self-report, behavioural or projective techniques in counselling and selection, or even in clinical work; hence much less is known about their potentialities and limitations. Thus we shall be concerned more with possible tools than well-tried ones; and in particular with applications or extensions of Q-technique, the Semantic Differential and the Rep test.

First, though, brief mention should be given to the diagnostic methods used by the authors of two other conceptual approaches to personality.

Leary's Interpersonal Diagnosis and Harvey, Hunt and Schroder's Conceptual System. Both of these systems rely on a combination of standard techniques; hence they need not detain us long. Leary (1957) plots a profile or circular chart of his Subject's or patient's standing on eight interpersonal variables, at three different levels (cf. p. 114). The top level Public Communications is covered by acquaintances' ratings of the person's overt behaviour, combined with certain situational tests and indices derived from the MMPI. The next level of Conscious Descriptions is diagnosed by self-report data – an adjective checklist, self-ratings, also ratings given by a clinical interviewer. The third level of Private Symbolizations is derived from TAT and other projective material. Although detailed instructions are provided, it is difficult to follow how the profiles are arrived at, how the test and other data are combined, and whether the scores are replicable or subjective, i.e. whether different diagnosticians would reach the same results.

Harvey and his colleagues (1961) do not advocate any specific methods of diagnosis, but mention a number of sources of data which should help to indicate a person's Stage or Level. These might include the Goldstein–Scheerer (1941) tests of abstract-concrete thought, Witkin's perceptual tests, the F-scale and other attitude tests, conformity situations like the autokinetic effect, also Rorschach, TAT and the Rep test. In one experiment they gave tests of conformity to social pressures, a questionnaire on reactions to frustration and a modified Rep test. There is no clear indication, however, of how congruent were the diagnoses reached from behavioural, self-report and projective devices, nor how they should be combined when they yield discrepant results.

Q-techniques. These may be thought of as bridging the gap between psychologist-determined and subject-determined tests. True, the psychologist chooses the initial set of items for the Subject to sort, but they are usually derived from statements made by other similar Subjects, and he is free to put any items that do not seem meaningful to him, positively or negatively, into the large middle piles. The psychologist may, of course, interpret or classify the items that are strongly accepted or rejected in terms of his own theoretical categories, in which case the Self-sort becomes merely a glorified forced-choice questionnaire. However, we have seen that it is usually scored 'ipsatively' by means of its correlations with the person's own Ideal or other sorts. Its special virtue is that the person's Self-concepts are compared with his own norms.

The Q-technique eliminates acquiescence response sets, but it is obviously subject to social desirability effects. Indeed the Self-Ideal correlation is intended to measure self-acceptance or self-esteem, which one might expect to be linked with desire for favourable evaluations by others. Kenny (1956) obtained judgments of the social desirability of a set of 25 traits, and showed that both Self and Ideal sorts tended to correlate strongly with this variable. However, his data bring out an an interesting point which he fails to note: in a small group of eight Subjects, the Self-Ideal correlations were closely parallel to social desirability scores based on each Subject's own judgments, but quite unrelated to desirability as measured by the average or group judgment. Apparently, then, Self-Ideal Discrepance or Congruence is not merely equivalent to an ordinary personality inventory score, though it is still far from clear how the counsellor should interpret it.

Levy (1956b) suggests that Discrepance reflects some discord not only in a person's perceptions of himself, but also in his attitudes to his environment. He obtained actual and ideal sorts of items describing his Subjects' home towns, as well as sorts of items dealing with Self. The correlation between the two Discrepance coefficients was 0·70, indicating that those who are dissatisfied with themselves are also dissatisfied with the town in which they lived. Surely one might have expected that this kind of criticalness in a person's concepts would be rather general.

Wylie (1961) has strongly criticized both Q-sort and other techniques employed in the study of self-concepts, on the grounds of lack of clear definition of the constructs which are being measured, and of unsuspected weaknesses and artifacts in the instruments. There is little or no evidence of the reliability of the latter, and studies that claim to show their validity have generally used other self-report measures as criteria, so that their results are contaminated. Discrepance or congruence scores, she maintains, are full of pitfalls, just as are the analogous difference-scores employed in research on social perception and insight (cf. Chap. 4). She objects too to Q-sort judgments being forced onto a normal distribution, since most Subjects prefer a U-shaped distribution. However, this objection surely means that the Q-sort technique is successful in controlling acquiescent and extremeness response sets. Certainly Wylie's criticisms deserve serious attention, though they seem unduly destructive in view of the useful results that this approach has yielded in studies of therapeutic change, and in researches on identification, projection and other aspects of personality development.

Applications of Q-sorting. The possible applications of the technique in diagnosing individual differences, especially among relatively normal individuals, have so far been little explored. Following Levy's result, we would suggest that a set of statements or items should be chosen to refer to everyday activities, vocational and leisure interests and values, as well as to common social-emotional problems. These should be taken from free written self-descriptions by ordinary counsellees, rather than from clinical interview records. The total number of statements should be kept fairly small, say 60, so that several ratings would not occupy too much time. The following sorts and their interrelations should be of interest, and might help towards specifying what F. Allport designates as the person's main trends:

1. Self-sort.
2. Self-sort for what he expects to be in, say, 10 years' time when settled in his career.
3. How he thinks the typical person of his own age, sex and social background would sort.
4. How his acquaintances would describe him.

No. 3 would be compared with the actual average sort by a group of similar individuals. It would also be quite feasible to correlate No. 1 with averaged sorts by persons representing different vocations, different pathological groups or other types of people, and thus to throw light on the important question of whom he identifies with (academics, delinquents, those older or younger than himself, and so on). While this would be almost equivalent to the Strong VIB or MMPI, the freedom from acquiescent response sets would be an advantage.

A second set of items might cover a variety of aspects of environment – opinions on social issues, people, institutions, etc., which would be sorted for Self and Perceived Others, as well as by actual Others. This would indicate what he sees as right or wrong with the world, what he thinks others think, and how these deviate.

Conceivably such sets of items could fruitfully be factor-analysed in a sample population, and the person's present or idealized standing on sub-groups of items, corresponding to the various factors, could be measured.

One attempt to analyse the dimensions of Self-concepts along these lines was carried out by Smith (1960). Seventy pairs of adjectives were taken from current Self-concept tests, and the self-ratings of 120 male psychiatric patients were intercorrelated. Five factors were obtained:

1. Evaluation, satisfaction with self, success vs. sense of failure, self-denigration.
2. Tension-anxiety, feelings of tiredness, emptiness, fear, confusion.
3. Independence, felt leadership and intelligence vs. inadequacy, conformity.
4. Estrangement, sense of distance from others.
5. Body image of potency, concept of bodily size and strength.

Rather different categories might have been obtained with normals, and with a broader set of items. However, such research differs little from factorizing items in a personality questionnaire, and it might be expected to yield factors similar to those in Cattell's 16 PF test. They represent consensual dimensions, or common elements in the Self-pictures of a group of people, not individual patterns of Self-interpretation.

The Semantic Differential. One weakness in all these applications of Q-sorting is that they encourage a somewhat artificial introspective attitude. The Subject's response is mainly in terms of 'Do I feel like that?' (though we have suggested adding, 'Do others feel like that?'). This seems likely to restrict the range of concepts that find expression. Osgood's semantic differential has the advantage of a more indirect approach. A great variety of items can be taken – Myself, my father, my employer (or school-teacher), different vocations, studying, outdoor sports, girls, Jews, stealing, ethical principles, etc. etc. And each of these is rated on a series of adjectival scales – good-bad, light-dark, excitable-calm, complex-simple, youthful-mature, etc., rather than just for likeness to me (or to others).

The technique has been applied mainly in the study of group phenomena, and it is not clear how best to utilize the information it yields about individuals, except in the clinical setting (as in the example quoted on p. 135). The adjectives could be grouped on the basis of a factor analysis such as Osgood describes; each concept could then be scored for evaluation or liking (Factor I) and for potency and activity. Thus the sizes of the factor scores would tell us something of the individual's attitudes to these concepts, and a plot would show the neighbouringness or distance between concepts (e.g. whether Self and father, or school work and sports, were widely separated). Alternately each individual's structure of epithets could be factorized by itself, and the make-up of his dimensions might be significant. It should be possible to categorize the patterns of various groups of people – normal and abnormal, in different vocations, etc. – to observe the resemblance of the individual's pattern to these, and thus to interpret him normatively. So far, however, there is little information on the behavioural correlates of people's semantic structures.

Another possibility would be, instead of exploring the same concepts or items with all individuals, to select for semantic analysis the goals and anxieties which had been found to be particularly significant to him in a previous interview, or to combine some of these with a standard list.

Osgood's technique can cope with relatively few concepts at a time, because of the arduousness of rating each one on at least 15 adjectives (usually many more); but it provides somewhat greater flexibility of dimensions. Maybe, though, this is insufficient. Because the pooled attitudes of a group of Subjects can be largely reduced to the evaluative dimension, plus one or two others (which are rather unstable), it does not follow that plotting a person's key concepts against these dimensions adequately portrays the wealth of his feelings towards them. For example, it may not show which concepts he finds worrying, embarrassing, exciting, curious, trivial, sources of fantasies and ambitions, and so on: or perhaps, for most practical purposes, it does.

Kelly's Rep test. The third approach, that of G. Kelly (1955), seems so flexible as to be almost unmanageable, though it has the merit of arising directly from the author's psychological and therapeutic theory. Kelly's methods of diagnosis are similar to those of most clinicians, including interviewing, case-history, projective testing, analysis of autobiographical materials, etc., but he also relies largely on his Role Construct Repertory, or Rep test.

Now an essential feature of his theory is that all constructs are dichotomous or bi-polar: they imply that two things are seen as alike in some way, and that they differ from a third thing in this respect. A fairly standard set of figures or persons is taken – Self, father, spouse, a liked teacher, a disliked employer, and other relatives or acquaintances meeting certain specifications. These are then sorted somewhat along the lines of a Goldstein object-sorting or Weigl concept-formation test. The tester presents a succession of triads, and asks the Subject to say in what way two members of a triad are alike, and different from the third. Kelly claims that some 15 to 25 such triads provide a sufficient sampling of the main constructs in terms of which the Subject groups and differentiates people, and that further comparisons yield little additional information. If the concept-structure is to be analysed quantitatively, each of the figures has then to be assessed as positive or zero in respect of each of the constructs; and a simple form of non-parametric factorization allows the constructs to be grouped, usually under three to six main dimensions (cf. also Levy, 1956a; Levy and Dugan, 1956).

Comments. Note that this procedure is wholly intra-individual. Its aim is to allow the subject to display his own constructs, not to force them on to dimensions provided by the tester, or by other people in general, nor to facilitate comparisons with the constructs of other Subjects. Kelly appears to use the results much like those of TAT, as a source of therapeutic hypotheses, and gives scarcely any indication of how the factors can be interpreted. Presumably they represent the ways in which the Subject groups qualities: e.g. if intelligent, then trustworthy and likeable, etc. – something which might be found out equally well by correlating his ratings of acquaintances on a standard list of traits.

Since a major object of the technique is to provide the clinician with a framework for viewing his client in terms of the client's own 'vocabulary', it offers little scope for predicting how the client will measure up against vocational or other external criteria. It could, presumably, be used purely idiographically – to guide the psychologist's understanding of the person; but its value would then depend wholly on the psychologist's skill. Kelly seems to claim that Rep test results are *more* communicable to other clinicians than are the finding of other diagnostic techniques. This may be true of the raw data: the test is easily administered either to an individual or a group, and easily 'processed'. But there are even fewer rules for interpreting and communicating the implications of such data, or relating them to the case-study and other material, than with Rorschach or TAT. It is interesting that the only evidence of the value of the method, apart from clinical usefulness, that Kelly quotes is that Rep test results can be matched successfully with diagnoses based (*a*) on TAT, or (*b*) on observing the Subjects in brief role-playing sessions.

A further limitation of the Rep test is that its constructs refer solely to people; and even if the people listed include most of the key figures in the individual's adjustment, it ignores many other important attitudes – likes and dislikes for different kinds of work, for leisure pursuits, for types of people rather than particular acquaintances, etc. Perhaps these could be covered by additional sortings; but all the objects included in any one sort have to be alike or unlike in some respect.

A strong point in favour both of the semantic differential and the Rep test, which cannot be claimed for Q-sorting, is that they may reveal concepts of which the person is barely aware, or which normally operate at the emotional rather than the verbally formulated level; i.e. they penetrate to our third level of Self. For example he may be construing his wife in much the same way as his mother, and the test helps him to realize such connections. In this respect one might reasonably claim that the Rep test involves less subjective interpretation by the clinician than does TAT.

In many ways the Rep test resembles the Word Association or Sentence Completion tests. All three yield samples of the person's concepts and linkages which often give the clinician valuable leads. But though the responses can be classified or quantified in various ways, the resulting *scores* convey very little useful information to the diagnostician. Sentence Completion has indeed worked better than the other two (cf. Chap. 10), since it is comparatively easy to score for personality conflict or neuroticism vs. stability; whereas there is no evidence so far that the Rep test can be interpreted other than idiographically.

Autobiographical materials. Written autobiographies or self-characterizations are often required in clinical counselling, and doubtless provide the counsellor with a valuable starting point and overview. In so far as they are capable of revealing all shades of attitude to all significant objects – Self, other people, activities, etc., and all the person's major trends, they are richer than any of the more formal techniques that we have been discussing. Correspondingly, they are more intractable to objective assessment, and are narrowly limited to the consciously verbalized level of the Self. It would seem fairly straightforward to apply some type of content analysis, in order to bring out the major themes or foci of interest, whose significance could be followed up by psychometric techniques. Little has been done along these lines, however, probably because the kind of content and treatment vary so much from one Subject to another. Differences in literacy also make it difficult to secure comparable material from different Subjects.

Baldwin (1942) showed that it was possible to analyse personal documents (in this case a series of letters written by one Subject) by a technique which anticipated the Rep test. A number of major topics and of attitudes expressed towards these was selected, and their frequencies were counted over successive time periods. Moreover contiguities were tabulated, i.e. the frequency with which any pair of items occurred together in a single passage; and the statistical significance of such linkages was calculated. Baldwin claimed then to have developed a statistical method of analysing a single personality, and showed that the frequencies and contiguities were congruent with a clinician's interpretation of the Subject's personality. However, the method does not seem to have been taken up by others, partly because of its laboriousness, but also because it is still essentially idiographic. No rules can be laid down regarding what to do with the results.

Linguistic analyses, such as those applied to oral interview material (Verb/Adjective quotient, etc., cf. p. 134) would likewise be feasible, even if too tedious for routine diagnostic purposes. But their construct validity is not encouraging (Doob, 1958).

Kelly advocates asking the client for a sketch of himself written in the third person, as if by an intimate and sympathetic friend. This instruction helps to produce much significant material, which can be analysed systematically for choice and repetition of themes, underlying constructs (e.g. powerful figures), choice of terms and associations of particular words, vocabulary level, sequences and organization of topics, and the relations of each statement to the whole. Such interpretation is, of course, wholly subjective. A similar but simpler device often employed by British vocational psychologists is to get their clients to write brief (1–2 minute) descriptions of themselves as seen (a) by a friend, (b) by a critic. Another instruction which appears to be fruitful is to ask for an imaginary autobiography written ten years hence, describing their lives in the interim. This can reveal much about the person's trends and goals, and his purposiveness in pursuing them; though no detailed system of scoring either for formal or content characteristics has been developed (cf. Veness, 1962).

Wylie (1961) suggests that open-ended questions about the Self are apt to produce mainly uninformative clichés. While this is often true, much must depend on the instructions given and on the Subjects' motivation.

A proposal. It would be of interest to follow up the applications in selection and counselling situations of any of the techniques discussed in this Chapter. None of them, however, seems quite to meet the need for a device which will:

(a) Supplement the self-report test or inventory by allowing the person to express his spontaneous concepts;

(b) direct his attention to other persons, groups and activities as well as to his Self-picture, trends and goals;

(c) be sufficiently structured to produce comparable material from many counsellees, which could be categorized or scored, and its construct validity investigated.

The best approximation that the present writer can suggest might work as follows. After a preliminary interview to help establish rapport, or even a group session with a number of counsellees, each would be asked to write for 10–15 minutes on four topics:

1. What I most like about the world in which I live.

2. What I most dislike about it, and what I do about these dislikes.
3. What I most like about myself.
4. What I most dislike, and how I hope to change.

Brief suggested headings would help the client to cover all important areas, without restricting him. The material would be expanded in individual interviews, particularly with the less literate. It would then be subjected to a detailed content analysis, including vocational and leisure-interest areas, social attitudes, family and interpersonal relations, self-attitudes, conflicts, etc. The key words 'like' and 'dislike' are chosen on the basis of Osgood's demonstration of the predominance of evaluation in most personal constructs, but they should not inhibit the display of a variety of other attitudes such as the Rep test helps to elicit. While the material can be treated nomothetically or normatively, it should also bring out unique trends and structures. However, no trials have been made of the feasibility of such a technique, and we cannot say whether Q-sorts of statements prepared by the tester would not be equally effective, as well as more convenient.

Projective techniques. The evidence surveyed in Chapter 10 indicated that the introduction of standard projective techniques such as Rorschach and TAT into vocational selection or counselling, or other practical decision situations, would be more likely to lower than enhance the validity of any conclusions, although there is ample justification for using them for exploratory-therapeutic purposes. At the same time the projective approach can help to penetrate the façades that a person normally maintains about himself, or presents to his counsellor. Thus there are good grounds for employing non-verbal stimulus materials (pictures), or non-verbal responses (drawings), which may appear less threatening, and be reacted to less self-consciously, than the techniques outlined in this Chapter. We also saw that better results are likely to be obtained from tests that are focused on particular needs and attitudes than from generalized instruments, though at the same time the clearer structuring must mean that their object is more easily discerned and that they are therefore more open to faking.

Ammons *et al.* (1950) describe a Vocational Apperception test consisting of eight pictures for men, ten for women, each portraying in rather vague form activities characteristic of a common job-type. This is given orally and responses are analysed for liking-disliking each activity, reasons for entering, areas of conflict, and final outcome. There is but little information on its effectiveness, and the test does not seem to have been taken up widely. Others have tried out pictures in teacher selection, designed to illustrate various adult-child inter-actions. Even a rather superficial (non-depth) classification of the relevant attitudes expressed in the Subject's stories seems to have some diagnostic value. However, much more research is needed on the most suitable kinds of picture, what instructions to give, and what interpretations are justified.

Also in the teaching field, Stern, Stein and Bloom (1956) asked students in training to draw: 'a picture of a teacher at work in a classroom', using stick figures if need be so as to reduce the effects of differences in drawing skill. Students rated as more successful teachers introduced greater individuality among the children portrayed, and tended to draw them as active among themselves or with the teacher. The less successful differentiated the teacher figure more clearly in terms of size and status symbols, introduced more order and regu-larity (e.g. the children sitting at desks), and paid relatively more attention to such physical details as blackboards and books. No definite evidence on validity is forthcoming, but the technique successfully avoids any verbalization; and it could obviously be extended to, and validated against, a number of vocational or other criteria.

Conclusion. In conclusion, it may be seen that there is a wealth of instruments which can be of value to the counsellor; and, of course, better ones will be devised when we are more clear about our objectives. At the moment we know more about the weaknesses of tests than about their potentialities, since research has concentrated so largely on the futile aim of proving or disproving their validity as measures of specified internal dispositions. Instead they should be accepted at their face value as samples of acquaintances' observations and interpretations, or of behaviour in social or job situations, or of self-concepts, etc., and the justifiable inferences that can be drawn from them determined by research. Simultaneously we need a more comprehensive psychological system of the trends – both common and unique – that underly behaviour patterns and self-concepts, as far as possible avoiding assumptions regarding inner dispositions. This should be linked up, on the one hand with learning theories and studies of child development, and on the other with the aims and procedures of counselling the relatively normal individual and other decision-making. If the information obtainable from the kind of instruments we have discussed could be fitted into such a framework, we might hope for real progress in the scientific assessment of personality.

BIBLIOGRAPHY

ABT, L. E., and BELLAK, L. (1950) *Projective Psychology*. New York: Knopf.

ADAMS, H. B., and COOPER, G. D. (1961) 'Barron's MMPI Ego Strength scale, Klopfer's Rorschach Prognostic scale, and Cartwright's Strength score as measures of Ego Strength.' *Amer. Psychologist*, **16**, 391.

ADAMS, H. F. (1927) 'The good judge of personality.' *J. abnorm. soc. Psychol.*, **22**, 172–81.

ADORNO, T. W., FRENKEL-BRUNSWIK, E., *et al.* (1950) *The Authoritarian Personality*. New York: Harper.

AINSWORTH, M. D. (1954) 'Problems of validation.' In B. Klopfer *et al.*, *Developments in the Rorschach Technique*. Yonkers, N.Y.: World Book Co., 405–500.

AINSWORTH, M. D., ANDRY, R. G., *et al.* (1962) *Deprivation of Maternal Care*. Geneva: WHO.

ALLEN, R. M. (1958) *Personality Assessment Procedures*. New York: Harper.

ALLPORT, F. H. (1937) 'Teleonomic description in the study of personality.' *Char. & Person.*, **5**, 202–14.

ALLPORT, F. H., and FREDERIKSEN, N. (1941) 'Personality as a pattern of teleonomic trends.' *J. soc. Psychol.*, **13**, 141–82.

ALLPORT, G. W. (1960) *Personality and Social Encounter*. Boston, Mass.: Beacon Press.

ALLPORT, G. W. (1961a) *Pattern and Growth in Personality*. New York: Holt, Rinehart & Winston.

ALLPORT, G. W. (1961b) 'The unique and the general in psychological science.' In Ross, J. A., and Thompson, R. (edit.) *Proceedings of the Summer Conference*. Western Washington State College, pp. 25–37.

ALLPORT, G. W., and CANTRIL, H. (1934) 'Judging personality from the voice.' *J. soc. Psychol.*, **5**, 37–55.

ALLPORT, G. W., and KRAMER, B. M. (1946) 'Some roots of prejudice.' *J. Psychol.*, **22**, 9–39.

291

ALLPORT, G. W., and ODBERT, H. S. (1936) 'Trait-names: a psycho-lexical study.' *Psychol. Monogr.*, **47**, No. 211.

ALLPORT, G. W., and POSTMAN, L. P. (1947) *The Psychology of Rumor*. New York: Holt.

ALLPORT, G. W., and VERNON, P. E. (1933) *Studies in Expressive Movement*. New York: Macmillan.

AMMONS, R. B., BUTLER, M. N., and HERZIG, S. A. (1950) 'A projective test for vocational research and guidance at the college level.' *J. appl. Psychol.*, **34**, 198–205.

ANASTASI, A. (1961). *Psychological Testing* (2nd ed.). New York: Macmillan.

ANDERSON, H. H., and ANDERSON, G. L. (1951) *An Introduction to Projective Techniques*. New York: Prentice-Hall.

ANDREW, G., HARTWELL, S., et al. (1953) *The Michigan Picture Test*. Chicago: Science Research Associates.

ANDRY, R. G. (1960) *Delinquency and Parental Pathology*. London: Methuen.

ANSBACHER, H. L. and ANSBACHER, R. W. (1956) *The Individual Psychology of Alfred Adler*. New York: Basic Books.

ANSTEY, E., and MERCER, E. O. (1956) *Interviewing for the Selection of Staff*. London: Allen & Unwin.

ARBOUS, A. G. (1955) *Selection for Industrial Leadership*. London: Oxford University Press.

ARNHOFF, F. N. (1954) 'Some factors influencing the unreliability of clinical judgments.' *J. clin. Psychol.*, **10**, 272–5.

ASCH, S. E. (1946) 'Forming impressions of personality.' *J. abnorm. soc. Psychol.*, **41**, 258–90.

ASH, P. (1949) 'The reliability of psychiatric diagnoses.' *J. abnorm. soc. Psychol.*, **44**, 272–6.

ATKINSON, J. W. (edit. 1958) *Motives in Fantasy, Action and Society*. New York: Van Nostrand.

BALDWIN, A. L. (1942) 'Personal structure analysis: a statistical method for investigating the single personality.' *J. abnorm. soc. Psychol.*, **37**, 163–83.

BALDWIN, A. L., KALHORN, J., and BREESE, F. H. (1945) 'Patterns of parent behavior.' *Psychol. Monogr.*, **58**, No. 268.

BALES, R. F. (1950) *Interaction Process Analysis*. Cambridge, Mass.: Addison-Wesley.

BANDURA, A. (1961) 'Psychotherapy as a learning process.' *Psychol. Bull.*, **58**, 143–59.

BANDURA, A., and WALTERS, R. H. (1959) *Adolescent Aggression.* New York: Ronald Press.

BARNES, E. H. (1955) 'The relation of biased test responses to psychopathology.' *J. abnorm. soc. Psychol.*, **51**, 286–90.

BARNES, E. H. (1956) 'Factors, response bias, and the MMPI.' *J. consult. Psychol.*, **20**, 419–21.

BARRON, F. (1953a) 'An Ego-strength scale which predicts response to psychotherapy.' *J. consult. Psychol.*, **17**, 327–33.

BARRON, F. (1953b) 'Complexity-simplicity as a personality dimension.' *J. abnorm. soc. Psychol.*, **48**, 163–72.

BARRON, F., and LEARY, T. F. (1955) 'Changes in psychoneurotic patients with and without psychotherapy.' *J. consult. Psychol.*, **19**, 239–45.

BARTLETT, F. C. (1932) *Remembering.* Cambridge University Press.

BARTLETT, N. (1950) 'Review of research and development in examination for aptitude for submarine training, 1942–5.' *Medic. Res. Lab. Rep.*, **9**, 11–53, No. 153. New London, Conn.: U.S. Naval Submarine Base.

BASS, B. M. (1954) 'The leaderless group discussion.' *Psychol. Bull.*, **51**, 465–92.

BAUGHMAN, E. E. (1958) 'The role of the stimulus in Rorschach responses.' *Psychol. Bull.*, **55**, 121–47.

BAYROFF, A. G., HAGGERTY, H. R., and RUNDQUIST, E. A. (1954) 'Validity of ratings as related to rating techniques and conditions.' *Personnel Psychol.*, **7**, 93–113.

BECK, S. J. (1953) 'The science of personality: nomothetic or idiographic?' *Psychol. Rev.*, **60**, 353–9.

BECKER, W. C. (1960) 'The matching of behavior rating and questionnaire personality factors.' *Psychol. Bull.*, **57**, 201–12.

BELL, J. E. (1948) *Projective Techniques.* New York: Longmans Green.

BENDER, I. E., and HASTORF, A. H. (1953) 'On measuring generalized empathic ability (social sensitivity).' *J. abnorm. soc. Psychol.*, **48**, 503–6.

BENJAMIN, J. D. (1950) 'Methodological considerations in the validation and elaboration of psychoanalytical personality theory.' *Amer. J. Orthopsychiat.*, **20**, 139–56.

BERG, I. A. (1959) 'The unimportance of test item content.' In Bass, B. M., and Berg, I. A., *Objective Approaches to Personality.* New York: Van Nostrand, pp. 83–99.

BERNSTEIN, L. (1956) 'The examiner as an inhibiting factor in clinical testing.' *J. consult. Psychol.*, **20**, 287–90.

BIERI, J. (1955) 'Cognitive complexity-simplicity and predictive behavior.' *J. abnorm. soc. Psychol.*, **51**, 263–8.

BIERI, J., and BLACKER, E. (1956) 'The generality of cognitive complexity in the perception of people and inkblots.' *J. abnorm. soc. Psychol.*, **53**, 112–17.

BLAKE, R. R., and RAMSEY, G. V. (edit. 1951) *Perception: An Approach to Personality.* New York: Ronald Press.

BLUM, G. S. (1960) 'The Blacky pictures with children.' In Rabin, A. I., and Haworth, M. R., *Projective Techniques with Children.* New York: Grune & Stratton, pp. 95–104.

BLUM, G. S., and HUNT, H. F. (1952) 'The validity of the Blacky pictures.' *Psychol. Bull.*, **49**, 238–50.

BOWLBY, J., *et al.* (1956) 'The effects of mother-child separation: a follow-up study.' *Brit. J. med. Psychol.*, **29**, 211–47.

BRAMMER, L. M., and SHOSTROM, E. L. (1960) *Therapeutic Psychology: Fundamentals of Counseling and Psychotherapy.* New York: Prentice-Hall.

BRONFENBRENNER, U. (1958) 'The study of identification through interpersonal perception.' In Tagiuri, R., and Petrullo, L., *Person Perception and Interpersonal Behavior.* Stanford University Press, pp. 110–30.

BRONFENBRENNER, U., HARDING, J., and GALLWEY, M. (1958) 'The measurement of skill in social perception.' In McClelland, D., *Talent and Society.* New York: Van Nostrand, pp. 29–111.

BRONFENBRENNER, U., and RICCIUTI, H. N. (1960) 'The appraisal of personality characteristics in children.' In Mussen, P., *Handbook of Research Methods in Child Development.* New York: Wiley, pp. 770–817.

BROWN, J. A. C. (1961) *Freud and the Post-Freudians.* London: Penguin Books.

BROWN, W. (1916) 'Individual and sex differences in suggestibility.' *Univ. Calif. Publ. Psychol.*, **2**, No. 6.

BROWN, W. P. (1961) 'Conceptions of perceptual defence.' *Brit. J. Psychol. Monogr. Suppl.*, No. 35.

BRUNER, J. S. (1948) 'Perceptual theory and the Rorschach test.' *J. Person.*, **17**, 157–68.

BRUNER, J. S., SHAPIRO, D., and TAGIURI, R. (1958) 'The meaning of traits in isolation and in combination.' In Tagiuri, R., and

Petrullo, L., *Person Perception and Interpersonal Behavior*. Stanford University Press, pp. 277–88.

BRUNER, J. S., and TAGIURI, R. (1954) 'The perception of people.' In Lindzey, G., *Handbook of Social Psychology*. Cambridge, Mass.: Addison-Wesley, pp. 634–54.

BUGENTAL, J. F. T. (1952) 'A method for assessing self and not-self attitudes during the therapeutic series.' *J. consult. Psychol.*, **16**, 435–9.

BULLOUGH, E. (1908) 'The "Perceptive Problem" in the aesthetic appreciation of single colours.' *Brit. J. Psychol.*, **2**, 408–63.

BURDOCK, E. I., SUTTON, S., and ZUBIN, J. (1958) 'Personality and psychopathology.' *J. abnorm. soc. Psychol.*, **56**, 18–30.

BURROUGHS, G. E. R. (1958) 'A study of the interview in the selection of students for teaching.' *Brit. J. educ. Psychol.*, **28**, 37–46.

CAMPBELL, D. T., and FISKE, D. W. (1959) 'Convergent and discriminant validation by the multitrait-multimethod matrix.' *Psychol. Bull.*, **56**, 81–105.

CAMPBELL, D. T., and TYLER, B. B. (1957) 'The construct validity of work-group morale measures.' *J. appl. Psychol.*, **41**, 91–2.

CANTRIL, H. (1957) 'Perception and interpersonal relations.' *Amer. J. Psychiat.*, **114**, 119–26.

CAPLAN, G. (1954) 'Clinical observations on the emotional life of children in the communal settlements in Israel.' In *Problems of Infancy and Childhood*. New York: Josiah Macy Foundation.

CARR, H. A., and KINGSBURY, F. A. (1938) 'The concept of traits.' *Psychol. Rev.*, **45**, 497–524.

CARRIGAN, P. M. (1960) 'Extraversion-introversion as a dimension of personality: a reappraisal.' *Psychol. Bull.*, **57**, 329–60.

CARTWRIGHT, R. D., and VOGEL, J. L. (1960) 'A comparison of changes in psychoneurotic patients during matched periods of therapy and no therapy.' *J. consult. Psychol.*, **24**, 121–7.

CATTELL, R. B. (1951) 'Principles of design in "Projective" or misperception tests of personality.' In Anderson, H. H. and G. L., *An Introduction to Projective Techniques*. New York: Prentice-Hall, pp. 55–98.

CATTELL, R. B. (1957) *Personality and Motivation Structure and Measurement*. Yonkers, N.Y.: World Book Co.

CATTELL, R. B. (1961) 'Theory of situational, instrument, second order, and refraction factors in personality structure research.' *Psychol. Bull.*, **58**, 160–74.

CHAMBERS, G. S., and HAMLIN, R. M. (1957) 'The validity of

U

judgments based on "blind" Rorschach records.' *J. consult. Psychol.*, **21**, 105–9.

CHANCE, J. E., and MEADERS, W. (1960) 'Needs and interpersonal perception.' *J. Person.*, **28**, 200–9.

CHAPMAN, L. J., and BOCK, R. D. (1958) 'Components of variance due to acquiescence and content in the F scale measure of authoritarianism.' *Psychol. Bull.*, **55**, 328–33.

CHI, P. L. (1937) 'Statistical analysis of personality rating.' *J. Exper. Educ.*, **5**, 229–45.

CHILD, I. L., FRANK, K. F., and STORM, T. (1956) 'Self-ratings and TAT: their relations to each other and to childhood background.' *J. Person.*, **25**, 96–114.

CHRISTIE, R. (1956) 'Eysenck's treatment of the personality of communists.' *Psychol. Bull.*, **53**, 411–30.

CHRISTIE, R., HAVEL, J., and SEIDENBERG, B. (1958) 'Is the F scale irreversible?' *J. abnorm. soc. Psychol.*, **56**, 143–59.

CLINE, V. B. (1955) 'Ability to judge personality assessed with a stress interview and sound-film technique.' *J. abnorm. soc. Psychol.*, **50**, 183–7.

CLINE, V. B., and RICHARDS, J. M. (1960) 'Accuracy of interpersonal perception – a general trait.' *J. abnorm. soc. Psychol.*, **60**, 1–7.

CLINE, V. B., and RICHARDS, J. M. (1961) Fourth Annual Report: *Variables Related to Accuracy in Interpersonal Perception*. University of Utah, Department of Psychology, ONR Contract 19288 (04).

COLBY, K. M. (1958) *A Skeptical Psychoanalyst*. New York: Ronald Press.

COLBY, K. M. (1960) *An Introduction to Psychoanalytic Research*. New York: Basic Books.

CONRAD, H. S. (1932) 'The validity of personality ratings of nursery school children.' *J. educ. Psychol.*, **23**, 671–80.

COPPLE, G. E. (1956) 'Effective intelligence as measured by an unstructured sentence-completion technique.' *J. consult. Psychol.*, **20**, 357–60.

COTTLE, W. C. (1950) 'A factorial study of the Multiphasic, Strong, Kuder and Bell inventories, using a population of adult males.' *Psychometrika*, **15**, 25–47.

COUCH, A., and KENISTON, K. (1960) 'Yeasayers and Naysayers: agreeing response set as a personality variable.' *J. abnorm. soc. Psychol.*, **60**, 151–74.

CRONBACH, L. J. (1948) 'A validation design for qualitative studies of personality.' *J. consult. Psychol.*, **12**, 363–74.

CRONBACH, L. J. (1949) 'Statistical methods applied to Rorschach scores: a review.' *Psychol. Bull.*, **46**, 393–429.

CRONBACH, L. J. (1953) 'Correlations between persons as a research tool.' In Mowrer, O. H., *Psychotherapy Theory and Research*. New York: Ronald Press, pp. 376–88.

CRONBACH, L. J. (1955) 'Processes affecting scores on "Understanding of Others" and "Assumed Similarity".' *Psychol. Bull.*, **52**, 177–93.

CRONBACH, L. J. (1958) 'Proposals leading to analytic treatment of social perception scores.' In Tagiuri, R., and Petrullo, L., *Person Perception and Interpersonal Behavior*. Stanford University Press, pp. 353–79.

CRONBACH, L. J. (1960) *Essentials of Psychological Testing* (2nd ed.). New York: Harper.

CRONBACH, L. J., and GLESER, G. C. (1957) *Psychological Tests and Personnel Decisions*. University of Illinois Press.

CRONBACH, L. J., and MEEHL, P. E. (1955) 'Construct validity in psychological tests.' *Psychol. Bull.*, **52**, 281–302.

CROW, W. J. (1957) 'The effect of training upon accuracy and variability in interpersonal perception.' *J. abnorm. soc. Psychol.*, **55**, 355–9.

CROW, W. J., and HAMMOND, K. R. (1957) 'The generality of accuracy and response sets in interpersonal perception.' *J. abnorm. soc. Psychol.*, **54**, 384–90.

CROWNE, D. P., and STEPHENS, M. W. (1961) 'Self-acceptance and self-evaluative behavior: a critique of methodology.' *Psychol. Bull.*, **58**, 104–21.

CURR, W., and GOURLAY, N. (1953) 'An experimental evaluation of remedial education.' *Brit. J. educ. Psychol.*, **23**, 45–55.

DAHLSTROM, W. G., and WELSH, G. S. (1960) *An MMPI Handbook*. University of Minnesota Press.

DAILEY, C. A. (1951) 'The clinician and his predictions.' *J. clin. Psychol.*, **7**, 270–3.

DARLEY, J. G., and HAGENAH, T. (1955) *Vocational Interest Measurement: Theory and Practice*. University of Minnesota Press.

DAVIDS, A., and PILDNER, H. (1959) 'Comparison of direct and projective methods of personality assessment under different conditions of motivation.' *Psychol. Monogr.*, **72**, No. 464.

DAVIDSON, M. A., MCINNES, R. G., and PARNELL, R. W. (1957) 'The distribution of personality traits in seven-year-old children.' *Brit. J. educ. Psychol.*, **27**, 48–61.

DEUTSCH, F., and MURPHY, W. F. (1955) *The Clinical Interview.* New York: International Universities Press.

DOERING, C. R., and RAYMOND, A. F. (1934) 'Relation of observation in psychiatric and related characteristics.' *Amer. J. Orthopsychiat.*, **4**, 249–57.

DOLLARD, J., and AULD, F. (1959) *Scoring Human Motives: A Manual.* New Haven, Conn.: Yale University Press.

DOLLARD, J., and MILLER, N. E. (1950) *Personality and Psychotherapy.* New York: McGraw-Hill.

DOLLIN, A., and REZNIKOFF, M. (1961) 'TAT stories and the social desirability variable.' *Amer. Psychologist*, **16**, 392.

DOOB, L. W. (1958) 'Behavior and grammatical style.' *J. abnorm. soc. Psychol.*, **56**, 398–401.

DORFMAN, E. (1958) 'Personality outcome of client-centered child therapy.' *Psychol Monogr.*, **72**, No. 456.

EBEL, R. L. (1961) 'Must all tests be valid?' *Amer. Psychologist*, **16**, 640–7.

EDWARDS, A. L. (1957) *The Social Desirability Variable in Personality Research.* New York: Dryden Press.

EDWARDS, A. L. (1959) 'Social desirability and personality test construction.' In Bass, B. M., and Berg, I. A., *Objective Approaches to Personality.* New York: Van Nostrand, pp. 100–18.

EISENBERG, P. (1937) 'A further study in expressive movement.' *Char. & Person.*, **5**, 296–301.

ELLIS, A. (1946) 'The validity of personality questionnaires.' *Psychol. Bull.*, **43**, 385–440.

ELLIS, A., and CONRAD, H. S. (1948) 'The validity of personality inventories in military practice.' *Psychol. Bull.*, **45**, 385–426.

ERIKSEN, C. W. (1958) 'Unconscious processes.' In Jones, M. R., *Nebraska Symposium on Motivation.* University of Nebraska Press, pp. 169–227.

ESCHENBACH, A. E., and BORGATTA, E. F. (1955) 'Testing behavior hypotheses with the Rorschach; an exploration in validation.' *J. consult. Psychol.*, **19**, 267–73.

ESTES, S. G. (1938) 'Judging personality from expressive behavior.' *J. abnorm. soc. Psychol.*, **33**, 217–36.

EYSENCK, H. J. (1947) *Dimensions of Personality.* London: Kegan Paul.

EYSENCK, H. J. (1952a) 'The effects of psychotherapy: an evaluation.' *J. consult. Psychol.*, **16**, 319–24.

EYSENCK, H. J. (1952b) *The Scientific Study of Personality*. London: Routledge & Kegan Paul.

EYSENCK, H. J. (1953) *Uses and Abuses of Psychology*. London: Penguin Books.

EYSENCK, H. J. (1955) 'The effects of psychotherapy: a reply.' *J. abnorm. soc. Psychol.*, **50**, 147-8.

EYSENCK, H. J. (1956a) 'The psychology of politics: a reply.' *Psychol. Bull.*, **53**, 177-82.

EYSENCK, H. J. (1956b) 'The psychology of politics and the personality similarities between fascists and communists.' *Psychol. Bull.*, **53**, 431-8.

EYSENCK, H. J. (1959) 'Scientific methodology and "The Dynamics of Anxiety and Hysteria".' *Brit. J. med. Psychol.*, **32**, 56-63.

EYSENCK, H. J. (1960a) 'A rational system of diagnosis and therapy in mental illness.' In *Progress in Clinical Psychology*, Vol. IV, 46-64. New York: Grune & Stratton.

EYSENCK, H. J. (1960b) *The Structure of Human Personality* (2nd ed.). London: Methuen.

EYSENCK, H. J. (edit. 1960c) *Experiments in Personality*. London: Routledge & Kegan Paul.

EYSENCK, H. J. (1960d) 'The effects of psychotherapy.' In Eysenck, H. J., *Handbook of Abnormal Psychology*. London: Pitman, pp. 697-725.

EYSENCK, H. J. (1962) 'Response set, authoritarianism and personality questionnaires.' *Brit. J. soc. clin. Psychol.*, **1**, 20-4.

EYSENCK, H. J., GRANGER, G. W., and BRENGELMANN, J. C. (1957) *Perceptual Processes and Mental Illness*. London: Chapman & Hall.

EYSENCK, H. J., and PRELL, D. (1951) 'The inheritance of neuroticism; an experimental study.' *J. ment. Sci.*, **97**, 441-65.

EYSENCK, S. B. G., EYSENCK, H. J., and CLARIDGE, G. (1960) 'Dimensions of personality, psychiatric syndromes, and mathematical models.' *J. ment. Sci.*, **106**, 581-9.

FAIRWEATHER, G. W., *et al.* (1960) 'Relative effectiveness of psychotherapeutic programs.' *Psychol. Monogr.*, **74**, No. 492.

FARRELL, B. A. (1951) 'The scientific testing of psycho-analytic findings and theory.' *Brit. J. med. Psychol.*, **24**, 35-41.

FARRELL, B. A. (1961) 'On the character of psychodynamic discourse.' *Brit. J. med. Psychol.*, **34**, 7-13.

FESTINGER, L. (1957) *A Theory of Cognitive Dissonance*. Evanston, Ill.: Row, Peterson.

FIEDLER, F. E. (1950) 'The concept of an ideal therapeutic relationship.' *J. consult. Psychol.*, **14**, 239–45.

FIEDLER, F. E. (1953) 'Quantitative studies on the role of therapists' feelings towards their patients.' In Mowrer, O. H., *Psychotherapy Theory and Research*. New York: Ronald Press, pp. 296–315.

FILLENBAUM, S. (1959) 'Some stylistic aspects of categorizing behavior.' *J. Person.*, **27**, 187–95.

FISHER, S. (1956) 'Plausibility and depth of interpretation.' *J. consult. Psychol.*, **20**, 249–56.

FLANAGAN, J. C. (1954) 'The critical incidents technique.' *Psychol. Bull.*, **51**, 327–58.

FLANAGAN, J. C., *et al.* (1954) 'Situational performance tests (a symposium).' *Personnel Psychol.*, **7**, 461–97.

FORGY, E. W., and BLACK, J. D. (1954) 'A follow-up after three years of clients counseled by two methods.' *J. counsel. Psychol.*, **1**, 1–8.

FREDERIKSEN, N. (1960) 'In-basket tests and factors in administrative performance.' *Invitational Conference on Testing Problems*. Princeton, N.J.: Educational Testing Service, pp. 21–37.

FREDERIKSEN, N., and MELVILLE, S. D. (1954) 'Differential predictability in the use of test scores.' *Educ. Psychol. Measmt.*, **14**, 647–56.

FREDERIKSEN, N., and MESSICK, S. (1959) 'Response set as a measure of personality.' *Educ. Psychol. Measmt.*, **19**, 137–57.

FREEMAN, F. S. (1955) *Theory and Practice of Psychological Testing* (rev. ed.). New York: Holt.

FRENCH, J. W. (1953) *The Description of Personality Measurements in Terms of Rotated Factors*. Princeton, N.J.: Educational Testing Service.

FRENCH, T. M. (1944) 'Clinical approach to the dynamics of behavior.' In Hunt, J. McV., *Personality and the Behavior Disorders*. New York: Ronald Press, pp. 255–68.

FRENKEL BRUNSWIK, E. (1949) 'Intolerance of ambiguity as an emotional and perceptual personality variable.' *J. Person.*, **18**, 108–43.

FRENKEL BRUNSWIK, E., and SANFORD, R. N. (1945) 'Some personality factors in anti-semitism.' *J. Psychol.*, **20**, 271–91.

FROM, F. (1960) 'Perception of human action.' In David, H., and Brengelmann, J. C., *Perspectives in Personality Research*. London: Crosby Lockwood, pp. 161–74.

FRUCHTER, B., ROKEACH, M., and NOVAK, E. G. (1958) 'A fac-

torial study of dogmatism, opinionation, and related scales.'
Psychol. Rep., **4**, 19–22.

FULKERSON, S. C., and BARRY, J. R. (1961) 'Methodology and research on the prognostic use of psychological tests.' *Psychol. Bull.*,
58, 177–204.

FURNEAUX, W. D. (1962) 'The psychologist and the university.'
Univ. Quart., **17**, 1, 33–47.

GAGE, N. L. (1952) 'Judging interests from expressive behavior.'
Psychol. Monogr., **66**, No. 350.

GAGE, N. L., and CRONBACH, L. J. (1955) 'Conceptual and methodological problems in interpersonal perception.' *Psychol. Rev.*, **62**,
411–22.

GARDNER, R. W., HOLZMAN, P. S., *et al.* (1960) 'Cognitive control:
a study of individual consistencies in cognitive behavior.' *Psychol.
Issues*, **1**, No. 4.

GATES, G. S. (1923) 'An experimental study of the growth of social
perception.' *J. educ. Psychol.*, **14**, 449–61.

GESELL, A., ILG, F. L., *et al.* (1946) *The Child from Five to Ten.*
New York: Harper.

GETZELS, J. W., and WALSH, J. J. (1958) 'The method of paired
direct and projective questionnaires in the study of attitude structure and socialization.' *Psychol. Monogr.*, **72**, No. 454.

GIBSON, J. J. (1951) 'Theories of perception.' In Dennis, W., *Current
Trends in Psychological Theory.* University of Pittsburgh Press, pp.
85–110.

GLOVER, E. (1961) 'Review of "Freud and the Post-Freudians" by
J. A. C. Brown.' *Brit. J. Psychol.*, **52**, 395–6.

GLUECK, S., and GLUECK, E. (1950) *Unraveling Juvenile Delinquency.* New York: Commonwealth Fund.

GOFFMAN, E. (1956) *The Presentation of Self in Everyday Life.* University of Edinburgh: Soc. Sci. Res. Centre, Monogr. No. 2.

GOLDMAN EISLER, F. (1950) 'Breast-feeding and character formation.' *J. Person.*, **19**, 189–96.

GOLDSTEIN, K., and SCHEERER, M. (1941) 'Abstract and concrete
behavior.' *Psychol. Monogr.*, **53**, No. 239.

GOUGH, H. G. (1953) 'The construction of a personality scale to
predict scholastic achievement.' *J. appl. Psychol.*, **37**, 361–6.

GOUGH, H. G. (1957) *Manual, California Psychological Inventory.*
Palo Alto, Calif.: Consulting Psychologists Press.

GRANGER, G. W. (1953) 'Personality and visual perception: a review.' *J. ment. Sci.*, **99**, 8–43.

GRANT, M. Q., IVES, V., and RANZONI, J. H. (1952) 'Reliability and validity of judges' ratings of adjustment on the Rorschach.' *Psychol. Monogr.*, **66**, No. 334.

GREBSTEIN, L. C. (1961) 'A study of clinical judgment.' *Amer. Psychologist*, **16**, 377.

GREGORY, W. S. (1945) 'The application of teleonomic description to the diagnosis and treatment of emotional instability and personal and social maladjustments.' *Char. & Person.*, **13**, 179–211.

GROSS, L. R. (1959) 'Effects of verbal and nonverbal reinforcement in the Rorschach.' *J. consult. Psychol.*, **23**, 66–8.

GRUEN, A. (1957) 'A critique and re-evaluation of Witkin's perception and perception-personality work.' *J. gen. Psychol.*, **56**, 73–93.

GUILFORD, J. P. (1959) *Personality*. New York: McGraw-Hill.

GUILFORD, J. P., and LACEY, J. I. (edit. 1947) *Printed Classification Tests*. Washington, D.C.: Government Printing Office.

GUILFORD, J. P., SHNEIDMAN, E. S., and ZIMMERMAN, W. S. (1954) 'A factor analysis study of human interests.' *Psychol. Monogr.*, **68**, No. 375.

HAGGERTY, M. E., OLSON, W. C., and WICKMAN, E. K. (1930) *Haggerty–Olson–Wickman Behavior Rating Schedules*. Yonkers, N.Y.: World Book Co.

HAIRE, M., and GRUNES, W. F. (1950) 'Perceptual defenses; processes protecting an organized perception of another personality.' *Hum. Rel.*, **3**, 403–12.

HALL, C. S. (1954) *A Primer of Freudian Psychology*. Cleveland, Ohio: World Publishing Co.

HALL, C. S., and LINDZEY, G. (1957) *Theories of Personality*. New York: Wiley.

HAMMER, E. F., and PIOTROWSKI, Z. A. (1953) 'Hostility as a factor in the clinician's personality as it affects his interpretation of projective drawings (H-T-P).' *J. Proj. Tech.*, **17**, 210–16.

HARRIS, J. G. (1960) 'Validity.' In Rickers-Ovsiankina, M. A., *Rorschach Psychology*. New York: Wiley, pp. 380–439.

HARRIS, R. E. (1956) 'Clinical methods: psychotherapy.' *Ann. Rev. Psychol.*, **7**, 121–46.

HARSH, C. M., and SCHRICKEL, H. G. (1950) *Personality Development and Assessment*. New York: Ronald Press.

HARTMAN, A. A. (1949) 'An experimental examination of the Thematic Apperception technique in clinical diagnosis.' *Psychol. Monogr.*, **63**, No. 303.

HARVEY, O. J., HUNT, D. E., and SCHRODER, H. M. (1961) *Conceptual Systems and Personality Organization*. New York: Wiley.

HASTINGS, D. W. (1958) 'Follow-up results in psychiatric illness.' *Amer. J. Psychiat.*, **114**, 1057–66.

HASTORF, A. H., and BENDER, I. E. (1952) 'A caution respecting the measurement of empathic ability.' *J. abnorm. soc. Psychol.*, **47**, 574–6.

HASTORF, A. H., BENDER, I. E., and WEINTRAUB, D. J. (1955) 'The influence of response patterns on the "Refined Empathy Score".' *J. abnorm. soc. Psychol.*, **51**, 341–3.

HASTORF, A. H., RICHARDSON, S. A., and DORNBUSCH, S. M. (1958) 'The problem of relevance in the study of person perception.' In Tagiuri, R., and Petrullo, L., *Person Perception and Interpersonal Behavior*. Stanford University Press, pp. 54–62.

HATHAWAY, S. R. (1956) 'Clinical intuition and inferential accuracy.' *J. Person.*, **24**, 223–50.

HATHAWAY, S. R. (1959) 'Increasing clinical efficiency.' In Bass, B. M., and Berg, I. A., *Objective Approaches to Personality*. New York: Van Nostrand, pp. 192–203.

HATHAWAY, S. R., and MEEHL, P. E. (1951) *An Atlas for the Clinical Use of the MMPI*. University of Minnesota Press.

HEBB, D. O. (1946) 'Emotion in man and animal: an analysis of the intuitive processes of recognition.' *Psychol. Rev.*, **53**, 88–106.

HEBB, D. O., and THOMPSON, W. R. (1954) 'The social significance of animal studies.' In Lindzey, G., *Handbook of Social Psychology*. Cambridge, Mass.: Addison-Wesley, pp. 532–61.

HEIDER, F. (1958) *The Psychology of Interpersonal Relations*. New York: Wiley.

HEIDER, F., and SIMMEL, M. (1944) 'An experimental study of apparent behavior.' *Amer. J. Psychol.*, **57**, 243–59.

HENRY, E. M., and ROTTER, J. B. (1956) 'Situational influences on Rorschach responses.' *J. consult. Psychol.*, **20**, 457–62.

HENRY, W. E. (1960) 'Projective techniques.' In Mussen, P., *Handbook of Research Methods in Child Development*. New York: Wiley, pp. 603–44.

HENRY, W. E., and FARLEY, J. (1959) 'The validity of the Thematic Apperception test in the study of adolescent personality.' *Psychol. Monogr.*, **73**, No. 487.

HERON, A. (1954) 'The objective assessment of personality among factory workers.' *J. soc. Psychol.*, **39**, 161–85.

HERTZ, M. R. (1960) 'The Rorschach in adolescence.' In Rabin,

A. I., and Haworth, M. R., *Projective Techniques with Children.* New York: Grune & Stratton, pp. 29–60.

HEWITT, L. E., and JENKINS, R. L. (1946) *Fundamental Patterns of Maladjustment: The Dynamics of their Origin.* Springfield, Ill.: State of Illinois.

HILGARD, E. R. (1949) 'Human motives and the concept of the self.' *Amer. Psychologist,* **4**, 374–82.

HILL, A. B., and WILLIAMS, D. J. (1947) 'Reliability of psychiatric opinion in the Royal Air Force.' In *Psychological Disorders in Flying Personnel of the Royal Air Force.* London: H.M. Stationery Office, pp. 308–20.

HOFFMAN, P. J. (1960) 'The paramorphic representation of clinical judgment.' *Psychol. Bull.,* **57**, 116–31.

HOLLAND, J. L. (1958) 'A personality inventory employing occupational titles.' *J. appl. Psychol.,* **42**, 336–42.

HOLT, R. R. (1951) 'The Thematic Apperception test.' In Anderson, H. H., and G. L., *An Introduction to Projective Techniques.* New York: Prentice-Hall, pp. 181–229.

HOLT, R. R. (1954) 'Implications of some contemporary personality theories for Rorschach rationale.' In Klopfer, B., *et al., Developments in the Rorschach Technique,* Vol. I. Yonkers, N.Y.: World Book Co., pp. 501–60.

HOLT, R. R. (1958) 'Clinical *and* statistical prediction: a reformulation and some new data.' *J. abnorm. soc. Psychol.,* **56**, 1–12.

HOLT, R. R., and LUBORSKY, L. (1958) *Personality Patterns of Psychiatrists.* New York: Basic Books.

HOLTZMAN, W. H. (1959) 'Objective scoring of projective techniques.' In Bass, B. M., and Berg, I. A., *Objective Approaches to Personality.* New York: Van Nostrand, pp. 119–45.

HOLTZMAN, W. H. (1962) 'Methodological issues in *P* technique.' *Psychol. Bull.,* **59**, 248–56.

HOLTZMAN, W. H., and SELLS, S. B. (1954) 'Prediction of flying success by clinical analysis of test protocols.' *J. abnorm. soc. Psychol.,* **49**, 485–90.

HOLTZMAN, W. H., THORPE, J. S., *et al.* (1961) *Inkblot Perception and Personality: Holtzman Inkblot Technique.* University of Texas Press.

HOLZBERG, J. D. (1960) 'Reliability reexamined.' In Rickers-Ovsiankina, M. A., *Rorschach Psychology.* New York: Wiley, pp. 361–79.

HONKAVAARA, S. (1961) 'The psychology of expression.' *Brit. J. Psychol. Monogr. Suppl.*, No. 32.

HOWARD, R. C., and BERKOWITZ, L. (1958) 'Reactions to the evaluators of one's performance.' *J. Person.*, **26**, 494–507.

HUNT, W. A. (1959) 'An actuarial approach to clinical judgment.' In Bass, B. M., and Berg, I. A., *Objective Approaches to Personality*. New York: Van Nostrand, pp. 169–91.

HUNT, W. A., WITTSON, C. L., and HUNT, E. B. (1955) 'The relationship between amount of presenting symptomatology and severity of disability.' *J. clin. Psychol.*, **11**, 305–6.

HUNTLEY, C. W. (1940) 'Judgments of self based upon records of expressive behavior.' *J. abnorm. soc. Psychol.*, **35**, 398–427.

HYMAN, H. H., and SHEATSLEY, P. B. (1954) 'The authoritarian personality – a methodological critique.' In Christie, R., and Jahoda, M., *Studies in the Scope and Method of 'The Authoritarian Personality'*. Glencoe, Ill.: Free Press, pp. 50–122.

ICHHEISER, G. (1949) 'Misunderstandings in human relations.' *Amer. J. Sociol.*, **55**, No. 2, Pt. ii.

INGHAM, J. G., ROBINSON, J. O., and RAWNSLEY, K. (1961) 'Psychological field studies in defined populations.' *Advancement of Science*, **18**, 265–72.

INKELES, A., and LEVINSON, D. J. (1954) 'National character: the study of modal personality and sociocultural systems.' In Lindzey, G., *Handbook of Social Psychology*. Cambridge, Mass.: Addison-Wesley, pp. 977–1020.

ITTELSON, W. H., and SLACK, C. W. (1958) 'The perception of persons as visual objects.' In Tagiuri, R., and Petrullo, L., *Person Perception and Interpersonal Behavior*. Stanford University Press, pp. 210–28.

JACKSON, D. N., MESSICK, S. J., and SOLLEY, C. M. (1957) 'How "rigid" is the "authoritarian"?' *J. abnorm. soc. Psychol.*, **54**, 137–140.

JENKIN, N. (1957) 'Affective processes in perception.' *Psychol. Bull.*, **54**, 100–27.

JENSEN, A. R. (1958) 'Personality.' *Ann. Rev. Psychol.*, **9**, 295–322.

JESSOR, R., and HAMMOND, K. R. (1957) 'Construct validity and the Taylor Anxiety scale.' *Psychol. Bull.*, **54**, 161–70.

JOHNSON, D. M., and VIDULICH, R. N. (1956) 'Experimental manipulation of the halo effect.' *J. appl. Psychol.*, **40**, 130–4.

JONES, E. E., and THIBAUT, J. W. (1958) 'Interaction goals as bases of inference in interpersonal perception.' In Tagiuri, R., and

Petrullo, L., *Person Perception and Interpersonal Behavior*. Stanford University Press, pp. 151–78.

KAGAN, J. (1960) 'Thematic apperception techniques with children.' In Rabin, A. I., and Haworth, M. R., *Projective Techniques with Children*. New York: Grune & Stratton, pp. 105–29.

KAGAN, J., *et al.* (1958) 'Personality and IQ change.' *J. abnorm. soc. Psychol.*, **56**, 261–6.

KAHN, R. L., and CANNELL, C. F. (1957) *The Dynamics of Interviewing*. New York: Wiley.

KELLEY, H. H. (1950) 'The warm-cold variable in first impressions of persons.' *J. Person.*, **18**, 431–9.

KELLY, E. L., and FISKE, D. W. (1951) *The Prediction of Performance in Clinical Psychology*. Ann Arbor: University of Michigan Press.

KELLY, E. L., and GOLDBERG, L. R. (1959) 'Correlates of later performance and specialization in psychology.' *Psychol. Monogr.*, **73**, No. 482.

KELLY, G. A. (1955) *The Psychology of Personal Constructs*. New York: Norton.

KELLY, G. A. (1958) 'The theory and technique of assessment.' *Ann. Rev. Psychol.*, **9**, 323–52.

KENNARD, M. A. (1953) 'The electroencephalogram in psychological disorders: a review.' *Psychosom. Med.*, **15**, 95–115.

KENNY, D. T. (1956) 'The influence of social desirability on discrepancy measures between Real Self and Ideal Self.' *J. consult. Psychol.*, **20**, 315–18.

KENNY, D. T., and GINSBERG, R. (1958) 'The specificity of intolerance of ambiguity measures.' *J. abnorm. soc. Psychol.*, **56**, 300–4.

KLEIN, G. S. (1950) 'The personal world through perception.' In Blake, R. W., and Ramsey, G., *Perception: An Approach to Personality*. New York: Ronald, pp. 328–55.

KLOPFER, B., *et al.* (1954) *Developments in the Rorschach Technique*, Vol. I. Yonkers, N.Y.: World Book Co.

KLOPFER, B., *et al.* (1956) *Developments in the Rorschach Technique*, Vol. II. Yonkers, N.Y.: World Book Co.

KNOPF, I. J. (1956) 'Rorschach summary scores in differential diagnosis.' *J. consult. Psychol.*, **20**, 99–104.

KOHLBERG, L. (1963) 'Moral development and identification.' *Yrbk. Nat. Soc. Stud. Educ.*, 62.

KRUMHOLTZ, J. D., and FARQUHAR, W. W. (1957) 'Reliability and validity of the n-Achievement test.' *J. consult. Psychol.*, **21**, 226–8.

LEARY, T. (1957) *Interpersonal Diagnosis of Personality*. New York: Ronald Press.

LECKY, P. (1945) *Self-consistency: A Theory of Personality*. New York: Island Press.

LEEPER, R. W., and MADISON, P. (1959) *Toward Understanding Human Personalities*. New York: Appleton-Century-Crofts.

LESSER, G. S. (1957) 'The relationship between overt and fantasy aggression as a function of maternal response to frustration.' *J. abnorm. soc. Psychol.*, **55**, 218–21.

LEVITT, E. E. (1956) 'The water-jar Einstellung test as a measure of rigidity.' *Psychol. Bull.*, **53**, 347–70.

LEVITT, E. E. (1957) 'The results of psychotherapy with children: an evaluation.' *J. consult. Psychol.*, **21**, 189–96.

LEVITT, E. E., BEISER, H. R., and ROBERTSON, R. E. (1959) 'A follow-up evaluation of cases treated at a community child guidance clinic.' *Amer. J. Orthopsychiat.*, **29**, 337–49.

LEVY, L. H. (1956a) 'Personal constructs and predictive behavior.' *J. abnorm. soc. Psychol.*, **53**, 54–8.

LEVY, L. H. (1956b) 'The meaning and generality of perceived actual-ideal discrepancies.' *J. consult. Psychol.*, **20**, 396–8.

LEVY, L. H., and DUGAN, R. D. (1956) 'A factorial study of personal constructs.' *J. consult. Psychol.*, **20**, 53–7.

LEVY, L. H., and ORR, T. B. (1959) 'The social psychology of Rorschach validity research.' *J. abnorm. soc. Psychol.*, **58**, 79–83.

LINDZEY, G. (1952) 'Thematic Apperception test: interpretative assumptions and related empirical evidence.' *Psychol. Bull.*, **49**, 1–25.

LINDZEY, G. (1959) 'On the classification of projective techniques.' *Psychol. Bull.*, **56**, 159–68.

LINDZEY, G. (1961) *Projective Techniques and Cross-Cultural Research*. New York: Appleton-Century-Crofts.

LINTON, H. B. (1955) 'Dependence on external influence: correlates in perception, attitudes, and judgment.' *J. abnorm. soc. Psychol.*, **51**, 502–7.

LITTLE, K. B., and SHNEIDMAN, E. S. (1959) 'Congruencies among interpretations of psychological test and anamnestic data.' *Psychol. Monogr.*, **73**, No. 476.

LOEVINGER, J. (1955) 'Some principles of personality measurement.' *Educ. Psychol. Measmt.*, **15**, 3–17.

LOEVINGER, J. (1959) 'Theory and techniques of assessment.' *Ann. Rev. Psychol.*, **10**, 287–316.

LOEVINGER, J., and OSSORIO, A. (1959) 'Evaluation of therapy by self-report: a paradox.' *J. abnorm. soc. Psychol.*, **58**, 392–4.

LORD, E. (1950) 'Experimentally induced variations in Rorschach performance.' *Psychol. Monogr.*, **64**, No. 316.

LORR, M., O'CONNOR, J. P., and STAFFORD, J. W. (1957) 'Confirmation of nine psychotic symptom patterns.' *J. clin. Psychol.*, **13**, 252–7.

LOVELL, C. (1945) 'A study of the factor structure of thirteen personality variables.' *Educ. Psychol. Measmt.*, **5**, 335–50.

LOWE, C. M. (1961) 'The Self-concept: fact or artifact.' *Psychol. Bull.*, **58**, 325–36.

LUBORSKY, L. (1953) 'Intraindividual repetitive measurements (P technique) in understanding psychotherapeutic change.' In Mowrer, O. H., *Psychotherapy Theory and Research*. New York: Ronald Press, pp. 388–413.

LUCHINS, A. S. (1948) 'Forming impressions of personality: a critique.' *J. abnorm. soc. Psychol.*, **43**, 318–25.

LUFT, J. (1950) 'Implicit hypotheses and clinical predictions.' *J. abnorm. soc. Psychol.*, **45**, 756–9.

LUMSDEN, J. (1961) 'The construction of unidimensional tests.' *Psychol. Bull.*, **58**, 122–31.

LUNDIN, R. W. (1961) *Personality: An Experimental Approach*. New York: Macmillan.

LUNZER, E. A. (1960) 'Aggressive and withdrawing children in the normal school.' *Brit. J. educ. Psychol.*, **30**, 1–10, 119–23.

LURIA, A. R. (1932) *The Nature of Human Conflicts*. New York: Liveright.

LYNN, R. (1959) 'Two personality characteristics related to academic achievement.' *Brit. J. educ. Psychol.*, **29**, 213–16.

MCARTHUR, C. (1954) 'Analyzing the clinical process.' *J. counsel. Psychol.*, **1**, 203–8.

MCCLELLAND, D. C., et al. (1953) *The Achievement Motive*. New York: Appleton-Century.

MACCOBY, E. E., and MACCOBY, N. (1954) 'The interview: a tool of social science.' In Lindzey, G., *Handbook of Social Psychology*. Cambridge, Mass.: Addison-Wesley, pp. 449–87.

MCCONNELL, J. V., CUTLER, R. L., and MCNEILL, E. B. (1958) 'Subliminal stimulation: an overview.' *Amer. Psychologist*, **13**, 229–42.

MACFARLANE, J. W., and TUDDENHAM, R. D. (1951) 'Problems in the validation of projective techniques.' In Anderson, H. H., and G. L., *An Introduction to Projective Techniques*. New York: Prentice-Hall, pp. 26–54.

MCGEE, R. K. (1962) 'Response style as a personality variable: by what criterion?' *Psychol. Bull.*, **59**, 284–95.

MCGHIE, A. (1961) 'A comparative study of the mother-child relationship in schizophrenia.' *Brit. J. med. Psychol.*, **34**, 195–221.

MACKINNON, D. W. (1958) *An Assessment Study of Air Force Officers, Part V. Summary and Applications*. Wright Air Development Centre: WADC Technical Report 58–91 (V).

MACKINNON, D. W. (1960) 'The highly effective individual.' *Teach. Coll. Rec.*, **61**, 367–78.

MACKINNON, D. W. (1962) 'The personality correlates of creativity: a study of American architects.' *Proc. XIV Intern. Congr. appl. Psychol.*, Vol. II, 11–39. Copenhagen: Munksgaard.

MACLEOD, R. B. (1960) 'Person perception: a commentary.' In David, H., and Brengelmann, J. C., *Perspectives in Personality Research*. London: Crosby Lockwood, pp. 226–44.

MCQUITTY, L. L. (1953) 'A statistical method for studying personality integration.' In Mowrer, O. H., *Psychotherapy Theory and Research*. New York: Ronald Press, pp. 414–62.

MCQUITTY, L. L. (1959) 'Differential validity in some pattern analytic methods.' In Bass, B. M., and Berg, I. A., *Objective Approaches to Personality*. New York: Van Nostrand, pp. 66–82.

MALAN, D. (1959) 'On assessing the results of psychotherapy.' *Brit. J. med. Psychol.*, **32**, 86–105.

MANN, R. D. (1959) 'A review of the relationships between personality and performance in small groups.' *Psychol. Bull.*, **56**, 241–70.

MANNHEIM, H., and WILKINS, L. T. (1955) *Prediction Methods in Relation to Borstal Training*. London: H.M. Stationery Office.

MARK, J. C. (1953) 'The attitudes of the mothers of male schizophrenics toward child behavior.' *J. abnorm. soc. Psychol.*, **48**, 185–9.

MASLING, J. (1960) 'The influence of situational and interpersonal variables in projective testing.' *Psychol. Bull.*, **57**, 65–85.

MEEHL, P. E. (1954) *Clinical vs. Statistical Prediction*. University of Minnesota Press.

MEEHL, P. E. (1956) 'Wanted – a good cookbook.' *Amer. Psychologist*, **11**, 263–72.

MEEHL, P. E. (1961) 'Review of "Clinical Inference and Cognitive Theory", by Sarbin, Taft & Bailey.' *Contemp. Psychol.*, **6**, 389–91.

MEEHL, P. E., and ROSEN, A. (1955) 'Antecedent probability and the efficiency of psychometric signs, patterns, or cutting scores.' *Psychol. Bull.*, **52**, 194–216.

MEHLMAN, B. (1952) 'The reliability of psychiatric diagnoses.' *J. abnorm. soc. Psychol.*, **47**, 577–8.

MENSH, I. N. (1950) 'Statistical techniques in present-day psycho-diagnostics.' *Psychol. Bull.*, **47**, 475–92.

MESSICK, S., and FREDERIKSEN, N. (1958) 'Ability, acquiescence and "authoritarianism".' *Psychol. Rep.*, **4**, 687–97.

MESSICK, S., and JACKSON, D. N. (1961) 'Acquiescence and the factorial interpretation of the MMPI.' *Psychol. Bull.*, **58**, 299–304.

MICHOTTE, A. E. (1946) *La Perception de la Causalité*. Paris: J. Vrin.

MILLER, D. R. (1953) 'Prediction of behavior by means of the Rorschach test.' *J. abnorm. soc. Psychol.*, **48**, 367–75.

MILLER, D. R., SWANSON, G. E., et al. (1960) *Inner Conflict and Defense*. New York: Holt.

MILLER, R. E., MURPHY, J. V., and MIRSKY, I. A. (1959) 'Relevance of facial expression and posture as cues in communication of affect between monkeys.' *Arch. Gen. Psychiat.*, **1**, 480–8.

MORTON, R. B. (1955) 'An experiment in brief psychotherapy.' *Psychol. Monogr.*, **69**, No. 386.

MOSIER, C. I. (1947) 'A critical examination of the concepts of face validity.' *Educ. Psychol. Measmt.*, **7**, 191–205.

MOSIER, C. I. (edit. 1951) 'Symposium: the need and means of cross-validation.' *Educ. Psychol. Measmt.*, **11**, 5–28.

MOWRER, O. H. (1953) *Psychotherapy Theory and Research*. New York: Ronald Press.

MURPHY, G. (1947) *Personality: A Biosocial Approach to Origins and Structure*. New York: Harper.

MURRAY, H. A. (1933) 'The effect of fear upon estimates of the maliciousness of other personalities.' *J. soc. Psychol.*, **4**, 310–29.

MURSTEIN, B. I., and PRYER, R. S. (1959) 'The concept of projection: a review.' *Psychol. Bull.*, **56**, 353–74.

MUSSEN, P. H. (edit. 1960) *Handbook of Research Methods in Child Development*. New York: Wiley.

MUSSEN, P. H., and NAYLOR, H. K. (1954) 'The relationship between overt and fantasy aggression.' *J. abnorm. soc. Psychol.*, **49**, 235–40.

MYERS, J. K., and ROBERTS, B. H. (1959) *Family and Class Dynamics in Mental Illness*. New York: Wiley.

NEWCOMB, T. M. (1958) 'The cognition of persons as cognizers.' In Tagiuri, R., and Petrullo, L., *Person Perception and Interpersonal Behavior*. Stanford University Press, pp. 179–90.

NEWMAN, S. H., BOBBITT, J. M., and CAMERON, D. C. (1946) 'The reliability of the interview method in an officer candidate evaluation program.' *Amer. Psychologist*, 1, 103–9.

NOTCUTT, B., and SILVA, A. L. M. (1951) 'Knowledge of other people.' *J. abnorm. soc. Psychol.*, 46, 30–7.

OLDFIELD, R. C. (1941) *The Psychology of the Interview*. London: Methuen.

O'NEIL, W. M., and LEVINSON, D. J. (1954) 'A factorial exploration of authoritarianism and some of its ideological concomitants.' *J. Person.*, 22, 449–63.

ORLANSKY, H. (1949) 'Infant care and personality.' *Psychol. Bull.*, 46, 1–48.

OSBURN, H. G., LUBIN, A., *et al.* (1954) 'The relative validity of forced choice and single stimulus self description items.' *Educ. Psychol. Measmt.*, 14, 407–17.

OSGOOD, C. E. (1962) 'Studies on the generality of affective meaning systems.' *Amer. Psychologist*, 17, 10–28.

OSGOOD, C. E., and LURIA, Z. (1954) 'A blind analysis of a case of multiple personality using the semantic differential.' *J. abnorm. soc. Psychol.*, 49, 579–91.

OSGOOD, C. E., SUCI, G. J., and TANNENBAUM, P. H. (1957) *The Measurement of Meaning*. Urbana, Ill.: University of Illinois Press.

O.S.S. (Office of Strategic Services) Assessment Staff (1948) *Assessment of Men*. New York: Rinehart.

PALMER, J. O. (1951) 'A dual approach to Rorschach validation: a methodological study.' *Psychol. Monogr.*, 65, No. 325.

PARKYN, G. W. (1959) *Success and Failure at the University*. Wellington, N.Z.: New Zealand Council for Educational Research.

PAYNE, R. W. (1955) 'L'utilité du test de Rorschach en psychologie clinique.' *Rev. de Psychol. Appliq.*, 5, 255–64.

PAYNE, R. W. (1960) 'Cognitive abnormalities.' In Eysenck, H. J., *Handbook of Abnormal Psychology*. London: Pitman, pp. 193–261.

PEARSON, J. S., and SWENSON, W. M. (1951) 'A note on extended findings with the MMPI in predicting response to electro-convulsive therapy.' *J. clin. Psychol.*, 7, 288.

PEMBERTON, C. (1952) 'The closure factors related to temperament.' *J. Person.*, 21, 159–75.

x

PENA, C. D. (1959) 'Influence of social desirability upon Rorschach content.' *J. clin. Psychol.*, **15**, 313–16.

PETERSON, C. H., and SPANO, F. L. (1941) 'Breast feeding, maternal rejection and child personality.' *Char. & Person.*, **10**, 62–6.

PHILLIPS, E. L. (1960) 'Parent-child psychotherapy: a follow-up study comparing two techniques.' *J. Psychol.*, **49**, 195–202.

POWERS, E., and WITMER, H. (1951) *An Experiment in the Prevention of Delinquency*. New York: Columbia University Press.

RABIN, A. I., and HAWORTH, M. R. (1960) *Projective Techniques with Children*. New York: Grune & Stratton.

RADKE, M. J. (1946) 'The relation of parental authority to children's behavior and attitudes.' *Instit. Child Wel. Monogr.*, No. 22. University of Minnesota Press.

RAIMY, V. C. (1948) 'Self-reference in counseling interviews.' *J. consult. Psychol.*, **12**, 153–63.

REES, W. L. (1960) 'Constitutional factors and abnormal behaviour.' In Eysenck, H. J., *Handbook of Abnormal Psychology*. London: Pitman, pp. 344–92.

RICHARDSON, S. A., DORNBUSCH, S. M., and HASTORF, A. H. (1961) *Children's Categories of Interpersonal Perception*. Nat. Inst. Mental Hlth. Research Grant M-2480, Final Report.

RICKERS-OVSIANKINA, M. A. (edit. 1960) *Rorschach Psychology*. New York: Wiley.

RICKMAN, J. (1951) 'Methodology and research in psycho-pathology.' *Brit. J. med. Psychol.*, **24**, 1–7.

RODGER, A. (1961) *Occupational Versatility and Planned Procrastination*. London: Birkbeck College.

ROGERS, C. R. (1939) *The Clinical Treatment of the Problem Child*. Boston, Mass.: Houghton Mifflin.

ROGERS, C. R. (1951) *Client-centered Therapy*. Boston, Mass.: Houghton Mifflin.

ROGERS, C. R. (1960) 'Significant trends in the client-centered orientation.' In *Progress in Clinical Psychology*, Vol. IV, pp. 85–99. New York: Grune & Stratton.

ROGERS, C. R., and DYMOND, R. F. (edit. 1954) *Psychotherapy and Personality Change*. University of Chicago Press.

ROGERS, C. R., KELL, B. L., and MCNEIL, H. (1948) 'The role of self understanding in the prediction of behavior.' *J. consult. Psychol.*, **12**, 174–86.

ROHDE, A. R. (1957) *The Sentence Completion Method*. New York: Ronald Press.

ROKEACH, M. (1956) 'Political and religious dogmatism: an alternative to the authoritarian personality.' *Psychol. Monogr.*, **70**, No. 425.

ROKEACH, M. (1960) *The Open and Closed Mind.* New York: Basic Books.

ROKEACH, M., and FRUCHTER, B. (1956) 'A factorial study of dogmatism and related concepts.' *J. abnorm. soc. Psychol.*, **53**, 356–60.

ROKEACH, M., and HANLEY, C. (1956) 'Eysenck's tendermindedness dimension: a critique.' *Psychol Bull.*, **53**, 169–76.

ROMMETVEIT, R. (1960) *Selectivity, Intuition and Halo Effects in Social Perception.* Oslo University Press.

ROSENTHAL, D. (1955) 'Changes in some moral values following psychotherapy.' *J. consult. Psychol.*, **19**, 431–36.

ROSENZWEIG, S. (1943) 'An experimental study of "repression" with special reference to need-persistence and ego-defensive reactions to frustration.' *J. exper. Psychol.*, **32**, 64–74.

ROSENZWEIG, S. (1945) 'The picture-association method and its application in a study of reactions to frustration. *J. Person.*, **14**, 3–23.

ROSENZWEIG, S. (1951) 'Idiodynamics in personality theory with special reference to projective methods.' *Psychol. Rev.*, **58**, 213–23.

ROSENZWEIG, S. (1954) 'A transvaluation of psychotherapy – a reply to Hans Eysenck.' *J. abnorm. soc. Psychol.*, **49**, 298–304.

ROSENZWEIG, S., and KOGAN, K. L. (1949) *Psychodiagnosis.* New York: Grune & Stratton.

ROTHNEY, J. W. M., and ROENS, B. A. (1950) *Guidance of American Youth: An Experimental Study.* Harvard University Press.

ROTTER, J. B. (1951) 'Word association and sentence completion methods.' In Anderson, H. H., and G. L., *An Introduction to Projective Techniques.* New York: Prentice-Hall, pp. 279–311.

RYANS, D. G. (1960) *Characteristics of Teachers.* Washington, D.C.: American Council on Education.

SACKS, J. M., and LEVY, S. (1950) 'The Sentence Completion test.' In Abt, L. E., and Bellak, L., *Projective Psychology.* New York: Knopf, pp. 357–402.

SAMUELS, H. (1952) 'The validity of personality-trait ratings based on projective techniques.' *Psychol. Monogr.*, **66**, No. 337.

SANDLER, J., and ACKNER, B. (1951) 'Rorschach content analysis: an experimental investigation.' *Brit. J. med. Psychol.*, **24**, 180–201.

SANFORD, R. N., et al. (1943) 'Physique, personality and scholarship.' Monogr. Soc. Res. Child Devt., 8, No. 34.

SARASON, S. B. (1950) 'The test-situation and the problem of prediction.' J. clin. Psychol., 6, 387-92.

SARASON, S. B., et al. (1960) Anxiety in Elementary School Children: A Report of Research. New York: Wiley.

SARBIN, T. R. (1943) 'A contribution to the study of actuarial and individual methods of prediction.' Amer. J. Sociol., 48, 593-602.

SARBIN, T. R., TAFT, R., and BAILEY, D. E. (1960) Clinical Inference and Cognitive Theory. New York: Holt, Rinehart & Winston.

SAUL, L. J. (1944) 'Physiological effects of emotional tension.' In Hunt, J. McV., Personality and the Behavior Disorders. New York: Ronald Press, pp. 269-305.

SAUNDERS, D. R. (1960) 'Evidence bearing on the existence of a rational correspondence between the personality typologies of Spranger and of Jung.' Research Bulletin 60-6. Princeton, N.J.: Educational Testing Service.

SCHAFER, R. (1954) Psychoanalytic Interpretation in Rorschach Testing. New York: Grune & Stratton.

SCHMIDT, H. O., and FONDA, C. P. (1956) 'The reliability of psychiatric diagnosis: a new look.' J. abnorm. soc. Psychol., 52, 262-7.

SCHOFIELD, W. (1953) 'A further study of the effects of therapies on MMPI responses.' J. abnorm. soc. Psychol., 48, 67-77.

SCODEL, A., and MUSSEN, P. (1953) 'Social perceptions of authoritarians and nonauthoritarians.' J. abnorm. soc. Psychol., 48, 181-4.

SEARS, R. R. (1936) 'Experimental studies of projection. I. Attribution of traits.' J. soc. Psychol., 7, 151-63.

SEARS, R. R. (1944) 'Experimental analysis of psychoanalytic phenomena.' In Hunt, J. McV., Personality and the Behavior Disorders. New York: Ronald Press, pp. 306-32.

SEARS, R. R. (1951) 'A theoretical framework for personality and social behavior.' Amer. Psychologist, 6, 476-83.

SEARS, R. R., MACCOBY, E. E., and LEVIN, H. (1957) Patterns of Child Rearing. Evanston, Ill.: Row, Peterson.

SECORD, P. F., and BACKMAN, C. W. (1961) 'Personality theory and the problem of stability and change in individual behavior.' Psychol. Rev., 68, 21-32.

SECORD, P. F., DUKES, W. F., and BEVAN, W. (1954) 'Personalities in faces: an experiment in social perceiving.' Genet. Psychol. Monogr., 49, 231-79.

SEEMAN, J. (1961) 'Psychotherapy.' Ann. Rev. Psychol., 12, 157-94.

SEEMAN, J., and EDWARDS, B. (1954) 'A therapeutic approach to reading difficulties.' *J. consult. Psychol.*, **18**, 451-3.

SEEMAN, J., and RASKIN, N. J. (1953) 'Research perspectives in client-centered therapy.' In Mowrer, O. H., *Psychotherapy Theory and Research*. New York: Ronald Press, pp. 205-34.

SEN, A. (1950) 'A statistical study of the Rorschach test.' *Brit. J. statist. Psychol.*, **3**, 21-39.

SEWELL, W. H. (1952) 'Infant training and the personality of the child.' *Amer. J. Sociol.*, **58**, 150-9.

SHIELDS, J. (1954) 'Personality differences and neurotic traits in normal twin schoolchildren.' *Eugen. Rev.*, **45**, 213-46.

SHOBEN, E. J. (1949) 'Psychotherapy as a problem in learning theory.' *Psychol. Bull.*, **46**, 366-92.

SHOBEN, E. J. (1953) 'Some observations on psychotherapy and the learning process.' In Mowrer, O. H., *Psychotherapy Theory and Research*. New York: Ronald Press, pp. 120-39.

SIEGEL, L. (1956) 'A biographical inventory for students.' *J. appl. Psychol.*, **40**, 5-10, 122-6.

SILVERMAN, L. H. (1959) 'A Q-sort study of the validity of evaluations made from projective techniques.' *Psychol. Monogr.*, **73**, No. 477.

SINNETT, E. R., and ROBERTS, R. (1956) 'Rorschach approach type and the organization of cognitive material.' *J. consult. Psychol.*, **20**, 109-113.

SMITH, M. B., BRUNER, J. S., and WHITE, R. W. (1956) *Opinions and Personality*. New York: Wiley.

SMITH, P. A. (1960) 'A factor analytic study of the self-concept.' *J. consult. Psychol.*, **24**, 191.

SNYGG, D., and COMBS, A. W. (1949) *Individual Behavior*. New York: Harper.

SPITZ, R. A. (1945) 'Hospitalism: an inquiry into the genesis of psychiatric conditions in early childhood.' *Psychoanal. Stud. Child.*, **1**, 55-74.

SPRANGER, E. (1928) *Types of Men*. Halle: Niemeyer.

STAINES, J. W. (1958) 'The self-picture as a factor in the classroom.' *Brit. J. educ. Psychol.*, **28**, 97-111.

STANTON, F., and BAKER, K. H. (1942) 'Interviewer-bias and the recall of incompletely learned materials.' *Sociom.*, **5**, 123-34.

STEPHENSON, W. (1953) *The Study of Behavior: Q-technique and its Methodology*. University of Chicago Press.

STERN, G. G., STEIN, M. I., and BLOOM, B. S. (1956) *Methods in Personality Assessment*. Glencoe, Ill.: Free Press.

STEVENSON, I. (1957) 'Is the human personality more plastic in infancy and childhood?' *Amer. J. Psychiat.*, **114**, 152–61.

STONE, L. J., and CHURCH, J. (1957) *Childhood and Adolescence*. New York: Random House.

STORMS, L. H., and SIGAL, J. J. (1958) 'Eysenck's personality theory with special reference to "The Dynamics of Anxiety and Hysteria".' *Brit. J. med. Psychol.*, **31**, 228–46.

STOTT, D. H. (1958) *The Social Adjustment of Children: Manual to the Bristol Social Adjustment Guides*. University of London Press.

STRAUSS, F. H. (1961) 'Analytic implications of the test situation.' *Brit. J. med. Psychol.*, **34**, 65–72.

STRICKER, L. J., and ROSS, J. (1962) 'A description and evaluation of the Myers–Briggs type indicator.' *Research Bulletin* 62–6. Princeton, N.J.: Educational Testing Service.

SULLIVAN, H. S. (1953) *The Interpersonal Theory of Psychiatry*. New York: Norton.

SUMMERWELL, H. C., CAMPBELL, M. M., and SARASON, I. G. (1958) 'The effect of differential motivating instructions on the emotional tone and outcome of TAT stories.' *J. consult. Psychol.*, **22**, 385–8.

SUPER, D. E. (1951) 'Vocational adjustment: implementing a self-concept.' *Occupations*, **30**, 88–92.

SUPER, D. E., *et al.* (1957) *Vocational Development: A Framework for Research*. New York, Teachers College: Bureau of Publications.

SWANSON, G. E. (1961) 'Determinants of the individual's defenses against inner conflict: review and reformulation.' In Glidewell, J. C., *Parental Attitudes and Child Behavior*. Springfield, Ill.: C. C. Thomas, pp. 5–41.

SWENSON, C. H. (1957) 'Empirical evaluations of human figure drawings.' *Psychol. Bull.*, **54**, 431–66.

SZASZ, T. S. (1957) 'The problem of psychiatric nosology.' *Amer. J. Psychiat.*, **114**, 405–13.

TAFT, R. (1955) 'The ability to judge people.' *Psychol. Bull.*, **52**, 1–23.

TAFT, R. (1956) 'Some characteristics of good judges of others.' *Brit. J. Psychol.*, **47**, 19–29.

TAFT, R. (1959) 'Multiple methods of personality assessment.' *Psychol. Bull.*, **56**, 333–52.

TAFT, R. (1960) 'Judgment and judging in person cognition.' In

David, H., and Brengelmann, J. C., *Perspectives in Personality Research*. London: Crosby Lockwood, pp. 196–209.

TAYLOR, D. W. (1947) 'An analysis of predictions of delinquency based on case studies.' *J. abnorm. soc. Psychol.*, **42**, 45–56.

THOMPSON, J. (1941) 'Development of facial expression of emotion in blind and seeing children.' *Arch. Psychol.*, **37**, No. 264.

THORNE, F. C. (1961) *Clinical Judgment: A Study of Clinical Errors*. Brandon, Vermont: Journal of Clinical Psychology.

THOULESS, R. H. (1949) 'Some problems of terminology in psychological theory.' *Brit. J. Psychol.*, **40**, 41–6.

THOULESS, R. H. (1950) 'The place of theory in experimental psychology.' *Brit. J. Psychol.*, **41**, 14–24.

THOULESS, R. H. (1951) 'Methodology and research in psychopathology.' *Brit. J. med. Psychol.*, **24**, 8–12.

THURSTONE, L. L. (1944) *A Factorial Study of Perception*. University of Chicago Press.

THURSTONE, L. L. (1951) 'The dimensions of temperament.' *Psychometrika*, **16**, 11–20.

TOLMAN, E. C. (1951) 'A psychological model.' In Parsons, T., and Shils, E. A., *Toward a General Theory of Action*. Cambridge, Mass.: Harvard University Press, pp. 279–361.

TOMAN, W. (1955) 'The multiple attitude test: A diagnostic device.' *J. abnorm. soc. Psychol.*, **51**, 163–70.

TOMKINS, S. S. (1947) *The Thematic Apperception Test*. New York: Grune & Stratton.

TOULMIN, S. (1961) *Foresight and Understanding*. London: Hutchinson.

VALENTINE, C. W. (1956) *The Normal Child and some of his Abnormalities*. London: Penguin.

VENESS, T. (1962) *School Leavers: Their Aspirations and Expectations*. London: Methuen.

VERNON, M. D. (1952) *A Further Study of Visual Perception*. Cambridge University Press.

VERNON, M. D. (1955) 'The functions of schemata in perceiving.' *Psychol. Rev.*, **62**, 180–92.

VERNON, P. E. (1933a) 'Some characteristics of the good judge of personality.' *J. soc. Psychol.*, **4**, 42–58.

VERNON, P. E. (1933b) 'The biosocial nature of the personality trait.' *Psychol Rev.*, **40**, 533–48.

VERNON, P. E. (1935) 'Can the "Total Personality" be studied objectively?' *Char. & Person.*, **4**, 1–10.

VERNON, P. E. (1936) 'The matching method applied to investigations of personality.' *Psychol. Bull.*, **33**, 149–77.

VERNON, P. E. (1938) 'The assessment of psychological qualities by verbal methods.' *Industr. Hlth Res. Bd Rep.*, No. 83. London: H.M. Stationery Office.

VERNON, P. E. (1953) *Personality Tests and Assessments.* London: Methuen.

VERNON, P. E. (1958) 'Educational testing and test form factors.' *Research Bulletin* 58–3. Princeton, N.J.: Educational Testing Service.

VERNON, P. E. (1961) *The Structure of Human Abilities* (2nd ed.). London: Methuen.

VERNON, P. E., and PARRY, J. B. (1949) *Personnel Selection in the British Forces.* University of London Press.

VEROFF, J., *et al.* (1960) 'The use of Thematic Apperception to assess motivation in a nationwide interview study.' *Psychol. Monogr.*, **74**, No. 499.

VROOM, V. H. (1959) 'Projection, negation and the self-concept.' *Hum. Rel.*, **12**, 335–44.

WAGNER, R. (1949) 'The employment interview: a critical summary.' *Personnel Psychol.*, **2**, 17–46.

WALKER, A. S. (1955) *Pupils' School Records.* London: Newnes.

WALLACH, M. A., and GAHM, R. C. (1960) 'Personality functions of graphic constriction and expansiveness.' *J. Person.*, **28**, 73–88.

WARD, L. B. (1959) 'The business in-basket test.' *Research Bulletin* 59–8. Princeton, N.J.: Educational Testing Service.

WATTS, A. F. (1944) *The Language and Mental Development of Children.* London: Harrap.

WEINGARTEN, E. M. (1949) 'A study of selective perception in clinical judgment.' *J. Person.*, **17**, 369–406.

WERNER, H. (1948) *Comparative Psychology of Mental Development.* New York: International Universities Press.

WHYTE, W. H. (1956) *The Organization Man.* New York: Simon & Schuster.

WICKMAN, E. K. (1928) *Children's Behavior and Teachers' Attitudes.* New York: Commonwealth Fund.

WILLIAMSON, E. G., and BORDIN, E. S. (1941a) 'The evaluation of vocational and educational counseling: a critique of the methodology of experiments.' *Educ. Psychol. Measmt.*, **1**, 5–24.

WILLIAMSON, E. G., and BORDIN, E. S. (1941b) 'A statistical

evaluation of clinical counseling.' *Educ. Psychol. Measmt.*, **1**, 117–132.

WILSON, N. A. B. (1945) 'Interviewing candidates for technical appointments or training.' *Occup. Psychol.*, **19**, 161–79.

WINDLE, C. (1952) 'Psychological tests in psychopathological prognosis.' *Psychol Bull.*, **49**, 451–82.

WINTHROP, H. (1957) 'The consistency of attitude patterns as a function of body type.' *J. Person.*, **25**, 372–82.

WIRT, R. D. (1956) 'Actuarial prediction.' *J. consult. Psychol.*, **20**, 123–4.

WISHNER, J. (1960) 'Reanalysis of "Impressions of Personality".' *Psychol. Rev.*, **67**, 96–112.

WITKIN, H. A., et al. (1954) *Personality through Perception*. New York: Harper.

WITTENBORN, J. R. (1955) *Wittenborn Psychiatric Rating Scales*. New York: Psychological Corporation.

WITTENBORN, J. R. (1961) 'Contributions and current status of *Q* methodology.' *Psychol. Bull.*, **58**, 132–42.

WITTENBORN, J. R., and HOLZBERG, J. D. (1951a) 'The generality of psychiatric syndromes.' *J. consult. Psychol.*, **15**, 372–80.

WITTENBORN, J. R., and HOLZBERG, J. D. (1951b) 'The Rorschach and descriptive diagnosis.' *J. consult. Psychol.*, **15**, 460–3.

WITTENBORN, J. R., et al. (1956) 'A study of adoptive children. III. Relationships between some aspects of development and some aspects of environment for adoptive children.' *Psychol. Monogr.*, **70**, No. 410.

WITTMAN, M. P. (1941) 'A scale for measuring prognosis in schizophrenic patients.' *Elgin Papers*, **4**, 20–33.

WITTSON, C. L., HUNT, W. A., and STEVENSON, I. (1946) 'A follow-up study of neuropsychiatric screening.' *J. abnorm. soc. Psychol.*, **41**, 79–82.

WOLFF, W. (1943) *Expression of Personality*. New York: Harper.

WOLPE, J. (1958) *Psychotherapy by Reciprocal Inhibition*. Stanford University Press.

WOODGER, J. H. (1956) *Physics, Psychology and Medicine*. Cambridge University Press.

WRIGHT, H. F. (1960) 'Observational child study.' In Mussen, P., *Handbook of Research Methods in Child Development*. New York: Wiley, pp. 71–139.

WYLIE, R. C. (1961) *The Self-Concept*. Lincoln, Neb.: University of Nebraska Press.

x*

YARROW, L. J. (1961) 'Maternal deprivation: toward an empirical and conceptual re-evaluation.' *Psychol. Bull.*, **58**, 459–90.

YATES, A. J. (1958) 'Symptoms and symptom substitution.' *Psychol. Rev.*, **65**, 371–4.

YONGE, K. A. (1956) 'The value of the interview: an orientation and a pilot study.' *J. appl. Psychol.*, **40**, 25–31.

ZAX, M., and KLEIN, A. (1960) 'Measurement of personality and behavior changes following psychotherapy.' *Psychol. Bull.*, **57**, 435–48.

ZUBIN, J. (1953) 'Evaluation of therapeutic outcome in mental disorders.' *J. nerv. ment. Dis.*, **117**, 95–111.

ZUBIN, J., DERON, L., and SULTAN, F. (1956) 'A psychometric evaluation of the Rorschach experiment.' *Amer. J. Orthopsychiat.*, **26**, 773–82.

SUBJECT INDEX

(including titles of tests)

AUTHOR INDEX

327